# Eternal Life

# ETERNAL LIFE

A STUDY OF ITS
IMPLICATIONS AND APPLICATIONS

BY
BARON FRIEDRICH VON HÜGEL

Archivum

San Rafael, Ca

Second, facsimile edition
Archivum, 2007
First edition, T & T Clark, 1912


For information, address:
Archivum, P.O. Box 151011
San Rafael, California 94915, USA


Library of Congress Cataloging-in-Publication Data

Hügel, Friedrich, Freiherr von, 1852–1925.
Eternal life: a study of its implications and applications
/Baron Friedrich von Hügel.

p. cm.
Originally published: Edinburgh: T & T Clark, 1912.
Includes bibliographical references and index.
ISBN-13: 978-1-59731-404-6 (pbk.: alk. paper)
ISBN-13: 978-1-59731-429-9 (hardcover: alk. paper)
1. Future life—Christianity. I. Title.
BT921.3.H84 2007
236'.21—dc22      2007027172

# PREFACE

THE history of the following book is indeed simple yet somewhat unusual. The Rev. Dr. James Hastings invited me to contribute to his *Encyclopædia of Religion and Ethics*; and his instructions concerning " Eternal Life," the first of the articles thus undertaken by me, were to make the paper as long as the subject-matter might seem to deserve or require. He was, in this, doubtless thinking primarily of his Encyclopædia as a whole; whereas I myself became so engrossed in my subject that I allowed my composition to grow as long as its great subject-matter pressed it to become. The result, anyhow, was that the article, when sent in, was found to be far too long for the scope of the Encyclopædia; and Dr. Hastings kindly arranged with Messrs. T. & T. Clark, the publishers of the Encyclopædia, to issue my article as a separate book—the present volume. Both Dr. Hastings and Messrs. Clark have been very patient and truly generous in their dealings with me throughout these agreements; and I now beg to thank them cordially.

This little private history is recounted here in order to explain how any writer possessed of even average modesty could venture on so bewilderingly vast a subject. I sincerely doubt whether I would ever have dared directly to undertake a volume upon this subject-matter. Yet this task, thus originally undertaken as but one of several articles, did not, somehow, appear preposterously ambitious; the work, once it was started, seemed to grow under my hands; and nothing as yet attempted by me has flowed so readily from my pen. The subject had doubtless been occupying my mind and life for many a year; and thus there is some reason to hope that these pages may, in their turn, live for a while and that they may, here and there, help some religious students and strugglers.

This is presumably the right place for saying a few words about certain peculiarities of the book, in the order of their appearance within its pages.

The Method is very deliberately an analysis of more or less advanced states of soul—of considerable spiritual experience and of considerable articulation of such experience; it is not a history claiming to begin with the beginnings, or at least with the really early experiences and utterances of mankind. Much is now made of the savage, the supposedly brute-like beginnings of man; and a purely historical, an entirely genetic method and account is now often demanded. Yet, as a matter of simple fact, we really *know* man only as man; and the interior significance of his earlier and earliest acts and utterances we understand, where we understand them at all, only from analyses of his more advanced and more articulate condition. I am, of course, fully aware that Buddhism and the Dionysiac Cult appeared late in the history of man. Yet at this, comparatively late, stage we are offered an amount of experience, and of articulation of this experience, sufficient, when explained in the light of still later experiences and articulations, for us to arrive at some sober, reasonably certain conclusions; whereas much further back we do not get such volume and such clearness of material.

I have striven hard throughout the book never to lose sight of the very important element of truth embodied, even, I think, exaggerated, in the attempts at a "purely genetic method," and in such Naturalism in Anthropology. Hence I have endeavoured to remain continuously alive to the profound need and continuous action of the body, of the senses, of sensible objects and of the physical environment, within and for man's mental, spiritual, religious life. And I have attempted, on reaching at last the very late period at which this fundamental fact has been systematically recognized even to excess, sincerely to appraise the strength and the weakness of this Method and Naturalism.

A strong insistence will be found throughout these pages upon the *Parousia*, the Proximate Second Coming—upon the Eschatological Element operative in the life and teaching of Our Lord and in all genuine and fruitful Christianity. The problem involved is so delicate and so far-reaching that we cannot wonder if the great majority of believers have, ever since the first enthusiastic age, turned away from it with instinctive fear or sickening dismay. Yet no repudiation of historico-critical scholars, however audacious or one-sided they may be in part of their conclusions, will prevent the battle concerning Christianity—the testing of its claim abidingly to supply the full sanity and truth of religion and of life—from turning, more and more, in this and the next two or three generations, around the precise significance, place, and range of this element in Christian teaching. In any case, the writer could not, in a serious study of Eternal Life, pass over this, the deepest and most operative revelation concerning the Temporal and the Eternal ever vouchsafed to man. And here he would take his stand very deliberately with those who indeed find a genuine and full eschatological element in Our Lord's life and teaching, yet who discover it there as but one of two movements or elements,—a gradual, prophetic, immanental, predominantly ethical element; and this sudden, apocalyptic, transcendental, purely religious element. Indeed, the interaction, the tension, between these two elements or movements, is ultimately found to be an essential constituent, and part of the mainspring, of Christianity, of religion, and (in some form) even of all the deepest spiritual life.

It is, surely, very interesting to note how that brilliant German-French teacher and writer, Albert Schweitzer, who insists, more exclusively again than Professor Loisy, upon one single element, the Eschatological and Apocalyptic, in Our Lord's life and teaching, has found even this picture of Christ so deeply fascinating for his own soul, that he has abandoned his high posts and brilliant prospects in Europe, and has gone, as a simple medical missionary—the Lutheran

Church authorities having refused him a clerical ordination and appointment—to labour at winning the heathen to this purely ascetical and transcendental Messiah-Christ and Saviour. This picture of Our Lord is deeply repulsive—I am convinced, most rightly repulsive—to the large majority of believers. And yet the Eschatological element will have to be apprehended, accepted, and practised with renewed vigour and a new range —within a larger, more varied world than ever before, as one out of two movements in the Life of our life. And so practised, as an enriching heroism and wise enthusiasm apprehensive of the Eternal God, it will reawaken Christianity to its fullest attractiveness and vigour.

I have had much trouble as to where to draw the line between Modern Times and the Present Day—as to how to group Kant and his derivatives. I first attempted to take Kant, his four great successors (Fichte, Schleiermacher, Hegel, and Schopenhauer), and Ritschl, all together; as already conjointly forming part of our contemporary life. But this arrangement refused to work well. So then I tried to treat Kant and his four immediate successors as concluding the Historical Retrospect, and to retain Ritschl alone in the Contemporary Survey. I found, however, that especially Schleiermacher and Schopenhauer, and indeed also Fichte and Hegel, are more copiously and more directly operative within our own lives than is Kant; and, again, that Ritschlianism, though it could never have existed without Kant, is, nevertheless, largely determined by a quite un-Kantian attitude towards the Historic Christ and towards the Christian Community. I continue to dislike the break between Kant and those four great followers of his, and, still more, the position, so far away and so far down, of Ritschlianism. Yet Kant, those four Kantians, and Ritschl appear thus at last to occupy the places naturally marked out for them by their origins and affinities. Especially does Ritschlianism really belong to the group of Institutional Religion, in spite of its largely forced interpretation and its grave impoverishing of the experience and tradition furnished by these Institutions.

There is throughout the book a vigilant attention to the nature, range, and implications of our knowledge—to *Epistemology*, especially to the ontological character and witness of Religion—the central position occupied, in the fullest experiences and articulations of Religion, by the Reality, the Difference, and yet the Likeness, of God. A critical Realism—a Realism not of Categories or Ideas but of Organisms and Spirits, of *the* Spirit, a purified but firm Anthropomorphism are here maintained throughout as essential to the full vigour and clear articulation of Religion. It is plain that this difficult subject is indeed inexhaustible, and that much discussion and discrimination will be required in this matter from ourselves and from our successors; yet it is, surely, quite as plain that Subjectivism has had its day for a good long while to come. Certainly, nothing can well be more arid, more drearily reiterative and useless, in face of the entrancing richness and the tragic reality of life, than is most of the still copious literature, not seldom proceeding from thinkers of distinction and technical competence, which attempts to find or to make a world worthy of man's deepest, ever costly and difficult, requirements and ideals, within avowedly mere projections of himself. We have thus everywhere man's wants and man's illusions—illusions which, at their best, are of a tribal or even racial range and utility, but which, one and all, convey no trustworthy intimation of any trans-subjective, more than merely human validity and reality whatsoever.

The chapter on our present-day Social Problems does not, of course, aim at any description or solution of these problems as such, but only endeavours to elucidate the causes at work here against or for the experience and conception of Eternal Life. The largely still obscure, but abiding and deep, instincts and needs of a spiritual kind struggling for expression in the present acute social agitations and troubles appear to fit in well with the Theory of Knowledge articulated in this book, and especially with the Two Movements found here to be essential to all fully fruitful religion. And thus these very agitations and troubles contribute powerful, because quite spontaneous and unexpected, additional reasons for holding those analyses of philosophy and of religion to be substantially true and adequate to the central facts of life. We have up to this point simply sought and sincerely followed the lines of the fullest life and of continual rebirth: and hence the joys as well as the pangs of expansion can now be ours, and not the sorry pleasures and dreary pains of contraction or, at least, of rigidity in face of the agitated present and the dim future apparently confronting our race. And that joy, pang, and expansion is, each and all, in the closest touch with, and is occasioned and sustained by, the experience of Eternal Life—the reality of the Abiding God.

I much wished to avoid the acute problems and conflicts of the present concerning Church Authority, and thus to keep myself and my reader in regions undisturbed by such immediate and embittering controversies. But I soon discovered that I could only escape the questions concerning Religious Institutions on the hypothesis that Eternal Life can be vividly experienced and clearly conceived outside all such Institutions. Yet all sane and full Epistemology, and all the more complete, characteristic and fruitful religious experiences and personalities imperatively demand, in the writer's judgment, some genuine Institutionalism. And the excesses and defects traceable in Epistemology and in Religion compel us to search out the precise place, function, need, and checks of Institutionalism within the full religious complex, and especially within the experience of Eternal Life—as these have been, and continue to be apprehended by earnest and saintly souls. If man's spirit is awakened by contact with the things of sense, and if his consciousness of the Eternal and the Omnipresent is aroused and (in the long run) sustained only by the aid of Happenings in Time and in Space, then the Historical, Institutional, Sacramental must be allowed a necessary position and function in the full religious life. No cutting of knots however difficult, no revolt against, no evasion of abuses however irritating or benumbing, are adequate solutions. Only the proper location, the heroic use, the wise integration of the Institutional within the full spiritual life are really sufficient. The writer is no Quaker, but a convinced Roman Catholic; and hence, do what he will, he cannot avoid, he cannot even minimize these for himself utterly intrinsic questions.

The Bibliography has been kept very short and sober—only such works have been mentioned here as appeared to be of first-rate importance for the elucidation of the subject, and amongst these, generally only such as have been fully assimilated by the writer's mind. The book makes no pretension to exhaustiveness; and bibliographies, in proportion as they are at all complete, readily distract both writer and reader from the experiences and realities professedly in view.

I regret, however, not to have found room for the following authors and writings so entirely within my two conditions.

After Kierkegaard, it would have been well briefly to have quoted and analysed the utterances concerning Eternal Life to be found in *Paul de Lagarde's* Paper on the Relation of the German State to Theology, Church, and Religion, first published in 1873 and finally reprinted in his

"Deutsche Schriften," ed. 1886. Amidst much that is prejudiced, wayward, even perverse, we get here a poignant sense of the continuous real presence of the Eternal, and of our persistent need and search of the Eternal, within all religious History and Succession—a sense all the more striking since it proceeds from one engrossed throughout a lifetime in the most minute textual and linguistic studies.

There ought to have appeared, perhaps as the conclusion to the remarks upon Naturalism in Anthropology, a grateful acceptance of the admirable pages of *C. P. Tiele*, in his "Elements of the Science of Religion," 1897, vol. ii., concerning the Infinite present within man—pages which sprang so fresh and deep and admirably adequate from the pen of that great scholar and genuine believer.

It would have been right, perhaps in connection with Kant's Epistemology, to have made appreciative mention of *Oswald Külpe's* "Einleitung in die Philosophie." For this little volume, first published in 1895, and already at its fifth edition in 1910, is a cheering proof that a carefully self-consistent, sober, and non-subjectivist theory of knowledge can, in the Germany of our day, be furnished in a short handbook, and that it can find there a large world of appreciative readers.

And, finally, some careful attention ought probably to have been given, at the end of the Feuerbach section, to Professor *Paul Natorp's* positions in his "Religion innerhalb der Grenzen der Humanität," 2nd ed. 1908. This exquisitely written booklet is indeed but a variant (distinguished by greater sobriety, elasticity, and pædagogic, accommodating tact) of the Feuerbachian Illusionism. Yet the attempt to "save" Religion by the elimination of all Ontology, and by reducing it to a purely human-social Moralism, is too characteristic of the atmosphere of our times, and is too subtly and completely destructive of religion, not to deserve the most repeated study and refutation.

The Contents and Index, on the contrary, err, if at all, on the side of over-copiousness; yet such a book as the present, if serviceable at all, seemed to require ready aids to its study in almost any reasonable direction and combination.

There now remain only two obligations, as pressing as they are pleasant.

I have very gratefully to thank the friends who have most kindly helped me to make this work less unworthy of its great theme.

Mr. Edmund G. Gardner, Lecturer on Dante at University College, London, aided me especially in the sections on St. Thomas, Darwin, and Marx, and in the chapter on Institutional Religion. I remain indeed alone responsible for everything printed here; yet I am anxious to acknowledge the support which I have derived from the careful reading of this my fellow-Roman Catholic.

Mr. Clement C. J. Webb, Wilde Lecturer on Natural and Comparative Religion in the University of Oxford, was of much service on points connected with Plato and Aristotle, in regard to the translations from Spinoza, and also as to Kant and Schopenhauer, and concerning Epigenesis and Evolution.

And two other friends have most patiently and skilfully criticized throughout the form and sequence of the book; and it is to their generous aid that the reader largely owes such clearness and simplicity as these pages may now show.

And I have once again, as in the case of my *Mystical Element*, to submit these my conclusions—conclusions which cannot fail to be at least imperfect in many ways and degrees—to my fellow-workers, and above all to the test and judgment of my fellow-Christians and of the Catholic Church.

FRIEDRICH VON HÜGEL.

KENSINGTON,
   1st October 1912.

# CONTENTS

## INTRODUTION

|  | PAGES |
|---|---|
| A generous range and development necessary in any fruitful study of Eternal Life . . . . . | 1 |
| Eternal Life, an experience and conception latent, and in various degrees patent, throughout all specifically human life; but fully operative and vividly recognized in religion alone . . . . . . . | 1, 2 |
| It involves, in proportion to such fulness and vividness, Simultaneity, a complete Present and Presence . | 2 |
| Indication of the three parts of this work—an Historical Retrospect, a Contemporary Survey, and Prospects and Conclusions . . . . . . . | 2, 3 |

## PART I

### HISTORICAL RETROSPECT

Rough division into evidences furnished by the Oriental religions, properly so called, and those supplied by the Græco-Roman and the Jewish-Christian worlds and their intermixtures, inclusive of Mediæval and Modern West European and North American civilization . 7

### CHAPTER I

#### THE ORIENTAL RELIGIONS

| | |
|---|---|
| The writer without first-hand experience or knowledge here. Range of his competence and contribution . . | 7, 8 |
| Four Oriental complexes of life and doctrine of special interest for Eternal Life . . . . . | 8 |

## Contents

                                                                            PAGES

1. *Buddhism.* The Nirvana described and analyzed by Lehmann and Oldenberg . . . . 8, 9
   Belief in Nirvana and apprehension of life as sheer flux strictly interconnected. Lesson of this interconnection, with respect to Eternal Life . . . 10
2. *Hindooism. Ramanuja* largely escapes from Monism into Theism and belief in Free-Will and Grace . 10–12
   The apprehension and conception of Eternal Life traceable here . . . . . . 12
3. *Zarathustra*: the *Gatha-hymns* may well go back to him. Their doctrine profoundly ethical and dualistic. The *Yasht-hymns* teach an Eternal Light . . 12, 13
   How far Eternal Life is apprehended here . . 13
4. The old Egyptian religion articulates or implies with certainty little or nothing concerning Eternal Life. Illustration: the God Râ and the souls identified with him . . . . . . . 13, 14

## CHAPTER II

### ISRAELITISH RELIGION

First of seven chapters devoted to the Jewish-Christian, Græco-Roman, and Modern European revelations, conceptions, civilizations . . . . . 15
Range of Israelitish times; considerably narrower range of the Israelitish utterances concerning Eternal Life . 15, 16
1. Utterances of the Israelitish *Jahvist* writer, and the history of *Elijah's* conflict with the Baal worship . 16, 17
   The prophet *Amos*: Israel's special responsibilities and moral dispositions, declared more central than all ritual observance . . . . . 17
   *Isaiah* of Jerusalem: the vision of his vocation; his parable of God and His vineyard . . . 17, 18
   The prophet *Micah*: the ethical character of God . 18
2. *Jeremiah*: God the fountain of living waters . . 18
   *Deuteronomy*: man is to love God with all he is and has . . . . . . . . 18
3. *Ezekiel*: God as the good shepherd; as re-animating the dead; as the boundless healing waters . . 19, 20
   The *Priestly Code*, akin to Ezekiel's spirit . . 20
4. Lateness of Israel's awaking to conviction of soul's full, indeed heightened, life after death. Reasons and profound instructiveness of this fact . . 21, 22
   The Greeks in full contrast with all this. Yet the Greeks gradually contribute much towards articulation and completion of the Jewish spiritual outlook . 22, 23

*Contents*　　　　　　　　　　　　xxi

## CHAPTER III

### THE HELLENIC EXPERIENCES

|  | PAGES |
|---|---|
| Their range in time | 23 |

1. The *Orgiastic Cultus of* Dionysus, as described by Rohde: ecstatic states here awaken apprehension of the Non-successive, the Eternal . . . 23–25
   The soul here felt itself immortal, divine—the soul as out of the body, in spite of the body . . . 25, 26
   Centre of the experience is here the apparent timelessness, eternity of the trance state . . . 27
2. The *Orphics* utilize and transform the Dionysiac cult; their doctrine of the Dionysian and the Titanic elements in man . . . . . 27, 28
   The soul's escape from the wheel of births, like yet unlike here to Buddhism . . . 28, 29
   The soul here is to regain memory of her earthly life in the Beyond—oblivion is here an evil . 29, 30
   Two currents of conception in the Orphic Tablets; traces in the mystical current of two characteristics of ecstatic states . . . . . 30, 31
3. *Parmenides* first precisely formulates the *Totum Simul* of Eternity    The clearest of all purely abstract and monistic, static, and determinist professions . . 31, 32
4. *Plato* attains the most vivid apprehension and formulation of Eternity as distinct from Time . . . 32
   Three stages of his growth and corresponding three groups of his writings    Only last two groups furnish teachings concerning Eternal Life . . 32, 33
   (1) Passages concerning Eternal Life in the *Phædrus* and *Republic*; in the *Theætetus*; in the *Sophist*; and in the *Parmenides* . . . 33, 34
   The passages concerning Purgation in this second group . . . . . 35
   (2) Passages in the third group—the *Symposium* and the *Timæus* . . . . . 35–37
   Plato's two defects. The four great insights, combined in Plato for the first and the last time amongst Græco-Roman non-Christian souls: the position of philosophy well within a large national and individual life; the need of purification and the function of the *Thumos*; the continuous search for the organism in all reality; and a deep sense of an inexhaustible transcendent Beauty, Truth, and Goodness, man's love of which constitutes all his worth . . . . . 37, 38

5. *Aristotle* drops Plato's Purification and his Thirst after the Transcendent. Yet conception of the Unmoving Energy here a profound contribution to expression of the experiences concerning Eternal Life . . 38
   (1) The Pure *Energeia* of God, in the *Ethics* and the *Metaphysics*. Dr. Schiller's analysis of the doctrine . . . . . . 38–40
   (2) *Nous* and *Energeia* as operative in human life . 40, 41
   Intolerably abstract features of this scheme. Yet abiding greatness of intuition that succession not an essential, but a defect, of life. The richness of the life will, however, alone give full worth to the simultaneity, as the simultaneity gives same to the richness . . . . . . . 41, 42

## CHAPTER IV

### JEWISH HELLENISTIC TIMES

Range of these times, and stages of interaction between the Pagan and the Jewish currents . . . . 42, 43
1. Stoicism. Oriental, partly Semitic, origin of all its earlier chiefs and the historical circumstances of its beginnings largely explain its three peculiarities.
   (1) Its Pantheistic-materialistic basis. The system has no room for Eternal Life . . . . 43–45
   (2) Its Ethical Rigorism and abstractness of outlook . 45, 46
   (3) Yet its deeply organic conception of human society prepares and eventually aids articulation of experiences concerning Eternal Life . . 47, 48
2. The Post-Exilic Biblical, Apocryphal, and Pseudepigraphic Jewish books, upon the whole less rich and pregnant than the Israelitish writings . . . 48
   But there are here—
   (1) A series of magnificent utterances in the Psalms, most of which probably belong to this period ; . 48
   (2) The first explicit mention of "Eternal" or "Everlasting Life," with a clear enunciation of the resurrection of some souls to it, and of some other souls to "everlasting contempt," in the book of *Daniel*; and statements in *Ecclesiasticus*, the *Second Book of Maccabees*, the *Apocalypse of Baruch* and the *Psalms of Solomon* ; . . 49, 50
   (3) Clear indications of the qualitative conception of Eternal Life in the *Wisdom of Solomon*. Two remarks concerning such qualitativeness . . 50

*Contents* xxiii

PAGES

3. The Alexandrian Jew *Philo*: his attempt to interpret the Israelite and Jewish religion by means of Platonic, Aristotelian, and Stoic categories . . 50, 51
  (1) God, as Pure Action and as Eternal—outside of Time . . . . . . . 51
  (2) God's relation to Life conceived in two-fold manner. God possesses fullest Life; hence He can and does communicate it in a lesser degree and kind . 52, 53
  Or God is above, more than Life; He is He Who *is* 53
  Yet the devoted Jew Philo often pictures God as self-communicative, and man as insufficient to himself . . . . . . 53, 54
  (3) The Stoic Apathy far too influential here. Yet, on this point also, the spontaneity and richness of the Jewish religion predominates . . . 54

## CHAPTER V

### PRIMITIVE CHRISTIANITY

The Primitive Christian utterances form three groups, as proceeding from Jesus Himself, or from St. Paul, or from the Johannine writer . . . . . 55
1. The actual utterances of *Our Lord*—the three conditions of their right apprehension; their abiding power . . . . . . . 55, 56
  (1) The Kingdom of God in the foreground here, and nowhere clearly pictured as a pure simultaneity . 56
  The Kingdom is future, imminent, sudden, a pure gift of God (and apparently successive) . . 56, 57
  Relation of "Life" and of "Life Everlasting" to the Kingdom . . . . . . 57, 58
  Certainty of presence and operativeness of the four-fold conviction concerning the Kingdom within Our Lord's life and teaching. Difficulty, since early times, especially concerning the imminence. Yet this teaching of Our Lord, if taken generally, and as one of two essential movements, found to convey the deepest religious experience and truth 58, 59
  (2) This purely religious, intensely transcendental outlook certainly prevalent in Our Lord's teaching from Peter's confession at Cæsarea Philippi onwards. But another, relatively immanental, predominantly ethical outlook on to present, slow, humanly operative realities, also to be admitted, especially in earlier period of Jesus's life . . 59, 60

|   | PAGES |
|---|---|
| This results from His attitude concerning the exorcisms | 60 |
| from His plant-parables | 60, 61 |
| from His references to His personal presence | 61, 62 |
| (3) Our Lord conceives the Kingdom everywhere as a social organism: four sets of indications | 62, 63 |
| (4) And the Future Life also to be rich, indeed complete, as to each soul's powers, and social as to each soul's occupation with other souls amidst the same soul's vision and adoration of God | 63, 64 |
| (5) Yet God here, everywhere, beginning, centre, medium, and end of the entire final life. The soul's self-donation to Him, effected in utter dependence upon His aid, yet with fullest actuation of its noblest feelings, motives, passions, supremely exemplified by Our Lord's own life | 64, 65 |
| The negative movement thus planted right within even the purest attachments to the best of things; with the whole impelled by, and culminating in, apprehension and lovingly awed acceptance of the deepest Reality, a holy Love and all-wise Will | 65, 66 |
| 2. *St. Paul's* teachings, though affected only by a part of Our Lord's life and revelation, generally more complex or systematic than Jesus's sayings. Yet enthusiastic absorption in most fundamental dispositions and aims of the historic Jesus, and in development of Christian organism gives to St. Paul's speculation a deep experimental content | 66, 67 |
| Dominating double fact of St. Paul's life—his conversion to a present Christ, yet without having known the earthly Jesus. He turns away from the past, earthly, Jewish Messiah to the present, eternal Christ, the universal Saviour; his dominant category becomes, not Kingdom of God, nor Eternal Life, but *Pneuma*, the Spirit | 67 |
| (1) St. Paul's fully developed anthropological scheme: *Psyche* and Flesh; and *Pneuma* and Body: their connotations | 67–69 |
| (2) A certain de-personalization observable in the Pauline Christ-image. Christ-Spirit taken as though an element | 69 |
| (3) The presence of this, intrinsically eternal, Spirit within us here and now, our surety of immortality and resurrection. The Kingdom of God thus, here also, partly a present possession | 70 |
| (4) This Christ-Spirit effects and maintains the universal human brotherhood: its articulation in | |

|                                                                                                                                                                  | PAGES   |
| ---------------------------------------------------------------------------------------------------------------------------------------------------------------- | ------- |
| the Christian Church. The Stoic World-City here far exceeded in tenderness, vitality, spirituality                                                               | 71, 72  |
| (5) And Stoicism again overcome by an amazing range of experience, and by sense of prevenience and omnipresent holiness and love of God                          | 72      |
| 3. The Johannine Writings—Pauline in their central Christian convictions, Philonian in their general conception of God and of His worship, and in their free allegorical treatment of O.T. | 73 |
| Utilization of the *Logos* conception; the earthly life of Jesus here set in a frame of Eternity                                                                 | 73, 74  |
| (1) All true existence comes from above, as already in St. Paul; but heightened stress laid here upon "knowing" and "truth"                                       | 74, 75  |
| (2) Eternal Life here the culminating conviction. Its meaning, compared with the Synoptic and Pauline sayings                                                     | 75–77   |
| Eternal Life, an already present possession                                                                                                                       | 77, 78  |
| (3) The interpenetration of spirits; the abiding of the Father in the Son, and of the Son in the Father; and the prevenience of God in His relations with man    | 78, 79  |
| (4) Range and variety of perfect life here much restricted, as compared with life actually lived and proposed by Jesus Himself. Yet here everywhere a keen sense of the two great concrete Realities—God fully extant and operative independently of our apprehension and action; and Jesus, who actually lived in the flesh here below, the lowly servant of human souls | 79, 80 |

## CHAPTER VI

### CHRISTIAN HELLENISTIC TIMES

|                                                                                                                                                         | PAGES   |
| ------------------------------------------------------------------------------------------------------------------------------------------------------- | ------- |
| Their range and three representatives                                                                                                                   | 81      |
| 1. *Plotinus*: Instructiveness of conflict throughout his writings between profound religious experiences and intensely abstract philosophy             | 81, 82  |
| (1) Thus God, utterly transcendent; nevertheless the soul consists and breathes in Him, and strives after contact with Him. But nowhere here does the One strive after us | 82–84 |
| (2) Plotinus drives home the trend of Greek philosophy, increasingly abstractive from Plato onwards, concerning God, man, the extant world, and relations between God and man—all in contradiction to |  |

|   | PAGES |
|---|---|
| his, Plotinus's, own deep experiences and intuitions . . . . . . | 85 |
| (3) What to retain from Plotinus's teaching : spaceless, timeless nature of God ; His distinct reality and otherness, and yet immense nearness to, and contact with, human soul ; and priority and excess of all reality over all theory concerning it . | 86, 87 |
| 2 St. Augustine—the historical circumstances of his life . | 87 |
| (1) He takes over and deepens Plotinus's apprehensions concerning non-spatial and non-temporal nature, the Eternity, of God . . . . | 87–89 |
| (2) Experience of Eternity achieved by St. Augustine in time . . . . . . | 89, 90 |
| (3) Sense of Eternity, of Beatitude, proceeds from immediate presence of God within our lives | 90, 91 |
| Insistence upon God's prevenience . . . | 91, 92 |
| (4) Keen apprehension of Historical Element of religion —the self-humiliation of the Eternal in Time and Space . . . . . . . | 92, 93 |
| (5) Emphasis upon need of Social Organism—the Church. The Two Cities : certain excesses here ; yet the fierceness intermingled with the very spirit of Jesus Christ . . . . | 93, 94 |
| Here again our Lord's own statements alone quite full and balanced . . . . . | 94 |
| 3. *Pseudo-Dionysius*, the last great expression of thirst after Eternal Life of ancient European and Near Eastern world. His profound, abiding influence. His country, position, date, character. He takes over Proclus on the largest scale. | |
| (1) *Proclus*, the great Neo-Platonist scholastic, a hierophant. The circular process of Plotinus here everywhere articulated in triadic development. Beings perfect in proportion to poverty of their attributes. Especially the One is even above Being. But the intermediaries between the One and man's even highest constituents more numerous than in Plotinus . . . | 95, 96 |
| But Proclus, as against Plotinus, sometimes censures those who hold that the soul can become the very One . . . . . . . | 96 |
| (2) Pseudo-Dionysius assimilates practically all the chief doctrines, terms, similes of Proclus ; and forms a compound of Christian priestly and sacramental organization and of Proclian ultra-transcendence and abstractiveness. Yet tender truth of Plotinus's experiences and supreme reality of Jesus's life and teaching vivify much of this strange amalgam . . . . | 97–99 |

(3) And in about one-fourth of his text Dionysius adopts Aristotle's general identification between relative elevation in scale of reality and relative richness of attributes; and applies this principle, in full contradiction to Neo-Platonism, to God Himself . . . . . . 99
(4) But Dionysius, following here many Greek Fathers, speaks with almost as little reserve as Plotinus of the "Deification" of the perfect soul . . 100
(5) Absence of historic sense, and purely negative character attributed to Evil, here grave defects; but these partly balanced by Platonist and Christian insistence upon the need of purification by the soul that would experience Eternal Life . 100

## CHAPTER VII

### MIDDLE AGES

Two teachers selected here . . . . . 100
1. *St. Thomas Aquinas*: His antecedents, times, character, life-work, and fortunes  His strength and limitations . . . . . . 101, 102
   (1) Aquinas compared with Augustine, as to temper, sources, and authorities of his religion . 102, 103
   (2) His usual, and his exceptional but deeper, teaching concerning man's knowledge of God . 103, 104
   (3) Aquinas follows Boëthius on Eternity. His position concerning *Aevum*, as between Time and Eternity, a groping after *Durée* . . . 104–106
   (4) His two currents of teaching concerning the perfect life:
      (*a*) The *solus cum Solo*, abstractive, more intellectualist, Aristotelian and Neo-Platonist current . . . . 107, 108
      (*b*) The social, concrete current, which finds perfection in creative power and love, and is deeply Christian . . 108, 109
   (5) Within latter current, a deep sense of right and dignity of true individuality . . . 109
   (6) Evil mostly held to be negative, in wake of Dionysius; the estimate of human nature, milder than in Augustine, yet still rather Pauline than Synoptic . . . . . 109, 110
2 *Joannes Eckhart*: His antecedents and character . 110
Vivid apprehension of one, and predominant blindness to other, of two movements of religious life. The

|   | PAGES |
|---|---|
| Monistic instinct has here largely the last word, and hence acts destructively . . . | 110, 111 |
| (1) His fundamental position: absolute identity of God and Being . . . . . | 111 |
| (2) His anthropology: the soul's highest powers touch Eternity, the lower touch Time. The Reason more truly God's servant than the Will or Love. This Reason penetrates to the simple, unmoving Divine Being which neither gives nor takes | 112, 113 |
| (3) 'God' and 'Godhead' sharply contrasted in more characteristic passages. Abstractive nature of this contrast . . . . | 113, 114 |
| (4) God's relation to the world: impressive and inadequate representations of it. Time and space here frequently without any function in spiritual life. Monistic conception of Creation, and Neo-Platonist insistence upon mere negativity of Evil . . . . . . | 115, 116 |
| (5) Eckhart's Ethics— | |
| (a) partly rich, religious, Christian; . . | 116 |
| (b) partly monistic to vanishing-point . . | 117 |
| (6) Completion of Circle by soul's return to its Origin— the bare Godhead . . . . | 117, 118 |
| General considerations. The three thirsts in Eckhart: they presuppose a mighty thirster, and a profound Cause or Causer, and a Quencher, of all this thirst. The religious thirst by far the deepest, and implies volitional and positive character of Evil. Eckhart drawn away, not by experience but by abstractive logic, from all history and concreteness, from all richness in reality—especially the supreme richness of God | 118, 119 |
| Rome's condemnation objectively deserved. Indeed the further experiences concerning conditions governing spiritual fruitfulness point away from Eckhart's scheme. . . . | 119, 120 |

## CHAPTER VIII

### MODERN TIMES

| | |
|---|---|
| The two thinkers chosen here . . . . | 121 |
| 1. *Baruch Spinoza*: Circumstances of his life . | 121 |
| Stoicism, Neo-Platonism, Mathematical Physics and strongest prejudice against historic and dogmatic elements of Jewish and Christian religion continuously operative in his mind . . . . | 121, 122 |

## Contents  xxix

PAGES

Yet he is perennially instructive through combination of deeply religious temper, a keen instinct as to man's constant need of purification, and a steady sense of help supplied towards such discipline by Determinist Science, with mistaken conception as to character of deepest Reality apprehended by man, as to means, categories, tests appropriate to this apprehension, and hence as to place and range of such Science within man's Spiritual Life . . . . 122, 123

(1) Ultimate object of philosophy conceived Stoic-wise with strain of Neo-Platonism : as directly ethical, practical, individual ; as difficult and of rare attainment . . . . . 123, 124

(2) Method everywhere mathematical (geometrical); the test, utter clearness . . . 124, 125

(3) Fundamental category, Substance. Its Attributes varyingly conceived . . . 125, 126

The Attributes apprehended by us in countless Modes, none of which necessarily involve existence or eternity . . . . . 126, 127

Eternity, in logic of system, rather a simultaneous infinite spatial extension ; and Time here ever considered as clearly as possible, *i.e.* as merely Clock-Time. Thus the system as such without depth of life, hence without Eternal Life . . 127

(4) Utter Determinism and purely negative conception of Evil pervade the system . . 128, 129

(5) Spinoza's self-contradictions concerning the Attributes and Modes, the Human Passions, and Reality and Perfection . . . . 130

(6) Culminating inconsistency : admission of ethical emancipation by individual soul . . 130, 131

Spinoza here especially utterly sincere, and driven to acute self-contradiction by facts of deeper life and by his sensitiveness to their significance . . . . . . 131, 132

(7) He is also ceaselessly awake to continuous influence and importance of human body ; to organic character and irreplaceable educative worth of human society ; and to necessity for inclusion within highest perfection of right self-seeking 132, 133

But this self-seeking here far too superficial—penetration by God's Spirit, and Christ's Cross badly wanted here . . . . . . 133

Determinist Science useful for purification only in middle distance and as means. And test of truth of convictions, not utter clearness, but richness and fruitfulness . . . . 133, 134

Yet Faith and Libertarianism themselves require

|  | PAGES |
|---|---|
| Fate and Science to be largely operative within seeking and finding of Eternal Life | 134, 135 |

2. *Immanuel Kant*: his greatness lies not in Religion, but in Epistemology and Ethics, and even here more in detection of precise nature and position of certain crucial problems than in consistency and adequacy of proposed solutions . . . . 135, 136
His origin and chief life-dates; his three periods; restriction of present study to his *critical* period 136, 137
His nobly ethical motive against Hume . . 137, 138
(1) Kant's Epistemology: its most important positions for present purpose.
 (*a*) Assumption of possibility of conceiving knowledge as independent of an object 139, 140
 (*b*) Contradiction between fundamental principle that reason cannot be used assertively concerning any *Noumena*, and ceaseless assertive conviction that Reality is entirely heterogeneous to our conception of it . . . . . . 140, 141
 (*c*) Assimilation of cognition to manufacture or building . . . . 141, 142
 (*d*) Wise admission, with Leibniz, of immeasurable range of our obscure apprehensions, as compared with narrow extent of our clear apprehensions . . 142, 143
 (*e*) And fruitful retention of certain parallelism, even at deeper levels of life, between Space and Time; but failure to discriminate, in each, between the real and the conceptual, and to consider them of any importance in soul's deepest, *i.e.* its religious, life . . . . . 143, 144
(2) Kant's Ethics bring one great help and two grave obstacles to experience and conception of Eternal Life.
 (*a*) Evil here everywhere not privation, or a substance; but positive, and an act or habit of the will . . . 144, 146
 (*b*) Ethics here formalist, monotonous—virtue recognized only where laborious and distasteful, and the affective element treated with suspicion. Causes of this . 146, 147
 (*c*) Excessive individualism of these Ethics arises from same causes . . 147, 148
Life's experience far richer than Kant's prescriptions . . . 148, 149
(3) The *Critical* Kant's Religion, hardly more than his *critical* Epistemology and Ethics applied to a

## Contents xxxi

PAGES

subject-matter recalcitrant to both, yet which says nothing specific to him and raises no suspicion in him as to truth or applicability of those tests . 150
(a) Kant's opposition to Ontological Argument for Existence of God, the inevitable consequence of his epistemological principles 150, 151
His objections . . . 151, 152
Traditional (Anselmian) form of argument, largely unsatisfactory. Yet the argument, at its best, covers three great abiding facts and necessities of life and mind . 152, 153
All knowledge, knowledge of reality. Our knowledge of things, ever accompanied by sense of their contingency, insufficiency, not furnished by themselves, even in their totality. Thorough failure of attempts to explain this sense as mere projection of man's empty wishes . . 153, 154
Kant's position here instructively halting. Continuous inconsistency of scepticism 154, 155
What the Ontological argument, taken alone, does and what it does not prove . 155, 156
(b) Kant's declarations, where he is *critically* active and unchecked by his more religious apprehensions, concerning Grace. 156, 157
    Religious Worship . . 157, 158
    Religious History . . 158, 159
Kant's motives here also understandable and high. Yet abuses of Religion satisfactorily curable only by deepening of Religion . . . 159, 160
Religion ever centrally Adoration . 160, 161
Is a Certainty, proclaims a Givenness. Hypothesis and Stoicism no equivalents . 161
Kant's objections with regard to Grace, refuted by experience of life also in non-religious fields . . . 161, 162
His objections to Religious Worship stand and fall with his Epistemology . 162, 163
And those against History disclose difficulties and dangers of appeal to contingent happenings, but leave need of concrete persons and events as strong as ever 164, 165
Kant's hostility to treatment of Jesus Christ even as simply unique, again inevitably results from his theory of knowledge. Lessing's self-contradiction concerning religious equivalence and religious uniqueness . . . . 165, 166

xxxii           *Contents*

PAGES

Nevertheless Kant's deepest strivings against an impossible universal equivalence of religion. Religion deep and strong only as a particular religion. . 167

## PART II

### CONTEMPORARY SURVEY

Four Philosophies derivative from Kant, and their main present-day utilizations, to be taken together. Next a great Biological Doctrine. Then Socialism and other now prevalent social problems and conditions. And lastly Institutional Religion . . . . 171

### CHAPTER IX

### PHILOSOPHIES DERIVATIVE FROM KANT

Fichte, Schleiermacher, Hegel, Schopenhauer to be studied in conjunction here. Reasons why . . . 172
1. *J. G. Fichte.* His violently ethical character, and change from Spinoza to Kant. His Epistemology more uniformly conceives knowledge as independent of its object than Kant; and his Religion as entirely rooted in Categorical Imperative as with Kant. Yet Fichte increasingly possesses a deeper religious apprehension than Kant . . . 172, 173
  (1) Fichte's entirely Immanental Critical System articulates wide-spread present-day feelings of constraint from whatever is not somehow my own mind or its creation . . . 173, 174
  (2) Yet he insists upon a Moral Ordering outside finite moral beings, but opposes conception of an Orderer . . . . . 174
    Nevertheless this Ordering is conceived religiously 174, 175
    Deeply religious sayings of his later stage concerning Love, the Blessed Life and Death 175, 176
  (3) Close interdependence of souls, and even self-subsistence of the Absolute affirmed; and Kant's rigorism overcome . . . . 176, 177
    Yet mysterious uniqueness attaching to all History never adequately recognized . . . 177
  (4) Accusation of Atheism against Fichte not altogether unfair. His account in 1792 of origin and worth of idea of God as sceptical as anything to be found in Kant . . . . 177, 178

| | PAGES |
|---|---|
| Fichte re-stated by *Hugo Münsterberg*: weaknesses of Fichtean positions even here . . | 178, 179 |
| *Rudolf Eucken* blends a Fichtean trend with Platonist and Hegelian doctrines; and a continuous keen sense of significance of History and of Evil makes him very largely satisfactory. Yet even here Fichte's influence unfortunate upon two points . . . . . | 179, 180 |

2. *Friedrich Schleiermacher.* His nature more æsthetic than religious, and more religious than ethical. His upbringing and career . . . . 180, 181
His times. Moravian, then Spinozist influences affect him throughout his two periods, of the *Reden* and of the *Glaubenslehre* . . . . 181–183

(1) In the *Reden*,
  (*a*) Essence of Religion : Intuition and Feeling of Infinite, of the Universe . . 183, 184
    This Intuition-Feeling, an influence of the universe contemplated . . 184, 185
    The generative moment of Religion 185, 186
    Consideration of these positions. Satisfactory points . . . . . . 186
    Yet we still have here an anti-dogmatic dogmatist Epistemology . . 186–188
    And the intuition is hardly religious . 188, 189
  (*b*) Intuition ever something simple, separate. Not religion but its systematizers have filled the world with strife . . . . 189
    Indeed religious feelings naturally paralyse man's energy of action. Yet religious feelings also vehement and shattering : men should do nothing from Religion but everything with Religion. Yet love, compassion, gratitude, humility, contrition, are not Morality but Religion . . 189, 190
    These positions considered :
    As to Intuition-Feeling . . 190, 191
    and as to Religion and Practical Action 191, 192
    Schleiermacher, however, sees greatly further than Kant in that Religion here is also contemplative and recollective, and that the deep worth and religious root of love, humility, contrition are laid bare . . 192
  (*c*) History in strictest sense, the highest object of Religion—all here to be organic life . 192
    Yet God only one of many religious ways of viewing universe . . . 192, 193
    And Immortality considered as mostly taken in a spirit directly contrary to Religion 193, 194

xxxiv                    *Contents*

                                                                    PAGES
           Here the emphasis upon History shatters
             entire Pantheistic scheme and temper. In-
             difference to Theism and Immortality be-
             come then impossible or affectatious      194, 195
    (2) The *Glaubenslehre* : its four changes.
        (*a*) Religion now the consciousness of our
             unlimited dependence, *i.e.* of our relatedness
             to God       .       .       .       .    195, 196
             Persistent inadequacy traced here    .         196
        (*b*) Everywhere now we have God; but the
             determinations concerning Him are Spin-
             ozistic. So too with Sin and with Prayer  .    197
        (*c*) Now Christ and Christianity enclose, in their
             past and future, the entirety and finality of
             religion. Schleiermacher here goes even
             beyond average orthodoxy. Double danger
             of this intense Christocentrism      .    197, 198
        (*d*) And now root of Religion found in the
             experience of the religious community.
             This change a profound improvement    .        198
        Ernst *Troeltsch* considers himself largely a suc-
             cessor of Schleiermacher, yet his superiority
             great. Troeltsch's four profound apprehensions.  199
        His declarations concerning Eternal Life—tension
             and polarity of religion     .       .    199, 200
 3. *G. W. F. Hegel* : main dates of his life.    .    .    201
    All-important influence of Schelling     .       .   .    201
    Change to opposition against the Identity-Philosophy.
        Yet Hegel adopts an anti-identity principle, but
        retains two positions of identification    .    201, 202
    (1) His profound, rich principle : Reality not substance
        but subject, system; it is self-subsisting, definite,
        self-knowing     .       .       .       .       .    202
        This a deliberate traversing of the Identity-
             Philosophy .       .       .       .       .    203
        Hegel's admirable survey and comparison of the
             categories of the human mind, from emptiest to
             fullest, *i.e.* most real—bare Being to Spirit
             (Absolute Spirit and Absolute Knowledge no
             more belong to this principle)    .       .    203
        So far, rock-ground. We *know* God is *at least* all
             our fullest categories carry with them    .  203, 204
        Thus a Critical Anthropomorphism, the sole self-
             consistent escape from sheer mythology  .  204, 205
        Also outside Philosophy, insistent evidences and
             motives for such Anthropomorphism    .  205, 206
        In any case, sincerity demands admission that our
             imperishable requirements are truly of this
             Theistic kind   .       .       .       .       .    206

## Contents xxxv

PAGES

(2) But Hegel prevented from this logical consequence of his own anti-identity principle by his two positions of identification . . . 206, 207
    (a) Identification of Thinking and Reality—transformation of Logic into Metaphysic, indeed Life . . . 207, 208
    Trendelenburg's analysis of this procedure 208, 209
    The crucial passages containing this transition from abstractions to realities. 209, 210
    Impossibility of such a jump . 210, 211
    (b) Identification of human and Absolute Reason and Consciousness . . . 211
    How Hegel arrives at this identification 211, 212
    Crucial passages . . . 212, 213
    He shrinks from, yet ventures upon, full identification of human history and of history of the Absolute, and then attempts some distinction . . . 213, 215
    Absolute Knowledge indeed the system's culmination; Religion here never more than the penultimate end and standard of man . . . . 215, 216
    Identification here of two very distinct, even different things—the need and reality of history for durational man, and the nature and operation of the Eternal God 216, 217
    Accumulation of improbabilities thus introduced . . . 217, 218
(3) The deceased English Hegelians: *T. H. Green, R. L. Nettleship, John* and *Edward Caird*. How much they owed to Hegel, and how much Hegel owed to them . . . . 218–220
Yet even here Hegel's influence not simply beneficent:
    Insufficient recognition of the senses, the body, the material world—their function within the mind's life . . . . . 220
    Of essentially ontological character of the religious affirmations—adoration and sense of sin . . . . . 220, 221
    Of insistent need of the Institutional in religion. . . . . 221, 222
    And of abiding distinction between Philosophy and Religion . . . . 222, 223
(4) *T. E. M'Taggart's* peculiar combination of convictions . . . . 223, 224
    (a) His declarations concerning—
        The need of metaphysics in Life and in Religion. . . . . 224

|                                                                                                                                                                                                                          | PAGES    |
| ------------------------------------------------------------------------------------------------------------------------------------------------------------------------------------------------------------------------ | -------- |
| His declarations concerning—                                                                                                                                                                                             |          |
| Personal identity, as consisting in identity of substance                                                                                                                                                                | 224      |
| A non-omnipotent, non-creative God, as a conception worthy of serious consideration                                                                                                                                      | 224, 225 |
| A perfect community of spirits as the actual reality and as excluding any single omnipotent Person                                                                                                                       | 224, 225 |
| Immortality as necessarily coupled with Pre-existence, and lapse of memory as no bar to identity of lives thus separated; and Time and Existence as two distinct, separable characteristics                              | 225, 226 |
| (b) Consideration of these declarations.                                                                                                                                                                                 |          |
| Satisfactoriness of Metaphysical attitude                                                                                                                                                                                | 226, 227 |
| But strange revival here of a Monadism less interior than Leibniz's own                                                                                                                                                  | 227, 228 |
| The Realized Perfection thus resides at any one moment not in Hegel's highest category, self-consciousness, but in lower category, substance. Reason of this choice                                                      | 228, 229 |
| Man here great even simply in himself—contrary to Christianity and experience                                                                                                                                            | 229      |
| The God here refused and the God considered possible, only mannikins, as against God of Christianity and Roman Church who alone penetrates depths of human mind and will                                                 | 229, 230 |
| The scheme leaves virtually unexplained and unutilized the characteristic, indelibly human sense of the Infinite, the Other,—of dissatisfaction with all that is merely human                                            | 230      |
| What admissions appear to be necessary here                                                                                                                                                                              | 230–232  |
| The Christian consciousness finds multiplicity of Persons in God's Unity; but 'Person' here not as in Dr. M'Taggart's construction                                                                                       | 232      |
| (5) *Ludwig Feuerbach*, ablest exponent of destructive implications of Hegelian Absolutism. Lesson fully cogent only by inclusion of contrast between his *Essence of Christianity* 1841, and his *Essence of Religion* 1851 | 233      |
| (a) His main positions in 1841.                                                                                                                                                                                          |          |
| Our consciousness of Infinite, merely consciousness of Infinity of our consciousness                                                                                                                                     | 233, 234 |

|   |   |
|---|---|
| God a purely human presupposition. Yet that man alone the true Atheist to whom the predicates of the Divine Being—Love, Wisdom, Justice—are nothing, not he to whom merely the subject of these predicates is nothing | 234 |
| But religion knows nothing of anthropomorphisms; they are pronounced such only by the understanding which reflects on religion | 235 |

(*b*) Consideration of these positions.

|   |   |
|---|---|
| At last here the human mind unambiguously knows nothing whatsoever but itself, and attains this real self-knowledge by means of no other realities than itself | 235, 236 |
| Yet in actual life we never know ourselves alone, but only with, on occasion of, by means of, other realities | 236, 237 |
| Our consciousness of Infinite cannot, then, be straightaway declared necessarily nothing but consciousness of Infinity of this our consciousness. And the specifically religious consciousness testifies to a different Infinite—to a Perfect Present Reality | 237, 238 |
| Soul's consciousness of this Infinite awakes only with consciousness of mind and of senses to their several objects and activities. But this true of our every other consciousness and knowledge | 238, 239 |
| Man's religious apprehensions never entirely adequate, and often erroneous, as are also his apprehensions in Physical Science. Yet no necessary connection between some error and all illusion: in both cases reality really apprehended from first | 239 |
| Conditions and effects of religious attestation witness strongly against a conclusion of all illusion | 240, 241 |
| Painful sense of inadequacy of all merely human apprehension left unexplained | 241, 242 |
| Yet this sense, noblest, costliest, most fruitful possessed by man: special intolerableness of scepticism here | 242, 243 |
| Religion, as sense of Infinite, *does* know of anthropomorphisms—*e.g.* St. Paul and St. John of the Cross | 243 |

(*c*) Feuerbach's own final utter scepticism and materialism, in 1851, a tragic proof that

|  | PAGES |
|---|---|
| denial of an abiding subject to predicates love, wisdom, goodness, *does* matter most profoundly . . . . | 243, 244 |
| 3. *Arthur Schopenhauer*, to be studied here in four of his positions . . . . . | 244, 245 |
| His antecedents and character. Practically author of one single book . . . . . | 245 |
| (1) His Epistemology as a Metaphysical Dualism | 245, 246 |
| Leading to an Oriental Dreaminess . . | 246, 247 |
| A strangely un-Kantian conclusion from Kantian premises . . . . . | 247 |
| One admirable epistemological instinct here: preference of intuition to abstraction . . | 248 |
| (2) His Epistemology as radically inconsistent in its attainment of the Thing-in-itself. This Thing-in-itself, the will—a will bereft of all reason and logic. . . . . . | 248, 249 |
| Angry denunciation of Pantheism. Its reason. Fine insight into special intolerableness of Pantheistic Optimism . . . . | 249 |
| History everywhere to be driven out . . | 249, 250 |
| The three self-contradictions of this position . | 250 |
| Its two truths . . . . . | 250, 251 |
| (3) Schopenhauer's Pessimism: its general character . | 251 |
| Opposition to Hegelianism, Judaism, Mohammedanism, as optimistic; esteem of Christianity and Buddhism as pessimistic . . | 251, 252 |
| Condemnation of anti-celibate Protestantism and rationalist Christianity . . . . | 252 |
| The Fall, the one valuable doctrine of O.T. . | 252, 253 |
| Criticism.—Truth and need of a pessimistic and ascetical movement. But this movement must stand within larger whole of two interdependent movements . . . . . . | 253 |
| Need of movement of attachment for awakening sense of Infinite . . . . . | 254 |
| The asceticism here, not Christian but Gnostic: purificableness of body, essential to Christianity . | 255 |
| Consequent injustice to Judaism and Islam. Fulness of spiritual life requires both preliminary Pessimism and final Optimism . . . | 255, 256 |
| (4) His *Nirvana*: statements concerning it . | 256, 257 |
| Schopenhauer's intensity of yearning after, and real faith in, an unutterable Perfect Life and Abiding Reality appear thus at the last . . . | 257 |
| And we learn weakness and strength, with respect to religion, of such dim, mostly despairing outlooks. Their weakness . . . . | 258 |
| Their strength . . . . | 258, 259 |

|   |   | PAGES |
|---|---|---|
| | The double requirement of Religion with regard to Philosophy here is advantageous to Philosophy | 259 |
| | Relation to Schopenhauer of Richard Wagner and Leo Tolstoi, but especially of Kierkegaard and Nietzsche | 260 |
| (5) | *Sören Kierkegaard.* His historic affinities: his special interest—combination of deep modernity of mind with massively ontological religion | 260 |
| | His declarations concerning God's Reality and Difference, and our utter need of Him | 261 |
| | Lesson of his life: all-importance for Religion of Reality and Difference, but also of Likeness of God; the last wanting in Kierkegaard | 262 |
| | Ibsen's *Brand*, suggested by Kierkegaard's figure, vividly drives home this lesson | 262 |
| (6) | *Friedrich Nietzsche.* Primary causes of his great vogue. Which of his writings are likely to live. His anti-religious excesses spring doubtless largely from a thirst for what religion alone can satisfy—*e.g.* his Super-man | 263–264 |

## CHAPTER X

### BIOLOGY AND EPIGENESIS

|   |   |   |
|---|---|---|
| Range of present study on Darwin and the thinkers especially influenced by him | | 264, 265 |
| 1. *Charles Darwin's* declarations concerning his own sense of religion, of poetry, of metaphysics | | 265, 266 |
| | Theism | 266, 267 |
| | Immortality | 268 |
| | Conscience, Duty, Sin | 268 |
| 2. Study of these declarations and their implications. | | |
| (1) Profound difference between Evolution proper and *Epigenesis* | | 268, 269 |
| | Darwin confuses the two | 269, 270 |
| | His one great obstacle to full continuous adhesion to Theism: its probable origin | | 270, 271 |
| (2) The Sciences recommend some doctrine of Descent; but precise character and mechanism of this Descent certainly very complex and still predominantly obscure for us. Kernel of the riddle lies in continuous presence of the necessary beginnings of useful variations (*Weissmann*) | | 271 |
| | We are thus thrown back upon some Providing Power. Purely mythological character of the alternatives | | 272 |

|   |   |
|---|---|
| (3) *A. R. Wallace* on the faculties special to man; on three stages in development of organic world where some new cause must necessarily have come into action: and on reality of these changes, however imperceptible at their origin | 272, 273 |
| Even greater definiteness of statement desirable here | 273, 274 |
| Significance of Dr. Wallace's example | 274 |
| (4) *Professor Huxley*: original position and question of his Romanes Lecture | 274, 275 |
| A direct challenge to inevitable concomitant of every doctrine of Descent taken as self-explanatory | 275 |
| Professor *Andrew Seth* completes and guards the challenge | 275 |
| Only one further requirement here: a plurality of worlds | 276, 277 |
| The Huxley-Seth positions alone furnish a sufficient home for Darwin's own sense of duty | 277 |
| (5) Anthropology and Comparative History of Religions still largely influenced by Naturalism. This all but inevitable | 277, 278 |
| *R. R. Marrett's* "Anthropology" instructively combines all the insights and some of the imperfections here considered | 278, 279 |
| The finest of the analytic historical workers apparently penetrate deeper into humanity, present and past, than do even the most learned "purely genetic" biological explorers | 279 |
| 3. Confirmation and growth brought, in three respects, to apprehension and formulation of religious and moral experience, by biological-evolutionary movement. | |
| (1) The movement, at its best, brings scientific attention back from dead or abstract things to concrete, living beings. Illustrations from Darwin's own life | 280, 281 |
| Full adhesion here of all fruitful Epistemology, Ethics, Religion, Life in general | 281 |
| This graduated love of the graduated realities of the rich, real world will triumph over the fierce passion for levelling all reality down to abstraction of purely mechanical causality. *Ernst Haeckel*: his main positions | 281, 282 |
| His cheery destruction of all "dualism," *i.e.* religion | 282, 283 |
| The more abstract and unreal the notions, the more they here oust concrete, experienced reality. Three causes of vogue of such materialistic Monism | 283 |

## Contents

|     | PAGES |
| --- | --- |
| (2) The Rev. *F. R. Tennant's* attempt to elucidate experiences of temptation and guilt by Descent Theory: its interest . . . | 283, 284 |
| Main positions of Tennant and of Archdeacon Wilson . . . . . | 284, 285 |
| Insufficiencies and satisfactory points of this attempt . . . . . | 285, 286 |
| (3) Continuity and Immediacy of Divine Action involved in adequate doctrine of Creation, allowed, indeed required, by an Epigenesis content to be a process and description . . . | 286 |
| The Rev. *Philip Waggett's* statements . | 286, 287 |
| Two additions suggested here . . | 287, 288 |
| 4. Two philosophers, Herbert Spencer and Henri Bergson, might be considered here. *Henri Bergson* chosen out . . . . . . | 288 |
| Grateful acceptance of his central conception—*Durée* as distinct from Clock-time; of his more restricted descriptions of both; and specially of his insistence on essential rôle played by Duration in man's entire life. Here only certain still more fundamental applications or conceptions of Bergson to be considered: as to Time and Space, and as to Finalism and place and character of Transformism . . . . . | 288, 289 |
| (1) Bergson's *Essai*: its fundamental antinomy—the Durational (Qualitative) and the Extensional (Quantitative). Origin of latter . . | 289, 290 |
| Time as really experienced and Time as clearly pictured. Function of Space . . | 290, 291 |
| Considerations. Difference of method pursued here as to Time and as to Space . | 291, 292 |
| Intense abstractness of the two "realities" here remaining . . . . . | 292 |
| Bergson himself indicates that Duration is not sheer Becoming . . . | 293, 294 |
| He has broken our living organic consciousness into two separate worlds, each unreal, and jointly exclusive of personality . | 294 |
| (2) Bergson's *Évolution Créatrice*: its fundamental thesis: utter heterogeneity and unpurposive character of all Duration and Life; Transformism essentially a dissociation and distinction of elements . . . . . | 294, 295 |
| Yet, here too, indications of persistence, purpose, graduated worth . . . . | 295, 296 |
| Nevertheless the system here conceives existence as strictly for existence only; change or advance here only in the means, not in the end of life | 296, 297 |

(3) General conclusions.
 Man requires Real Space and Conceptual Space as well as Real Time (Duration) and Conceptual Time; and, in his consciousness of Duration, a sense of Simultaneity as well as of Succession . 297, 298
 Duration at its highest in its element of Permanence . . . . . . . 298
 Bergson's conception of Liberty too "pure," *i.e.* artificially one-sided . . . 298, 299
 This shown by facts of consciousness, especially of conation . . . . . 299
 And by insufficiency of reasons given for his high esteem of the Free Act . . 299–301
 He has removed the mechanical obstacles to Liberty, but has not discovered its spiritual conditions . . . . . . 301
 As to Eternal Life: the distinctive being of personality is inversely as its dependence on successiveness (*Bosanquet*) . . 301, 302
 Religion can and must experience and conceive full Eternity as the characteristic of the Eternal God present and operative within man's durational, *i.e.* quasi-eternal spirit. . . 302

## CHAPTER XI

### SOCIALISM AND PRESENT SOCIAL PROBLEMS

The world of the West European and North American workmen genuinely new. Chief causes operative here 303, 304
This complex to be studied here only in its relation to Eternal Life—in its anti-transcendental trend; in the reasons productive of such secularism; and in the conditions and dispositions here hopeful or already satisfactory for religion . . . . . 304
1. *Karl Marx*: his two great discoveries—the Materialistic Conception of History and the secret of Capitalist Production. The former derived from Hegel through Feuerbach . . . 304, 305
 Yet this conception pushed by Marx and Engels to the full materialism and anti-religiousness of Feuerbach's last period . . . . . 304, 305
 Capitalistic question here passed over. Yet reminder necessary that original Marxist Socialism wages relentless war against all the natural organizations other than the State, omnipotent and sole . . . . . . 306–307

## Contents

PAGES

2. Three causes generally operative within these classes and movements in direction of Secularism.
    (1) Man's limited capacity of attention and interests ordinarily extended only by great, unbroken traditions of spiritual experience and training. These traditions practically unknown here; men absorbed here in other needs which appear to be more immediately important . . . 307
    Baffling complexity, scale, acuteness of these needs . . . . . 307, 308
    Only a great moral miracle could preserve such a world from all Secularism . . 308, 309
    (2) A positive revulsion against the Churches and Sects here frequent; predominantly social and political in origin, it is largely religious (*i.e.* anti-religious) in effect . . . . . . 309
    (3) A peculiar atrophy and deformation of the soul. First, widespread ignorance or misunderstanding of religion and of perennial spiritual needs of man . . . . . . 309, 310
    Clear superficial abstraction thus wins against dimmer deep reality . . . . 310
    Leads to highly militant, acutely problematic creed of purely immanental yet apocalyptic millennial character . . . . . 310, 311
    Allows a superficial expectation of soul's full satisfaction by entire realization of such purely earthly programme, as against John Mill's deepest insight 311
    And, by concentration of entire man upon this admittedly difficult realization, it greatly increases the Secularism already furnished by the absorption and revulsion already considered . . 312
3. Three sets of conditions and dispositions here religiously hopeful.
    (1) Certain general effects operative within all men throughout the countries concerned :
        Our confrontation by masses of men free from the maladies of the more fully educated mind, and possessing a certain sincerity, simplicity, self-sacrifice; . . 312, 313
        and the awakening of upper classes by the socialist militancy in various much-needed ways . 313
    (2) This double general gain can be specially advantageous to religious souls, particularly as regards Eternal Life. For thus we attain insight into large dependence of religion of average man upon certain social and physical conditions. The "poor" declared blessed by our Lord and by the *Poverello* . . . . . . 314

|  | PAGES |
|---|---|
| This dependence parodied by the Socialists and more wisely apprehended by the Christian social workers | 315 |
| And thus too we are thrown anew upon the costly two-fold movement — Christianity's renovative power. For religion thus forced to be more than ever Temporal—Spatial—Immanental | 315, 316 |
| Yet also more than ever Eternal and Omnipresent —Transcendent | 316, 317 |
| Only the two movements together of the real, durational soul supported by the real Eternal God here adequate | 317 |
| Sir Charles Booth's testimony concerning London | 317, 318 |
| And only such Transcendence in Immanence can preserve enthusiasm from fanaticism followed by cynicism | 318, 319 |
| (3) Symptoms amongst Socialist leaders and masses of subsidence of angry Secularism, perhaps also of indifference to religion— | |
| in Germany | 319, 320 |
| Belgium and Italy | 320 |
| France : M. Georges Sorel— | |
| on mystery and pessimism ; on Pantheism ; and on Institutional Christianity | 320, 322 |
| on the Encyclopedists ; on monastic asceticism ; on the Christian tradition | 322, 323 |
| Sorel not far from fuller experience and clearer conception of Eternal Life | 323 |

## CHAPTER XII

### INSTITUTIONAL RELIGION

| | |
|---|---|
| To be studied only as home and training ground of Eternal Life—as bringing help or occasioning obstacles, or as itself purified and checked by this life. Three groups of facts and questions to be studied | 323, 325 |
| 1. Increasing clearness as to central position held in religion by *Cultus*—Social Worship, and by Symbols and Sacraments—contacts between spirit and matter | 325 |
| Instances of powerful operation of the Institutional | 325, 326 |
| This Social Institutional need really treble : | |
| (1) Need of common worship : Professor Troeltsch's utterances | 326, 327 |
| Our Lord's institutions and the intrinsic needs of religion | 327, 328 |

|     | PAGES |
| --- | --- |
| (2) Need of efficacious sensible signs and contacts: weakness of Liberal Protestantism here | 328, 329 |
| The anti-sacramental passion historically understandable; yet it has not resolved the problem and has exceeded the facts and necessities of human nature and of religion | 329 |
| Use and commendation of such signs by Our Lord, St. Paul, the Fourth Gospel; and the intrinsic requirements of religion here | 329, 330 |
| (3) And need of interrelation between Religion and the other complexes and organizations of human life | 330 |
| Wilhelm Hermann here essentially inadequate in his opposition to all Mysticism | 330, 331 |
| And in his reduction of Religion to recognition of Categorical Imperative and the Historic Jesus | 331, 332 |
| Impossible for religion to ignore or suppress the other activities, or for these activities to suppress religion. Especially impossible for Christianity | 332 |
| Increasing impossibility of such reduction amongst educated West Europeans. Official Church persistently conceives and practises life in an all-inclusive manner | 332, 333 |
| (4) Yet the fully developed Institutional Religions losing ground for many a day— |  |
| in Germany | 333, 334 |
| France, Portugal, Spain, Italy | 334 |
| United States | 334 |
| and in England | 335 |
| These losses not all simply ascribable to perversity of human nature | 335 |
| Where, then, besides the social causes already studied, are we to seek the inhibition? | 335, 336 |
| 2. Essential strength and incidental weakness of Institutional Religion, studied from within Roman Catholic Church, appears in five pairs of closely related power and defect | 336 |
| (1) Large continuous utilization by Religion of Philosophy and Science. Its antiquity and advantages | 337, 338 |
| Yet two great weaknesses here: |  |
| Philosophy essentially free | 338 |
| but Theology often oppressive towards Philosophy | 338, 339 |
| And Aristotelianism in particular profoundly unhistorical in temper | 340 |
| As to Natural Science: a tolerable latitude appears finally assured to it | 340, 341 |
| (2) Close connection of Religion with History: rightness, necessity, fruitfulness of this | 342, 343 |

| | PAGES |
|---|---|
| The difficulties of all the Institutional Religions here | 343, 344 |
| Rome's special difficulties from her rejection of Pietism | 344, 345 |
| and from her very large and ancient toleration of the uncertain and legendary in history | 345 |
| No grave intrinsic difficulty with respect to earliest, mostly sober constituents of such beliefs, within secondary subject-matters. But more or less grave trouble surrounds questions concerning factual character of certain constituents of the complex of Christian doctrine | 346 |
| The Church's abiding insistence apparently covers three points. Limits to reasonable demands of theologians in historical and documentary matters. Parallel of the Heliocentric controversy | 346, 347 |
| (3) Insistence upon supreme importance of Religious Truth and Unity. Deep, abidingly precious insight thus manifested | 348 |
| The corresponding trouble: persecution. Instances of it throughout Church History | 348, 349 |
| Yet contrary current also very real in ancient Church | 349, 350 |
| amongst Popes of late antiquity and of Middle Ages | 350 |
| in the great Jesuit theologian Cardinal de Lugo and Pope Pius IX. | 350, 351 |
| Implications of the Church's solemn self-commitment to entire O.T. as divinely inspired | 351 |
| Excommunications. Schisms. Cardinal Manning on supernatural grace amongst non-Roman Catholic Christians | 351, 352 |
| And great variety of spiritual types within Roman Church also aids this wider, gentler outlook | 352 |
| Permanent predominance of the gentler current would again render the Roman Church fully lovable. In any case, scepticism and indifference only excuse and aggravate bigotry and persecution. A vigilant sense of Reality of Abiding God are here alone of sufficient avail | 352, 353 |
| (4) Persistence, consolidation, domination of Canon Law. | |
| Religion rightly conceived as also concerned with Law. Christianity contrary to Gnosticism here. Evidence of Acts of the Apostles. Hence only the spirit, position, and effects of such law can reasonably be called in question | 353, 354 |

## Contents

|   | PAGES |
|---|---|
| Yet Church's persuasiveness now for long in inverse ratio to her coercive character. | |
| Contentions of Lutheran Canonist *Rudolf Sohm* : | |
| Catholicism essentially the non-discrimination between Church in the religious sense and Church in the legal sense . . | 354, 355 |
| Christians knew from first only one Church, the same Catholic Church; the only change since, an all-pervading interior transformation of this One Church from an entirely free, charismatic body into a predominantly coercive, legalist organisation . . . . | 355, 356 |
| Considerations : | |
| Primitive Christian, average Roman Catholic, Lutheran, and Curialist attitudes towards relation between Visible and Invisible Church. Neither simple identity nor complete independence are primitive or fruitfully possible solutions . . . | 356, 357 |
| Here again all superfine Idealism, all "pure" spirituality a snare . . . | 357 |
| Yet Canon Law largely late medieval, *i.e.* strongly theocratic. It was *then* largely checked and completed by other forces still vigorous in those times . . | 357, 358 |
| The Protestant Reformation, still more the French Revolution, have changed habits of mind operative when this part of Canon Law flourished, and yet have also abolished the checks within Church upon this Law's full development. Operative constitution of visible Roman Church now an autocracy . . . . | 358, 359 |
| Three reflections and encouragements as to future possibilities . . . | 360 |
| (5) Insistence upon connection between Religion and Politics. Undeniable as a general principle . | 361 |
| Yet no modern, Western attempt at a direct connection long successful. Hostility of the finest of present-day religious minds to such combination . . . . . | 361, 362 |
| Apparent deathlessness of political ambitions within Roman Curia . . . . | 362, 363 |
| Hopes with regard to this trouble . . | 363, 364 |

3. How the experiences and convictions of Eternal Life, which Institutions alone fully awaken, can aid against the evils incidental to Institutionalism to be now described and illustrated. Limitations of this double study.

*Contents*

|   | PAGES |
|---|---|
| (1) The complex of vivid operative convictions connected with Eternal Life, fundamentally fivefold: | |
| Double sense of Abidingness— | |
| Divine Eternity, human Duration | 365, 366 |
| Special work effected by this sense | 366 |
| Sense of Otherness in Likeness— | |
| We are like and are unlike the Realized Perfection | 360 |
| Function of this sense | 366, 367 |
| Sense of Other-Worldliness in contrast with This-Worldliness—spiritual personality begun here, consummated hereafter | 367 |
| Effect of this sense | 367, 368 |
| Sense of Reality—realities environing us, real beings, and *the* Reality of realities sustaining all | 368 |
| Consequences of this sense | 368, 369 |
| Finally, sense of Unity in all multiplicity and of multiplicity in all Unity—organisms everywhere in the real world | 369, 370 |
| Operation of this sense | 370, 371 |
| (2) Illustrations of Institutions awakening, and their operation kept pure by, strong sense of Eternal Life. | |
| Sir Charles Booth's London experiences | 371 |
| Poignant literary expression of this sense in recent Jewish, Anglican, Greek-Russian Church writings | 371, 372 |
| Four recent Roman Catholic examples dwelt on in some detail. | |
| Father Damien at Antipodes slowly dying amongst the lepers | 372 |
| The Beatified Curé d'Ars, J. B. Vianney—his sayings as to Prayer, God alone, and Suffering | 372, 373 |
| Eugénie Smet, Mère Marie de la Providence, her heroic life and painful blissful death | 373, 374 |
| And the Abbé Huvelin. His personality and life-work | 374, 375 |
| His sayings in connection with— | |
| S. François de Sales | 375, 376 |
| Père de Condren | 376 |
| M. Olier | 376 |
| S. Vincent de Paul | 376, 377 |
| and the Trappist Abbé de Rancé | 377 |
| General conclusion concerning all these examples | 377, 378 |

## PART III

### PROSPECTS AND CONCLUSIONS

### CHAPTER XIII

#### FINAL DISCRIMINATIONS

PAGES

Attempt at sketch of lines along which consciousness of Eternal Life has been revealed to us and requires to grow . . . . . . . 381

1. Operative conviction of Eternal Life primarily a matter not of speculation but of characteristically human experience awakened and illuminated by Religion . 382
2. Not an ultimate cause evolving. living subjects, but simply the effect of a living Reality within other realities . . . . . . . 382, 383
3. Eternal Life in fullest sense involves plenitude of all goods and energizings that abide, entire self-consciousness of Being which constitutes them, and pure activity, non-successiveness, of this Being. It excludes space and clock-time : reasons why . . 383
4. Eternal Life, in a real but not the fullest sense, attributable to man ; Duration its true form . 383, 384
5. Man's apprehension of Eternal Life ever achieved only more or less in, contrasting with, finite, changing things ; and obscurely, but with immense range of influence. Its ultimate cause : the actual presence of the Eternal Living Spirit within man's durational spirit . . . . . . 384, 385
6. Hence necessity of Real Time, Duration, for development of human consciousness of Divine Eternity 386, 387
7. Necessity also of spatial imagery and concepts : the reasons of this . . . . 387, 388
Place of Mathematics in full spiritual life. Preliminary Pantheism, the preservative against Ultimate Pantheism . . . . . . 388
8. Material things also continuously check or stimulate durational human spirits—in this life at least. Matter and things—a rich, wise contact with them—as occasions and means of soul's awaking to Eternal Life . . . . . . . 389
9. The sole self-consistent alternative to such costly acceptance of Eternal Life, a more or less obscure but real and profoundly operative evasion of man's true call, of his deepest requirements—a self-stultification and spiritual death . . . 389, 390

*d*

## Contents

PAGES

     Eventual difference of souls thus quantitative as well as qualitative: almost fully eternalized spirits and almost entirely phenomenalized souls . . 390, 391
10. Eternal Life requires deep sense of human weakness and sin, and of our constant need of God's prevenience and purification, but excludes conceptions of total corruption of human nature or of essential impurity of human body. Our Lord's own practice and utterances give the normative balance and combination . . . . . 391, 392
11. And Eternal Life not simply a Moralism *plus* a reference to God as its source and sanction, but centrally Religious—Adoration, a Cultus, and a Finding of God in Art, Speculation, and Analysis, in the Senses and the Body, as well as in Ethics and Heroic Self-dedication . . . . . 392
12. All this seems hopelessly to bind us to exclusive ecclesiasticism, indeed to persecution and oppression. But three strong counteractions against this continuously operative in religion as here conceived 392, 393
     Religion true in its degree exists and functions here in various stages . . . . . 393
     Religion, even in its totality, here not the only activity and response of man's spirit . . . 393, 394
     And Religion here ever conscious of a real interdependence between all these various realities and complexes as all caused and sustained by the Reality of realities, the self-giving Eternal God . 394
13. Apparently intolerable complexity of all this. Parallel of all simple-seeming life and its attempted ever elaborate analysis. Three essentials of Religion continually bring to it expansion and simplicity . 395
     Religion social horizontally—a division of labour amongst souls . . . . . . 395
        Social vertically—a sustainment of the soul by God 395, 396
        And essentially also other-worldly—a life beyond the grave for fullest energizing of durational man within the utterly Abiding God, pure Eternal Life . . . . . . 396

# INTRODUCTION

# ETERNAL LIFE

—•—

## INTRODUCTION

ETERNAL Life cannot be studied with any fruit, except a generous range and a careful, many-sided development be allowed to its study. For the direct subject-matter here is not, indeed, Time and Eternity, nor Body and Spirit, nor the Supreme Good, subjects predominantly philosophical. Nor is it Immortality or Eschatology, nor the Kingdom of God, nor Ecstasy or Pure Love, all primarily religious matters. Yet something about all these things will have, all but continuously, to be implied, said, and decided here. We shall have to begin by roughly assuming and defining, and we hope to end by clearly exhibiting, Eternal Life as an experience, requirement, force, conception, ideal which is, in endless degrees and ways, latent or patent in every specifically human life and act; which, in its fullest operativeness and its most vivid recognition, is specifically religious; and which, in proportion to such fulness and recognition, is found to involve the consciousness, or possession, of all the highest realities and goods sought after or found by man, and the sense (more or less) of non-succession, of a complete Present and Presence, of an utterly abiding Here and Now.

Let us, then, in a First Part, look back, at some length, upon the chief types and stages of this experience and conception, as furnished by the great religious revealers and the chief philosophical formulators of the past. Precise leading utterances will here be given some precise consideration or criticism. Let us next, in a Second Part, look round at the present-day situation, the chief needs, forces, aids, and difficulties operative now in religious and philosophical and also in apparently quite non-religious or non-philosophical departments, for or against that experience and conception. Here again we shall be busy with specific, characteristic declarations, although we can more confidently attempt to reach back, through these, to the forces moving the personalities that uttered them. And let us finally, in a Third Part, attempt a more abiding and systematic elucidation of the elements and realities involved in Eternal Life, and some forecast of, and some demands upon, the future, in this case simply in our own words and with a direct reference to practice. Here again we shall have to utilize philosophy; yet what we now, at last, attempt directly to make explicit, and thus to strengthen, appears, in this its fulness, as a specifically religious sense—a sense of the closest of relations, of the most delicate difference within affinity, between two, the deepest and most real of all realities really known to us, our finite, *durational* spirit, and the infinite, *eternal* Spirit, God.

# PART I
HISTORICAL RETROSPECT

# PART I

## HISTORICAL RETROSPECT

We can conveniently, though somewhat artificially, divide the historical evidences into those furnished by the Oriental religions, properly so called; and those supplied by the Græco-Roman and the Jewish-Christian worlds and their intermixtures, inclusive of the Mediæval and the Modern European (and American) civilization and philosophies, which are still so predominantly derived from these two worlds and their manifold conflicts and combinations.

## CHAPTER I

### THE ORIENTAL RELIGIONS

Introductory—Buddhism—Hindooism—Zarathustrism—Egyptian Religion.

The present writer cannot pretend to any first-hand experience, or knowledge of, the Oriental religions, and must restrict himself to a reproduction of some translations of texts and of the most sober conclusions maintained by careful and sympathetic specialists in these difficult subject-matters, with simply the addition of certain general applications of his own. We can, in strictness, ignore Mohammedanism, since its orthodox type hardly seems to contain any clear or vivid apprehension of non-successiveness, whilst the Sufis are indeed important, as exhibiting a religious life full of the sense of Eternity; but the articulation of this life is probably derived from, and certainly like either Vedantic Pantheism, or the Buddhist Nirvana, or Neo-Platonism. We arrive thus at four, predominantly original and characteristic, Oriental types of experience and conception which, really or seemingly, are concerned with Eternal Life.

1. In *Buddhism* (Gautama Buddha died B.C. 477) we appear to get, in the Nirvana,—in so far as we can take it as not simply annihilation,—a state or condition ultimate, abiding, eternal. Yet, as Professor Lehmann impressively puts it, "in the Buddhist *Weltanschauung* we have colossal dimensions, innumerable worlds, a vertiginous succession of endlessnesses constituting the course of time,—everything without beginning and without end, everything in process of be-

coming and of passing away. It knows no Brahma, no Atman, as the World-spirit,—no Being that consists in itself and through which other things exist. There is here no fixed point for existence, no genuine being." And Professor Oldenberg says strikingly: "The speculation of the Brahmans finds Being in all Becoming; the speculation of the Buddhists finds, in all apparent Being, nothing but Becoming." Thus "an Ego," declares Lehmann, "exists only apparently for the Buddhist; there exists, for him, a series of concepts and of other forms of consciousness, but a self-subsisting subject of all these conditions can neither be traced nor thought" in this system. The Nirvana is the condition in which the suffering life's endless reincarnations are abolished. It is declared to involve the extinction of Desire and of Cognition; and though we are not told that it also includes the extinction of Life, such an extinction would be in the logical consequence of Buddhism, since the evil from which man is to save himself, namely, suffering, consists precisely in existence. The Nirvana can," however, "only be defined negatively: not Desire, and not Consciousness, not Life, yet also not Death. Only this can be said positively concerning it,—that it is the condition in which the soul is freed from transmigration;

only from the point of view of the endless births, with their life and death and death and life, is it possible to attach any conception whatsoever to the term Nirvana."[1]

Thus, even if the Nirvana still be life of some kind, and even though all succession appears to be eliminated from it, we do not get here any positive affirmation of Eternal Life. Yet we are here given perhaps the most impressive of all exemplifications of the intolerable horror felt, by the wide-awake human soul, for mere succession of any kind. The pain of such sheer flux, already simply because it *is* sheer flux, is here seen to be such that the soul, which is haunted by the image and sense of such a flux, is too much absorbed in the relief afforded by any and every complete escape from this pain to move on towards the apprehension of full spiritual life,—of *duration*, and of perfect *Simultaneity*, as respectively the ceaseless characteristic and the deepest implication of that life. And yet that horror eloquently expresses this very characteristic and this very implication of the human soul's deeper and deepest life.

2. In *Hindooism* there is the great *Ramanuja* who, in the eleventh century A.D., founded a

---

[1] Edvin Lehmann, in Chantepie de la Saussaye's *Lehrbuch der Religionsgeschichte*, 3rd ed., 1905, vol. ii. pp. 90, 91, 93, 96, 97 ; Oldenberg, *Buddha*, 3rd ed., 1897, pp. 304-328.

sect which indeed conceives the world, as does the orthodox Vedanta, thoroughly monistically. There exists nothing but the one, all-comprehending Being. Yet this Being is not mere Thought and Existence without qualities; Existence and Thought are here not the substance, they are simply qualities, of Being; the Absolute does not consist of Existence and Thinking, but is a Being which exists and thinks and which possesses all other qualities, and these in so perfect a way that they confer upon it absolute power and absolute worth. Thus Brahma is here conceived as an all-penetrating, all-powerful, all-knowing, all-merciful Being. He is not an undifferentiated Unity, for the manifold world of reality exists in Him; souls and the material elements form His body but not His nature; they are subordinate to Him as our body is to our spirit, and *exist in Him with a relative independence.* All that lives is in process of transmigration (*samsāra*), from which the soul can free itself, — through the knowledge of Brahma, not through good works; the soul is then raised into the world of Brahma, to an eternal, blessed life, and participates in Brahma's divine qualities, except in His power to emit and to rule the world and to receive it back into Himself. Sometimes it is even said, not that souls exist in Brahma, but that Brahma dwells in them as their constitutive principle. And the soul here does not attain liberation from transmigration, through recognizing Brahma and being absorbed in Him by means of its own power, but through its learning to know and to contemplate His nature by the gracious aid of Brahma Himself, and thus attaining to the highest condition of eternal liberty and beatitude in His heaven.[1]

Here indeed, especially in so far as Brahma's own life may be considered to be non-successive in itself, we clearly have Eternal Life, its apprehension and conception.

3. *Zarathustra* lived in North-Western Media, probably between 700 and 650 B.C.; and the oldest parts of the Avesta, especially the *Gatha-hymns*, may well go back to him or to his immediate disciples. In these *Gathas* the supreme God does not yet bear the proper name of, but is already qualified as, Ahura Mazda, the *Lord* possessing *Wisdom*, — the perfect discrimination between Good (Faith) and Evil (Delusion). Or

[1] Edv. Lehmann, *ibid.* p. 143. See the actual texts of Rāmānuja, in his Commentary to the Vedanta-Sutras, tr. by G. Thibaut, Oxford, 1904, esp. p. 208: "The Brahman . . . is nothing else but the highest Person capable of the thought 'of becoming many' by manifesting himself in a world comprising manifold sentient and non-sentient creatures."

he is called the Holy Spirit, and we are told: "In the beginning were the two Spirits, which were there as twins and each by itself." "And when the two Spirits met each other they created, as first created things, Life and Death, and that, at the last, Hell should be for the Wicked and Heaven for the Just." And in the younger *Yasht*-hymns the soul of the departed just man is led, by his religion, his own profession of faith, to his good thoughts, to his good words, to his good works; and, through these three forecourts of Paradise, he arrives at the Eternal Light."[1]

Here, in the insistence upon Good and Evil, as equally powerful; upon these positive forces, as productive of abiding consequences; and upon good works, as the fullest and most final of the essentials for salvation; we get some elements of an even excessively ethical religion, yet which, as such, is in fruitful contrast to the thin intellectualism, and to the conception of Evil as merely negative, so dominant elsewhere. And Eternal Light may here, apparently, be taken as non-successive Life, apprehended as such in God, or even lived by the soul itself.

4. The old Egyptian religion, so bewilderingly rich in its habits and conceptions with regard to

[1] Edv. Lehmann, *ibid.* pp. 170, 171, 174, 188, 199, 223.

the dead and to a life beyond or in the grave, appears to articulate, or even to imply with certainty, little or nothing of Eternal life. For the Gods are here, apparently, all and always, conceived as occupied in purely successive actions; and the texts from all periods (right back to the most ancient pyramid-texts), which identify the individual dead with a God, ever represent this individual as occupied, together with or in this God, in such purely successive, even if monotonously repeated, actions. Thus the dead can be completely identified with Râ, the Sun-God, the dispenser of all life; but this confers upon them no more than the God himself possesses and does,—for the dead man now arises in the heavens, courses through them, descends in the West and arises again in the East.[1]

We have, here, Immortality indeed, but, apparently, not a touch of Eternity.

[1] H. O. Lange, in Chantepie de la Saussaye's *Lehrbuch der Religionsgeschichte*, 3rd ed., 1905, vol. i. pp. 124, 200.

## CHAPTER II

### ISRAELITISH RELIGION

The Jahvist Narratives and the first Prophets: Elijah, Amos, Isaiah, Micah—Deuteronomy and Jeremiah—Ezekiel and the Priestly Code—Late appearance of belief in a fulness of life after death, and abiding significance of this fact.

IN now taking the Jewish-Christian, the Græco-Roman, and the Modern European revelations, conceptions, civilizations, in so far as these are concerned with Eternal Life, we shall do so as constituting seven periods, stages, and conditions of inter-relation, help, and check. Continuing our numeration from our Chapter on the Oriental Religions we thus get Chapters concerned with the following times: II. Israelitish; III. Hellenic; IV. Jewish Hellenistic; V. Primitive Christian; VI. Christian Hellenistic; VII. Mediæval; and VIII. Modern.

The Israelitish times range from, say, B.C. 1320, the Israelite Exodus from Egypt under Moses, to B.C. 597, the first deportation of the Jews and their King Jehoiachin to Babylon, indeed to B.C. 538, the return of the Jews from the Captivity. But we find little or nothing to our purpose till about B.C. 880 (the Book of the Covenant in its present form, Exodus xxi.–xxiii.), and about B.C. 850 (the Jahvist document of the Pentateuch),—the times of King Omri's building of Samaria and of the activity of the great prophets Elijah and Elisha.

1. The *Jahvist* tells us, in the beautiful story of Hagar's desolation in the wilderness, of "the well of the Living One who seeth me" (Gen. xvi. 14, xxiv. 62, xxv. 11); and however much the occasion of the interpretation may be a previous, pagan, proper name of the well, the Jahvist writer himself is evidently full of the sense of God's living presence. Indeed *Ezekiel*, after B.C. 593, still makes God asseverate, "As I live, I have no pleasure in the death of the wicked" (xxxiii. 11): God's power and His merciful love are thus bound up with His livingness. The magnificent account of *Elijah* (1 Kings xvii.–xix., xxi.) doubtless goes back, by oral tradition, to eye-witnesses, and, even in its written form, must be almost entirely as old as about B.C. 790. And here we see how for Elijah "there existed everywhere only *one* holy, only *one* mighty Power, that revealed Itself, not like Baal, in the life of mere nature, but, like Jahveh, in the ethical

requirements of the spirit."¹ In the great ordeal upon Carmel, Jahveh is apprehended by Elijah as so alive and active, and Baal as so dead and inert, that, throughout that long day, the prophet mockingly invites the throng of Baal-priests to invoke Baal and to sacrifice to him (1 Kings xviii. 25–29).

The oldest of the literary prophets, *Amos*, with his eyes fixed upon the approach of the Assyrians (about B.C. 760), makes Jahveh announce to the Israelites: "You only have I known of all the families of the earth: therefore—it is you I will punish for all your iniquities." And again: "Seek good and not evil, that ye may live." And finally: "Though ye offer Me burnt offerings and your meat offerings, I will not accept them. . . . Take thou away from Me the noise of thy song . . . but let judgment roll along as waters, and righteousness as a mighty stream" (iii. 2, v. 14, 22–24). Here the Israelite's special privileges are made the very ground of special responsibilities, and the living God is one to whom moral dispositions are above all ritual observance.

And then the great *Isaiah* of Jerusalem tells us how, in about B.C. 740, he "saw the Lord sitting upon a throne, high and lifted up, and the hems

---

¹ J. Wellhausen, *Abriss der Geschichte Israels und Judas*, 1884, p. 33.

of His garment filled the temple. Seraphs stood before Him, each with six wings. With twain each covered his face . . . And one cried to the other: Holy, holy, holy is Jahveh of hosts, all lands His glory fills." And Isaiah exclaims: "Woe is me, I am undone; for I am a man of impure lips" (vi. 1–3, 5). The living God is thus realized to be transcendent as well as immanent, and man, in His presence, feels himself painfully weak and sinful. And then the prophet, with his lips purified, not by himself but by an angel of God, addresses, in God's name, a parable to God's people: "Now judge, I pray you, betwixt Me and My vineyard. What more could have been done to My vineyard, that I have not done in it?" (v. 4). Thus this overflowingly living, all-powerful God truly cares for weak, sinful man.

*Micah*, in about 696 B.C., exclaims: "Will the Lord be pleased with thousands of rams? . . . shall I perchance give my firstborn . . . in penance for my life? He hath told thee, O man, what is good; and what doth Jahveh demand of thee, but to do justice, and to love mercy, and to walk humbly before thy God?" (vi. 7, 8). The ethical character of the all-powerful, living One is here again magnificently emphasized.

2. *Jeremiah*, called to the prophetical office in 628 B.C., makes God declare Himself "the fountain of living waters," which His people have forsaken; and insists that "the Lord is the living God and an everlasting King; at His wrath the earth shall tremble" (ii. 13, x. 11). Thus God more clearly appears as One possessing the reason of His existence within Himself, and who, as such, is ceaselessly, perfectly active. And then *Deuteronomy* reasserts, and interprets by means of some two and a half centuries of prophetic teaching, and closely in the spirit of Jeremiah, the earlier (Mosaic, Covenantal, Jahvist, and Ephraimite) teachings, and exhorts Israel "Thou shalt love the Lord thy God with all thine heart, and with all thy soul, and with all thy might" (vi. 5), and thus strenuously insists, as central to man's life, upon the most living of relations with the Living One.

3. And, finally, at the beginning of the Exile, the priest-prophet *Ezekiel* (called in B.C. 593, his book completed in 573 B.C.) announces in the name of Jahveh: "Behold, I am against the shepherds, and I will require My flock at their hands. Behold, I Myself will search My sheep. I will deliver them out of all places where they have been scattered in the cloudy and dark day.

I will feed My flock; I will seek that which was lost, and will bind up that which was broken. Ye are My flock, . . . and I am your God" (xxxiv. 10–12, 16, 31). And in the prophet's vision of the valley full of bones, it is God, "the everlasting," who "will put breath into them, and they shall live" (xxxvii. 1, 6). And finally, in his vision of the new temple, the prophet is shown waters that issue from under the threshold of the temple-house, and these, flowing eastward, rapidly become "a river that could not be crossed over." And the interpreting angel explains to Ezekiel: "These waters go down into the Araba, and when they come into the sour waters" of the Dead Sea, "the waters shall be sweetened. And everything that liveth, whithersoever the waters shall come, shall live; and there shall be a very great multitude of fish,—they shall be as the fish of the great sea" (xvii. 1, 5, 8, 9, 10). Thus here God Himself, all life, purity, health, expansion, self-donation, moves out to the weak, the impure, the stricken and contracted, and Himself vivifies, heals, purifies, and infinitely fructifies all He touches. The *Priestly Code* too contains, amidst much detailed legalism and dry schematism, passages of magnificent insight and outlook, akin to those of the priest Ezekiel.

4. It is especially impressive to note how, throughout these eight centuries, the emphasis and the detail of the religious experience and teaching are ever upon God, not upon man, and, nevertheless, upon this life, not upon the next. The various heathen round about had, indeed, much of necromancy, animism, preoccupation with a temporal beyond of all kinds, and little sense of anything otherwise beyond nature,—they had, as yet, but a very slender spiritual and ethical sense. But Israel, in spite of not a few still lingering traces of analogous worship (here, of a mountain- and storm-god) and a largely hard and fierce social code, is, by the prophets, made to abstain from all such animistic practices and indeed from any active thought concerning the individual soul's beyond; and nevertheless it is made to realize, with, at that time, incomparable power and purity, the Other Life of God, present somehow within the soul, here and now, and the unique joy and self-realization, to be found by man's soul, in belonging to Him alone in all its acts and states. And we shall find that it is these spiritual-ethical "this-life" experiences and teachings, and not those naturalistic-magical guesses and practices as to a subsequent life, which heralded, prepared, and entered into the substance of, whatever was fully fruitful and abiding in the further, eventually also

"next-life," teachings concerning Eternal Life. In a word, it is the convictions of the reality and the spiritual-ethical character of God, of a spiritual-ethical soul in man, and of this soul's relation to that God—the reality of a spiritual-ethical kind, already within this life before the body's death—that are the root of every sane and spiritual apprehension of Eternal Life. And though these convictions involve logically, and in the long run are developed by, the faith in the soul's non-diminished life after the body's death, it is not this faith in survival after death that is the basis of these great convictions, but it is, contrariwise, these great convictions that support and postulate that faith.[1]

And yet, as our third Chapter will now show, how much light has been thrown upon the workings of man's mind and spirit, and how much noble, at bottom deeply religious, aspiration, precisely concerning Eternal Life, has been contributed by the Greeks! Indeed how much, after the dross and fever of their earlier experiences and speculations had been dropped and

---

[1] For an admirable account of the long abstention of the Jewish religious world from all other-life speculations and practices, and of the causes and effects of this strikingly persistent religious concentration and reserve, see Dr. R. H. Charles's *Critical History of the Doctrine of a Future Life*, 1899; or his quite short "Rise and Development in Israel of the Belief in a Future Life," *Expositor*, January 1903.

overcome, did they aid in helping even the Jewish saints and seers to articulate and to complete their spiritual outlook!

## CHAPTER III

### THE HELLENIC EXPERIENCES

The Dionysiac Cult—Orphism—Parmenides—Plato and his four abiding contributions—Aristotle and the Unmoving *Energeia*.

THE Hellenic experiences here considered range, from about 550 B.C., to the deaths of Alexander the Great and Aristotle, 323, 321 B.C.

1. The precise local and temporal antecedents and occasions of Orphism are still, in some measure, matters of debate. I shall here, for these questions, follow chiefly Miss Jane Harrison and Professor Gilbert Murray. But the psychic experiences, disagreeably *maladif* or even immoral though they doubtless largely were, can be securely traced; and in this, the point that alone directly concerns us, Erwin Rohde's great *Psyche* book remains a guide, unsurpassed in delicate penetration and power of sympathetic re-evocation.

It is, in any case, certain that the orgiastic

worship of Dionysus, was one of the occasions of Orphism, so largely different in its attitude and spirit. Rohde describes the beginnnigs of that worship in the change that came over Greek thought in the sixth and fifth centuries B.C. : "The continuous life of the soul, which the cultus of the dead presupposes and guarantees, is," so far, "completely tied to the memory of the survivors upon earth, to the care which these survivors may choose to devote to the soul of the predeceased ancestor. If this memory ceases, if the reverent care of the living relaxes, the element is withdrawn from the soul of the departed, in which alone it still possessed a shadow of existence. Not from such a cultus could the idea arise of a true immortality of the soul, of its persistent life, working independently within its own energy. If the soul is truly *immortal*, it is, in its essential quality, equal to *God*. He who, amongst the Greeks, says *immortal*, says *God*; the conceptions are interchangeable. And, in the religion of the Greek people, it is a *fundamental* principle that, in the divine order of the world, humanity and Divine Being are locally and essentially separate and distinct, and are intended to remain so. The religious relation of man to the Divine is essentially based upon this difference; the ethics of the Greek popular consciousness are rooted in willing resignation to the limitation and relativity of human capacity and of human claims to happiness and power,—all this as essentially different from the life and lot of the world of the Gods." And yet, "since a certain time there appears in Greece, and nowhere so early in such clear articulation as in Greece, the thought of the divinity of the human soul, and of the immortality resulting from this, its divine, nature. This thought belongs entirely to Mysticism, a second kind of religion which, but little noticed by the popular religion, created a field for itself in isolated sects, influenced certain philosophical schools, and was able, thence, to convey to far-away posterity in the West and in the East the doctrine of the essential unity, of the union to be striven for by religion, between the divine and the human spirit—of the divine nature of the soul, and of its eternity."

The orgiastic night-worship of Dionysus Sabasios in the Thracian mountain-forests leads to the experience of, here a wild, feverish, thus all the more easily observed, "possession," κατεχόμενοι ἐκ τοῦ θεοῦ, ἔνθεοι: and an absence of the mind, ὁ νοῦς οὐκέτι ἐν αὐτῷ ἔνεστιν: the soul's going out, standing out, of the body, ἔκστασις (Plato, *Meno*, 99 D; *Ion*, 534 B). This ecstasy is here a sacred madness, in which the soul unites itself with the Godhead: ἱερομάνια (Clemens Alex., *Protrept.* 9 D; Plato, *Phædr.* 253 D). And this experience could not fail strongly to aid a peculiar development of belief in the immortality, indeed in the eternity, of the soul. Thus Herodotus and others tell of Thracian tribes whose faith "made men immortal"—Γέται οἱ ἀθανατίζοντες (4. 93, 94). Transmigration of souls appears to have been taught. But it is the cultus itself, its aim and its return-effect upon the worshipper's conviction, that we can follow out clearly. "The aim, indeed the task, of the cultus, was to drive its participants as far as 'ecstasy,' to tear their souls out of their ordinary, humanly limited, mode of existence, and to raise them, as free gods, to communion with the God and his satellites. This experience could be gained in ecstasy by the soul, but by it alone,—the spiritual being living invisibly within man,—not by the entire human being, composed of body and soul. The feeling of its own divinity, of its eternity, which, in the ecstasy, had revealed itself, as in a lightning-flash, to the soul, could develop into the abiding conviction that this soul is of a divine nature, called to a divine life, as soon as the body leaves it free—as in ecstasy for a short while, so in death for ever."[1]

---

[1] Erwin Rohde, *Psyche*, 2nd ed., 1898, vol. ii. pp. 1, 2, 11, 12, 28, 32, 33. The entire section, pp. 1-37, is a classic of the purest water

I would only insist, even more than Rohde, upon the fact that all states of trance, or indeed of rapt attention, notoriously appear to the experiencing soul, in proportion to their concentration, as timeless; *i.e.* as non-successive, simultaneous, hence as *eternal*. They appear thus to the soul, if not during, at least soon after, the experience. And hence the eternity of the soul is not, here, a conclusion drawn from the apparent God-likeness, in other respects, of the soul when in this condition, but the eternity, on the contrary, is the very centre of the experience itself, and is the chief inducement to the soul for holding itself to be divine. The soul's immortality cannot be experienced in advance of death, whilst its eternity, in the sense indicated, is, or seems to be, directly experienced in such "this-life" states; hence the belief in immortality is here derivative, that in eternity is primary.

2. It was the religious sect of the *Orphics* that took over this experience and conviction from those orgiastic Dionysus-worshippers, whilst greatly altering, in part directly reversing, the cultual acts and the ethical practice and dispositions. Orphic communities appear to have formed themselves in Greek regions soon after 550 B.C.; certainly Onomakritos established such

a community in Athens, under the Peisistratidæ, about 530–510 B.C., and presents the Orphic doctrines in poetic form. In the poetry and cultus of the sect a long genealogy of the Gods ended with Dionysus or Zagreus, the son of Zeus and Persephone, entrusted by his father with the rule of the world. The Titans, Zeus's enemies, attack Dionysus, who escapes in various disguises; but at last, in the form of a bull, Dionysus is overcome, torn to pieces, and devoured by his savage enemies. Zeus destroys the Titans with a thunderbolt; and out of their ashes arises the human race, possessing the good which descends from Dionysus, mixed up with the evil derived from the Titans. Thus the good, in the several human souls, is so many fragments of one single soul, broken up by a crime; and man's task is to free himself from the Titanic element in his present nature, and to bring his Dionysian part back pure to the God of whom, essentially, it forms a part.

Thus the soul will escape "the circle of necessity," "the wheel of births," ὁ τρόχος τῆς γενέσεως, endless transmigrations; here we have a truly Buddhist feeling. But this escape can only be brought by Orpheus and his Bacchic initiations. It is Διόνυσος λύσιος, θεοὶ λύσιοι, and

### Orphism like and unlike Buddhism

not man's own strength, which here liberate man,
—here we get beyond Gautama's teaching.[1]

Now this Orphic cultus and life are full of abstinence and purification, and are as intensely dualistic in their attitude towards the body as is Buddhism itself. The σῶμα-σῆμα play-upon-words, the body, the soul's grave, is Orphic, as Plato tells us, *Cratylus*, 400 C. Yet the Orphics not only very certainly believed in a future life, but the remains of their actual cultus and practice (as distinguished from literary utilizations and eclectic transformations of their teachings, such as those of the largely sceptical Euripides) show us how important, how alive and intense an element in their religion was this belief, and also how decidedly not a Nirvana, not an unconsciousness or lowered consciousness, this future life was conceived by them to be.

Thus, in the absolutely authentic, contemporary Orphic Tablets the soul, on coming, at its death, into the Beyond, declares that "I am son of Earth," the Titans, "and of starry Heaven," Zeus, through Dionysus; that "out of the pure," from Orphic purification, "I come, pure queen of them below," Persephone; and that "I have" in consequence "flown out of the sorrowful weary

---

[1] For all this, see Miss Jane Harrison's careful account in *Prolegomena to the History of Greek Religion*, 1908, pp. 478–496.

wheel" of flux and transmigration. But how utterly non-Buddhist is the life here, which the Orphic expects, and desires, to live after death! For the soul, thus arrived in the Beyond, is not to approach a certain Well-spring there, but is to draw near to another, "by the lake of Memory," and to beseech the guardians of it "Lo, I am parched with thirst and I perish, give quickly the cold water flowing forth from the lake." The first well is doubtless Lethe, Forgetfulness, since already Hesiod, in about 720 B.C., holds Lethe to be bad (*Theog.* 227); and in Plato the river Ameles or Lethe brings pollution to those who do not succeed in crossing it successfully (*Rep.* x. 621*a*, *c*), and the soul that refuses to soar, sinks to earth "full" simultaneously "of forgetfulness (λήθη) and vice" (*Phædr.* 248*c*).[1]

The world presented by these tablets is a complicated one, since the soul, in spite of its divinity, requires, even when freed from the body, first to find and to utilize certain means for regaining the memory of its own past. And, again, the soul seems thus, even when it has attained this memory, to find its bliss, not in a vision of, and

[1] Jane Harrison, *op. cit.* pp. 572–599, and Prof. Gilbert Murray, *ibid.* 659–673, give a most careful and full account and elucidation of these eight tablets, the former not, I think, without a considerable over-estimate of the elevation of religion here attained.

intercourse with, the Gods, but in the regaining of its past joys and insights. Perhaps, however, the memory here intended is primarily the soul's re-awakening to its pre-natal experience and knowledge. Yet, even so, we miss any simple consciousness, not of its own past or future, but of a present Reality, and any non-successiveness or eternity in this its consciousness. I take it that the popular, non-mystical Greek religion, with its conception of a merely shadowy continuance after death, has been strongly operative here, and has been respectively reinforced and overcome by the two apparently contradictory characteristics of all concentrated or ecstatic states—an apparent oblivion of all things, even including the object fixed by the mind, and a finding of delightful freshness both in this object and in all other things.

3. It is in *Parmenides*, who owes so much to the Orphics and Pythagoreans (he was born in Greek Southern Italy about 544 B.C.) that we get the first quite plain and precise discrimination, still accessible to us, between an Eternal Now and all Succession.

μοῦνος δ' ἔτι μῦθος ὁδοῖο
λείπεται ὡς ἔστιν· ταύτῃι δ' ἐπὶ σήματ' ἔασι
πολλὰ μάλ', ὡς ἀγένητον ἐὸν καὶ ἀνώλεθρόν ἐστιν

οὖλον μουνογενές τε καὶ ἀτρεμὲς ἠδ' ἀτέλεστον.
οὐδὲ ποτ' ἦν οὐδ' ἔσται, ἐπεὶ νῦν ἔστιν ὁμοῦ πᾶν,
ἕν, συνεχές.[1]

" There remains then still only to give an account of One way—that Being exists indeed. Many directing posts stand upon it: because unborn, it is also indestructible, entire, only-begotten, unshakable, and without end. It never was and it will never be, since it is, all of it together, only present in the Now, one and indivisible." Thus the first clear promulgation of the *Totum Simul* of Eternity is also the clearest of all purely abstractive and Monistic, utterly static and determinist, professions of faith,—and, like all such professions, takes Mathematical transparency and lucid spatial picturings as directly applicable to the deepest of realities, and as the test and measure of our attaining to the truth concerning them.

4. But it is in *Plato* (born in Athens about 427 B.C., died there in 347) that the apprehension of an Eternal Now, and the conception of a *Totum Simul*, attain their greatest vividness and clearness, though far from their greatest richness of content, so far for all time. Let us accept as

[1] 8. 1-3, 5, 6. Diels, *Fragmente der Vorsokratiker*, 2te Aufl., 1906, vol. i. pp. 118, 119.

now established, in at least their main outlines, the three stages of Plato's growth, and the three corresponding groups of the Platonic writings. The first, beginning with the *Lysis* and ending with the *Meno*, is a continuation of Socrates's work, and hardly more articulated than it; the second, beginning with the *Gorgias* and ending with the *Phædrus*, turns away from the *Here* to the *There*; and the third, beginning with the *Symposium* and ending with the *Laws*, is a compromise between the later orientation towards the Beyond and the earlier position in the visible world. Hence only in the second and third groups do we find teachings to our purpose. The *Republic* is a mosaic of contributions from all three periods.

(1) In the second group, then, we get the passages in the *Phædrus* and *Republic*, which are already mentioned as hostile to forgetfulness, and so strongly insist upon how Remembering-Again, ἀνάμνησις (like unto the Orphic μνημοσύνη, Memory), and not Unmindfulness or Forgetting, is the lot of the purified soul in the Beyond. In the *Theætetus* (176*a*, *b*) Socrates affirms: "It behoves us to attempt to escape hence thither, as swiftly as possible; and this flight thither consists in a likeness to God (ὁμοίωσις τῷ θεῷ) as far as possible; and this likeness consists in becoming just and

holy and wise." Thus the soul is not identical with God: it can attain to some likeness to Him; and He is possessed of ethical qualities in a supreme degree and way. Indeed in the *Sophist* (248*d*, 249*a*), the Eleatic stranger breaks out with: "Can we, O heavens, ever be made to believe that motion and life and soul and mind are not present in Absolute Being? Can we imagine Being to be devoid of life and mind, and to remain a venerable, holy, mindless, unmoving fixture (ἀκίνητον ἑστός)?" The clear, cold, fixed, empty abstraction of Parmenides has, here at least and for a little while, been replaced by a vivid, warm apprehension of the Reality, as full of life and energy and as rich in self-communication. And the *Parmenides* vigorously criticizes, surely, as a *reductio ad absurdum*, the doctrine of One, or of the One, when taken strictly, as exclusive of all multiplicity and relations, and thus criticizes it also in respect to its view of Time. "The One cannot exist in Time at all," it is argued (141 A); the various forms of Time are each examined and rejected, and amongst such forms appears also "is,"—"is not 'is' simply the form of Time when now present?" (141 E); and hence, these forms of Time being the only possible modes of Being, "the One" of Parmenides, it is concluded, "cannot possibly partake of Being" (141 E).

It is in this second group also that we find most of Plato's utterances and picturings as to an after-death purification from bad habits in souls that are good in their active, dominant intention at the moment of death, a purification deliberately chosen by such souls. These intrinsically necessary purifications, freely willed by the soul itself, most advantageously replace the quite un-intrinsic delay in attaining to a blissful consciousness noted by us in the Orphic Tablets. These chief purgatorial passages occur in the *Gorgias*, pp. 525*b*, *c*, 526*c*, *d*; the *Phædrus*, p. 249*b*; the *Republic*, x. pp. 617*e*, 619*e*, 920*e*; and the *Phædo*, pp. 110*b*–114*d*.[1]

(2) It is, however, in the third period and group of writings that Plato most strenuously strives after, and most nearly attains to, a way from the Contingent to the Necessary, and gives us a clear definition of the essential nature of, and contrast between, Time and Eternity. In the *Symposium*, Diotima, in her great speech as to the soul's mounting up, by

[1] For the sequence of the *Dialogues*, see Prof. Henry Jackson's "Plato's later Theory of Ideas," *The Journal of Philology*, Cambridge, vols. x.–xv., 1882–1886. I have accepted the three stages in the composition of the *Republic* demanded by Rohde, *Psyche*, ed. 1898, vol. i. pp. 266, 269 note, and E. Pfleiderer, *Socrates und Plato*, 1896, pp. 124–136. For Plato's Purgatorial teachings, see my *Mystical Element of Religion*, 1908, vol. ii. pp. 123–126, 205–211.

ever greater purification and abstraction, to the momentary vision of, and union with, Eternal Beauty, tells us how, when the purified seeker "comes towards the end, he will suddenly perceive a Nature of wondrous beauty, neither growing nor decaying . . . but Beauty absolute, separate, simple and everlasting"—ἀεὶ ὂν καὶ οὔτε γιγνόμενον οὔτε ἀπολλύμενον (210 E, 211 A). Here we have indeed an Eternal that truly *is*, and indeed that is even, somehow, supremely beautiful. Yet not all the rapture of the loving soul can prevent that Eternal from here appearing cold and unattractive; for it is not here possessed, as, for a moment, it was in the *Sophist*, of energy and life and, at least by implication, of self-communication. Erōs, the soul's movement up to the Eromenon, the beloved One, is indeed here; but the Eromenon is not an Erōn, there is no previous movement down to the soul from the One; no longing for our longing, no "He hath first loved us," hardly the dawn of *Agape*, is as yet discoverable here.

It is in the *Timæus* that Plato achieves the clearest extant contrast between Eternity and Time. For, in the account of the fashioning of the world, we see how the Father who begat the world "whilst he was ordering the universe, made, of Eternity which abides in unity, an eternal image moving according to number, even that which we have named Time. . . . Days and nights and months and years, are all portions of Time; and *was* and *shall be* are forms of Time that have come to be, although we are wont wrongly to ascribe them to the Eternal Essence. For we say that It was and shall be, yet, in truth, *is* alone belongs to It" (37 E). "Is," taken thus strictly, is here no more one of the forms of Time, but is the characteristic form of Eternity. Hence Eternity is essentially simultaneous, and quite distinct from everlasting duration, from succession, from Time.[1]

In spite of his distressing insensibility to the odiousness of certain Pagan vices, and of his dangerous, because excessively abstractive, method and temper, especially during his middle period, Plato, at his best, remains the first and last of the Græco-Roman non-Christian souls and thinkers to unite, especially also in his thirst and search after Eternal Life, four things never to be disunited without a great impoverishment of experience and outlook. Philosophy with him stands in the midst of a great social and political as well as individual life, and strives to understand and to aid this life; it ever retains the need and

[1] For the passage in the *Timæus*, see Archer Hind's good notes, 1880.

practice of purification, whilst enlisting in this struggle all the nobler passions, the *Thumos* as well as the Reason, against the lower passions; it ever strives to find multiplicity in all unity, and unity in all multiplicity; and it never ceases to be kept profoundly alive, and very largely humble and sweet, by the sense of an inexhaustible, transcendent Beauty, Truth, and Goodness, our love of which constitutes all our worth.

5. In *Aristotle*, Alexander the Great's great tutor, 384-322 B.C., we miss much of what, in Plato, deep souls will never let die,—especially the κάθαρσις, the turning of the whole soul, as ever the essential condition for its attainment of spiritual truth and life; the retention and training of the Thumos, as the born auxiliary of reason in its difficult fight against ignoble passion; and the, already largely theistic, thirst after more than all merely human, merely contingent, things and states. Yet, in his conception of the Unmoving Energy, Aristotle also has made a profound and permanent contribution to the expression and stimulation of the experiences and problems involved in Eternal Life.

(1) In the *Nicomachean Ethics* there are such sayings as that "to be is to be active," ἐσμεν δ' ἐνεργείᾳ (ix. 1168a, 3); that "men are unable to be

continuously active, and hence pleasure does not continuously arise in their lives, for pleasure follows upon *energeia*" (x. 1175a, 9); and that "all men have held the gods to be alive and to energize, and not to be asleep like Endymion" (x. 1178b, 7). God alone is always completely and actually all that He can be; hence the divine *energeia* is kept up inexhaustively, and ever generates the supreme pleasure of self-contemplation (νόησις νοήσεως) which constitutes the divine happiness. It follows, as a matter of course, that this ἐνέργεια is above κίνησις—it is ἐνέργεια ἀκινησίας or ἠρέμια. Hence "if the nature of anything were simple, the same action would ever be sweet to it. And this is the reason why God always enjoys a single and simple pleasure; for there is not only an activity of motion but also one void of motion, and pleasure is rather in constancy than in motion. And change of all things is sweet" to us men "because of a certain defect" in us (vii. 1154b).

And in the *Metaphysics* we have the account of the divine life: "And life subsists there; for the activity of pure reason (ἐνέργεια νοήσεως) is life and He is sheer activity (ἡ ἐνέργεια); and His activity, ever busy with itself, constitutes His perfect and eternal life. We say, then, that God is an eternal perfect being, so that life, and continuous and eternal duration (αἰὼν συνεχὴς καὶ ἀΐδιος), pertain to God, for God is indeed all this" (xi. 1072b).

We have in the above, especially also in the important translation of ἠρέμια by "constancy," been following Dr. F. C. Schiller, in his admirable study of the Unmoving Energy. And it is he also who, most instructively, points out how "Aristotle does not, as we commonly do, regard a 'function' (ἐνέργεια) as a sort of 'process' (γένεσις), or try, materialistically, to reduce all things to 'matter' in 'motion.' He does the very opposite. Instead of classifying ἐνέργεια under κίνησις, he simply makes ἐνέργεια the wider and supremer notion, and subsumes κίνησις under it as a particular species, *viz.* an *imperfect ἐνέργεια*."[1]

(2) Applying his principles of *Nous* and *Energeia* to human life, Aristotle declares "such a life" (of philosophy, as described by him) "would be a life superior to ordinary human life; for it cannot be lived in so far as man is merely man, but only in so far as a divine element (θεῖόν τι) subsists in him." This element is pure intelligence (ὁ νοῦς); and in proportion as such *Nous* exceeds man as a composite being, in the same proportion does the activity of this element exceed the activity

[1] F. C. Schiller, "Activity and Substance," in *Humanism*, 1903, pp. 204–227.

directed to the virtues of the practical life. "Wherefore, in so far as we can, we must live the immortal life (ἀθανατίζειν) and do our utmost to live according to the highest principle within us" (*Ethics*, x. 1177*b*, 8).

Especially the Christian revelation and experience will show us presently how intolerably thin and shadowy, in this entire Aristotelian scheme, is this "Thinking of Thought," and this isolating of intelligence from all the emotive and operative activities and outgoing interests of the soul. Yet the great intuitions that succession is not essential to, but a defect of, life, and that the perfect human life will approximate to such non-successiveness, prove all the more, indeed only then really, satisfactory, when we keep and make the human life as rich as possible with variously picturing, reasoning, cognizing, emotive, volitional, operative activities, interests, sufferings, and joys; and when we hold that the fundamental causes and final objects of all that is truest and best in these our experiences and necessities are somehow present in God, in a most real, though for us quite unpicturable, manner. The simultaneity of ten thousand different activities applied to myriads upon myriads of mutually differing creatures is no more incredible, no more anthropomorphic, than is the simultaneity of a sheer thinking of sheer thought; and only such an infinitely rich content gives its true value to the simultaneity, just as the simultaneity, in its turn, gives its full worth to that richness. But only an immense increase of light as to man's spiritual needs and miseries, and as to the nature of the deepest ethical perfection, could break up, to any advantage, the thin, deistic constituents of this Aristotelian outlook; and this light was not to be for yet awhile.

## CHAPTER IV

### JEWISH HELLENISTIC TIMES

Introductory—Stoicism—O.T. Apocrypha—Philo.

THE pre-Christian Hellenistic experiences and conceptions range, in strictness, from the death of Alexander at Babylon (323 B.C.), to our Lord's public ministry in Galilee (about A.D. 30). Let us, however, here take the Pagan and the Jewish developments (even though these latter begin already with the return from the Exile, in 538 B.C.) in close juxtaposition; and this because of the considerable influence, at least after Alexander's death, exercised probably by each upon the other. And let us consider thus successively Stoicism, the Old Testament Apocrypha, and Philo, as the most important sources for our present purpose.

1. The Oriental, partly Phœnician, hence Semitic, origin of all the earlier Stoic chiefs—especially *Zeno*, the founder (Cyprus), about 342–270 B.C.; *Cleanthes* (Troas), about 331–251 B.C.; and *Chrysippus* (Cilicia), about 281–208 B.C.—is very striking. And the rapid up-building, and the as rapid break-up, of Alexander's world-empire occurs at this time. The ethnic origin and the historical occasion help to explain the school's otherwise strangely persistent combination of an emphatically materialistic Pantheism, a deep moral earnestness, an intuitive, prophetic habit of mind, and a both sad and enthusiastic, largely non-political, non-patriotic, yet, for the most part, socially organized, cosmopolitanism.

(1) The pantheistic-materialist basis of Stoicism is described by Diogenes Laertius (vii. 40): "The Stoics liken philosophy to a living creature—the Logic to the bones and muscles, the Ethics to the fleshy parts, and the Physics to the soul"; and by Cicero (*Acad. post.* I. 11): "Zeno differs from his predecessors in holding that nothing that effects anything, and nothing that is effected, can

be other than a body." The First Principle is ether or fire, a fiery ether or warm fluid; and this moves through a regular change from fire to air, air to water, water to earth, and back again to fire—to a conflagration (ἐκπύρωσις) which, at the end of each age of the world, destroys all that has been produced between whiles, inclusively of all souls and of all consciousness. Thus pure matter without any quality, fire, is, after each such inevitable crisis, all that exists (Diog. Laert. vii. 136, 142, 157).

The Stoics, indeed, call God "an immortal, living being, endowed with reason (λογικόν), with forethought for the world and for all things in the world" (Diog. Laert. 147). But all this, taken as part of the system, means no more than the necessity, the law, entirely immanent in the material universe. God *is* the Universe, and the Universe *is* God.

Hence we cannot, here, consistently speak of Eternal Life, in the sense of an abiding consciousness on the part of the human soul, or even of a momentary consciousness on the part of the First Principle, of the Infinite God. The finite spirit here survives the body, at longest, up to the Ecpyrosis only; and an Infinite Spirit, self-conscious and distinct from the world, exists at no time, since, when implicit, such spirit as is allowed at all is but pure material fire, and, when explicit, this fire moves through material changes, or itself constitutes these changes, having, during part of this time, self-conscious finite minds for its concomitants and effects. A certain appearance of livingness and richness is, indeed, introduced through the conception of the First Principle as also the Logos, as Reason, which permeates, conjoins, sustains all things, and which thus resembles Plato's World-Soul, but is in strong contrast with the Platonic supreme Idea, conceived as outside of all movement and becoming. Yet the identification of this Logos with material fire, its complete immanence in the world, and its lack of consciousness effectually disqualify it from acceptance as the sufficient bearer, cause, and object of Eternal Life, in the fuller sense of the word.

(2) And the Ethical Rigorism also takes us farther away from Eternal Life than was Plato, if we hold such Life to retain, indeed to consummate, the development, purification, harmony and organization of all man's nobler passions and emotions, or of their deepest roots and equivalents. "Whilst the earlier philosophers did not abolish perturbations of soul from out of man, but only restricted their range, Zeno required his sage to be free from them all, as so many diseases

of the soul," says Cicero (*Acad.* i. 10, 38). The objects to be striven after or avoided are also greatly restricted: "Good things consist for the Stoics in the virtues," prudence (φρόνησις) standing first; "evil things consist in the opposite," thoughtlessness coming first; "and the things that are neither good nor evil are those that neither benefit nor damage us, such as life, health . . . and their opposites, death, disease . . ." Again, the perfect life and its acts have here lost indefinitely in variety, dramatic contrast, and fruitful tension. "The Stoics declare that the sage practises all the virtues in each one of his acts, since his entire activity is perfect," Stobæus tells us (*Ecl.* ii. p. 116). The outlook on mankind is terribly simplified: "Zeno holds that there exist only two classes of men, the class of the earnest (the good) and that of the worthless; and that, throughout their respective lives, the former practise the virtues, the latter the vices" (Stobæus, *Ecl.* ii. p. 198). And above all, there is no deep richness of relation between spirits, because there is no sufficiently intimate dependence of spirit upon Spirit: "monstro quod ipse tibi possis dare," "I here prescribe what you yourself can give yourself," says Juvenal, truly Stoically, of the very highest devotedness and resignation.

(3) And yet the system nobly preaches the profound necessity of self-control and of the renunciation of all petty or low desires. And, in its deeply organic conception of human society, it directly prepares, and eventually aids, the powerful articulation of the requirements and of the conception of Eternal Life as effected by Christianity. "They consider the world to be, as it were, a common city and state of men and of Gods, and that each one of us constitutes a part of that world, whence it follows that we should put the common advantage above our own," says Cicero (*de Fin.* iii. 19, 64). And the Stoic Seneca tells us: "We are members of one great body"; "it behoves thee to live for thy neighbour, if thou wouldst live for thyself" (*Ep.* 95, 52, 47, 3). From Zeno's work, the *Politeia*, through the writings of Polybius and Cicero, up to the school's culmination, as to tenderness, in the discourses of the freedman Epictetus, and as to mournful, moral splendour of human outlook, in the memoirs of the emperor Marcus Aurelius, we get this most fruitful perception of the essentially organic character of human society, and insistence upon finding its image in the human body, which is constituted by, and which still more constitutes, the several, yet interdependent and mutually complementary,

parts and members and their differing specific positions, functions, and characters.[1]

2. The experiences and conceptions of the Jews since the return from the Exile, 538 B.C., and especially since their submission to Alexander the Great, 332 B.C., and to his successors, are, upon the whole, less rich and pregnant than are the deepest of the previous Israelitish prophetic teachings.

(1) There is, indeed, a series of magnificent utterances in the Psalms, of which the greater part probably belong to this period, such as, "With Thee is the fountain of Life, and in Thy light we shall see light" (xxxvi. 9); and "Whom have I in heaven but Thee? and, having Thee, I delight not in aught that is on earth. My flesh and my heart faileth, but God is the rock of my heart and my portion for ever" (lxxiii. 25, 26). Thus here, without any speculation concerning time and eternity, we have the fundamental elements of Eternal Life, the human spirit finding its peace and support in the Divine Spirit, its origin and home.

---

[1] E. Zeller's standard account in his *Philosophie der Griechen*, part iii. vol. i., ed. 1880, has been the chief help here. Von Arnim's *Stoicorum Veterum Fragmenta* gives Zeno in vol. i., 1905, pp. 1-71, and Cleanthes, pp. 103-139. See also James Adam in *The Vitality of Platonism*, 1911, pp. 104-189, for a beautiful account of Stoicism at its best.

(2) The Book of *Daniel* (an apocalyptic consolatory address, which but little resembles the pre-Exilic prophecies, written between 168 and 165 B.C.) gives a description of the era of salvation: "Many of them that sleep in the dust of the earth shall awake, some to everlasting life, and some to everlasting contempt" (xii. 2)—the only passage in the Old Testament which explicitly speaks of "everlasting" or "eternal" life. The resurrection extends here as yet only to "many"—apparently only to the Jewish martyrs and to their persecutors; and still we cannot press the "everlasting" as involving simultaneity.

Amongst the Apocryphal and the Pseudo-Epigraphic writings, *Ecclesiasticus*, originally written in Hebrew between 190 and 170 B.C., still articulates only the quantitative conception, the soul's endless duration, together with the resurrection of the body. God is "He that liveth for ever" (ὁ ζῶν εἰς τὸν αἰῶνα); and "He gave the law of life for an inheritance" (xviii. 1). The *Second Book of Maccabees* (about 100–80 B.C.) has "the Lord of life and spirit" (xiv. 46); and the *Apocalypse of Baruch*, possibly as late as A.D. 40–70, has "Thy deep thoughts, O God, that are full of life" (liv. 12). The *Psalms of Solomon*, so strongly Pharisee, of about 65–45 B.C., also have the quantitative conception: "the life of the just lasteth for ever" (xiii. 11); "the law which He hath vouchsafed to our life."

(3) It is in the *Wisdom of Solomon*, doubtless written in Egypt, probably between 100 and 50 B.C., that, in addition to the *quantitative* conception,—endless duration: "the just live for ever" (εἰς τὸν αἰῶνα ζῶσι), v. 45,—we find also clear indications of the *qualitative* conception. Thus God created man unto "incorruption" (ἀφθάρσια), ii. 23; "to know Thy power is the root of immortality" (ἀθανάσια), xv. 3; and, above all, "incorruption maketh us near to God," vi. 20.

It is important, however, clearly to realize, that simultaneity of itself is as little spiritually qualitative a conception as is succession by itself; and to note how again, in these passages, it is God, His purity and power, who centrally occupies the soul: intercourse with, proximity to, Him—this is Eternal Life.[1]

3. And lastly the Alexandrian Jew *Philo*, who lived from about 30 B.C. to A.D. 50, is deeply interesting in his attempt to retain, indeed to propagate, the intensely personalist, racial and

---

[1] See the excellent collection of translations with introductions and notes, *Die Apokryphen und Pseudepigraphen des A.T.*, edited by E. Kautzsch, 2 vols., 1900.

theistic, Israelite and Jewish, religion, within and by means of the categories of Greek philosophy—especially those of Platonism, so largely impersonal, and those of Stoicism, so strongly materialist, pantheistic, and cosmopolitan.

(1) Philo, then, insists, adopting Aristotle's terms, upon how " God never ceases from action ; as the fire's property is to burn, so God's property is to act"; indeed "He is the origin of the activity of all things." And He ceases not from this His activity even on the Sabbath (*Leg. Alleg.* 3, 6; Cohn and Wendland's ed. of *Philo*, vol. i., 1896, pp. 62, 65). And, following Plato, he describes God's Eternity as exclusive of all succession: "God is withdrawn from both ends of Time. For His Life is not so much Time as Eternity (αἰών), the archetype and pattern of Time. And in Eternity there is nothing past and nothing future, but only present" (*Quod Deus sit Immut.* 6; CW. ii. 63).

(2) As to Life, Philo is subject to two currents of thought. Along one current God is possessed of the fullest life, and, because of this, can and does communicate it, in a lesser degree and kind : " There are three kinds of life : life as it concerns God ; life as it concerns the creature ; and a third, intermediate life, a mixture of the former two. Now life as it concerns God has not descended

to us, nor has it entered into the necessities of the body." The second kind of life is "life according to sense," "life as resident in the blood (ζωὴ ἔναιμος)." But only those who live the third kind of life are "truly living": for Moses tells us that "the soul's nature is double: that of the soul generally is blood, that of its most leading part is divine spirit" (πνεῦμα θεῖον). And Philo finds, here following the Stoics, this Pneuma to be Logos. "Hence there are two kinds of men—those living by the divine spirit and reason (λογισμός), and those living by the blood and the lust of the flesh" (*Quis rer. div. heres*, 9, 11, 12; CW. iii. 11, 13, 14). "God" Himself "breathed into man's earthly mind the power of the true life; thus it is that man becomes a mental, a truly living soul." Hence God is the fountain of reason, and such a reasonable life is a life of God (*Leg. Alleg.* 1, 12; CW. i. 69; *Poster. Cain*, 20; CW. ii. 15). Indeed this divine life, even as man can begin to live it here by a holy life, and still more as, after such a life, he will live it in the Beyond, is sometimes characterized as strictly eternal, *i.e.* non-successive. "Is not the flight to true Being (τὸ ὄν) Life Eternal?" To such souls "Moses promises incorruption: 'Ye shall live to-day,' for 'to-day' is boundless and inexhaustible eternity (αἰών)." "They participate in the immaterial and incorruptible life of the Unbegotten and Incorruptible" (*Profug.* 15; CW. iii. 126; *de Fuga*, ii.; CW. iii. 122; *Gigant.* 3; CW. ii. 44).

Yet Philo follows also another current in which, fully adopting and pushing home certain tendencies of Plato, he already largely anticipates the exclusive transcendence and excessive abstraction of Plotinus, perhaps even of Proclus. God, here, is indeed "the cause of soul and life"; but "God" Himself "is something more than life; He is, as He says Himself, the ever-flowing fountain of life" (*de Fuga*, 36; CW. iii. 152). For Philo, in this his more strictly philosophical mood, God is not the Living One, but He Who Is (ὁ ὤν, τὸ ὄν, ὁ ὄντως ὤν, τὸ ὄντως ὄν, τὸ πρὸς ἀλήθειαν ὄν).

And yet this devoted Jew is too sensitively religious with the great, historical religion of the Old Testament, not also (and then enthusiastically) to picture God as graciously self-communicative to man's spirit, which spirit, in deliberate difference from Stoicism, is here not sufficient to itself. Thus "often," beyond all man's endeavours and in spite of all man's temptations and corruption, "God, by His grace, pours a sweet flood of waters, in place of its salt flood, into the soul"; "it is God who moves and leads the soul's chariot whither He chooses"; and "the soul must confess that, not its own power has effected the moral good, but He who vouchsafed to it its very love for this good" (*Leg. Alleg.* ii. 9, 21; CW. i. 97, 107, iii. 46; CW. 143).

(3) The Stoic Apathy, again, influences Philo far too much. Thus "Moses considers it necessary that all desire shall be excised from the soul, since he loves not a moderation of the passions but a complete apathy." Yet on this point also the spontaneity and richness of the Jewish religion mostly predominates, *e.g.*, "virtue is naturally a matter of delight, and he who possesses it rejoices continually" (*Leg. Alleg.* iii. 46; CW. i. 143; *de Mutat. nom.* 31; CW. iii. 185).[1]

[1] James Drummond's *Philo Judæus*, 2 vols., 1888, remains the fullest, and an excellent, account: "Time and Eternity," i. 292–295; "The Two Conceptions of God," i. 1–64; "Apathy and the Higher Anthropology," ii. 320–324. J. Grill, *Untersuchungen über Entstehung des vierten Evangeliums*, 1902, "'Life' in Philo," 207–211

## CHAPTER V

### PRIMITIVE CHRISTIANITY

The utterances of Jesus : the Kingdom—Teachings of St. Paul : the Spirit—Conceptions of the Johannine writer : Eternal Life.

THE chief Primitive Christian teachings fall into three groups, according as they proceed from Jesus Himself, from St. Paul, or from the Johannine Writer.

1. The actual utterances of Our Lord, as we can still find them in the Synoptic Gospels, cannot be rightly estimated unless they are first taken as entirely occasional—hence are interpreted within their context of special circumstances; as utterly exoteric—homely words addressed to the homely spiritual and ethical experiences and needs of simple unlettered folk, or to the (almost as homely) preachers' requirements of His apostolic little band; and as specifically not philosophical nor even moral, but religious. Studied, above all practised thus, as far as possible in the spirit of their first enunciation, they reveal, across the experience of the ages, within their grandly baffling simplicity, a richness of elements, indeed

a tension of apparently irreconcilable antinomies, which keep them, in their substance, as operative and soul-transforming now as on the day when He uttered His sacred spirit through them.

(1) Now in Jesus' personal teaching, not Eternal Life, but the Kingdom of God is in the foreground. And this Kingdom is presented, directly and emphatically, as, not present but future; not distant, but imminent; not gradual, but sudden; not as at all achieved by man, but as simply given by God. Nor is this Kingdom presented as consisting, for man, when it does come to him, of an Eternal Now; indeed, the life of God Himself is here nowhere clearly pictured as a pure Simultaneity.

The Kingdom is future: "many shall come . . . and shall recline . . . in the Kingdom of heaven"; "ye shall sit upon twelve thrones"; "then shall the just shine like the sun in the Kingdom of their father"; and "I shall drink the generation of the vine with you anew in the Kingdom of God" (Matt. viii. 11, xix. 28, xiii. 43; Mark xiv. 25). The Kingdom is imminent: "Amen I say unto you, there are some here standing who shall not taste of death until they see the Son of Man coming in His Kingdom"; "Amen I say unto you, this generation shall not pass until all these things shall be fulfilled";

"henceforth ye shall see the Son of Man coming upon the clouds of heaven" (Matt. xvi. 28, xxiv. 33, xxvi. 64). The Kingdom is sudden: "as the lightning cometh forth from the east and shineth unto the west," "as men in the days of Noah knew not till the flood came," "so shall the coming," the presence, παρούσια, "of the Son of Man be"; and "if the master of the house knew at what hour the thief would come, he would watch" (Matt. xxiv. 27, xxxix. 43). Everywhere, here and in other places, the Kingdom is not a human achievement but a pure gift of God, as also in the Apocalypse of John, xxi. 2, the "New Jerusalem" descends "from heaven, from God, prepared as a bride for her husband." And Life in the Kingdom appears as simply successive: "many shall recline with Abraham, Isaac, and Jacob" at the Messianic banquet; indeed God's own life seems to be successive, since it includes the very feeding of the fowls of the air, and the clothing of the grass of the field (Matt. viii. 11, vi. 26, 30). Where "life" or "life everlasting" occurs in Jesus' own sayings, it is ever placed in the future, as a reward for previous virtue, and expresses the totality of good to be conferred in the Kingdom of God. "Good master, what shall I do, that I may inherit eternal life?" Jesus is asked. And He answers, "Thou knowest the commandments," and "sell all thou hast and give to the poor, and thou shalt have treasure in heaven"; and declares "how hardly shall they that have riches enter into the Kingdom of God!" (Mark x. 17, 19, 21, 23).

Nothing can well be more certain than the presence and deep operativeness of this conviction, as to the futurity, imminence, suddenness, and pure God-givenness of the Kingdom of God, within our Lord's life and teaching. One especially amongst the features of this outlook—the imminence—has, almost from the first, been a grave difficulty for those whom reason and conscience constrain to combine a frank acceptance of the textual evidences with a deep conviction of Our Lord's profound spiritual insight and supreme normality. And yet this His attitude of mind and will, if taken generally, and as one of two essential spiritual movements, is found, by the spiritually fully awake and earnest soul, to inflict upon it, and ever anew to awaken within it, an easily overlooked or forgotten, yet most necessary, utterly abiding, element and requirement of the deepest spiritual life. Detachment, even from the very things to which also we owe attachment; the irremediable inadequacy of even the totality of all our present earthly conditions, though improved to the utmost,—in so far as these conditions do not include, or lead up to, God and His presence,—to satisfy the soul's wants; our utter dependence upon a Will, a Spirit, distinct from our own, Who precedes, and from Whom proceed, all our very capacities for good, and Whose very "rewards" are rooted in an order of pure creative donation, indeed of self-donation: all this and more, of specifically *religious* truth and fact, is given us here. And it is all presented with so forcible a dramatic vividness, and with such richness of Jewish details, as easily to obscure, for even religious spirits, in our own lands and times, the sobriety in sublimity of the abiding substance thus conveyed.

(2) Now the purely religious, intensely transcendent and dualistic, outlook, with its apocalyptic form, as just described, appears to have been attained and developed by Our Lord's humanity under the stress of the resistance to His teaching, and of the approach of a violent death and apparently utter defeat. Certainly it is from the great scene of Peter's confession at Cæsarea Philippi onwards (Mark viii. 31 = Matt. xvi. 21 = Luke ix. 22) that this outlook prevails in His teaching. Nevertheless, especially in the earlier period, another outlook which is, relatively, immanental, monistic, and ethical, and possesses prophetical form, must also be admitted in Jesus's

temper and teaching, unless we would, more or less violently, explain away texts no less certain than those of the transcendental and apocalyptic kind, and would thus artificially unify His life.

Thus, on Jesus's very first public appearance, "all marvelled saying . . . 'He even commands the impure spirits and they obey Him'" (Mark i. 27); whilst Jesus declares, even considerably later, "if I cast out devils in the spirit of God, the Kingdom of God has indeed come to you" (ἔφθασεν ἐφ' ὑμᾶς) (Matt. xii. 28), and He can then tell His disciples, who assure Him "the devils also obey us in Thy name," "I saw Satan fall like lightning from heaven" (Luke x. 17, 18). The Kingdom of God is thus in process of establishment, in proportion as the kingdom of Satan is driven back and broken up. Hence the disciples are bidden simultaneously to "preach that the Kingdom of heaven is at hand," and to "heal the sick" and "cast out devils" (Matt. x. 7, 8; Luke x. 9).

Again, the plant-life parables (as truly characteristic of this first, relatively peaceful, period as are the expectancy parables of the second, storm-and-stress period) are full of corresponding conceptions. The fundamental parable, that of the Sower (Mark iv. 3–9 and parallels), indicates how the Kingdom of God is subject, in its growth, to laws analogous to those obtaining in the natural world; since the results of the preaching of the Kingdom depend upon the differing dispositions of the hearers' hearts, much as the results of sowing plant-seed depend upon the nature of the soil sown upon. And the profoundly authentic and fresh parable of the Seed that grows of itself (Mark iv. 26-29) lays the stress of the comparison upon the gradual unfolding and prosperity of the seed which takes time to grow. Thus similarly the Kingdom of God, once it is planted, rises slowly but surely to an ever-richer development, and reaches maturity simply through the divine power immanent within it.

And finally, Jesus's answer to the Baptist's messengers as to whether He is the Messiah—a simple reference to the cures, awakenings, preachings they see Him perform (Matt. xi. 4)—also implies that the Kingdom is already present. Indeed, Jesus's very presence involves, in a very real degree and way, the presence of the Kingdom. "The acceptable year of the Lord" (Luke iv. 19) is itself *already* present; the disciples cannot fast, since "the bridegroom is" *already* now "with them" (Mark ii. 19); and "blessed are the eyes that see what you are" *actually* "seeing" (Luke x. 23). Hence Jesus can speak of when they "shall see the Kingdom of God coming in power" (Mark ix. 1), in contradistinction to the Kingdom as already come in obscurity and weakness.[1]

(3) The Kingdom of God, whether insisted upon apocalyptically or prophetically, is throughout conceived by Our Lord as a social organism. For the Kingdom of God, present wheresoever God's will is done on earth as in heaven (Matt. vi. 10, 11), evidently coincides with the totality of those through whom God's will is accomplished—we have thus, not one soul but many. If the Kingdom is primarily an interior disposition, it must contain many differently situated, yet similarly disposed, souls—since only thus can there be lesser and greater (Matt. v. 19, xi. 11). And if the perfection of the Kingdom consists in the greatest within it being he who is the servant of all (Matt. xx. 26, 27), it must again be an organized community. And indeed Jesus forms and sends out a special little

---

[1] H. J. Holtzmann's *Lehrbuch der N.T. Theologie*, 2nd ed. 1911, vol. i. pp. 284-295, in its admirable sobriety as to the Kingdom of God, has, after much independent study of my own, been chiefly followed above. Brilliant, very instructive, but, I think, too exclusive, insistence upon the apocalyptic element, in Albert Schweitzer's *Von Reimarus zu Wrede*, 1907; Eng. trans., *The Quest of the Historic Jesus*, 1909; and even in Alfred Loisy's *Les Évangiles Synoptiques*, 2 vols., 1901, a work of quite extraordinary penetration, in most of its treatment of the discourses.

band of apostles to aid them in winning this larger community (Matt. ix. 35 – x. 16, and parallels). These apostles are, in the future world, to sit with Jesus as judges over the tribes of Israel (Matt. xix. 28); and meanwhile they are to be the salt of the earth, the yeast that is to leaven the Jewish people (Matt. v. 13, xiii. 33).[1]

(4) And the future, final life of souls is to remain, and more than ever to become, not only social as between soul and soul, but also complete as regards each soul's powers. Nowhere is there a trace, in Our Lord's conception of this ultimate life, of the *solus cum solo,* or of the survival of the abstractive intellect alone, as we found the latter in Aristotle, and as we shall find the former in Plotinus. Thus the very angels who "see in heaven, without ceasing, the face of God," are also simultaneously attentive to any contempt shown towards their human charges upon earth (Matt. xviii. 10); and "there is joy before the angels of God over one sinner doing penance" upon earth (Luke xv. 10). Indeed, everywhere these popular sayings, with their current imagery of the Messianic banquet and the thrones and other strongly spatial pictures, vividly portray and insist on the great fact and truth that the inner spiritual life, to be deep and genuine, per-

[1] See H. J. Holtzmann, *Lehrbuch der N.T. Theologie*, pp. 265-268.

manently requires a rich variety and organization within a strongly social life with fellow-souls.

(5) Yet it is not man or men, but God Who, here as everywhere in Jesus's experience and teaching, is the beginning, centre, medium, and end of the whole of this final life. " Have you not read what was said to you [Ex. iii. 6] by God: 'I am the God of Abraham and the God of Isaac and the God of Jacob'? He is, then, 'not the God of the dead but of the living'" (Matt. xxii. 32). The Simultaneity, as well as the Self-Identity, of the intensely living God is doubtless here implied, as alone upholding, because exceeding and enclosing, the minor aliveness and successiveness of the generations of men. The soul's perfection is thus practised and proclaimed by Jesus as its complete self-donation to the service of man for God and of God in man. And this self-donation is effected in utter dependence upon God's aid, and yet with the fullest actuation of all the feelings, motives, and passions of chaste fear, tender pity, manly wrath, childlike simplicity and humility, homely heroism, joy in God, love of our very enemies, sense of and contrition for sin, and trust in God's fatherly care even in deep desolation and an agonizing death. The expansive happiness of His early ministry; the loving observation of flower and bird, sky,

## Eternity in Time, Transcendence in Immanence

wind, and wave; the lonely night-watches on the mountain-side; the delight in children; the mercifulness to publicans and sinners; the standing in the midst of the disciples as a servant (Luke xxii. 27); the emphatic anger in purifying the temple; the sadness of the Last Supper; the craving for the disciples' sympathy and the terror of death in Gethsemane; the lofty silence before Caiaphas and Pilate; the cry of desolation on the Cross: are here all constituents, occasions, and expressions of a ceaseless sense, possession, and operativeness of Eternal Life.

Thus the negative movement, of detachment and renunciation, is planted here, by the devoted soul, not outside of, but right within, even the purest attachments to the best of things, in order to keep them and itself (ever, in itself, so weak and changeable) pure and fruitful. A wise and noble, warm because ever love-impelled, asceticism is here the instrument, concomitant and guardian, though never the first motive or last end, of the entire life, in precise proportion to this life's depth and richness. Plato's wisely wide acceptance of the *Thumos* is here far surpassed by the delicacy, elasticity, and depth with which the entire gamut of the soul's impulsions and necessities is utilized, cultivated, and organized; and the Stoic renunciation is practised here, within a boundless, richly difficult material, with infinite variety, tension, and fruitfulness. And both the acceptance and the renunciation, each in and through and with the other, are not here caused by, nor do they here end in, the sorry superficiality of a mere self-culture, but they follow upon, or lead up to, the vivid apprehension and awed acceptance of the deepest Reality as Spirit, a holy Love and all-wise Will. All here comes from, or leads to, a life lived, within the more or less successiveness of our own mode of existence, in willed touch and deliberate union with God, the Simultaneous and Eternal.[1]

2. St. Paul's spontaneous self-communications and formal teachings, whilst demonstrably affected by, and occupied with, only a part of the immense range and depth of Our Lord's life and revelation, are mostly far more complex or systematic than Jesus's sayings. They are, in their form, where at all doctrinal, utterances of a rabbinically trained theologian, in which Philo-like, Platonic, and Stoic ingredients are often not

---

[1] The above insistence upon two complementary movements, as equally necessary to the deepest religion and Christianity, has been largely learnt from Ernst Troeltsch's great writings, especially his "Was ist Wesen des Christenthums?" in *Die Christliche Welt*, 1903, i., coll. 583, 584.

difficult to trace. And yet it is the manner and degree in which his great soul is filled with the love and reproduction of the most fundamental of the dispositions and aims of the historic Jesus, and with the conception and development of the spiritual organism of the Christian community, which give to these and to the other currents of his reflective thought an experimental content and rich sobriety far beyond what they bring by themselves alone.

The dominating double fact of St. Paul's life, his conversion to enthusiastic faith in a present Christ, yet this without ever having known the earthly Jesus, led him to concentrate all his attention and love, away from the earthly, the past, the Jewish Jesus, upon the heavenly, the present and eternal Christ, the Saviour of Mankind. Indeed, in the earthly life only the Passion and Death and the Resurrection of Jesus were retained, as constituting, respectively, the sowing and death, and the up-springing and life, of the Seed—of the Second Adam, the heavenly Man. And since Christ had revealed Himself to Saul on the way to Damascus, in a substantially *pneumatic* manner, the convert Saul's, Paul's dominant category is, henceforth, not the Kingdom of God, not Eternal Life, but Pneuma, the Spirit.

(1) St. Paul's fully developed scheme as to

man's natural endowments and supernatural gifts says relatively little about man's highest natural endowment, his νοῦς, or Mind, but insists much upon two strongly contrasted, indeed mutually exclusive, couples: a couple of natural, strictly human, incurably mortal constituents, ψυχή, the sensual soul, and σάρξ, the flesh; and a couple consisting of Πνεῦμα, Spirit, which is essentially divine and eternal, and of σῶμα, Body, which is potentially immortal, ever capable of being rewoven, of being raised to life, by the Pneuma which first constituted it. Thus "the *psychic* man receiveth not the things of the Spirit of God, for they are a foolishness unto him; neither can he know them, because they are (only) spiritually discerned. But he that is *pneumatic* judgeth all things, yet he himself is judged of no man" (1 Cor. ii. 14, 15). "Ye are not in the flesh but in the Spirit, since the Spirit of God dwelleth in you" (Rom. viii. 9). Only where certain comparisons require it, and in loosely worded popular passages, is pneuma, spirit, also attributed to man, as such. "The pneuma of man knows the things of man and the Pneuma of God knows the things of God," is said in 1 Cor. ii. 11; but here we find also the even looser terms, πνεῦμα τοῦ κόσμου, "the spirit of the world" (ver. 12) (like "the God of this world" applied to the devil,

2 Cor. iv. 4), and νοῦς Κυρίου, "the mind of God" (ver. 16).

(2) Although it was the precise deeds, words, and character of the historic Jesus of Nazareth, and their specific effect upon the dispositions of particular human witnesses which gave its richness and tenderness to St. Paul's image of the Christ, the special circumstances of his conversion and apostolate occasioned a certain depersonalization of his conception of this same Christ. Thus St. Paul can teach that, in His resurrection, Christ, "the Second Adam, was made a life-giving Spirit" (1 Cor. xv. 45); man, living no more for the flesh or the *psyche*, can, by and with that quickening Spirit, become spirit too. And Spirit and spirit, unlike material things, can be each within the other. Human spirits can be "in Christ" (Rom. viii. 1), or "Christ," "the Spirit of God," can be "in them" (Rom. viii. 10, 9). This formula, ἐν Χριστῷ, parallel to ἐν πνεύματι, is often used by St. Paul in a pregnant mystical sense, with a strongly local suggestion—Christ-Spirit is here the element by which the human spirit is surrounded and penetrated, as man is by the air which he breathes and by which he lives. Thus we are baptized, dipped, into Christ, Spirit; we can drink Christ, the Spirit (Rom. vi. 3; Gal. iii. 27; 1 Cor. x. 3, 4).

(3) It is the presence of this intrinsically immortal, eternal Spirit within us that constitutes our surety of immortality, ever accompanied, in St. Paul's conviction, by the resurrection of the body. "If the Spirit of Him that raised Jesus from the dead dwelleth in you, He . . . will give life to our mortal bodies through His Spirit that dwelleth within you" (Rom. viii. 11); "I die daily"; "daily we bear about in our bodies the death of Jesus, in order that," in a measure already here and now, "also the life of Jesus may be manifested in our bodies" (1 Cor. xv. 31; 2 Cor. iv. 10, 11).

The Kingdom of God is thus, with St. Paul also, in part a present possession; "the Kingdom of God consists not in word but in power," "it is justice and peace and joy in the Holy Spirit" (1 Cor. iv. 20; Rom. xiv. 17); yet still more is it a future gift: "flesh and blood," the unrighteous, "shall not inherit the Kingdom of God" (1 Cor. xv. 50, vi. 9). Hence "whether we live or whether we die, we are the Lord's"; "to me to live is Christ"; already "not I but Christ liveth in me" (Rom. xiv. 8; Phil. i. 21; 1 Cor. ii. 20). And the Corinthian Christians can be told that "Jesus Christ is" already "within you" (2 Cor. xiii. 5).

(4) And it is in and through this element and

medium of the Christ-Spirit that the universal brotherhood of mankind is effected and maintained: "there is not among you Jew or Gentile, slave or freeman, male or female; for all of you are one—in Christ Jesus" (Gal. viii. 28). And this Spirit-Christ articulates, locates in particular posts and functions, keeps in continuous interchange of selfless love and service, and thus develops and constitutes, the several human spirits, as variously necessary parts and members of the one Christian Society and Church. The Stoic conception of the human body-politic, constituted by, and constituting, the several sexes, orders, capacities of mankind, has here attained the greatest possible elasticity, tenderness, and vitality. For an all-embracing self-conscious Spirit—the Spirit of one who loved, and immolated Himself, wholly and to the end—is here the link and medium by and in which all human spirits, in proportion to their awakeness and acceptance, are bound and fitted together. And further, the conception presupposes throughout, not the self-sufficingness of the individual spirit, but the utter, pressing need, for each human spirit, of all the others, and, for the totality of human spirits, of the Christ, the Spirit, God—of His initiation, purification, sustainment, and crowning of it all. "As the body is one and hath many members, and all the members of that one body, being many, are one body, so also is Christ"; "ye are the body of Christ, and members of it severally"; and "whether one member suffer, all the members suffer with it; or one member is honoured, all the members rejoice with it" (1 Cor. xii. 12, 27, 26). The Stoic cosmopolitanism has here widened and deepened to an outlook into the Invisible and Eternal: "our citizenship is in heaven" (Phil. iii. 20).

(5) And we have here, amidst some Stoic terms, an amazing range and richness of volitional and emotional attitude and experience—anger, scorn, pity, tenderness, zeal, joy, rapture, contrition, sadness, loneliness—the whole steeped in a manly humility and deepest *creatureliness*, and in a sense of the prevenience, the omnipresent holiness and love, of God. "I have learnt, in whatever circumstances I am, to be self-sufficing (αὐτάρκης); I have all strength—in Him who giveth me power." "All things are yours,—and ye are Christ's, and Christ is God's." "Christ is all things in all" (Phil. iv. 11, 13; 1 Cor. iii. 22, 23; Col. iii. 11).[1]

[1] See H. J. Holtzmann, *Lehrbuch der N.T. Theologie*, vol. ii. pp. 88-90, 218, 219, 260. The Pauline section of this great work is, in spite of Albert Schweitzer's vivid criticisms, probably the most thorough study of the difficult subject extant.

3. The Johannine writings may be briefly described as Pauline in their central convictions and emotions, and as Philonian in their general conception of God and of the worship of God, and in their, reverential yet astonishingly free, allegorical treatment of the Old Testament. "God is a Spirit"; "neither have ye ever heard His voice nor seen His shape" (iv. 24, v. 37); "My Father worketh until now"—ever, even on the Sabbath (v. 17, 16); "the hour cometh when men will adore the Father neither on this mount," Gerizim, "nor in Jerusalem," "the true adorers will adore Him in spirit and in truth" (iv. 21, 23). All this, in spite of the Theophanies, the one sole legitimate sanctuary, the Sabbath-rest of God, in Genesis and Deuteronomy. Indeed Philo's Life of Moses, as the mediator, reconciler, intercessor, the one great organ of divine revelation, the pattern and leader upwards of souls eager for salvation, is a true literary precursor of this pragmatic, mystical Life of Christ.

And by the utilization, and development to full personality, of the Heracleitean, then Stoic, and lastly Alexandrian conception of the Logos, the earthly life of Jesus is here set in a frame and background of an Eternity extant before, behind, and after this our earthly world of space and time. For the Prologue shows us the Eternal Son of

God blessedly resting in the bosom of the invisible Father (i. 18), as, towards the end, the ideal disciple, representative of all Christ's genuine followers, rests in the bosom of Jesus, the Logos hidden under human form (xiii. 23). We get thus a development of such Pauline passages as "Christ, the image of God," and "the image of the invisible God, the first-born of all creation" (2 Cor. iv. 4; Col. i. 15).

(1) All true existence, all "truth," thus comes from above, where is the real world, down to us here below, where is only the derivative, a blurred copy: a man is "born" spiritually "from above" (iii. 3). "Every one who is of the truth heareth My voice"—follows Me back to whence I came (xviii. 37). All this is conformable, in its intellectual framework, to Plato and to St. Paul.

But a heightened stress is laid here upon "knowing" and "truth"—thus γινώσκειν appears, in the short First Epistle alone, twenty-five times. "If ye are truly My disciples, ye shall know the truth, and the truth shall make you free"; "the spirit of truth shall lead you into all truth"; "for this I came into the world, that I might witness unto the truth" (viii. 31, 32, xviii. 37). This apparent hegemony given to truth and knowing is the feature which approximates this, otherwise deeply and deliberately anti-Gnostic, writer to the Gnostics, all characterized by their insistence upon γνῶσις. And this knowing is taken to be intuitive, as analogous to physical sight (ὁρᾶν, ἰδεῖν, θεᾶσθαι, βλέπειν, θεωρεῖν), and to conform to the Stoic principle that "like is apprehended by like" (Sextus Empiricus, 7. 92). "Only He who is with the Father, hath seen the Father"; "he who is of the earth, speaketh of the earth" (vi. 46, iii. 31).

(2) Yet it is not Knowledge, however intuitive, nor Truth, however heavenly, but Life, Eternal Life, which constitutes the culmination of the Johannine convictions. Christ here declares "I am the Way, the Truth, and the Life," in an ascending scale of values, and this is the inner meaning of the raising of Lazarus, the greatest and last of the seven great miracle-symbols of this gospel of Eternal Life (xi. 25).

True, in the direct teaching of Jesus, Eternal Life depends upon the observance of the twin commandments of the love of God and of man (Luke x. 25-28, and parallels), whilst here "this is eternal life, that men may know Thee the one true God, and Jesus Christ whom Thou hast sent." (xvii. 2, 3). Yet the great saying, "If any man willeth to do His will, he shall know of the doctrine whether it is of God" (vii. 17), is the precise equivalent of Jesus's actual words, "Blessed are the pure of heart, for they shall see God" (Matt. v. 8). The Johannine doctrine of Life has indeed taken over and refashioned the Synoptic conceptions of Life and of the Kingdom of God —the latter term appearing here in one passage only, iii. 3, 5. And though this gospel begins with the Logos conception, and attaches "Life" to that conception (i. 1, 4), yet, in the progress of the work, a richness of content is given to "Life" which it derives, not from the Stoic-Philonian categories, but from the life of Jesus, as actually lived by Him, and from this Jesus's teachings concerning the Kingdom of God and the conditions for entering it, as these teachings had reached the writer through persons who had actually heard them. Thus Life here means, in itself, indissolubility, though not as a consequence, but as a presupposition, of the resurrection: "that every one who seeth the Son and believeth in Him, may have eternal life; and I will raise him up at the last day" (vi. 40). For its possessor's consciousness, such Life means beatitude: "that they may have life and may have it abundantly" (x. 10). In its ethical relation, it is the immediate concomitant of all acts pleasing to God: "His commandment is eternal life" (xii. 50). And with respect to knowing, it is enlightenment: "This is eternal life, that they may know" (xvii. 3).

St. Paul's teaching, "In Christ all shall be made alive" (1 Cor. xv. 22), yields here, as developed in Christ's great speech (v. 21–29), a wondrously deep content for the conception of Life Eternal. "As the Father raises the dead and maketh them alive, so also the Son maketh alive whom He willeth"; for "the Spirit it is that maketh alive," and "the words that I have spoken to you are spirit and are life." Hence "he who hearkeneth to My word . . . hath eternal life, and hath passed over from death to life" (v. 21, vi. 63, v. 24). Such believer already *here and now* possesses eternal life; already *here and now* has accomplished the transition from death to life; he "has" *already* "tasted the powers of the coming age" (Heb. vi. 5). The believer "will not die for ever," will not die at all, whilst Martha, the ordinary Palestinian Jew, affirms that "he," her brother, "will rise again at the last day" (xi. 26, 24). "This" *already* "is eternal life," that men may know God and the Christ; "these things have I spoken to you, that . . . your joy may" *already* "be fulfilled" (xv. 11). The emphasis in the pre-Exilic Old Testament lies upon the past, upon the absence of all beginning in God; in Jesus's teaching it lies upon the future, the coming of the Kingdom, and upon the direct, explicit preparations for it; in the specifically Johannine passages, it lies upon an Eternal Now. Thus Christ, as God, is free from all successiveness: "before Abraham was (became), I," not was, but "*am*" (viii. 58). It is in the less characteristic passages of these writings that we get the very valuable, strictly necessary, compensatory movement,—an insistence upon the future,—the bodily resurrection and the increase of the soul's stability and joy in the beyond.

(3) The social, organically interconnected and variously graduated, life of spirits, of each with all the others, and of all in and through the Spirit, Christ, and God, so deeply embedded in our Lord's own teaching and so clearly articulated by St. Paul, is here explicitly insisted on by Christ Himself: "I am the true vine, ye are the branches, and My Father is the husbandman" (xv. 1, 5). And the Pauline vivid realization of the non-spatiality, the interpenetrability, of spirits appears here in fullest force: "I am in the Father and Thou, Father, art in Me"; "he who abideth in Me and I in him"; "I in them and Thou in Me" (xiv. 10, xv. 5, xvii. 23). And the human spirit's utter need of God, and the prevenience of God in the relations between man and God, are magnificently emphasized. "Not we loved God (first), but He

(first) loved us"; "let us love Him, because He first loved us" (1 John iv. 10, 19); "no man can come to Me, unless the Father draw him" (vi. 44). And this drawing effects a hunger and thirst for Christ and God (iv. 14, vi. 35). Thus man's spirit, so largely merely potential, can respond actively to the historic Jesus, because it has been already touched by, and thus made hungry for, the all-actual, eternal Spirit-God who created that human spirit akin unto Himself.

(4) Yet, finally, the range and variety of the perfect life is, in these writings, much restricted, as compared with the inexhaustible richness and spontaneity actually lived and proposed to us by Jesus Himself. In the Synoptists Jesus "grows in favour with God and man"; passes through a profoundly real individual experience in His Baptism and Temptation; prays alone on the mountain-side; suffers an agony of fear and seeks His disciples' sympathy in Gethsemane; and dies with a cry of desolation upon Calvary. In the Fourth Gospel the Logos's watchword is "I *am*"; there is no Baptism and no Temptation; He has deliberately to stir up emotion in Himself; He prays only for others; and in the Garden and on the Cross He shows naught but self-possession. And men's duty, although, besides the "knowing" and believing, it includes the loving of God and

of man, appears correspondingly to lack variety, spontaneity, tension, incident. Nevertheless, all through this great work's apparent thinness and abstractness, pulses the sense and the effect of the two great concrete Realities—God, the already fully extant and operative eternal Beauty, Truth, Love and Goodness, infinite Personality and Spirit, Who is all this independently of our apprehension and action; and Jesus, Who actually lived in the flesh here below amongst us, the lowly servant of human souls. Thus here the Christ tells us : "God so loved the world, that He gave His only-begotten Son, so that whosoever believeth in Him should . . . have everlasting life"; and that "the Father will give you another Helper, the Spirit of Truth, who will abide with you for ever" (iii. 16, xiv. 15). And perhaps the most solemnly introduced, and the most deeply felt, of all the scenes here given, is that of Christ washing the disciples' feet, and inculcating a similar service of each to all the others, a passage which expands words actually spoken in a parable by Jesus (Luke xii. 35–37) into an appealing summary and picture of the aim and disposition of His entire life and teaching (xiii. 1–17).[1]

[1] The most many-sided discussion of all the above and allied points is in H. J. Holtzmann's *Lehrbuch d. N.T. Theologie*, especially in the greatly improved 2nd ed. 1911, vol. ii. pp. 390–437. The above sketch, after much personal study of the texts,

## CHAPTER VI

### CHRISTIAN-HELLENISTIC TIMES

Plotinus—St. Augustine—Pseudo-Dionysius (Proclus).

WE will next take the three most typical and influential teachers of Eternal Life that flourished between the appearance of the Johannine literature and the closing of the Pagan schools of philsophy,—from about A.D. 100 to A.D. 529,—Plotinus, St. Augustine, Pseudo-Dionysius.

1. *Plotinus* (A.D. 204-270), who, born in Egypt, taught during his last twenty-five years in Rome, has left us, in his ever succinct, though generally obscure writings, utterances of the most delicate spiritual experience and of the noblest religious passion and tenderness. They are deeply instructive also because of the ceaseless conflict

---

and with certain value-judgments of my own, is based almost throughout upon these pages. Careful work is to be found also in Bp. Westcott's *The Epistles of St. John*, 1886, pp. 214-218; in A. Loisy's extraordinarily rich and suggestive *Le Quatrième Evangile*, 1903, pp. 151-199, 420-481; in Père Th. Calmes's *L'Evangile selon S. Jean*, 1904, pp. 81-144, 239-262; and in E. F. Scott's *The Fourth Gospel*, 1906, pp. 234-294 (the most incisive and clear of the English books upon the subject).

within them between the formal principles of the philosopher, which indeed are themselves in part determined by a sensitively spiritual sense of the distinct reality and qualitative difference of God, and the experiences of a profoundly religious soul. The philosopher Plotinus here leaves the First, God, without qualities, internal activities, or outgoing action whatsoever, and conceives man's approach to Him as a literal emptying of himself, even down to his ethical qualities. But Plotinus, the religious soul, ever turns to, thirsts after, and loves, that God Whom, in spite of those principles, he continuously discovers as a very ocean of Life and Loveableness, hence, surely, of Love also.

(1) Thus, as to the utter Transcendence of God, we are told: "The First had no desire of any kind, for otherwise it would have been imperfect; there was, too, nothing whatever extant, to which It might stretch Itself." "If anything is the simplest of all things, It will not think Itself, for otherwise It would possess multiplicity . . . nor can there be any thinking of It." "We say what It is *not*; what It is we do not say" . . . "It is neither . . . Intellect nor Soul, It neither moves nor stands still, It is neither in space nor in time, but It is . . . the Formless before all form, before all movement, before all rest" (v. 3. 12:

13; 14; vi. 9. 3). Nevertheless, this First can be experienced by man; indeed, the real contact of man's spirit with, and his self-surrender to, It, constitute that spirit's very life and sole true joy. In fact, in spite of the philosopher's insistence upon the emptiness of God, and the corresponding need of emptiness in the soul that would approach Him, Plotinus's words, where his own mystical experience speaks, really convey or imply the very opposite—the unspeakable richness of God in life, love, and joy; His ever immediate, protective closeness to man's soul; and this soul's discovery of Him, the Lover, by becoming aware of, and by completely willing, His actual contact, when it freely, heroically turns its whole being, away from the narrow self, to Him, its root and its true, overflowing life.

"The One can be apprehended only κατὰ παρουσίαν ἐπιστήμης κρείττονα, through a presence," an immediate contact, "which is above knowledge"; by "an ecstasy, a simplification, and a self-donation, a striving after contact (ἀφή), a quiet, and a musing upon union with It." "Bodies cannot enter into real communion with each other, but incorporeal things . . . are separated from each other, if at all, not by place but by difference and antagonism. When therefore this difference is absent, they are immediately present to each other." And as to the One, "we are always gathered around It, but we do not always gaze upon It. When, however, we do so gaze, we attain to the end of our desires and to the rest of our souls." "We are not cut off from It nor severed from It . . . but we breathe and consist in It, since It does not give and then withdraw, but ever bears and directs us ($\chi o\rho\eta\gamma\epsilon\hat{\iota}$) as long as It is what It is. . . . There the soul rests free from evils . . . and the true life is there." "For since the soul is different from God, but springs from Him, it longs after Him by a necessity of its nature" (vi. 9. 4; 11; 8; 9).

Yet we cannot accept the following as an adequate explanation of this supreme attraction and lovableness of God, and of the supreme joy thus imparted by His real touch of man's soul. "The One does not strive after us, so that It would encircle us, but we have to strive after It, so that we may circle around It." "If something came to be, after It, this something came to be, by the First remaining in Its own being." And "since the One is perfect, since It neither seeks nor possesses nor requires anything, it was, so to speak, an overflow of the One, Its overfulness, that brought forth other things" (vi. 3. 12; 2. 1; 9. 8).

(2) Thus Plotinus the philosopher drives home the increasingly abstractive trend of Greek philosophy from Plato onwards. Aristotle's God only thinks, and only thinks Himself; Aristotle's world, κινεῖ ὡς ἐρώμενον, is in motion, not as loved by God but solely as loving Him; and Aristotle's man approaches God, the abstract Thinker, by abstractive thought. But Plotinus's God does not even think at all, and Plotinus's man attains to the sheer One by the real cessation of every mental or even vital activity. And since Plotinus, the religious soul, shrinks concurrently from allowing any necessitation in God, even though a purely spiritual one resulting from His own nature, he has to treat the undeniably extant world as a quasi-physical, an automatic, result of God, unknown, unwilled by Him; and although love is evoked by Him in man, this love has nothing corresponding to itself in God. The entire relations between God and man consist here, in reality, in one relation and movement only,—from man up to God, since no such movement or relation is explicitly allowed from God down to man. And thus in Plotinus's philosophy God is exiled from His world and His world from Him, whilst Plotinus's experiences and intuitions find God to be the very atmosphere and home of all souls.

(3) It is, then, Plotinus's deep spiritual instincts and experiences, and the religious motive operative in the very excesses of his negation, that demand retention and development, whilst his abstractive method and theories require a corresponding check or rejection. What is here so specially valuable is doubtless Plotinus's constant, vivid sense of the spaceless, timeless character of God; of God's distinct reality and otherness, and yet of His immense nearness; of the real contact between the real God and the real soul, and of the precedence and excess of this contact before and beyond all theories concerning this, the actual ultimate cause of the soul's life and healing. Indeed, reality of all kinds here rightly appears as ever exceeding our intuition of it, and our intuitions as ever exceeding our discursive reasonings and analyses. And, on the other hand, the one-sided abstractiveness of the method leads to his profoundly unsocial conception of man's relation to God, and of the moments when this relation is at its deepest,—alone with the Alone,—and to the exclusion, from the soul's deepest, ultimate life, of all multiplicity and discursiveness of thought, and of all distinct acts and productiveness of the will. Here we have grave omissions, and here Plotinus compares most unfavourably with the frankly

social and serving condition of the blessèd, here and in the beyond, in Our Lord's own preaching.[1]

2. The great African-Roman, *St. Augustine*, born in A.D. 354, a convert from Manichæism and an impure life in 386, wrote his *Confessions* in 397. He had lived to see the Roman Empire united, for the last time, under Theodosius the Great, and soon again divided, between his two sons, in 394-395. And later on, in 410, came the capture and sack of Rome by the Visigoth Alaric. It was under the impressions of these immense events—the clear dissolution of a mighty past and the dim presage of a problematical future—that he wrote his great work, *The City of God*, in 413-427, and died in 430 at Hippo, his episcopal city, whilst the Vandals were besieging it.

(1) St. Augustine himself tells us how much he owes to "the Platonists"—*i.e.*, quite predominantly, to Plotinus—his final emancipation from Manichæan, variously materialistic, conceptions of God.

The *Confessions* especially are full of the noblest expressions as to the non-spatial character

---

[1] E. Caird's *Evolution of Theology in the Greek Philosophers*, 1904, vol. ii. pp. 210-233, 289-316, is the most balanced extant discussion of Plotinus on the above points.

of God, of the soul's dispositions, and of the relations between the soul and God. "What place is there within me, whither my God can come? ... I would not exist at all, unless Thou wert already within me." "Thou wast never a place, and yet we have receded from Thee; we have drawn near to Thee, and yet Thou wast never a place." "Are we submerged and do we emerge? Yet it is not places into which we are plunged and out of which we rise. What can be more like places and, yet, more unlike? For here the affections are in case" (*Conf.* i. 2. 1; x. 26; xiii. 7). "The spiritual creature can only be changed by times," by a succession within duration, "by remembering what it had forgotten, or by learning what it did not know, or by willing what it did not will. The bodily creature can be changed by times and places, say from east to west." "That thing is not moved through space which is not extended in space ... the soul is not considered to move in space, except it be held to be a body" (*De Genesi ad litteram*, viii. 39; 43; ed. Ben., col. 387 B, vol. iii. 389 A).

As to time, St. Augustine has gone much deeper than Plotinus, and indeed still remains unequalled in the delicate splendour of his insight. "Thou, O God, precedest all past times by the height of Thine ever-present Eternity; and Thou exceedest all future times, since these *are* future and, once they have come, will be past times. . . . Thy years neither come nor go; but these years of ours both come and go, that so they may all come. All Thy years abide together, because they abide . . . but these our years will all be, only when they will all have ceased to be. Thy years are but one day; and this Thy day is not every day but *to-day*. This Thy *to-day* is Eternity." "Who shall hold man's vain heart, and fix it, so that it may for a little abide, and may for a little grasp the splendour of ever-abiding Eternity, and may compare it with the never-abiding times, and may thus see how Eternity is not comparable with them?" (*Conf.* xi. 13. 2). "True Eternity is present where there is nothing of time" (*Tract. in Joann. Evang.* xxxiii. 9; ed. Ben., vol. iii. col. 1953 A).

(2) Yet moments of a vivid apprehension, of a real experience, of Eternity do occur, even in this life. In the great scene at the window in Ostia, autumn 387, Augustine and his mother Monica rise (in form by ever-increasing abstraction from, in reality by ever-increasing concentration upon, the deepest constituents of their actual experiences and necessities) to a vivid apprehension of Eternal

Life in the beyond. "And we transcended our very minds, so as to touch the region of unfailing plenty, where Thou feedest Israel for ever with the food of truth; and where life is the Wisdom," the Word, "by Which all things become that both were and are to be, yet Which, Itself, does not become, but Which *is* as It was and ever will be, . . . since It is eternal. . . . And we touched It slightly, by an impulse of all our heart (*modice, toto ictu cordis*); and we sighed, and returned to the sound of our own voices, to where the" human "word begins and ends. And what is there, O Lord, that is like unto Thy Word, that abideth within Itself without growing old, and yet reneweth all things? . . ." And "if that our touch, by our rapidly passing thought, of the Eternal Wisdom which abideth above all things . . . were to be continued . . . so that Eternal Life would be like that moment of intelligence,—would not *that* be the meaning of the words 'enter thou into the joy of thy Lord?'" (*Conf.* ix. 10. 2, 3). Hence "perchance . . . when 'we shall be like Him,' our thoughts will no more . . . go from one thing to another, but we shall see all we know simultaneously, in one intuition" (*De Trinit.* xv. 26; ed. Ben., vol. viii. col. 1492 D).

(3) And this sense of Eternity, of Beatitude, of God and His nature generally, proceeds, at

bottom, from His immediate presence in our lives. Thus the supremely Real, Rich, Concrete is before, is the cause, occasion, and object, of all abstractions, indeed of all rich and real consciousness concerning our own weakness, or sin, or support, or profoundest peace. "This day of ours does not pass within Thee, and yet it *does* pass within Thee, since all these things have no means of passing, unless, somehow, Thou dost contain them all." "In Thee abide the causes of all unabiding things, and the unchanging origins of all changing things; and in Thee live the eternal reasons of all things that are unpossessed of reason and are temporal" (*Conf.* i. 6. 3; 2).

"Behold Thou wast within, and I was without . . . Thou wast with me, but I was not with Thee." "Thou hast made us for Thyself, and restless is our heart until it rests in Thee." "Is not the blessed life precisely *that* life which all men desire? We evidently possess that life, I know not in what manner; and there is another manner in which a man possesses it when he is truly blessèd. Yet even those who only hope to be blessèd, would not, unless they, in some manner, already possessed the blessed life, desire to be blessèd as, in fact, it is most certain that they desire to be" (*Conf.* x. 27; xiii. 1).

Hence a strenuous insistence here upon the *pre-*

*venience* of God, and the soul's utter need of Him. "Thou hast not forgotten me, who have forgotten Thee. I call Thee into my soul which Thou hast prepared to receive Thee by means of the desire for Thee which Thou Thyself instillest into it. . . . Before I was, Thou wast; and here I am, the whole of me that Thou hast made, and everything out of which Thou hast made me, springing from Thy prevenient goodness." "There liveth in Thee, without any diminution, our Good which Thou art Thyself, O God; we need not fear to have nowhere whither we can return, after we have fallen away from thence. For whilst we were away from it, our home has not fallen,—our home Thy Eternity." "My soul is a land without water before Thee; it cannot enlighten, it cannot satiate, itself from itself or by itself. Thus 'with *Thee* is the fountain of life,' since 'in *Thy* light we shall see light.'" "O God, forsake not Thine own gifts" (*Conf.* xiii. 1; iv. 16. 5; xiii. 16; xi. 2. 3).

(4) And then there is the keen sense of the Historical Element,—of the self-humiliation of the Infinite in time and space, and of the irreplaceable appropriateness and greatness of humility in the finite spirits thus taught and loved. "Thy Word, the eternal Truth . . . built for Itself, in this lower world, a dwelling of our clay . . . healing thus our inflation and feeding our love."

"Where," in the Neo-Platonists teaching, "was that charity that builds itself up on that foundation of humility which is Christ Jesus? These pages have not the expression of this piety—the tears of confession, the sacrifice dear to Thee—a troubled spirit, a contrite and humbled heart, the salvation of Thy people, the bridal city, the first-fruits of the Holy Spirit, the chalice of our ransom" (*Conf.* vii. 18; 20. 2; 21. 2).

(5) And thus also the Social Organism, resulting from, and in return aiding and in part constituting, such a rich, strong life of the soul, becomes more and more developed and emphasized in his writings. The *City of God* is directly devoted to it, although the social conceptions here are, in some respects, even more strongly influenced by the Greek *Republic* of Plato, and its abstractiveness, and by the Roman Empire, with its massive coercion, now broken up before the writer's very eyes, than by the Kingdom of Heaven as preached to Galilæan fishermen and peasants. And yet it is from that deathless life and preaching that this, in part fierce, hard, and gloomy African, derived his melting tendernesses, humility, fullest spiritual fruitfulness, and splendidly perennial youth. "Two cities were built for themselves by two loves,—an earthly city by the love of self, up to the contempt

of God; and a heavenly city by the love of God, up to the contempt of self. . . . This entire time . . . from which men withdraw at death and to which men succeed at birth, is but the evolution of these two cities" (*De Civit. Dei*, xiv. 28; xv. 1). Great yet terribly dangerous conception, if applied directly to entire groups of men, with the one set thus easily assumed to be all angelic and ever right, the other set all diabolic and ever wrong; and here mostly thus interpreted, owing to this great convert's profound distrust of human nature!

Thus, when facing St. Augustine, we once more cannot but recognize that it is Jesus Our Lord Himself Who alone gives us the quite full and costingly balanced statement within which the experiences and doctrines as to the social organism and as to sin have to find their place and level. And yet a deep sense of the need of such an organism and of the reality of sin will constantly be necessary to a sane and solid conception and practice of Eternal Life; and such a sense is ever, even excessively though not uniformly, operative within the vast scheme of St. Augustine.[1]

3. The last great expression, by the ancient Western and Near Eastern world, of the thirst

---

[1] For St. Augustine's teachings, see the still most useful Index to the Benedictine edition of his works.

and search after Eternal Life, and which profoundly influenced the whole course of Mediæval, and hence largely of Modern thought, are the *Pseudo-Dionysian* writings. Composed probably in Syria, certainly by a Christian cleric, presumably by a bishop, somewhere between A.D. 490–500, they constitute the most wholesale adoption of non-Christian philosophy ever, so far, endorsed by the official Christian Church. It is especially *Proclus*, the last of the greater Hellenistic philosophers (A.D. 410–485, born in Constantinople, he taught in Athens after 430), who is thus taken over on the largest scale.

(1) Now Proclus, the great Neo-Platonist systematizer and scholastic, is as abstractive as Plotinus, and far more dominated, not by experiences and necessities of the human spirit, but by formal logic, an uncriticized philosophical tradition, and the latest Hellenistic theosophy. Genuine favourite sayings of his are that " he would, were he master, leave only the collection of the Divine Oracles " (Delphic, Orphic, and such-like sayings) "and Plato's *Timæus* in general circulation"; and " it behoves the philosopher to be the hierophant of the whole world." Plotinus's conception of the circular process of all things, the Many moving from the One back to the One, is rigorously carried out by Proclus, throughout, and for every stage

and province of, life, in its triadic development of μονή, the *abiding* of the produced in the producer—similarity, unity; πρόοδος, the *going-forth* of the produced from the producer—difference; and ἐπιστροφή, the *return* of the former to the latter—assimilation, unification. And here, too, all beings are perfect and powerful in proportion to the poverty of their attributes—the pyramid of our abstract thinking and regressive simplification represents the actual condition of reality. Thus here especially the First, the One, τὸ ῞Εν, is above all reason, life, goodness, even, strictly, ἐπέκεινα τοῦ εἶναι, "above being"; It is, too, ἀναιτίως αἴτιον, "Cause, yet not Cause" (*In Republic.* 429 middle). But the realities intermediary between the One and man's even highest constituents are here more numerous than in Plotinus, and both those intermediaries and these constituents are almost endlessly, most subtly sub-divided.

On only one, most important, point is there a greater sobriety than in Plotinus; indeed, we get here some sense of a glaring Neo-Platonist inconsistency: for Proclus at times censures those who hold that the soul, forsaking all that is lower, becomes the very One and the Intelligible (*In Tim.* 310 A).[1]

[1] See E. Zeller, *Philosophie der Griechen*, 1881, iii. 3, pp. 774-793, 823-826.

(2) Pseudo-Dionysius assimilates practically all the chief doctrines, terms, similes, of Proclus, far more than he takes from Aristotle or even from Plato or Plotinus; and forms a curious compound of Christian priestly and sacramental organization and of Proclian ultra-transcendence and abstractiveness. Yet the tender truth and beauty of Plotinus's experiences, and the supreme reality of Jesus's life and teaching, vivify much of this strange amalgam.

Thus also in Dionysius "the super-essential Illimitability is placed above things essential, and the Unity above mind is placed above the minds" (the angels); "and the Good above word is unutterable by word . . . and the Cause of being to all, Itself is not being." "To none who are lovers of the Truth above all truth is it permitted to celebrate the supremely divine Essentiality, either as word or as power, as mind, life, or essence, but only as pre-eminently separated from every condition . . . surmise . . . infinitude, all things whatsoever." "There is no contact ($\dot{\epsilon}\pi\alpha\phi\acute{\eta}$) with the Deity, nor has it any communion with the things participating in it" (*De Div. Nom.* i. 1; 5; ii. 5).

Yet here also "we are brought into contact ($\sigma\upsilon\nu\alpha\pi\tau\acute{o}\mu\epsilon\theta\alpha$) with things unutterable and unknown, in a manner unutterable and unknown."

"All things aspire to It: things intellectual, by means of knowledge; things inferior to these, through the senses; and other things, by living movement, or by substantial and habitual aptitude." And "the Divine Love whirls round, as it were an everlasting circle, because of the Good, from the Good, in the Good, and to the Good, ever advancing and remaining and returning" (*ibid.* i. 1; 5; iv. 14).

But the Christian here, in various degrees and ways, colours or modifies, in the direction of deliberate self-revelation and of direct preoccupation with His creatures, the Plotinian-Proclian concept of God's automatic overflowing. "Even as our sun, by its very being, enlightens all things able to partake of its light in their own degree, so too the Good, by Its very existence, sends, to all things that be, the rays of Its whole goodness, according to their capacity." "Love Itself . . . moved Itself to creation." "The very Author of all things . . . becomes out of Himself by His providences for all existing things" (*ibid.* iv. 1; iv. 10; 10). And, in return and imitation, "Divine love," that is, the creature's love for God, "is ecstatic, not permitting any to be lovers of themselves." "By all things the Beautiful and Good is . . . loved; and because of It, and for Its sake, the lesser things love the greater suppliantly; and those of the same rank, their fellows brotherly; and the greater the lesser, considerately." " The fulness of the perfect Peace passes through all existing things, yoking all together in one connatural friendship" (*ibid.* iv. 13; 10; xi. 2).

(3) In a fundamental point of general outlook indeed, Dionysius, in, say, one-fourth of his text, adopts the Aristotelian identification between relative elevation of position in the scale of reality and relative richness of attributes, and applies this principle, in complete opposition to Neo-Platonism, to God Himself. He finds, indeed, that Being has a wider application than Life, and Life a wider than Wisdom. "For what reason, then, do we affirm that Life is superior to Being, and Wisdom to Life?" "Things with Life," so answers the author, "are doubtless above things that merely exist, things sensible above those that merely live, and things rational above these last. . . . The things that participate more in the One, the boundless-giving God, are more near to Him . . . than those that come behind them" (in gifts). "Are not Life and Goodness more cognate (συγγενέστερον) to God than air and stone? And is He not further removed from debauch and wrath than He is from ineffableness and incomprehensibility?" (*De Div. Nom.* v. 1. 2; *Myst. Theol.* iii.).

(4) But in the important theological, indeed religious, matter as to the perfect soul's relation to God, Dionysius, following here many of the Greek Fathers, speaks with less reserve than Proclus and with almost as little as Plotinus. "The Deification (θείωσις) from Itself"; "the many who become Gods (θεοί)"; "the Deification of those that turn to Him" (*De Div. Nom.* ii. 11). It is as though the initial excess of distance avenged itself, at the end, in an excess of closeness.

(5) The absence of the historic sense,—of any intrinsic and necessary function, within the spirit's life, of apparently contingent happenings,—and the purely negative character attributed to Evil are as prominent here as in the entire Platonist tradition, and this in spite of certain orthodox saving clauses, and of the noble insistence, Platonist and Christian, upon the need of purification by the soul that would experience and obtain Eternal Life.[1]

---

[1] On Dionysius and Proclus: Hugo Koch, *Pseudo-Dionysius Areopagita in seinen Beziehungen zum Neuplatonismus und Mysterienwesen*, 1900, is a very careful, thoroughly conclusive study.

## CHAPTER VII

### MIDDLE AGES

St. Thomas Aquinas : the two currents in his teaching—
Eckhart's two tendencies.

For the Middle Ages, let us take St. Thomas and Eckhart, as specially influential and instructive teachers concerning Eternal Life.

1. *Thomas* (A.D. 1225 or 1227–1274), born to a noble, of Norman descent, in his castle of Rocca Secca, near Aquino, educated by the Benedictines of Monte Cassino, and early won to the Dominican Order, dedicated his life to the defence of the (now four centuries old) West-European Christian civilization and Church, both in his day at their apogee, against the sapping, then proceeding apace, of Mohammedan-Aristotelian science and philosophy. His adoption of Aristotle is almost as complete as that of Proclus by Pseudo-Dionysius. A sensible, solid, capacious, balanced mind, a sane, pure, equitable, laborious soul, which ever possessed, and never lost nor gained, the Christian and Catholic faith, and which embraced and embodied, in fullest sincerity, all the best knowledge and

method of his time, he most richly deserved his adoption as dominant exponent of Roman Catholic orthodoxy, from soon after his death onwards. Yet such security of traditional tenure, such restriction to the intellectual systematization of what, some eight centuries earlier, had been forced to prove the superiority of its very substance in agonizing wrestlings with the most formidable forces, and such peaceful, ingenious accommodation, have necessarily limited his helpfulness, as the ages have moved on. Especially is there here no adequate sense as to the intrinsic, ultimate trend and affinities of Aristotle, the least religious among the greater Greek philosophers, or as to the precise contexts and differences surrounding, and observable between, Synoptic and other New Testament sayings. And Eternal Life, in particular, is conceived, upon the whole, with less consistency and depth by Aquinas than by Augustine, yet, on one point, with additional richness.

(1) Everywhere Aquinas is primarily concerned with carrying through his fundamental, precise delimitation between doctrines of Natural Religion, directly accessible to, and demonstrable by, reason, and doctrines of Revealed Religion, capable only of being proved by reason to be actually revealed by God, and to be not contrary to reason. In

both cases, specific written authorities decide—*the* Philosopher, Aristotle, and Scripture and the Fathers, respectively. The same rigid delimitation is not present in Augustine: the appeal there is primarily to the human soul; and to Plato and Plotinus, so deeply penetrated by the twice-born temper, as hungerers after the Infinite, and the New Testament, as furnishing the full articulation of this hunger, and its true, complete assuagement. Hence in Augustine, at his best, a costly tension, *élan*, dynamism; in Thomas, practically everywhere, a comfortable balance, quiet circumspection, a static quality. Augustine cries: "Thou hast made us for Thyself, and restless is our heart until it rests in Thee"; Thomas reflects: "To know that God exists, in a certain general and confused way, is connatural to us, since God is man's beatitude, and what man naturally desires, man naturally knows. But this is not simply to know that God exists . . . since many hold man's beatitude to consist of riches, others of pleasures, and others again of other things" (*Confessiones*, i. 1. 1. *Summa Theologica*, i. qu. ii. art. 1, ad 1).

(2) Aquinas's usual teaching is that "Reason cannot attain to the Simple Form (God), so as to know *what* It is (*quid est*); but it can know *whether* It is (*an est*)" (*Summ. Theol.* i. qu. xii.

art. 12, ad 1, and often elsewhere). Yet, also generally, he allows that "the names that we give to God and to creatures, are predicated of God according to a certain" real "relation of the creature to God, as its Principle and Cause, in Which the perfections of all things pre-exist in an excellent manner" (*ibid.* i. qu. xiii. art. 5, concl. et in corp.). This still seems to exclude all real contact, however little analysable, between the soul and God. But in an important direct discussion of the point, Aquinas admits that "it is impossible, with regard to anything, to know *whether* it exists, unless we somehow know *what* is its nature," at least "with a confused knowledge"; whence "also with regard to God, we could not know *whether* He exists," which we do know, "unless we somehow knew, even though confusedly, *what* He is" (*In Librum Boëthii De Trinitate*: D. Thomæ, *Opera*, ed. veneta altera, 1776, pp. 341*b*, 342*a*). It is indeed clear that only such positive knowledge can justify the numerous confident assertions as to God not being this or that.

(3) Aquinas, as indeed is the case with the Middle Ages generally, derives his conception of Eternity predominantly from the same Boëthius, who, in his *Consolatio Philosophiæ*, written in prison at Pavia about A.D. 524, gives us the

definition: "Eternity consists in the completely simultaneous (*tota simul*) and perfect possession of interminable life." Thus, *e.g.*, Aquinas, in his *Summa Theologica* (i. qu. x. art. 1, ad 1), opens the discussion concerning the Eternity of God with the quotation of this strongly Platonist passage from that monument of late classical antiquity, so perplexing in its Christian origin and yet freedom from all specifically Christian conceptions.

And Aquinas insists, in an interesting fashion, upon a mode of existence lying between Time and Eternity, which he calls *Aevum*. "Even supposing Time to last for ever, we can still distinguish within it a beginning and an end, by noting various parts of it. Eternity, on the other hand, is all together (*tota simul*)." But "*Aevum* is intermediate between Time and Eternity, participating in each; since, whilst Time has a before and an after," and "Eternity neither has, nor can suffer, a before nor an after," "the *Aevum* has not," of necessity, "either a before or an after, although they can be conjoined to it." Now "spiritual creatures, as regards their affections and intellections, in which there exists succession, are measured by Time; as regards their natural being, they are measured by the *Aevum*; and as regards their vision of glory, they participate in Eternity"

(*Summ. Theol.* i. qu. x. art. 5, in corp. et ad 1).

We have here an interesting groping after what M. Bergson now describes under the designation of *Durée*, the succession which is never all change, since its constituents, in varying degrees, overlap and interpenetrate each other; a succession which can be anything from just above the chain of mutually exclusive, ever equal moments,—artificial, clock-time,—to just below the entire interpenetration and *Totum Simul* of Eternity. Taken thus, the conception appears indeed to account for all the experiences concerned. For it indicates that man, even in the beyond, will—*pace* St. Thomas—still remain more or less subject to *duration*, though there he will be indefinitely more penetrated by, or aware of, that Eternity, that Eternal God, Who already here and now supports and penetrates him through and through. And this same conception suggests that even here and now, in his deepest experiences, man apprehends and loves that Eternity by means of and within, and as akin to, yet contrasting with, his own *duration*, his quasi-eternity.

(4) Aquinas, again, has two, instructively contradictory, currents of teaching concerning the character of the perfect life, in God and for man.

(*a*) There is, first, the *solus cum solo* current, a compound, varying in its proportions, of the Aristotelian, abstractive, more or less purely intellectualist and contemplative ideal, and the, still more abstractive although mystical, Neo-Platonist aspiration. Thus "in the active life, occupied with many things, there is less beatitude than in the contemplative life, busy with one thing only—the contemplation of truth"; "beatitude consists essentially in the action of the intellect, only accidentally in the action of the will." "God's intelligence is His substance"; whereas "volition cannot but be in God, since there is intelligence in Him," and "love has to be there, since there is volition there." And "as God understands things other than Himself by understanding His own essence, so also does God will things other than Himself by willing His own goodness." "God enjoys Himself alone." Hence, correspondingly among men, "'he who knoweth Thee and creatures,' as Augustine says, 'is not happier than if he knew them not, but is happy because of Thee alone.'" "The perfection of love is" thus "essential to our beatitude, only with respect to the love of God, not with respect to the love of our neighbour; were there but one soul only to enjoy God, it would be blessèd, even if it had not a single fellow-creature whom it could love"

(*Summ. Theol.* I. ii. qu. iii. art. 2, ad 4; art. 4, concl.–I. qu. xiv. art. 4 in corp.; qu. xix. art. 1, concl.; qu. xx. art. 1, concl.–I. qu. xix. art. 2, ad 2; I. ii. qu. iii. art. 2, ad 4.–I. qu. xii. art. 3, ad 4; I. ii. qu. iv. art. 8, ad 3).

(*b*) But there is also a deeply Christian current, where the Saint keenly realizes that direct, detailed knowledge, love and care of individual things and souls, and the greatest possible operativeness, are absolute essentials of all true perfection. "To understand something merely in general, not in particular, is to know it imperfectly"; and "since Our Lord says that 'the very hairs of our head are numbered,' God must know also all other individual things with a distinct and proper knowledge." "A thing," again, "is most perfect, when it can make another like unto itself. Hence everything tends to be like God, in proportion as it tends to be the cause of other things." And "everything in nature has, with respect to its own good, a certain inclination to diffuse itself amongst others as far as possible; and this applies, in a supreme degree, to the Divine Goodness, from which all perfection is derived." "Love, Joy, Delight can be predicated of God"—love "which, of its own nature, causes the lover to bear himself to the beloved as to his own self." "He, the very cause of all things, moves out of Himself by the abundance of His loving goodness" (*Summ. Theol.* i. qu. xiv. art. 8, in corp.; art. 11, contra et concl.; art. 8, concl.; art. 11, concl.; *Contra Gentiles*, lib. iii. c. xxi. in fine; *Summ. Theol.* ii. ii. qu. iii. art. 4, ad 4; i. qu. xix. art. 2, in corp.; qu. xx. art. 1, ad 1; ad 3; art. 2, ad 1).

(5) And further, Aquinas has, in his concrete, Christian current, a deep sense of the right and dignity of true individuality. "The multitude and diversity of natures in the universe proceed directly from the intention of God, Who brought them into being, so as to communicate His goodness to them and to have it represented by them. And since this goodness could not be sufficiently represented by one creature only, He produced many and diverse ones, so that what is wanting in the one towards this office may be supplied by the other." Hence "the multiplication of the angels," each of whom constitutes a separate species, "adds more to the nobility and perfection of the universe, than does the multiplication of men," who differ only as individuals of one species (*Summ. Theol.* i. qu. xlvii. art. 1, in corp.; *Contra Gentiles*, lib. ii. c. xciv. init.; c. xciii.).

(6) The negative character of Evil is, for the most part, maintained, in the wake of the Pseudo-Dionysius. The estimate of human nature is

milder than in St. Augustine, but still rather Pauline than Synoptic.¹

2. *Joannes Eckhart* (b. about A.D. 1260; d. 1327), the son of a noble near Gotha, still an immediate disciple of Albert the Great, St. Thomas's master, is a Dominican, as pure of life, as ceaselessly active in teaching, and as unworldly in character, as Aquinas himself. And precisely on the subject-matter of Eternal Life Eckhart's preaching has, at the first hearing, a far greater persuasiveness than is to be found in the cautiously checked and counter-checked teaching of the Angel of the Schools. And again, Eckhart's deep religiousness, and his sincere conviction that his positions were fully compatible with, indeed that they only developed, the Christian, Catholic, Scholastic experiences and traditions, cannot be doubted. Nevertheless, the special interest of his life and writings, in particular his extraordinarily eloquent German Sermons, lies elsewhere. For Eckhart brings to poignantly full expression both the power of the Neo-Platonist outlook and method (so largely already operative in the Pseudo-Dionysius) to express *one* of the two

¹ Ueberweg-Heinze's *Grundriss der Philosophie d. patristischen u. scholastischen Zeit*, ed. 1898, contains, pp. 270–290, an admirable digest, elucidation, and criticism of Aquinas's doctrine. Schütz's *Thomas-Lexikon*, ed. 1895, is most useful.

fundamental apprehensions and movements of the deepest religious life and faith, and the terrible blindness and destructiveness of that same philosophy (if taken as complete and ultimate) as regards the *other*, the still deeper, apprehension and movement of that life and faith. And special interest lies here also in observing the way in which the distinctively modern passion for utter logical clearness and consistency—the hunger of the mind which seeks its satisfaction in the mathematical and physical sciences—here largely takes the place of the spirit's thirst after the Spirit, God, and gives a tragic intensity and substance to that negative current. The Monistic instinct, so entirely right and indirectly so necessary and fruitful even for religion, when it functions in its proper place, here appears, largely, as the first and last word of life, and hence as impoverishing and destructive.

(1) Eckhart's fundamental position is: "God and Being are one and the same thing. All things have being from Being Itself, as all white things are white from whiteness."[1]

(2) In Psychology he tells us: "The soul is created a thing between a first and a second. The first is Eternity, which ever holds itself

---

[1] Eckhart's *Lateinische Schriften*, ed. Denifle, *Archiv f. Litteratur- u. Kirchen-geschichte des Mittelalters*, 1886, ii. p. 537.

within itself and is uniform; the second is Time, which changes and is manifold. With its highest powers (memory, understanding, will, like unto the Father, Son, and Holy Ghost) the soul touches Eternity, that is God; and with its lower powers (apprehension, temperament, desire) it touches Time, and thus the soul becomes changeable and inclined to bodily things, and loses her nobility." More characteristically: "The *little spark* of reason is found only in God; in Him its birth occurs, and this not once in a year, or in a month, or in a day, but at all times—according to the 'Time' above, in which there is neither Here nor Now." With intense, abstractive intellectualism: "Reason is more truly God's servant than will or love. For will and love are directed to God, in so far as He is good, and, were He not good, they would not approach Him; but reason penetrates into His Being, before considering whether this Being is goodness, power, wisdom, or this or that which, accidentally, is applicable to God." Indeed, "Being and Cognition are entirely one: what is not, *that* one does not know; and what has most being, *that* one knows the most." Hence "Man is not blessèd because God *is* so near him, but because man *knows* how near God is to him." And "I advise you to grow in *under-*

## Eckhart's Intellectualism and Abstractiveness 113

*standing* how God has made you out of nothing into something (into being), and has united you with the divine nature. But, if you cannot thus understand the divine nature, *believe* in Christ and follow His holy image."

"The light in the soul which is increate apprehends God without means, without veil, as He is in Himself. . . . This *spark* is not satisfied with (knowledge of) the three Persons, in so far as each subsists in its difference, nor with the unity of a fruitful kind in the Divine Nature, nor with the simple, unmoving Divine Being that neither gives nor takes; but it is determined to know whence this Being comes, to penetrate into the Simple Ground, into the Silent Desert within which never any difference has lain . . . and *there* it is more at one than it ever is in itself."[1]

(3) *God* and *Godhead* are sharply contrasted in all the most characteristic passages, although the terminology is not always carried through. "So long as thy soul has any image, it is without simplicity; and as long as it is without simplicity, it does not rightly love God ( = the Godhead). How then am I to love God ( = the Godhead)? Thou shalt love Him as He is: a non-God, a

[1] Meister Eckhart, ed. Pfeiffer, 1857, pp. 170, 319, 320; 110; 221; 498; 193; 194.

non-spirit, a non-person, a non-image; as a sheer pure One; and in this One we are eternally to sink from nothing to nothing, so help us God." "The soul receives, from the Trinity, all that can be measured by the powers of the soul; (but) from the sheer Godhead, a simple light shines into the simple being of the soul, which the soul's powers cannot receive." And "when the soul" of man "comes to the sheer Being of the Godhead, it knoweth all things, down to the lowest creature." Nevertheless, "the Persons" in God "are Eternal, they are in no wise creatures, since they have no before nor after," and "wherever God is, there He must act and speak His Word" (Pfeiffer, pp. 320, 540, 541, 677; 11).

Hence, after all, we have but a mere abstraction in that conception of the "desert Godhead," except in so far as this conception emphasizes, however one-sidedly, the very real difference (in likeness) between the immensely rich and harmonious Spirit, God, and ourselves, the relatively ever poor, and now largely chaotic human spirits, and their unpurified apprehension of Him.

(4) God's relation to the world is represented in correspondingly varying fashion and adequacy. As to Eternity and Time, we have the fine saying: "The *Now* in which God made the

world, is as near to the present time, as is the *now* within which I am speaking; and the Last Day is as near to that Now as is our yesterday." With strong intellectualism and depreciation of history he says: "Reason" (*Vernünftigkeit*) severs us from "here" and from "now." "The (human) *now* is the smallest part of Time—yet all that Time touches must go." "'Here' is indeed a small Space . . . but it must go, if I am to see God." "Temporal becoming ends in eternal dissolution (un-becoming); and the Eternal Becoming is a work of the Eternal Nature, and hence has neither beginning nor ending." And Neo-Platonist and Monistic inadequacies in face of creation and of Evil appear strikingly in the startling sayings: "The prophet (Ps. lxi. 2) says 'God said *one* thing, and I heard *two* things.' Thus when God speaks, it is God (only); but here," in man's apprehension, "it is (God and) creature." "All things are the same in God, and are God Himself." "God alone has Unity. . . . The soul is all things—God is one." "Evil is nothing but a privation or absence of being. . . . Evil is not an effect, but a defect." "Since God, in a certain way, also wills that I shall have committed sins, I do not wish not to have committed them" (Pfeiffer, pp. 207, 323; Denifle, 602; Pfeiffer, 426).

(5) The Ethics taught by Eckhart are partly rich, religious, Christian; and in part are sublimated by Monism to vanishing-point.

(*a*) "That is beautiful which is well-ordered. The soul ought, with its lower powers, to be ordered under the higher, and, with the higher, under God." "The right and perfect state of the soul would be, not simply that it should practise virtues, but that all the virtues should constitute her state, without being practised with deliberation." Yet "Some men say 'if I have God and God's love, I can do whatever I like!' But they misunderstand this saying. For so long as you are capable of doing anything that is against God and His command, thou art without God's love." And "In proportion as thou hast love for Him, art thou certain that He has, out of all comparison, more love for thee, and is incomparably more faithful to thee, since He is indeed fidelity itself." Also "It is better, when there is a genuine necessity, to do the works of the outer man, in compassion towards oneself or others, than to place oneself in a condition of interior liberation from all particular knowledge and desire." And there is the deep saying: "An interior work (of the soul) is one that neither Time nor Space can limit or comprehend, and in this such a work is like to God."

(*b*) But then there are also sayings which, pressed, would dissolve all human endeavour, contrition, special work, and social contribution. "He who is still mounting and increasing in graces and in light, never comes to God, for God is not an increasing light." "Follow your bare nature, and seek no other abode than the undesiring Nothing. God, who created thee out of nothing, will Himself be thine abode, in His desireless Nothing and in His Unmovingness. There thou shalt become more immoveable than nothingness itself." "We are wont to say, '*this* man is not *that* man, *I* am not *you*, and *you* are not *I*.' But lay aside the nothing," your individuality, "and we are all One. What is this One? It is the Son, whom the Father generates." "There is not more than *one* natural outflowing of Sonship (in God); not two but *one* . . . ye must be an *only* Son,—not many Sons, but *one* Son." Hence "As little as the Heavenly Father can forsake His Son, can He forsake the soul in which He generates His Son" (Pfeiffer, pp. 514; 524; 232; 559; 330; 434. 510; 620; 157; 652.

(6) The Circle attains its completion by the soul's return to the bare Godhead whence it came. "I stood bare and empty, increate, in God; God created all things and I" was "with Him."

"Can God understand Himself without my soul? No ... I stand in the ground of the Eternal Godhead where He works out all His works, understandingly, through me, and all that is thus understood I am." "The soul is created ... that it may flow back into the bottom of the bottomless fountain whence it flowed forth," "where it will occupy itself as little with anything as it did before it existed" (Pfeiffer, pp. 581–583; 511; 242).

We thus find in Eckhart a deeply impressive and instructive combination of a religious, Platonist and Christian, thirst for spiritual purification and union with God; a scientific, still predominantly Proclian, thirst for intellectual utter simplicity and clearness, for the logical ladder and pyramid; and an apparent thirst, of a more or less Buddhist kind, for an utter Nothingness. Yet all three thirsts presuppose a mightily thirsting, hence an intensely real, and a richly endowed and experiencing, thirster, and, indeed, a still more real and operative prevenient Cause or Causer, and subsequent Quencher, of all this thirst. And especially the religious thirst, as it is by far the deepest, so is it also much the richest in content, and doubtless implies the positiveness, the volitional character, of Evil. Hence, not real experience, but the abstractive process of logical regression from, and the artificial, ever-increasing, impoverishment of, this real experience, and the subsequent attempt to explain reality and experience in terms of mere scheme and skeleton, take Eckhart away from all history and concreteness, and from the sense of their abiding value and necessity; and from all richness in reality, especially from the supreme richness in the Godhead.

No wonder that Rome, in 1329, condemned twenty-eight such propositions, as objectively incompatible with the Catholic faith. But, indeed, the further experiences, since then, of mankind in the spiritual life, and the various attempts that have been made to discover and describe, as precisely and unforcedly as possible, the fountains and channels of spiritual fruitfulness also point (and in our times increasingly) away from such a scheme. We cannot take bare Being, or any other such abstraction, as first, either in existence or in value. For we ever find more and more richness, vividness, and difficulty of definition in reality, the deeper and the more ultimate this reality is; and, contrariwise, we find the more poverty, clearness, and facility of definition, the shallower and less ultimate, or the nearer to a simple abstraction of our own minds, such a reality, genuine or supposed, may be.

Certainly Eternal Life, its practice and conception, can but suffer from any attempt to restrict the spirit's action to one of its two movements —to abstraction and negation only; or to cut religion loose from the mysteriously mighty stimulation accruing to it, in and through the very tension and difficulties, from historic personalities and the happenings and operations in time and space; or, above all, from the full, vivid conviction of the distinctness from our own spirits, and of the supreme, stupendous richness, of the life of the Spirit—of God, the Godhead.[1]

[1] On Eckhart generally, see the admirable digest of his teaching by Prof. A. Lasson, in Ueberwig's *Grundriss der Geschichte der Philosophie*[8], 1898, pp. 314-331; and the important elucidation of the even excessively scholastic character of his teaching by Fr. Denifle, in *Archiv f. Litteratur- und Kirchen-geschichte des Mittelalters*, 1886, ii. pp. 417-669.

## CHAPTER VIII

### MODERN TIMES

Introductory—Spinoza, his object, method, and fundamental category; his utter determinism; his primary inconsistencies; the abiding truths and lessons of his life and teaching—Kant, his Epistemology, Ethics, Religion, and their special strength and weakness.

LET us take Baruch Spinoza and Immanuel Kant as the two thinkers who, in their very paralogisms or insensibilities, are probably, for these modern times, the most typical, influential, and instructive, as to the experiences and conceptions concerning Eternal Life.

1. *Baruch Spinoza* was born in 1632, in Amsterdam, of Jewish immigrants, from Spain and its Inquisition, into relatively free, largely Deistic Holland; was excommunicated by the Synagogue for his doctrines in 1656; and died, amidst loneliness, poverty, and patient toil, at The Hague, in 1677. Within his great, pure, strong soul and throughout a strangely inadequate method there move, beneath a baffling clearness and sudden and serene self-contradictions, three great currents of previously extant (indeed, for the most

part, of very ancient) requirement and thought, and one very understandable, continuously operative prejudice. Thus *Stoicism* is here taken over in the largest quantities; yet the ultimate temper of the soul is rather Neo-Platonist. And *Neo-Platonism* is adopted, in its negative, abstractive trend and in its mystical *attrait*; yet the general mental affinities are rather with Stoicism, especially in the high importance here attached to the body. And these two ancient philosophies are here, for the first time fully and calmly, reinforced, supplemented, and permeated, by the method and ideal, taken as universally applicable, of absolutely clear, rigorously deductive, unrestrictedly determinist *Mathematical Physics*, as these had now been developed by distinguished natural philosophers. And the strongest prejudice, a coldly angry contempt is, unlike the Stoics, here everywhere at work, and occasionally patent, against the historic and dogmatic elements and temper of the Jewish and Christian religion and theology—feelings all but inevitable in one already naturally so devoid of the sense for the need and use of history, so largely the child of a profoundly unhistorical age, and so near to the terrible, apparently logical, consummation of those elements in the prisons and fires of the Inquisition.

Yet Spinoza is rendered perennially pathetic

by a rare combination of insights and inadequacies. There is a deeply heroic, indeed Religious Temper of soul, a delicately true instinct as to man's constant and immense need of Purification from his petty self, and a remarkable sense as to the helps towards such a discipline to be found in Mathematical, determinist Science. And there is also a mistaken conviction as to the nature of the deepest Reality apprehended by man, as to the means, categories, and tests appropriate to this apprehension and to its expression, and hence as to the place and range to be assigned, within the spiritual life of man, to such science.

(1) Now the ultimate object of Spinoza's philosophy is conceived predominantly Stoic-wise, with a strain of Neo-Platonism; hence as directly ethical, practical, individual. "The things which, for the most part, are considered amongst men as the Highest Good are reducible to three: riches, honour, lust. And by these three things the mind is distracted, so as to be unable to think of any other good." And "happiness or unhappiness resides alone in the quality of the object to which we adhere by love. Sadness, envy, fear, hate; all these affections occur in the love of perishable things. But the love of what is Eternal and Infinite feeds the soul with joy

alone—a thing greatly to be desired and sought" (*De Intell. Emend.*; *Opera*, ed. Van Vloten et Land, 1895, vol. i. p. 3).

And the noble conclusion of his *Ethics* warns us: "If the way that leads to the mind's power over the affections and to its liberty appears as excessively arduous, yet it can be found. And *that* indeed must be arduous which is so rarely found. For how could it happen, were salvation easy, that it should be neglected by almost every one? But, in truth, all things great are as difficult as they are rare" (*ibid.* p. 266).

(2) The method which he believes himself to be everywhere following is vividly described where he tells us: "When I applied my mind to Politics, I determined, in order that I might inquire into the matters of this science with the same liberty of mind as that with which we are wont to treat things mathematical, not to ridicule, to lament, or to detest the actions of men, but to understand them; and to contemplate their affections and passions, not as vices of human nature, but as properties pertaining to it, in the same way as heat, cold, storm, belong to the nature of the atmosphere" (*Tract. Polit.* § iv., ed. V. et L. i. p. 270). Indeed, "the truth" generally "might for ever have remained hidden from the human race, had not Mathematics,

which look, not to the final cause of figures, but to their essential nature and to the properties attaching to it, revealed another type of truth to man" (*Ethica*, i. prop. 36, App., V. et L. i. p. 68). His chief, last work is consequently entitled "Ethics demonstrated in Geometrical Order."

Everywhere utter Clearness is thus, following Descartes, the test and measure of truth; and Spatial imagery is everywhere sought, indeed is often, unconsciously, taken, even in contradiction of the system's logic, as itself a proof or corroboration of truth. And yet, as we shall see, a motive springing from depths utterly beyond the ken of mathematics is largely determining Spinoza thus persistently to sacrifice what he has come to think are mere feelings and prejudices, or fantastically apprehended facts and happenings, to such entirely clear, spatially figured, abstractions.

(3) The fundamental category here is, most characteristically, not Spirit, but Substance. "By *Substance* I understand what subsists in itself, and whose concept does not involve the concept of another thing; and by *Attribute* I understand the same thing, except that 'Attribute' is said with respect to the intellect that attributes such a nature to the Substance"

(Ep. xii. = olim xxix., V. et L. ii. p. 230). Here the Attributes seem to be merely refractions, within our minds, of a Substance free in itself from all Attributes; yet Spinoza's dominant doctrine is certainly that Attributes are intrinsic to the Substance. "The more of Reality a being possesses, the more Attributes are attributable to it; and the more Attributes I attribute to a being, the more I am compelled to attribute Existence to it" (*ibid.*). Yet the supreme, in the last resort the sole, Infinite Substance, God, only possesses, or at least is not known by us to possess more than, two Attributes—it is a *res cogitans* and a *res extensa*; Thought and Extension are absolutely equal, co-present, simply parallel, Attributes of God. All single thoughts anywhere have God as a thinking being for their cause, as all single bodies have Him, as an extended being, for *their* cause; the thoughts are never caused by perceived things, nor are things ever caused by thoughts. And "the order and connection of the Ideas is the same as the order and connection of the Things"; for the Attributes, from which each series follows, necessarily express the being of the One Substance (*Eth.* ii. props. i.–vii., V. et L. i. pp. 73–77).

The Attributes, again, are apprehended by us in various *Modes*, and these Modes do not, anywhere in Spinoza, necessarily involve Existence or Eternity. "We conceive the Existence of Substance as altogether different from that of the Modes; whence arises the difference between Eternity and Duration, since it is only the Existence of the Modes that we can explain by Duration, but the Existence of Substance we explain by Eternity—that is, the infinite fruition of existing or of being" (Ep. xii. = olim xxix., V. et L. ii. p. 230). And to such Modes belong all "Quantity, as it is in our imagination,—divisible, finite, composed of parts and manifold"; "quantity, as it is in our intellect, being found there infinite, indivisible, unique"; all Measure, Time, and Number; and all Configuration (*ibid.* p. 231; Ep. l., *ibid.* p. 361). Note how Eternity is here, in the logic of the system, not a Simultaneity of infinite Self-Consciousness, but ever, more or less, a simultaneous infinite Spatial Extension; and how Duration here is never differentiated from Time, which latter is also conceived as clearly as possible, *i.e.* under the Spatial imagery of a chain of equally long, mutually exclusive moments. Thus here too it is the *res extensa*, as the more clearly conceived, that dominates even where the *res cogitans* would have special claims. There is thus, in this system as such, no depth of life, and hence no Eternal Life.

(4) The position, everywhere present here, that "all determination is negation," and the resolution of all concretion and interiority into the abstractest of categories, necessarily empty God, Free-will, and Evil of all reality, and find everything equally perfect, in its precise place and time, as part and parcel of the one necessary, utterly determined and utterly determining Whole.

Thus "I do not assign to God any human attributes, such as will, intelligence, awareness." Indeed, "it is certain that he who declares God to be one or unique, has no true idea of God" (Ep. liv. = olim lviii., V. et L. ii. p. 370; Ep. l., *ibid.* p. 361).

"If we assume a little worm to live in blood, and capable of discerning the several particles of blood, lymph, etc., and the reactions of each particle under the impact of the others, such a worm would live in the blood, as we live in this part of the universe, and could not know that certain motions and changes in the blood spring really from causes external to it. . . . Yet the nature of the universe is not limited, as is that of the blood, but is absolutely infinite, and hence its parts are affected in infinite ways. And, as One substance, each part of the universe has a still closer union with its totality" (Ep. xxxii. = olim xv.; *ibid.* pp. 310, 311).

"Evil is a state of privation; and privation is named with respect to our human intelligence, not with respect to that of God. We comprise all single things of the same kind," say all individual visible men, "under a single definition; and we then judge all these things to be equally capable of the highest perfection deducible by us from our definition. And when we find one such thing which conflicts with such a perfection, we judge it to be deprived of this perfection, and as erring from its nature. . . . But God does not attribute to things more of reality than the divine intelligence and power has implanted in them" (Ep. xix. = olim xxxii. p. 254). In a word, "by Reality and Perfection I understand one and the same thing." "The whole of Nature is one and the same Individual whose parts, that is, all bodies, vary in infinite Modes without any mutation of the Individual." "All things, if viewed in themselves, or related to God," the whole, "are neither beautiful nor deformed. I do not know in what respect spirits express God more than do other creatures; the difference between the most perfect finite creature and God, the Infinite, is no other than that obtaining between God and the least creature" (*Ethica*, ii. Defin. vi., V. et L. i. p. 73; Lemma vi. Schol., *ibid.*; Ep. liv. = olim lxviii., *ibid.* ii. pp. 370, 371).

(5) Yet precisely with respect to these greatest ethical and spiritual matters, Spinoza's self-contradictions, in detail and in principle, are the most glaring, though all are quite unconscious and were doubtless produced by the pressure of the actual nature of reality upon his fine nature and quite inadequate system. Thus the two Attributes are ever to remain parallel, each closed to the other; yet the human minds, mere Modes of the one Attribute (of Thinking), here clearly and continuously conceive also the other Attribute (of Extension), with its various Modes. The human passions, painted with classic power in the great Fourth Book of the *Ethics*, are described as terribly, powerfully extant; and though all that *is* at all is assumed, by the system, to be in so far perfect, they are not treated as perfect, and to be accepted if we would be perfect, but, on the contrary, as to be combated, and as somehow so real that such combat is ever rare and heroic. And though no one thing, in this system, expresses Reality, Perfection, more than another, yet "God's Eternal Wisdom, which has manifested itself in all things, has done so most in the human mind, and supremely in Christ Jesus" (Ep. lxxiii. = olim xxi., V. et L. ii. 412).

(6) But the inconsistency which, above all, introduces an element of grave unreality into the

system precisely at its culminating, crucial point, is the admission of victory by the individual soul,—by but one amongst countless fleeting Modes of one of the Attributes of the Infinite Substance, a Substance bereft of all Will, Love, Self-Consciousness. For the soul, thus utterly determined, already necessarily perfect for and in its place within the Whole, somehow does achieve emancipation from this its lot, a lot somehow keenly felt to be somehow unworthy, and attains identification—for a little while—with, now, a somehow all-wise and all-holy Will, Love, Self-Consciousness. At least, the rapturous, partly Christian, partly Neo-Platonist, final outlook and appeal of the system, in its vibrating sincerity, doubtlessly means or implies all this, since otherwise it would be but empty words. "Even if we knew that our mind is not eternal, we should give the first place to piety, religion, and generally to all things that are connected with greatness and generosity of soul." "The free man thinks of nothing less than of death; his wisdom consists in a meditation, not of death but of Life." And "the mind's intellectual love of God is the very love with which God loves Himself" (*Eth.* v. prop. xli., V. et L. i. p. 264; iv. prop. lxvii., *ibid.* pp. 226, 277; v. prop. xxxvi., *ibid.* p. 260).

The fact is, very certainly, not that Spinoza,

in order to win toleration for his Mathematical Pantheism, here prudently adopts an ethical and theistic phraseology beyond his own sincerest convictions, but, contrariwise, that life is far too rich and Spinoza is far too sensitive to this its richness, for him not to be carried, quite without intention or awareness, entirely beyond the limits of his highly artificial system.

(7) Yet, over and above this most impressive lesson, Spinoza can teach us, more and better than the Stoics, on points where the Stoics have already taught us much, even though here again his antagonism to rival, in part richer, convictions tends to limit the fruitfulness of the teaching.

There is, then, a ceaseless sense of the presence and the immense, continuous importance of the human Body, for good as well as for evil. Not all the materialistic, and yet also dualistic, inadequacies of his formulations can rob Spinoza of the glory of this deep, wholesome, terribly neglected insight.

There is, too, the sense of the organic character, and of the irreplaceable educative worth, for all human beings, of human Society. "Men can desire nothing more helpful towards the preservation of their own being, than that the minds and bodies of all men shall compose, as it were, one single mind and body" (*Eth.* iv. prop. xviii. Schol., V. et L. i. pp. 193, 194).

And, above all, there is the constant sense that, somehow, the highest perfection must include a wise, right Self-seeking; that the initial self-seeking requires an arduous Purification; and that Determinist Science can and should contribute to this purification. Yet here especially the inadequacies of his execution readily obscure the delicate truth of his fundamental instincts.

The Self-seeking, for one thing, remains here, after all, far too much a rationalist fighting for what we, more or less explicitly, hold from the first. "To act from virtue is in us nothing else than to act, to live, to maintain our being as reason directs, and that on the principle of seeking what is useful to the self" (*Eth.* iv. prop. xxiv.; V. et L. p. 198). God, Spirit, and His penetration and support of our spirit in its search for its own depth in Him, and the Cross, a practice of death in life to attain the deepest life, are badly wanted here.

Determinist Mathematical Science and its utter clearness prove true and fruitful instruments of purification, only if these things are assigned, not the ultimate, but an intermediate place; if they remain means and do not become quite ultimate ends; if we accept and practise, as the deepest experiences of the soul, not perfect clearness but rich vividness, not interchangeableness but more or less of uniqueness, not automatic happenings but effortful doings, not Physics but History, not Determinism and Abstraction, not the principle that "all determination is negation," but Libertarianism and Concrete Apprehension, and the sense that all Reality involves Determination. And, in that case, a life will ever repose upon the conviction that it ever more requires to be built up, developed and defended anew, with never complete success; it will contain a sense of Sin and of its utter need of God—of God, not Substance but Spirit, and of His continuous prevenience. The soul will feel its deepest convictions to be inadequate, not because they are not clear, but because they are not sufficiently *rich*, as over against the great Reality, the ultimate, yet intimately present, source, support, and end of all we are. And the test of the growth in adequacy of our convictions will be their *fruitfulness*, their power of practically explaining, still more of effectuating, things and growths in and for life in the most disparate fields.

And yet even such a continuously renewed apprehension and practice of a more than purely human Libertarianism, will not, of itself, suffice to purify us from our immediate, less than nobly

## Kant's Greatness, Ethical, not Religious

human, wilfulness; but there must ever flow, between that noble background or groundwork and this petty foreground, a river of cleansing pain and discipline, such as, especially for some ages and civilizations, the absolutely clear, determinist Mathematical Physics can supply. In this way Faith will turn Fate itself into a means for the soul's growth in likeness, not to Fate, but to God, Free-willing Spirit; and that strict Determinism, ready Interchangeableness, utter Clearness can, and ought to, find a large abiding place and function in the experience of, and search after, Eternal Life.[1]

2. *Immanuel Kant* may well conclude our series of characters and minds which, in the past, have best or worst understood, and have most aided, deflected, or checked, the experiences and conceptions of Eternal Life. For Kant was the first, and remains still the most powerful, formulator of certain presumptions and of a frame of mind, which are now again, after a considerable break,

[1] Probably still the most balanced English estimate is Dr. E. Caird's "Cartesianism," *Essays Literary and Philosophical*, 1890, vol. ii. On the subtly swift transition from servitude to liberty in the Ethics, see V. Delbos' delicate study, *La Morale de Spinoza*, 1890. On Stoic constituents, W. Dithey's brilliant "Autonomie des Denkens im 17 Jahrhundert," *Archiv f. Geschichte der Philosophie*, 1894, pp. 74-91. Valuable general considerations are to be found in R. Eucken's *Problem of Human Life*, Eng. tr. 1911, pp. 362-379.

most largely operative, and which deprive those religious experiences and conceptions of most of their native character, and of the certainty of their function and vigour. Indeed, Kant's greatness undoubtedly lies, not in Religion, but in Epistemology and Ethics; and, even in these, more in his acute detection of the precise nature and whereabouts of certain crucial problems and complications, than in the consistency and satisfactory character of the solutions proposed. Three or more, mutually inconsistent, principles are often operative in what claims to be a single, self-consistent solution; and certain strong general prejudices, unbeknown to the author, can often be traced as largely deciding the starting-point. And then these epistemological, and other more or less inadequate solutions, confirm him in certain strong, specifically theological, antipathies and insensibilities, when he comes to religious matters, and render his attitude as regards Eternal Life particularly unsatisfactory.

Kant was born, the son of a saddler of Scottish descent and of a purely German mother, at Königsberg in 1724; was brought up in strict Lutheran pietism, and was tutor for a while in a Calvinist pastor's family; taught as Professor at Königsberg University, 1770–97, and died, in that far-away little seaport town, in 1804. His *rationalist* period, as a follower of Leibniz-Wolff, up to 1762, and his *empirical* time, up to 1769, were followed by his, alone fully characteristic, *critical* years and works. His chief work, the *Kritik der reinen Vernunft*, took twelve years of thinking but only some five months of writing, first edition 1781, second edition 1787. His *Religion innerhalb der Grenzen der blossen Vernunft*, 1793, and his *Metaphysik der Sitten*, 1797, are applications of these *critical* principles to Religion and Ethics respectively. For our purpose, we can, all but entirely, restrict ourselves to certain main passages in these three works, although any such selection is rendered specially difficult, for the reason already given. The Ethics shall stand between the Epistemology and the Religion.

First, however, we must fully realize, never to forget, the abidingly strong and deeply sincere, the nobly ethical, motive of Kant's bewilderingly complex, in a sense intensely scholastic, system-building. This Metaphysic was, once for all, to put an end to all Metaphysic, as the arch-imperiller, the arch-perverter, of all Knowledge, all Ethics, all Faith. Bishop Berkeley (1685–1753), in his overmastering desire once for all to abolish the very possibility of materialism, had attained to the conviction that percipient minds alone are real, whilst matter and the entire external world were but so many floating ideas utterly dependent upon these minds—their very essence consists in being perceived. Berkeley, thus extending Locke's conviction as to the purely mental and subjective nature of the *secondary* qualities of material objects (light, heat, colour, etc.), to these objects' *primary* qualities also (extension, resistance, figure), believed himself to be furnishing a final refutation of the materialist Mandeville. And so also Kant believed himself to have utterly demolished Hume, especially in the latter's contentions that all our ideas are but copies of perceptions; that the mere association and complex of these impressions and ideas constitutes our soul-life, which thus requires no unitary substrate; and that no conclusion from the empirically given to what exceeds the entire range of sensible experience, such as God and Immortality, is admissible. Kant thus comes to trace, in refutation, the intense operativeness of the Mind in its elaboration of sense-impressions, and to seek exclusively in this mind, so immensely productive of order, harmony, unity within the unordered manifold of sense, and, beyond this mind, in the implications and requirements of Moral Obligation, the motives and reasons for belief in Freedom, Immortality, and God.

(1) As to *Epistemology*, the following amongst often considerably varying, parallel positions seem to be the most important for our purpose.

(*a*) The question which appears to Kant as supremely legitimate and simply fundamental is: "What is meant by an Object corresponding to Knowledge and therefore distinct from it?" And he answers: "It is easy to see that this object must be thought of as something in general, as $x$, since we have nothing outside our knowledge that we can place opposite to this our present knowledge, as corresponding to it." That is to say,—of Things-in-themselves we only know *that* they are, not *what* they are; and hence, in any one case, as here, we can but infer an $x$. "But we find that our thought of the relation of all Knowledge to its Object carries with it something of necessity, since this Object is regarded as what prevents our knowings (*Erkenntnisse*) from being determined at random, since, in that they are to relate to an Object, they must have that unity which constitutes the conception of an Object" (*Kr. der r. Vern.* 1781, p. 104 = *Werke*, ed. Berlin Academy, 1903, vol. iv. p. 80).

Kant thus assumes the possibility of conceiving Knowledge as independent of an Object, and of studying such Knowledge as a sufficiently complete subject-matter of research. Yet Knowledge thus independent is simply unthinkable, hence not a legitimate subject of inquiry at all. The true question is not "*Can* I know?" or "How can I introduce an Object into my Knowledge?" but "How *do* I know?" "What are the ever-present constituents in all my knowledge?" I can but analyse such knowledge as is actually in my possession, as I have to presuppose in all my negations as well as affirmations, epistemological or otherwise. And the Thing-in-itself appears here to be somehow known, since the unity of its parts is known to us as such, and somehow constitutes the unity of our knowledge of it.

The fact is, it is not really possible for the mind to get, self-consistently, beyond the given complex of a somehow knowing subject and a somehow known object, in all and every act and state of Knowledge; and Kant himself manages to break up this given trinity, only at the cost of the most varied, subtle inconsistencies.

(*b*) "Things-in-themselves, *Noumena*, are," then, "to be thought of only under the name of an unknown something"; "the conception of a *Noumenon* is thus simply a limiting conception (*Grenzbegriff*), fit to keep within bounds the pretensions of the senses,—my reason cannot be used assertively concerning any objects outside the field of sense" (*ibid.* p. 255 = *Werke*, ed.

Berlin Academy, vol. iv. p. 166). Yet Kant habitually knows, most assertively, that reality is entirely heterogeneous to our conception of it. Thus in 1772 we find the view "that God has implanted into the human mind categories and concepts of a kind spontaneously to harmonize with things" to be "the most preposterous solution that we could possibly choose" (*Briefe*, ed. Berlin Academy, 1900, vol. i. p. 126).

Thus what, until contrary evidence be forthcoming, should be reckoned only the Epistemological Difference between Presentation and the Thing-in-itself, becomes, prior to any such evidence or even inquiry, a Metaphysical Exclusion of each by the other. We thus get an Exclusive Subjectivism of a "dogmatic" kind from the strongly anti-"dogmatic" Kant; and this, although there is no fact of experience or of thought to prevent what is *my* presentation from existing also, as to the content of that presentation, independently of such a presentation. Indeed, Epistemology has increasingly obliged us to abandon such excessive, indeed gratuitous, dualism.

(*c*) "The order and conformity to law in the phenomena which we call *Nature*, we introduce ourselves; and we could not find them there, had not we, or the nature of our mind (*Gemüth*), originally placed it there." Thus "without our human understanding (*Verstand*) there would nowhere exist Nature, that is, the synthetic unity of the manifold of phenomena according to rules" (*ibid.* pp. 125, 126; ed. Berlin Academy, vol. iv. p. 92).

Here cognition is assimilated to manufacture or construction, the synthesis being limited by the nature of the constructive mind, and by the nature of the constructional material, the manifold of sense; and consequently much stress is laid upon the "recognition" of the synthesis, and upon self-consciousness in the act of knowledge. Yet the nature of knowledge presupposes that what we know is already extant, even where we happen ourselves to make what we know.[1]

(*d*) It is but fair to Kant, otherwise so readily classable with Descartes as regards the demand and esteem for direct and clear apprehensions and concepts, to remember his declaration (in 1798), in full acceptance of the great facts methodically established by Leibniz in 1701–9: "We can be mediately conscious of an apprehension as to which we have no direct consciousness"; and "the field of such obscure apprehensions is immeasurable, whereas clear apprehensions constitute

---

[1] See J. Volkelt's penetrating *Immanuel Kant's Erkenntnisstheorie*, 1879, esp. p. 241; and H. A. Prichard's sane and solid *Kant's Theory of Knowledge*, 1909, esp. pp. 114, 124; 233–236.

but a very few points within the complete extent of our mental life." [1]

(e) The difficult, yet fundamentally important, questions as to the nature of Time and of Space, and as to their precise function and worth in the spiritual awakening of the soul, and hence in the growth of the sense of Eternal Life, have been undoubtedly much advanced since Kant's examination of them. In this place we would only insist upon the importance of keeping both Time and Space vigorously apprehended in our life, and clearly analysed in our philosophy ; and of distinguishing, in both cases, between Time and Space, as actually perceived and experienced, and Time and Space, as abstractively conceived by us. Not only the vivid perception of Time, but also that of Space (one or the other or both of them, ever actually experienced, in various degrees and ways, in all the finite things or realities which we apprehend at all), turns out to be most necessary for the awakening of any deep sense of the contrasting Other, of the Non-Contingent, the Infinite and Abiding. And not only the clear conception of abstract Space, but also that of abstract Time, though, as such, ever

[1] " Anthropologie," *Werke*, ed. Berlin Academy, 1907, vol. vii. pp. 135, 136. G. W. Leibniz, " Nouveaux Essais sur l'Entendement," in *Die philosophischen Schriften von G. W. L.*, ed. Gerhardt, 1882, vol. v. pp. 45, 69 ; 100 ; 121, 122.

artificial products of the reflecting mind, turns out to be, in different ways yet similar degrees, necessary to the greatest possible adequacy and clearness of philosophy. According to this, Kant was indeed right, as against such of his modern critics as Bergson, in retaining a parallelism, even at the deeper levels of life, between Time and Space; but he was wrong in not discriminating between them as perceived and as conceived, and in treating even the perception of them predominantly as indeed necessary but empty forms of the mind, and hence in refusing all importance to these experiences and categories when he came to the soul's deepest, *i.e.* to its religious life.[1]

(2) Kant's *Ethics* are characterized by one profound help towards, and by two serious obstacles to, the experience and conception of Eternal Life.

(*a*) Kant's imperishable service is that, strangely late in the day, he, with but some anticipations on the part of Plato, first amongst professed philosophers, has everywhere conceived Evil, not in terms of privation or of a substance, but as Positive; as capable of, indeed as essentially consisting in, flight from, or revolt against, the

---

[1] See the excellent discussion in J. M'Kellar Stewart's *Critical Exposition of Bergson's Philosophy*, 1911, pp. 212-245, 300, 301.

light, and hence as an act or habit of the Will. Here he indeed rises, head and shoulders, above all the previous or subsequent Enlightenment, indeed above the entire Neo-Platonist strain, present, in strange contrast with their deep Christian experience and directly personal teaching, even in St. Augustine's and Aquinas's pages. "Nowhere in this our world, nowhere even outside it, is anything thinkable as good without any reservation, excepting the good will alone," he exclaims, with an impressive one-sidedness. And, contrariwise, "that a corrupt inclination to evil is rooted in man, does not require formal proof, in view of the clamorous examples furnished to all men by the experience of human behaviour. If you would have such cases from the so-called state of nature," take "the unprovoked cruelties enacted in New Zealand or North-Western America." Or "if you prefer to study civilized humanity, you will have to listen to a long string of accusations, of secret treachery, even amongst friends; of an inclination to hate him to whom we owe much . . . so that you will prefer to turn away your look from human nature altogether, lest you fall yourself into another vice—that of hatred of mankind" ("Grundlegung zur Metaphysik der Sitten," *Werke*, ed. Berlin Academy, 1903, vol. iv. p. 393; "Religion innerhalb d. Grenzen der blossen Vernunft," Erstes St. iii., *ibid.* 1907, vol. vi. pp. 32–34). This nobly truthful, virile insight was unfortunately lost again by such post-Kantians as Hegel and Schleiermacher, who, in this deep matter, revert to Spinoza. Yet, without such an insight, there is wanting a sufficiently imperative motive for the soul to gain the greatest livingness in its turning utterly away from self to God, its strength and purifier.

(*b*) On the other hand, Kant's Ethics are distressingly formalist and *doctrinaire*, and remarkably lacking in richness and variety of motivation, especially in any consciousness that the highest virtue may be indeed easy and delightful to a spontaneously high nature or to a laboriously acquired disposition. "A man can advance his own happiness, not from inclination, but from the motive of duty; and only in such a case his behaviour possesses moral worth." And "Love, as inclination, cannot be commanded; but benevolence, from a sense of duty, even when no inclination drives a man to it, and indeed when natural and insuperable repulsion is struggling against it, is *practical* and not *pathological* love, and this can be commanded" ("Grundlegung zur Metaphysik der Sitten," Erster Abschnitt. *Werke*, ed. Berlin Academy, 1903, vol. iv. p. 399).

There is here a painful lack of spontaneously *affective* as well as effective love, of the beautiful tenderness of Our Lord or of St. Francis, where there is no thought of a law, but a joyous absorption in realities, spirits, persons, loving and loved, serving and served. The general thinness and formalism of Kant's moral outlook proceeds indeed largely from the artificiality of his Epistemology and the slightness of his specifically religious sense. For thus he is ever fearful lest, by any moving away from Ethics, consciously willed as so much costly Categorical Imperative, we fall into Sentimentality and Subjectivism, since here it is not spiritual realities other than ourselves, and the certainty of our relatedness to them, which constitute for us a world prior to our moral acts and life; but, on the contrary, it is our sense of ethical obligation alone upon which our assurance of, and approach to, any such world is built up.

(*c*) There is also, doubtless for the same reasons, an excessive individualism in Kant's Ethics. In one of the Fragments he declares: "There can be nothing more terrible than that the actions of a man should be required to be subject to the will of another. For the like of this does a child become embittered, if it is to do what others will, without their having striven to make the thing attractive to it." And indeed in his *Metaphysic of Morals*, 1797, he defines the Ends of action, which are at the same time Duties, as "our own Perfection" and "our neighbour's Happiness." And he explains how "all men indeed possess the End of their own Happiness, by an impulse of nature; but this End cannot, without a self-contradiction, be conceived as a Duty, since Duty is a compulsion to an End which is accepted without liking"; and how "it is a similar contradiction to make the Perfection of another my End, and to consider its furtherance as my Duty, since precisely in this consists the Perfection of my neighbour, as a person, that he is himself capable of determining his own End in accordance with his conceptions of Duty; and hence I cannot consistently be required to do what no other than he himself can do" (Zweiter Theil, Einleitung iv., *Werke*, ed. Berlin Academy, vol. vi. pp. 385, 386).

Such systematic non-interference would, however, render all education of children impracticable. Indeed, throughout life, there is no deep spiritual advance possible, without a break-up, not only of the soul's habits but even of its standards; and this break-up will often be occasioned by the "interference" of another soul, more advanced and more devoted than our own. Life, in short, is indefinitely richer than that Kantian distinction assumes; and this its richness here again depends upon our ability really to *know* and to love, to love and to know—in this case, our fellow-souls. Monica and Augustine, Clare and Francis of Assisi, and analogous minor experiences in the lives of us all, cry aloud against any necessary limitation, in one soul's knowledge of another, to impressions, of a simply hypothetical evidential value, made and received by each upon and from the other. For here again I get to know myself, ever incompletely yet in various degrees really, in the same act by which I get to know others really. And in this really known world of realities there is serving and commanding, as well as self-defensive equality; and thwarting, as well as careful abstention from all checks. Indeed, Kant himself was too full of devoted service for his Ethics not frequently to have a tone more richly true than the principles here considered would logically permit; and these principles themselves are, in part, most understandable reactions against certain contrary extremes.[1]

[1] On Kant's Ethics, see the excellent short annotations in Ueberweg-Heinze, *Grundriss der Geschichte der Philosophie der Neuzeit*, 1880, pp. 228–238; and James Seth's *A Study of Ethical Principles*, 1894, 11th ed. 1910, with its instructive contrast between *Eudæmonism*, retentive of the Supreme Good and finding Happiness in the elaboration of the raw material of sense by means of the Moral Law, and, at the one extreme, *Hedonism*,

(3) Now the Kantian *Religion,* where Kant treats it *ex professo*, contains strangely little of what history at large, and our own souls, where these are spiritually awake, show us as specifically religious; Kant's "Religion" is *then* but the Kantian Epistemology and Ethics applied to a subject-matter which says nothing specific to him, and which, hence, cannot awaken any suspicion within him as to the intrinsic truth, or as to the applicability here, of the tests thus ruthlessly applied by him to a strongly recalcitrant material. The following are probably the chief of such applications to be found in Kant, *qua* the *critical* philosopher of Religion.

(*a*) Among the three main arguments for the Existence of God, in the *Kritik der reinen Vernunft*, the Ontological, the Cosmological, and the Physico-Theological (or Argument from Design), Kant, in strict consistency with his fundamental epistemological principles, cannot but consider the Ontological argument as especially demanding, and as especially succumbing to, his destructive criticism. For if Knowledge, even of the least thing, is ever, for us men, not knowledge of that thing's Reality, but only of its appearance

engrossed in the sensational Material to the neglect of the Form, and, at the other end, *Rigorism* or *Rationalism* (Kant), neglecting the Material whilst engrossed in the Moral Form and End of action.

to our senses and of the elaboration of this appearance by our minds; if of Reality we only know, somehow, that it exists distinct from our senses and minds, and, somehow, that it is radically different from these our apprehensions and elaborations; if hence everywhere our strongest impressions that we know Reality are but illusions: then the Existence of an Infinite, Necessary Reality will, in a supreme degree and in a normative manner, be absolutely unreachable from any amount or kind of impressions or implications to that effect. For here we have the supreme application of, and trust in, that *minimum of a realistic conviction*, the denial of which indeed lands Kant, elsewhere, in continuous difficulties of various kinds, and, at this point, tears up the elementary experience and affirmation of religion by the roots.

"There exists here," says Kant, "the strangely irrational situation, that the conclusion from a Given Existence generally," *i.e.* a Being than whom no greater can be conceived, "to an unconditionally Necessary Existence, appears to be urgent and correct," since otherwise we *could* think of a greater Being; "and yet that we have all the conditions of our understanding, which are necessary for our conceiving the idea of such a necessity, entirely against us." True, "the analytic indication of Possible Existence, which consists in that simple positions (realities) do not generate contradictions, cannot be denied to a Supreme Being"; such a conception "is" even, "in many respects, a very useful idea": but, "precisely because a mere idea, it is quite incapable, by itself, of enlarging our knowledge concerning the Extant." For "if I think of a Being as the highest Reality, there still remains the question whether it exists or not; since, even if nothing be lacking in my conception of the possible real content of a thing, there may still be a lack with respect to the condition which underlies all my thinking, namely, that the knowledge of an object shall also be possible *a posteriori*." Now "our consciousness of all Existence belongs entirely to the Unity of our Experience; and an Existence outside of this field cannot, indeed, be declared simply impossible, but is a supposition which we cannot justify by anything."

Here we may note that the traditional (Anselmian) form of the Ontological Argument has, indeed, been largely unfortunate, and that Kant has taken full advantage of this. The addition of the predicate of Existence does *not* add to the content of the thing affirmed to exist; and certainly not any simple determination on our own part to think any particular thing involves that thing's Existence. Yet, this argument, at its best, covers three great abiding facts, general experiences and strict necessities of life and mind, which, taken together, remain unrefuted by Kant, and which indeed strongly influence him throughout his work.

As already seen,—in all Knowledge there is never that abstraction, simply knowledge of knowledge, or knowledge of phenomena which hide or travesty reality; there is knowledge of reality. All Knowledge is thus ever a trinity of Subject, Object, and the subject's Knowing which simultaneously includes knowledge of the Object and of itself, the Subject. We do not know the Thing-in-itself, in the sense that we know nothing exhaustively, and that we do not, of course, know the Thing as outside our Knowledge of it. But we *do* know the Thing in our Knowledge of it, and we there know it without further mediation. Again, in all our knowledge of Single Things there is ever concurrently, in contrast with, and entering into, the apprehension of them, a sense of their Finitude, Contingency, Incompleteness, Insufficiency, which is not furnished by themselves even in their totality,—since they each and all can and do furnish only endless varieties of such Contingency. It is not that we contrast a permanence, or an endless succession, of such contingent objects, with the fleetingness of any one of them; but that *all* mere Succession and Fleetingness is keenly apprehended and felt as contrasting with (and it spontaneously awakens) a sense of Simultaneity and Abidingness, as somehow superior to and normative of, as somehow alone giving dignity and worth to, all that flux and relativity. And finally, the attempts at explaining this sense as a mere projection of man's empty, undisciplined wishes, and at ridiculing it from out of all serious consideration, have certainly not succeeded, even in the limited sense of having been consistently practised by the very protagonists of such explanation and ridicule.

Indeed, Kant's own position has ever remained instructively halting. Halting in theory: for Things-in-themselves certainly exist; God, Freedom, Immortality must be postulated; yet we can never know what the Things are, and we can never proclaim the latter three great convictions as more than practically necessary and intellectually admissible as hypotheses. And halting in practice: for his deep awe before the starry heavens and the voice of conscience is quite obviously more than a contented ignorance, or even than a doubt, concerning the more than human yet still ethical character of more than human Spiritual Reality.

As a matter of simple fact, all that is deepest in human achievement and conviction,—the nobler, the most disinterested, negations included,—springs persistently from, and grows with, such an elementary belief and trust in a World and Reality more than even universally human. Only through and with such conviction does man become fully himself. And it is a useless ingenuity and a perverse excess of caution to try to build up any ultimate philosophy upon an assumption of the actual (or even the possible) illusion of that which, even to be sufficiently in earnest in affirming such illusion, we have to assume as true.

Kant, however, is no doubt right in refusing to accept the Ontological Argument as, of itself, proving Theism. It does not, alone, prove more than that, in all our knowledge of beings as finite and contingent, a contrasting knowledge of an Infinite and Necessary Reality is involved. And the more precise nature of this Reality will have to be revealed to us, at all fully and vividly, by the experience and testimony of the positive religions, where these latter, by their fruitful illumination and enrichment of the other stages of life, prove themselves to be authentic expressions of the deepest Knowledge of the deepest Reality: namely, of the Religious Knowledge of prevenient

Spirit. And yet the Ontological proof is one far beyond any simple deduction, and consists in an infinitely multipliable tracing of the Religious Knowledge in all our ordinary knowledge, and of the ceaseless elevating operation of this Religious Knowledge within our human lives. So far and no further philosophy seems both to be able to supply, and to be reasonably bound to accept, reasons for a first step towards Theism, and for a conviction which, apart from any such support, contributes much towards the faith in and practice of Eternal Life.[1]

(*b*) Again, where Kant is *critically* active and unchecked by his deeper, more religious apprehensions, we must expect a non-understanding of Grace, of Waiting upon God, of Religious Worship, of Religious History and Institutions. Indeed, all these things have to go, except in so far as they can be affirmed as demonstrably harmless or useful hypotheses, or can be practised as transparently human expressions of the all-devouring Moral Imperative.

Thus as to Grace. " Whether over and above all that *we* can do, there may not exist something

[1] See the still admirably fresh " Die Selbständigkeit der Religion" of Professor E. Troeltsch, *Zeitschrift f. Theologie u. Kirche*, 1895, pp. 361–436 ; my paper, "Experience and Transcendence," *Dublin Review*, April 1906 ; and Clement Webb's clear and firm discussion, in *Problems in the Relations between God and Man*, 1911, pp. 157–159, 179–188.

which God alone can do, in order to make us into men well pleasing to Himself, is not herewith decided negatively"; indeed, "at times certain movements, operative in the direction of morality, occur within ourselves, as to which our ignorance is forced to confess that 'the wind bloweth whither it listeth, but we know not whence it cometh.'" Yet "the persuasion that we are able to distinguish between the effects of Grace and those of Nature (Virtue) or even to produce the former within ourselves, is fanaticism, since we can neither recognize a super-sensible object within our experience, nor exercise an influence upon it"; and "a feeling of the immediate presence of the Supreme Being, distinct from every other, even moral, feeling, would mean a capacity for a perception, for which there is no place within human nature."

As to Religious Worship. "All that man thinks he can do, outside of a good life, towards pleasing God, is sheer religious illusion and false worship of God." "A disposition to execute all our actions *as though* they took place in the service of God is the spirit of praying 'without ceasing.' But to incorporate this wish, even interiorly, in words can, at most, only have the value of a means for the repeated awakening of that disposition within us." Indeed, any "devout but still, as regards pure religious conceptions, backward man, whom another would surprise even simply in the attitude indicative of praying aloud" would be expected "at once to become confused, as over a condition of which he has to be ashamed." In short, "It is a superstitious illusion to attempt to become pleasing to God by confessions of statutory articles of faith, observance of ecclesiastical discipline, etc., since merely natural, non-moral means have here been selected, which can effect simply nothing with respect to what is not nature, that is, the morally good."

And, finally, as to Religious History. "It is reasonable to assume that, not only 'the wise according to the flesh,' but also 'what is foolish before the world' should be able to lay claim to such a saving instruction and interior conviction. . . . Now there exists a practical cognition which, although reposing upon reason alone and requiring no historical information, lies, nevertheless, as near even to the simplest of men as if it were literally written on his heart,—a law which carries with it an unconditional obligation in the consciousness of every man,—namely, the law of morality. Moreover, this cognition either leads, already of itself, to belief in God, or at least it alone determines the concept of Him as of a moral law-giver; and hence it leads us to a pure religious faith, which is not only understandable but also supremely venerable to every man" ("Religion innerhalb d. Grenzen d. blossen Vernunft," Viertes Stück, §§ 2, 3, *Werke*, ed. Berlin Academy, pp. 170, 174, 175, 190, 194, 195 and n., 181, 182).

Here again let us be fair to Kant's motives, and not forget the terrible abuses—ascetical, mystical, hierarchical, and the checks, conflicts and oppressions introduced or furthered by them in the racial, political, social, and scientific life of mankind, such as Kant himself, with fairly complete oblivion of the immense beneficence of the positive religions, yet in large part truly and with deeply sincere indignation, describes here (in the second division of the Third Piece, *Werke*, ed. Berlin Academy, vol. vi. pp. 130, 131). To have done away for ever with the very possibility of religious pressure and persecution, and of attempts to force upon men a choice between insincerity towards growing Science and Criticism and insincerity towards cast-iron detailed professions of Historic faith; and yet to retain Ethics (increasingly pure and universally benevolent Ethics); and this still with the background, indeed the sanction, of God, Freedom, Immortality—this, Kant believed himself to be here achieving. And yet those abuses of Religion must evidently be met by a deepening of Religion *as such*; whereas here we get, unmistakably, a thinning out, and a violent explaining away, of Religion, in precisely its specific characteristics, especially as these concern the experience of Eternal Life and the habits of mind favourable to such experience.

Religion, indeed, has ever been, at its fullest and deepest, *Adoration*, hence apprehension and affirmation of, and joy in, what already *is*; and the Prevenience of God, His part in the religious act, has consequently, by the Prophets and Psalmists, by Jesus and St. Paul, by St. Augustine and Pascal, been dwelt upon almost to the exclusion of our own part. Kant, as usual, seizes the central difficulty here, and rightly rejects exclusively divine acts within our souls; doubtless the Divine Action must be conceived as ever inviting our own, and as, where an act pleasing to God is the result, ever accompanied by some human, presumably our own, activity. Yet that divine environment and prevenience, the all-in-all of God, Who Himself has deigned to limit Himself in order to leave to us the kind and degree of liberty He has chosen for us; the great fact, not of our own action, but of what renders that action possible, especially in forms and with motives too high and too wide for the world of simple sense or of unaided nature: these are the realities and truths central to the religious consciousness.

Where Kant's view remains religious, and he is reasoning *ex professo*, he at once becomes hypothetic. But who ever found the religious soul hypothetic? The very desolations of Gethsemane and Calvary imply certainty, not hypothesis. And, indeed, it is doubtless this grand sense of Givenness, of Grace, which, as much as anything, won the humanity of the Roman Empire from Stoicism, with its "Monstro quod ipse tibi possis dare," to Christianity, with its "Our sufficiency is from God." And thus any and every Stoicism, Kant's included, comes too late. As a matter of fact, we daily, in a lesser degree, experience, in any and every deep and pure human intercourse, the soul-enlarging mystery of the awakening of our mind and will, to fuller life and fruitfulness, by minds and wills stronger, where they are also more devoted, than our own; hence there is nothing unreasonable, nothing even simply without experimental parallel for us, in belief in an action of God's Spirit awakening the depths of our own.

Nor is the impossibility of deciding infallibly, at any moment, and concerning any particular thought or act, whether it is of Grace or of Nature, decisive, as Kant assumes; unless my inability to pick out infallibly precisely what I owe to my friend's influence is decisive against the reality of that influence, and stamps my belief in it as superstitious or unwholesome. Of course, if Nature is, with Kant, assumed, for this occasion, to be identical with Virtue, Grace will, to any pure Moralist, readily appear a superfluity. And yet the Givenness, and the sense of Givenness, will infuse a special character into all the virtues. There are, too, such heroic virtues as the forgiving of enemies, which postulate and require precisely such a realm of Divine Prevenience and generosity. Again, our very acceptance of never more than trust, than moral certainty, as to the supernatural character of any one of our acts or states adds a further touch of utterly appropriate humility to such an already rich outlook. And finally, such general, yet also practically precise, discriminations between Nature and Grace as are given, say, by Thomas à Kempis, remain founded upon an experience safe against all final overthrow.

As to Religious Worship, it is, of course, plain that without a God, the Spirit of Spirits of Theism, and a certainty of His Reality and Presence amongst us, it would no doubt be superstitious; and indeed we can hardly find any place for it in a world of *phenomena* that alone are certain and known, and of *noumena* known, at

## Givenness and Worship essential to Religion 163

most, just simply to exist. But in a world of diversely deep realities, from stone and tree up to animal and man, with a Supreme Reality upholding and penetrating it all, a world known really to one of these its real constituents, man, there is nothing necessarily superstitious in, there is indeed a need for, Cultual Acts. For if each and all finite objects and acts awaken in our souls the sense of the Infinite, we cannot but expect that finite objects and acts specially representative of specifically religious requirements and dispositions, and specially introduced by and commemorative of great religious teachers and revealers, will (though never alone, but only where used and spiritually willed by human souls, in and with a religious society) be the means, occasions, and vehicles of a more precise, deep, and expansive religious enlightenment and volition. Only if sense is simply cut off from Spirit, and if, say, close contact with mathematico-physical science can do nothing for the awakening and disciplining of the human soul, can we rule out non-moral things and acts as necessarily incapable of mediating spiritual benefit. Certainly, neither stocks nor stones can, as such and separately, profit my soul; but the element of inexorable Fate, of impersonal Law, and of opaque *Thing*, must be placed somewhere in the totality of my life, even of my spiritual life; and, placed in the middle-distance of this my life, and used rightly by me, so largely still a mere natural individual in the foreground, I can touch and pass through that element, ever again, as through an awakening and purifying river, out on to the background and heights, having become thus, more and more, a spiritual person.

And, finally, History most certainly introduces endless difficulties as to the evidence for, and as to the abiding applicability of, its facts, and many temptations to oppression and insincerity. Yet the broad fact remains that, in every department of experience, but supremely so in the very deepest, in that of religion, we men learn to know truth and goodness, not abstractly, as Laws, but concretely, as qualities of Persons. And what we thus learn most fully has cost their all, of sweat and tears and blood, to these our teachers, and costs anxiety, self-discipline, and humble docility of soul to us the learners. Those utterly concrete, ever more or less unique, experiences and revelations of the Infinite Spirit are thus offered and accepted, never automatically or compulsorily, but ever freely and expensively. And those great teachers and revealers, *qua* religious, ever enlighten and win us primarily with regard to *God's* reality, character, claims, and approachableness.

# Truth and Goodness revealed through Persons

For, even though, in proportion as the religion thus lived and announced is high and developed, the ethical requirements become increasingly exacting and continuous, they in no wise oust God from the centre, the beginning, and end of the entire life; but this life remains, with correspondingly increased consciousness, more than, though inclusive of, all these requirements.[1] And especially do the individual religious Historical Events not remain, or become, mere symbols of a stream or tendency; they are now, not less but more, conceived as expressive of the religious Personality which lived them, and such a Personality again is recognized as the vehicle and manifestation of abiding, self-conscious Spirit.

It is easy to trace, throughout his book on Religion (in spite of his deeply Christian attitude towards Evil, and of his finely suggestive ideal "the Son of God"), Kant's angry hostility to any treatment of Jesus Christ, we will not say as

[1] Certainly, in the case of the Buddha, we get an apparently complete exception to this rule. But this primitive Buddhism is, I think, most correctly taken as an extraordinarily immanental, self-absorbed, estimate of, and attitude towards, life, and as a spiritually attuned moralism; and not as directly a religion at all. All human life, all life, apprehended as a sheer wheel of generation and mere change—such a conception can but issue in the desire for a complete cessation of all life. A more healthy and adequate perception of the real content and evidences of human life has ever to precede, accompany, or succeed the religious sense, where this is at all fully awake.

God, but even simply as, somehow, unique. But we should carefully note that Kant's quarrel with orthodoxy here lies far further back, and extends much further afield, than the symbols of Nicæa and Chalcedon. What he, faithful to his general position, objects to, first and foremost, is the assumption of man's ability to know Reality of any kind in and through phenomena of any kind. Even the most general incarnational doctrine,—that Reality, especially Spirit, and supremely God, manifest their true natures to us, precisely in and through and on occasion of Sense, must, then, be Superstition or Fanaticism for him. Judaism and Mohammedanism, indeed Brahmanism and the later, theistically enriched, Buddhism cannot fail, for this general reason, to be also obnoxious to him. Indeed, the three golden rings in Lessing's *Nathan*, symbolizing the utter equivalence of the three great Theistic faiths, Christianity, Judaism, Mohammedanism, ought not, logically, to satisfy Kant, except with an evisceration which would leave each unrecognizable to itself and to the others; but he would have to exclaim, as does Sultan Saladin in that great play which, on this its central point, is so interestingly, because unconsciously, inconsistent: "If I could but find a man who would be satisfied with being ust simply a man!"

And yet, no. Kant himself is too great and deep ever consciously to work, or to wish, for such a sheer, fortunately impossible, *naturalization* of man. Indeed, his whole philosophy consists in one long, heroic attempt to regain, for and by the Practical Reason, those certainties of more than human realities and destinies which the Pure Reason had to abandon, yet which remain largely operative in all his deepest convictions. In any case, Lessing's man of no particular religion would be no more typically a man, than is the savage wearing no particular clothes, using no particular tools, owning to no particular family ties or sexual traditions. In all these cases, not to have these things in particular, is not to have them at all. And especially as to the soul's sense of the Infinite and Abiding,—these will be, *cæteris paribus*, at their deepest and keenest, in the soul's closest contacts, its most loving familiarity, its most heroic struggles, with and for the Concrete, Historical manifestations of such Eternal Life.[1]

[1] On Kant's attitude towards Grace, see Clement Webb, *op. cit.* pp. 92-117; on the necessity of Cultus in religion, Ernst Troeltsch, *Die Bedeutung der Geschichtlichkeit Jesu für den Glauben*, 1911, pp. 25-33; and on the need of History, the same deep thinker's *Das Historische in Kant's Religionsphilosophie*, Kant Studien, 1904. On Kant's "ignoring of religion, *i.e.* of the reality which historically is thus denominated," see the vivid picture and incisive criticism in Georg Simmel's *Kant*, 1904, pp. 125-135.

# PART II
CONTEMPORARY SURVEY

# PART II

## CONTEMPORARY SURVEY

### INTRODUCTION

LET us now attempt some characterization of such amongst the chief movements in philosophy, life, religion, as have come to their full expansion since Kant's zenith and are still at all powerfully among us, and as express or aid or hinder the experience and conception of Eternal Life. We will here take, first, four Philosophers and their main present-day followers; next, a great Scientist and a mighty biological doctrine; and lastly, those two massive things—Socialism (so largely still averse from all Transcendence) and Institutional Religion. We thus again move throughout, as far as possible, in historical order, although we keep for the last what, though doubtless still the home and training-school of an indefinitely larger number of religiously awake souls than are decisively influenced by all the previous groups put together, is, nevertheless, incomparably older than them all.

## CHAPTER IX

### PHILOSOPHIES DERIVATIVE FROM KANT

Introductory—J. G. Fichte, his radical *criticism* ; his acceptance of a Moral Ordering, not an Orderer ; his social, affective ethics ; his sceptical bent—Münsterberg, Eucken—Schleiermacher, his *Reden*, his *Glaubenslehre*—Troeltsch—Hegel, his fruitful anti-identity principle, and his two destructive identifications—The English Hegelians, J. E. M'Taggart, Feuerbach—Schopenhauer, his two main epistemological positions, his pessimism and asceticism, his *Nirvana*—Kierkegaard, Nietzsche.

LET us first, then, consider Fichte, Schleiermacher, Hegel, and Schopenhauer. We take these men thus together, since, however different in nature from each other and from Kant, they each and all build philosophically upon Kant's most characteristic assumptions. And we take them as influences of our own times, because all four are still, or again, largely operative, even if mostly through repulsion, especially by means of now living writers and movements of vast, though often veiled, present-day importance.

1. *Johann Gottlieb Fichte*, born in poverty, the iron-willed, violently ethical, heroic character and mind (1762-1814), moved, in 1790, away from

Spinoza's Determinism to Kant's Criticism, in order here to find room for Free Will. But whilst, from 1794 onwards, he elaborated a conception of knowledge more consistently independent of the object than ever Kant systematically propounded, and though, as strongly as ever Kant did, he found the root and worth of Religion entirely in the Categorical Imperative, he nevertheless retained, and increasingly (1801–6) articulated, a greater depth, delicacy, and range of specifically religious apprehension and feeling than are to be found in Kant.

(1) Thus, as to Knowledge and the Thing-in-itself, Fichte insists, already in 1794, that every philosophy is still "dogmatic" which admits anything as equal to, or as contrasted with, the Ego. In the (true) Critical System, the Thing is posited in the Ego; in the Dogmatic System, the Thing is that wherein the Ego itself is posited; hence the Critical System is immanent, placing everything within the Ego, the Dogmatic System is transcendent, going beyond the Ego. So does Fichte most fully articulate the feeling, unknown to the ancient and mediæval worlds, but so characteristic still of large tracts of modern life, of constraint from, and irritation against, whatsoever is not somehow his own mind or the creation of this his mind, empirical and limited or absolute—the

Absolute creating and seeing in and through this mind and its fellows.

(2) True, in 1798 and 1800 he insists upon the existence of "a Moral or Intelligible Order, contradistinguished from the Order of Nature" and outside of finite moral beings; and says that "here, in this necessary thought and demand of an Intelligible Order, through which all genuine morality has necessary consequences, is the *place* of Religious Faith." But he adds: "This faith is faith full and entire; that living and active Moral Order is itself God, we do not require, and we cannot apprehend, any other" (*Sämmtliche Werke*, 8 vols., 1845, 1846; vol. v. pp. 392, 394; 186).

Yet it is not simply "the demands of an empty system" (*ibid.* p. 180), but the spontaneous religious consciousness, that goes beyond this; and it is incumbent upon philosophy, if it would find room for religion, to derive its knowledge of the fundamentals of religion from the unadulterated religious sense itself. Indeed, Fichte's warmth of conviction that "without this active moral Ordering," which is in no wise an Orderer, "not a hair falls from my head and not a sparrow from the roof" (*ibid.* p. 188), undoubtedly proceeds from Religion, as distinct from Ethics and Philosophy. And, if such a belief is accepted from Religion by Philosophy at all, it also invites Philosophy to admit Religion's conjoint affirmation of a self-conscious Orderer, an affirmation more consistent with this belief, and one not less in accordance with our difficult life's experience.

Plainly here in Fichte there is no irritation against the conception of a Reality distinct from any apprehending spirit, so long as this Reality is a spiritual law and not a Spirit expressing Himself in a law, and so long as this law is conceived as fundamentally moral only, and as apprehensible by moral sense, in action, alone. Yet, especially in his later stage, his deep religious instinct allows Fichte and his readers often to forget his vehement, exclusive moralism and all the unnatural strain of a system that would make man, as subject, find the entire objective world simply by producing it in and through the purest self-activity, of, at deepest, an exclusively ethical kind. For we then get sayings which, taken separately, reveal a tender religious insight beyond the range of Kant. Thus, in the *Directions for a Blessed Life*, of 1806, we hear: "Thou, O Soul, art what thou lovest"; and "Blessedness consists in love and in the eternal satisfaction of love," where Fichte doubtless thinks of self-conscious spirits living on eternally, since no Ego that has ever really become —*i.e.* that has developed—something of universal and eternal validity can, according to him, ever be destroyed. And he here adds strikingly: "True, blessedness exists also beyond the grave, for the man for whom it has already begun here; and it exists there in no other way and kind than as it can begin on this side of the grave at any moment; by the mere getting oneself buried, one cannot arrive at blessedness" (*S.W.* vol. v. pp. 409, 403).

(3) Already, in the *Destination of Man*, 1801, he had impressively proclaimed the close interdependence of souls: "The individual finds and understands and loves himself only in another, and every spirit develops itself only in contact with other spirits"; and he had even, here, addressed God as "the life which binds spirits with spirits into one, as the air and ether of the one intelligible world" (*S.W.* vol. v. p. 316). And if such expressions in this apologetic, exoteric work cannot be pressed, we get, in his *Thatsachen des Bewusstseins*, amongst much of contrary import, the description of God as "the Absolute, the Self-Subsistent, that which does not enter into process and has never come into being" (*S.W.* vol. ii. p. 687).

In his latest stage Fichte gets clear of Kant's Ethical Rigorism: "'The inclinations which I have to sacrifice,' so thinks the religious man, 'are not really *my* inclinations, but are inclinations which are directed against myself and my higher being; they are my enemies that cannot die too soon'" (*S.W.* vol. vii. p. 234).

It is, however, instructive to note how Fichte's usual identification of the totality of individual souls with God fails to produce, doubtless it even tends to hinder, a sufficient recognition of the uniqueness of historical personalities. Thus, in the *Anweisung*, the Eternal Word becomes flesh, "in entirely the same way as in Jesus Christ, in every one who vividly recognizes his unity with God, and who truly and actually abandons his entire individual life to the Divine Life" (*S.W.* vol. v. p. 402). Only under the influence of patriotism, in his *Reden an die Deutsche Nation*, 1807–8, does he somewhat more adequately realize and express the mysterious uniqueness attaching to all History.

(4) Fichte is so heroic a character, and he is so largely moved by sensitively Christian tradition and feeling, that it is easy to be unfair to his adversaries in their accusations of Atheism, especially in their expulsion of him from Jena in 1799, 1800; and to forget the deliberately hypothetic and subjectivist foundation and limitation of his entire Philosophy of Religion. For he never appears to have fully and finally abandoned,

or to have pushed deeper down than, the position of his *Versuch einer Kritik aller Offenbarung* of 1792: "The idea of God, as lawgiver by means of the moral law within us, is based upon a transference of something subjective within us, to a being without us, and this projection (*Entäusserung*) is the specific principle of religion, in so far as it is to be used for determining our will" (*S. W.* vol. v. p. 55). It is plain that here we have Kant in his most hypothetic, indeed sceptical, mood; that, here again, we get simply the inevitable culmination of a complete attitude of mind—a conclusion inevitable if, but only if, that general attitude is held to be complete. It is plain too that it would be impossible, whilst retaining one of the elements of the religious consciousness, to deny more flatly, and reverse more violently, the sense attached to all those elements by this very consciousness, or more utterly to reduce its evidential value, from the deepest of truths, to a double-dyed error of the most childish kind.

Professor *Hugo Münsterberg* especially has now made vigorous attemps to restate Fichte with a foreground of modern psychology, and with a carefully equal emphasis upon the Æsthetic, Noetic, and Ethical requirements and values. But not all his earnest eloquence can hide a certain violence in the process of affirming, as binding at a great cost, a Law nowhere prepared and nowhere indicated in the entire range of the demonstrative and experimental sciences, and which we consciously project from ourselves; and a certain doctrinaire superiority to, or forcing of, evidence, in that here something is alone to be authentic, reasonable religion, which no positive religion has ever held or admitted.

The Fichtean trend in Professor *Rudolf Eucken* remains much less provocative, since it is blended with Platonist and Hegelian doctrines, and especially since it is checked by a continuous deep sense of the character and significance of History and of Evil. And indeed Eucken is ever nobly insistent on Religion as precisely our need; and on the presence of the Abiding and Eternal within all our persistent and passing (deeper) trials and sufferings, and in all the genuine productions (always so largely conditioned by History) of Science, Art, Philosophy, and Ethics. Yet even here the Kantian, Fichtean irritation against the very idea of any Reality not, in a sense, produced, and recognized as produced, by the mind which acknowledges it, and the resolute ignoring of the necessity of the mind's contact with *thing*, for the mind's awakening even to religion, remain, we think, weaknesses intrinsically hostile to the noble intention and large effectiveness of Eucken's virile stand against all Naturalism and sceptical Subjectivity.[1]

2. *Friedrich Schleiermacher* (1768-1834) offers us a combination of experience and formulation instructively unlike (whilst like), in their respective strength and inadequacy, to the combinations presented by Spinoza, Kant, and Fichte, even though it is these three powerful personalities, especially Spinoza, who everywhere suggest, and indeed for the most part determine, the theories and analyses of Schleiermacher.

Born at Breslau, the son of a Calvinist minister, Schleiermacher was brought up, 1783-86, by the Moravian brethren, the nearest German equivalent to our English Quakers. And here this ardent, impressionable and sensuous, rather æsthetic than

---

[1] There is a good short account of Fichte in Ueberweg-Heinze, *Grundriss d. Geschichte d. Philosophie der Neu-Zeit*, 1880, pp. 258-269. H. Rikert's *Fichte's Atheismusstreit*, 1899, is a finely balanced estimate ; and A. Seth's " Fichte," in his *Hegelianism and Personality*, ed. 1893, pp. 42-78, a sound criticism. E. Lask's *Fichte's Idealismus und die Geschichte*, 1902, is very careful ; and Fritz Medicus's *J. G. Fichte*, 1905, a reasonably enthusiastic, useful popular account. H. Münsterberg's *Philosophie der Werte*, 1909 (which exists also in English), especially in its last two chapters, and R. Eucken's *Der Kampf um einen geistigen Lebensinhalt*, 2nd ed. 1907, have been taken as the most Fichtean amongst these authors' works. Eucken is particularly striking concerning the Eternal and History, in his " Philosophie der Geschichte," *Kultur der Gegenwart*, i. 6, 1907 ; and in *The Truth of Religion*, 1911, pp. 270-273.

## Schleiermacher Æsthetic, Pietistic, Pantheistic

religious, and rather religious than ethical, nature received, amongst these pure, simple, out-of-the world and other-worldly souls (in however one-sidedly mystical, even fantastically individualist a form), the most precious insights of his rich life,—a life, for the rest, almost entirely beset by artistic and non-moral, by pantheistic and determinist, and by variously subjectivist or even sceptical minds and moods. A student at Halle University in 1788-89, tutor in a West-Prussian Calvinist noble family in 1790-93, he was, from 1796 to 1802, a Calvinist minister and pedagogue, and afterwards, from 1806 to the end, lived as a Professor of the University in Berlin.

Thus Schleiermacher's most varied life covered, in the first period, the last years of that "Beautiful Soul," the Moravian-minded Susanna von Klettenberg (d. 1774)—whose but slightly modified "Confessions" Goethe included, as a dainty pathological curiosity, in his *Wilhelm Meister's Lehrjahre*, 1796; the change of Goethe, in 1772-73, from habits of prayer, church-going, and Christian Theism generally, to a Spinozist-Pantheistic habit of mind (which did not indeed prevent his attainment, in maturity, of a wide range of moral and even religious insight, yet which undoubtedly leaves his utterances on religion bereft of the deepest notes); and (unknown to Schleiermacher at the time) the interview, July 1780, between Lessing and Jacobi, where Lessing also, as against Jacobi, showed himself much influenced by Spinoza. It was indeed from Jacobi's letters to Moses Mendelssohn, *On the Doctrine of Spinoza*, 1785, that Schleiermacher first learnt to know Spinoza. And in 1794 he writes a criticism of Kant, in which (finding that Kant considers the world of sense merely a product of the world of the understanding and of man) he thinks that for Kant "the world of *Noumena* is in the same way cause of the world of sense, as Spinoza's Infinite Thing is cause of finite things." And he even asks: "Is it then quite certain that a distinct *Noumenon* underlies every several consciousness? The individualizing consciousness extends only to the phenomenal level (*Erscheinung*)." There is now in Schleiermacher both an interior antagonism against any scientific or demonstratively philosophical completion of the world in which we live by a second, more valuable, and harmonious world, *and* a deep enthusiasm for the person and power of Christ, as the awakener of the religious life—of the moments "expressive of the highest feeling in our whole being."[1] This period of preparation results in his *Reden*

[1] W. Dilthey, *Leben Schleiermacher's*, 1873, from MS. material, pp. 149, 145.

*über die Religion*, 1799, and the *Monologen*, 1800, the former the religious, the latter the moral, manifesto of his early enthusiastic manhood.

And from 1806 onwards we have his second period, in which his later, more sober mind develops and expresses itself in the relatively cautious, compromise-loving, in some respects institutionally tempered work, *Der christliche Glaube nach den Grundsätzen der Evangelischen Kirche*, 1821.

It is the second of the *romantically* eloquent and boundlessly daring *Reden*, "On the Nature of Religion," and the corresponding, very technical and dry, first chapter of the Introduction to the *Glaubenslehre*, "Towards the Elucidation of Dogmatics," which alone here concern us. The former demands to be taken in its first text.[1]

(1) In the *Reden*, then, the following passages well express Schleiermacher's position towards the essence of Religion and of Eternal Life.

(*a*) "The Essence of Religion is neither Thought nor Action, but Intuition and Feeling. Religion desires to contemplate the Universe, devoutly to overhear it, in this Universe's own representations and actions; to let itself be seized and filled, in childlike passivity, by this Uni-

[1] Critical Edition by Pünjer, 1879.

verse's immediate influences. Metaphysics start from the finite nature of man, and desire deliberately to determine, from that nature's simplest concept, from the range of its powers and its receptivity, what the Universe can be for man, and how, of necessity, he must perceive it. Also Religion lives out its whole life in nature, but in the Infinite Nature of the Whole, the One and All. Morality starts from the Consciousness of Freedom, and desires to enlarge its kingdom to infinity and to subject all things to it. Religion breathes where Freedom itself has again become Nature; it seizes man beyond the play of his particular powers and personality, and views him from whence he must of necessity be what he is, whether he so wills or not" (pp. 50–52). Thus "Religion is opposed to Metaphysics and Morals, in all that constitutes its essence and that characterizes its effects. Practical Life is Art, Speculation is Science; Religion is Sense and Taste for the Infinite" (pp. 52, 53). Hence "the Intuition of the Universe is the widest and highest formula of Religion, from which you can most precisely determine its essence and its limits" (p. 55).

Now "all Intuition proceeds from an influence of the thing contemplated upon the contemplator; it is an original, independent action of the former, received, collected, and understood by the latter, according to the latter's nature. Did not the efflux of light, quite without action of your own, touch your visual organ, you would see nothing; yet what you see is not the nature of things, but these things' action upon you; and what you know or believe concerning these things lies far beyond the domain of intuition. So with Religion. The Universe is in ceaseless activity and self-revelation; every form, being, event produced by it, is an action of its own upon us. And thus to take every single thing as part of the Whole, everything limited as a representative of the Infinite—this is Religion; but what would penetrate beyond, into the nature and substance of the Whole, is no more Religion; and, if it insists upon being considered such, will inevitably sink back into empty Mythology" (p. 55).

And daringly vivid descriptions then drive home the reality of this contact, in undifferentiated intuition and feeling, between the Object and Subject. "Intuition without Feeling, and Feeling without Intuition, are both nothing; only then and therefore are they something, when and because they are one and indivisible. That first mysterious moment, which occurs in every sensible perception, before intuition and feeling separate, and where sense and its object have become one, is indescribable. . . . I lie at the bosom of the Infinite World; I am, in that moment, her soul, I feel all her infinite life as my own; and she is, in that moment, my body, for I penetrate her frame as though it were my own. . . . This is the generative moment of all that is living in Religion" (pp. 73, 64).

We have here a remarkably vivid, experimental knowledge of certain characteristics of Religion,—its intuitive-emotional quality and its difference from Speculation and Practice. The insistence on Religion, as a sense both of contact between finite realities and of the Infinite Reality within, and in contrast to, those finites, is indeed admirably conformable to the central constituent of the religious experience. Yet even at this crucial point a *critical* Subjectivism, here also largely and unconsciously inconsistent, prevents these perceptions from attaining, in two all-important respects, to adequate expression.

For one thing, Metaphysics are here reduced to an Epistemology of the anti-"dogmatic" dogmatist type. Here man knows indeed that the Universe *qua* Universe exists distinct from his perception and conception of it; yet Schleiermacher is so haunted by the, somehow necessary, unlikeness of this Universe itself to the perception and conception through which we know it, that he dares not affirm anything ontological about it. True, Religion seems, at first sight, to contrast with such "Metaphysics," not only as to its *mode* (Religion, purely intuitive and emotional, as against Metaphysics, so largely conceptual, analytic, speculative), but, above all, as to its reach (for Religion is insisted upon as *Contact* between Realities), with intuition and feeling as consequences of this contact. And so far we have the unadulterated testimony of the sense concerned. But Schleiermacher then vehemently checks the testimony directly furnished by the sense he has so vehemently endorsed. And as in the *critical* Kant we get a genuine knowledge only of human knowledge generally, as distinct from the objects through knowing which alone we have any knowledge, so here we are, correspondingly, shut up in a genuine feeling only of human feeling generally, without the unequivocal acceptance of any object distinct from, and the cause of, such feeling. And yet the religious experience in question is, essentially, an intuition and feeling of Reality as distinct from, as prior and subsequent to, as indefinitely more than, and as the cause of, the activities through which we apprehend it. In this sense, not of the affirmation of a detailed system, or of an abstract principle, but of an elementary instinct and affirmation of Reality, Religion is indeed unchangeably Metaphysical,

Dogmatic; and if all Ontology is illusion, then all Religion is so likewise.

And again, the sense we get here is rather of the Spatial Infinite, or, at most, of the connection between every and any, between *this* part of life and every other part. The strictly religious sense is, however, of *a depth of Reality greater and other than* any and all of these parts, or than the whole, in so far as it is made up of them. True, our mind's contact with the Finite is a necessary condition for the awakening of this our sense of the Infinite; the Infinite, however, to which we are thus awakened is then, as far as the experience is religious, not simply a boundless extension, in space or even in time, of that Finite—of life at its surface or middle depths, or even of the totality of such life—but of a Reality contrasting with, whilst partially expressing Itself in, those finitudes, a Reality helpful towards, because Itself possessing, in an unspeakable manner and degree, all that is highest in ourselves. Certainly, precisely the acknowledged classical exponents of Religion, as distinct from those of Metaphysics and Ethics, have thus articulated this sense of the Infinite; Augustine's great cry, "Restless is our heart until it rests in Thee,"—in a spiritual Reality present always and everywhere, but not simply the sum-total of the various parts of the

## The Religious Infinite, a Spiritual Reality

world,—well expresses this specifically *religious* sense.

(*b*) "Intuition ever remains something simple, separate—it is an immediate perception, and nothing more; to combine it with other things, to place it within a whole, is no more the business of intuition but of abstract thinking. Thus does religion restrict itself to its immediate experiences, of the existence and action of the Universe, through its single intuitions and feelings; derivation and connection are the things most repugnant to its nature. A system of intuitions, can anything be more fantastic? The Infinite Chaos of the starry heavens, with each point a world, is the fittest symbol of religion: in each, only the single is true and necessary" (p. 58). And it is the systematizers, "the adherents of the dead letter rejected by religion," who "have filled the world with strife and tumult. But the true contemplators of the Eternal were ever quiet souls, living alone by themselves with the Infinite; or, if they looked about them, granting to every one, provided he knew the great word, his own way" (pp. 64, 65).

Indeed, "the religious feelings, by their very nature, paralyse man's energy of action, and invite him to a still, engrossed enjoyment; whence the men who lacked other motives for action, and who were nothing but religious, forsook the world and completely abandoned themselves to idle contemplation." Yet "quiet and deliberateness are lost, if man allows himself to be driven to action by the vehement and shattering feelings of Religion." "All action, properly so called, should be moral and can indeed be such; but the religious feelings should (only) accompany all man's actions as a sacred music; man should do all things *with* Religion, nothing *from* Religion" (pp. 69, 68). But then "Morality cares not about love and inclination, but only for action proceeding entirely from its own law; condemns as impure acts produced by compassion or gratitude; despises humility; and treats contrition as a waste of time. And indeed none of these feelings aim at action, they end in themselves, as functions of our innermost, highest life;—they are Religion" (p. 111).

Here we have deeply instructive inconsistencies and insights. For the intuition here considered, whether or no it acts separately within the soul's life, is, according to Schleiermacher, precisely *not* an intuition of separate things, as such, but of connection, of a whole; although the connection is perceived and not derived. We thus have, not indeed a system of intuition, but still an intuition of a system. Indeed, Schleiermacher is himself steeped in a particular philosophical system—that of Spinoza—as shown by his enthusiastic apostrophe:

"Sacrifice reverently with me a lock to the *Manes* of the holy, repudiated Spinoza; the Universe was his sole, eternal love" (p. 55). Indeed, Schleiermacher's general attitude, especially towards Evil, is predominantly Spinozist: "Contemplate nothing separately, but rejoice over everything at the spot where it stands" (p. 91). And already St. Paul and the Johannine writer most largely utilize particular philosophical systems for the articulation of their deepest, abidingly religious experiences. In a word, the entire notion of absolutely pure and separate intuition-feeling, which becomes necessarily adulterated and weakened even by differentiation between the two constituents, and still more by any and every derivation, connection, system and speculation, is paradoxical and unworkable. Rather do each of the faculties of man's wondrous range aid all the others, though each does so only in certain ways, combinations, and antagonisms.

Again, religious feeling is here seen, at one moment, to be violent and to require exclusion from all direct control of action, as indeed all sober-minded Mystics, *e.g.* St. Teresa, have ever taught; at another moment it is held to be so peaceful, that only the system-building of reason is to blame for the spirit of persecution. Yet, here also, the just balance is, for man, an ideal never completely reached, but one which can be approximated only within and through the obstacles and not outside of them, and especially not at the cost of a denial of the reality of Evil. Certainly the Johannine and the Augustinian writings contain many a fierce denunciation, although they are amongst the chief religious classics.

And finally, as to Action, Jesus's curing of the sick and cleansing of the Temple were, surely, as religious as His night-watches and His Transfiguration. Schleiermacher, however, pierces to the very core of the facts by representing religion as normally occupied *also* (he attempts to make it *only*) with contemplation and recollection; and as alone furnishing sufficiently deep motives, and sufficiently vivid environment, for the steady persistence of such difficult, precious dispositions as love, humility, contrition. How immensely deeper does Schleiermacher here see than Kant!

(*c*) "History, in the strictest sense, is the highest object of Religion. In this territory lie its loftiest intuitions." "Nothing," in the intention of Religion, "is to be a dead mass, moved only by a dead impact, and resisting only by unconscious friction; all is to be genuine, organic, manifold, heightened life" (pp. 100, 103).

But "for me the Godhead can only be one out of many religious ways of viewing things; and from my standpoint there is no such alternative as 'no God, no Religion.'" "For most men, God is evidently merely the Genius of mankind. But mankind is only an infinitely small part, only one of the passing forms, of the Universe; can then such a God be what is highest in religion? A God conceived as an Individual entirely distinct from Mankind, a single specimen of a special genus, would still, as every genus with its individual, be subordinated to the Universe." No: "to possess Religion" simply "means to contemplate the Universe; and on the manner in which you contemplate it, and on the principle which you find in its actions, depends the value of your Religion. And since the idea of God accommodates itself to every such manner of contemplation, a religion without a God may be better than another religion with a God" (pp. 125, 126).

And "as to Immortality, it is taken by most men in a spirit directly contrary to Religion. For Religion strives, above all, that the clear-cut outlines of our personality shall gradually be lost in the Infinite—that, by the contemplation of the Universe, we may, as far as possible, become one with it; whilst those men oppose the Infinite and want to be nothing but just themselves." "Immortality has no right to be a wish, if it has not previously been a task which you have resolved. To become one with the Infinite and to be Eternal in a moment,—this is the true Immortality of Religion" (pp. 130, 131; 133).

Here we have an interesting inconsistency —an emphasis upon History as the highest object of Religion, hence as the deepest action of the Universe. For this emphasis, if carried out, utterly shatters the entire Pantheistic scheme and temper, since we have thus, not the Universe, but self-conscious Spirit revealing Itself, in various degrees and ways, throughout the Universe, yet with the greatest fulness in specifically human History. And indifference to Theism, and hostility to Immortality, then become impossible or affectations; since Determinist Laws, Mathematical Clearness, Boundless Extension, Spatial Concepts cannot now be accepted as the Richest known to us—the distinction of rich and empty being now admitted to be intrinsic and fundamentally important. Personality and its attainment by the soul have now to be admitted as higher than all these determinisms and their admission; however higher, in their turn, such determinisms and admission may be than all mere Individuality. Under, in, and through all that Determinism we now find Spirit, Will, Love in operation; and Individualism can now be lost, and Personality can be won, by the human spirit's abandonment of self and the development of its true self; by seeking, finding, willing God in and behind those intermediate, secondary Things, Laws, and Concepts.

(2) The *Glaubenslehre* of 1821, 1831, has made four changes, of which two are rather apparent than real, and two are real, one of these indeed being a pure gain.

(*a*) The Essence of Religion or of Piety is now "that we are conscious of our unconditional dependence, or (the same thing) of our relatedness to God." For "every" human "self-consciousness presupposes, besides the self, still something else, without which it would not be this particular self-consciousness," indeed, "not self-consciousness at all." "The sense that we *are*, and that we become, ourselves somehow from within, is our Feeling of Freedom; the sense that we have *become thus* from elsewhere, still more, that we could not become thus except from elsewhere, is our Feeling of Dependence." A feeling of unconditional freedom is impossible. For, as an activity of the self moving away out of the self, freedom supposes a given object, and "such an object never comes about absolutely through our own activity"; and, as an interior self-activity, "our existence is never felt by us as proceeding simply from such self-activity." But "a Feeling of Unconditional Dependence is possible, and indeed is actually present in our self-consciousness, which accompanies our entire self-activity and our entire existence, and contradicts all absolute freedom." Now "the *Whence* of our receptive and self-active being is expressed by the term God." "This *Whence* is not the world, in the sense of the totality of temporal being, still less of any one of its parts"; "nor is this sense of dependence conditioned by any previous knowledge of God." But "the feeling of unconditional dependence and the consciousness of one's relatedness to God, are one and the same thing"; "consciousness of God and self-consciousness are inseparable"—"God is given us in feeling, in a primitive way" (Sechste Ausgabe, 1884, vol. i. pp. 14-16, 18-20).

Thus the *Glaubenslehre* insists upon a Feeling of Unconditional Dependence, whereas the *Reden* emphasize the Intuition of the Infinite. But each is doubtless conceived as involving the other. And if the Feeling avoids the spatial connotation which unfavourably characterized the Intuition, this Feeling also appears strangely thin as an analysis of the religious consciousness, since there is no mention here of any sense of obligation to God, of affinity with Him, or of elevation to Him.

(*b*) Everywhere in the *Glaubenslehre* we have now God; yet the determinations concerning Him can readily be traced back to Spinoza. God is just the unity of the multiplicity which appears as world; everything is, and becomes, entirely through its natural connection (since each thing consists through everything), and everything is and becomes entirely through the Divine Omnipotence (since everything consists undividedly through the One); and all distinctions, attributes, and actions of God, are only such in our human consciousness of God, and have no foundation in the Divine Being Itself. Again, the sense of Sin is simply the predominance of the sensuous or sensual consciousness over the divine consciousness, and the inhibition of the latter by the former; and the sense of Grace is the predominance of the divine consciousness over the sensuous or sensual consciousness, and the liberation of the former from the latter: thus Sin is not here a contradiction of the spiritual law within the mind itself. And Prayer, indeed the soul's entire doings, affect only itself, not God in any way. We have thus still a predominantly Pantheistic doctrine and temper, as to God and Sin and Prayer.

(*c*) Instead of, as in the *Reden*, an endless, simultaneous and successive, qualitatively equal yet immensely diverse, self-differentiation of religion, we now get Christ and Christianity as enclosing, within their past and future experience and development, the entire and final culmination of all religion. Indeed, Schleiermacher here goes even beyond average orthodoxy, and insists upon the Johannine picture as so entirely historical and an eye-witness's testimony, and, generally, upon so intense a Christocentrism, as to prepare acute collisions with Biblical Criticism and with the patent presence of various lights and graces in the Old Testament and in the different ethnic religions and spiritual philosophies.

(*d*) And instead of basing all religion upon the individual consciousness, he now finds the root of religion in the experience of the religious community, whence his high estimate of Church life. This fourth change gives now an immensely heightened cogency and breadth to Schleiermacher's appeal to experience, and only requires to be combined with genuinely Theistic conceptions as to the first two points, and with a less Christocentric position as to the third, in order to show forth its profound fruitfulness.[1]

[1] W. Dilthey's *Leben Schleiermacher's*, 1870, vol. i., unfortunately reaching only to 1802, is a most brilliant, indeed exquisite, presentation of the very soul of Schleiermacher's life. See especially pp. 78–87, 365–377, 377–413. Mostly very sensible criticism of Schleiermacher can be found in O. Pfleiderer's *Entwicklung der Protestantischen Theologie*, 1891, pp. 42–53, 102–120.

Professor *Ernst Troeltsch* considers himself as largely a successor of Schleiermacher; yet it is impossible not to realize (in face of the abiding forces and necessities of religion and of life, and of the extraordinary extension and precision of documentary evidence, historical criticism, and of psychological and epistemological analysis since Schleiermacher's day) the great superiority of Troeltsch. For here we get a sensitive richness in the apprehension and analysis of the religious experience,—this experience ever here possessing a double *polarity*,—of *other-worldliness* and detachment, and of *this-worldliness* and attachment; a courageous persistence of the Ontological, Theistic sense; a continuous remembrance that God's Spirit works also outside of Christendom (even though we find here but an imperfect insight into the finer special gifts of Catholic Christianity); and a strenuous insight into the abiding need of association and external worship for a vigorous religious life.

Such a profound declaration as the following directly concerns Eternal Life: "The formula for the specific nature of Christianity cannot fail to be complex"; it will be but "the special Christian form," articulation and correction, "of the fundamental thoughts concerning God, World, Man, Redemption, which are found existing together," with indefinite variations of fulness and worth, "in all the religions. And the *tension* present in this multiplicity of elements is of an importance equal to that of the multiplicity itself; indeed in this tension resides the main driving-force of Religion. Christianity," in particular, "resembles, not a circle with one centre, but an ellipse with two focuses. It is" unchangeably "an Ethic of Redemption, with a conception of the world both optimistic and pessimistic, both transcendental and immanental, and an apprehension both of a severe antagonism, and of a close interior union, between the world and God. Neither of these poles may be completely absent, if the Christian outlook is to be maintained. Yet the original germ of the whole vast growth and movement ever remains an intensely, abruptly Transcendental Ethic, and can never simply pass over into a purely Immanental Ethic. And the importance of that classical beginning ever consists in continually calling back the human heart, away from all Culture and Immanence, to that which lies above both."[1]

[1] "Was heisst Wesen der Christenthums?" *Christliche Welt*, 1903, i. coll. 583, 584. Troeltsch's fullest work so far is his "Die Selbständigkeit der Religion" (*Zeitschrift f. Theologie u. Kirche*, 1895, 1896); "Geschichte u. Metaphysik" (*ibid.* 1898); the astonishingly rich and vivid " Protestantisches Christenthum u. Kirche in der Neuzeit" (*Kultur der Gegenwart*: "Geschichte der Christlichen Religion," 2nd ed. 1909); and his very lengthy but profound *Die Soziallehren der Christlichen Kirchen*, 1912.

3. *Georg W. F. Hegel*, born at Stuttgart in 1770, the son of a Government official, studied at Tübingen University 1788-93, was Lecturer in Jena University, 1801-3, and Professor, first in Heidelberg, 1816-18, and then in Berlin up to his death in 1831.

The all-important influence in Hegel's life was doubtless that of Schelling (1775-1854), in the direction of the latter's Identity-Philosophy, especially whilst the two men were together at Tübingen and at Jena. Thus, in his Dissertation "On the Difference between Fichte's and Schelling's Philosophical Systems," Hegel declares: "In philosophy the reason recognizes, and deals with, its own self alone"; "the essence of knowledge consists in the Identity of the Given under the two forms of Thought and of Being"; and "the principle of all genuine speculation, the Identity of Subject and Object," has been "expressed, with all clearness, in Kant's deduction of the forms of the understanding."

Gradually, from 1803 onwards, a sense of acute difference from Schelling arose in Hegel's mind, and, from the publication of the *Phenomenology of the Spirit* in 1806, Schelling looked upon Hegel as his antagonist. Hegel indeed insists, most freshly in this amazingly rich *Phenomenology*, but most fully in his longer

*Logic*, 1818, 1831, upon a principle directly opposite to the fundamental position of the Identity-Philosophy. Yet, already here, and still more in his later works, he is in part (more or less unconsciously) inclined to and haunted by, in part (deliberately) committed to, other two positions which undoubtedly belong to the Identity-Philosophy, and have no satisfactory place within Hegel's own anti-identity principle. Certainly the principle allows, and as certainly the positions refuse, room and expression for the experiences of vital religion, and especially of Eternal Life.[1]

(1) Hegel's profoundly rich, immensely applicable principle is that "the True" (Reality) "is to be apprehended, not as Substance, but as Subject"; God is self-conscious; and "since Form is as essential to Being as is Being itself, the Absolute must be conceived equally as Form, indeed as possessing the full richness of the developed Form; only thus is it apprehended as Real." "The True is real only as System"; "the Absolute is Spirit, Self-subsistent, the Definite; It is For-Itself, is Its own Object; It knows Itself" (*Phaenomenologie*, ed. 1907, pp. 12, 13, 17).

[1] For Hegel's early writings and publications, see G. Lasson's interesting introduction to the *Phaenomenologie des Geistes*, ed. 1907, especially pp. lxiv, lxv.

All this directly traverses the Identity-Philosophy, which "takes monotony and abstract universality for the Absolute," and "holds the dissolution of the discriminated and determined to be the true mode of speculation. In such an Absolute, $A = A$, we have the night in which 'all cows are black'" (*ibid.* p. 12).

And then Hegel undertakes a systematic survey and comparison of the fundamental Categories of the human mind, studying them simply from within and trusting them all equally, without Kant's hopeless attempt to get outside the mind and to discriminate between objectively true and only regulatively useful categories. And he takes the Categories in the order from the emptiest, least real and least "true," to the fullest, most real and "most true,"—from bare Consciousness (in the *Logic*, indeed, from bare Being) right on to Spirit, in Religion. (The culmination in Absolute Spirit and Absolute Knowledge does not belong to this principle.)

Now so far, with Hegel's deep sense here of the Concrete, of History, of Inner Experience and Personality, we are on bed-rock; and such a systematic survey of the Categories allows us to realize clearly their varying fulness and worth— some are "truer," *i.e.* more adequate to the deeper and deepest Realities. And thus we are preserved from conceiving God simply as Being or Infinite Substance, or as the First Mover or even the First Cause; for, though we cannot indeed adequately know God, we have richer, deeper categories than those, hence we *know* that God is more than those emptier concepts and that He is *at least* all that our fullest categories carry with them. We thus, here as everywhere, deliberately resist all artificial simplification of Reality by its reduction to simpler categories—all omission of essential features whilst claiming to express the whole truth.

And this settles the question of Anthropomorphism, since we here see that we cannot but be nearer to, not further from, an adequate apprehension of God, by conceiving Him as distinct, self-subsistent, self-conscious, than by eliminating all such attributes. We remain certain indeed that He possesses these characteristics in a degree and manner indefinitely superior to our own; somewhat as, in the opposite direction, we are sure that animals, and indeed plants, possess a consciousness or vitality not all unlike to, yet very different from, our own. In both cases, as everywhere, we apprehend and elucidate in and through what we are ourselves; yet now we do so, very deliberately, by the highest that we are and know. And if the world in which we find ourselves is inter-connected, and if philosophy is essentially an understanding of the less known and the lower (as far as this is possible) by the best known to, and the highest experienced by, the philosopher, such a procedure cannot fail to leave us, or to put us, in touch with reality, and to be truly philosophical. We can in no case escape Anthropomorphism; but by this procedure we can and do escape an uncritical Anthropomorphism, and a superfine and unconscious, hence quite unchecked, Anthropomorphism, indeed Mythology, such as we shall find in the huge mythical constructions of the Hegelians of the Left.

Indeed, also outside of Philosophy, the evidences and motives for such a critical Anthropomorphism are great and insistent. Certainly Religion, in its most articulate utterances, is profoundly, at its best nobly, anthropomorphic; and the cheery contempt for this evidence, if taken as in any way testifying to a corresponding distinct Reality, which is still so largely prevalent amongst cultured West Europeans, cannot be reason's last word. And the ethical, practical necessities of man, at his deepest, press strongly in the same direction. For it remains, in the long-run, impossible for man to accept, to act in accordance with, to abandon himself to, a world and a power, as the very ground, home, and end of his being, and as rightfully claiming the most difficult virtues and heroisms, if he sees it to be no more than, indeed to be a mere abstraction formed by, himself; and impossible for him not to note that mere " Being," " Substance," " Totality," " Law," " Life," " Evolution," are all in this case.

In truth, even if all the evidences of other facts and experiences were to rule out the satisfaction of these our requirements, full sincerity would still demand our admission that our requirements, hence *these* our human facts and experiences, are truly of the kind described. Those abstractions and half-truths doubtless derive such persuasiveness and power as they possess, either from the still persisting (though unperceived) influence of the old, rich Theistic convictions; or from the clearness, and the fruitfulness in other—the Mathematical and Physical—fields, of such abstractions; or, lastly, from a most understandable yet excessive (possibly an all but unconscious) fear of, and reaction against, the dangers and abuses apparently inseparable from Theism and Institutional Religion. Our sections on Schopenhauer, Darwin, and Institutional Religion will respectively consider these points.[1]

(2) But from such a logical development of his

---

[1] See, in Prof. A. Seth's *Hegelianism and Personality*, ed. 1893, the admirable pages 73-78 ; 84-94 ; 103, 104 ; 235.

own fundamental anti-identity *principle*, Hegel is prevented by his other two, almost as fundamental, *positions*. And by these two positions, taken in their full destructiveness of that principle, Hegel, doubtless much against his prevailing intention, became shortly after his death (through the ablest of his followers, the Hegelians of the Left) one of the fountain-heads of the indifference, hostility, and contempt, so largely extant against the entire Theistic tradition and evidences.

(*a*) We have, first, the Identity of Thinking and Reality,—the transformation of Logic into Metaphysic, of the analysis of the categories immanent to the human mind into an exhibition of the forces productive and constitutive of the real Universe. Thus Hegel is, indeed, aware, even to contemptuousness, of the artificial (*i.e.* abstractive) origin, and of the poverty of content, of such concepts as "Pure Being." Yet throughout the examination and comparison of all the categories (instituted for the very purpose of giving us a full sureness in the use of the richer categories for the explanation of the poorer, and in resistance to all inversion of this procedure) he is also haunted by what (even according to this, his root-principle and motive) is a delusion, and destructive of that principle. For in his practice he comes to hold that the richer categories are explained by, are even caused by, a combination of the poorer,—indeed that this world of the categories, which is (in varying degrees) ever abstract, secondary, and instrumental, itself apprehends and penetrates, indeed creates, even *is*, the Real World.

When in this mood, he thinks himself determined solely by "the coldly progressing necessity of the subject-matter itself"; "the difference between the philosophical systems" appears here as "the progressive development of the Truth, of Reality, itself" (*Phaenomenologie*, ed. 1907, pp. 7, 4). And thus step by step the Dialectic is and becomes something in itself alive, in itself productive of "Truth," of Reality. Yet Trendelenburg has fully shown how the notions of this logic are but the instruments of daily thought, ranged in the inverse order of their richness and adequacy; how the earlier, more abstract notions here seem to live, and to insist upon their own growth by the incorporation of their "contradictory," simply because the man who thinks them is aware of their abstract (*i.e.* artificial) character, and strives to regain for them their natural complements; and finally how these complements are not (as Hegel describes them) logical contradictories, but *real* contraries, determinations of, and within, the organism of the real thing. For example, "*Pure*

*Being*, ever self-identical, is rest; *Nothing*, also ever self-identical, is also rest. Out of these admitted abstractions it is impossible that *Becoming* shall suddenly arise, this concrete perception, which presides over life and death."[1]

Indeed, Hegel himself admits that "every beginning has to be made with the Absolute, and all advance is but its exposition"; "the movement forward is a movement backward to the *Ground* of the whole, to the Original and the True," the Real, "on which depends our beginning" ("Logik," *Werke*, v. 334, iii. 64). Nevertheless, the logical abstractions and successions imperceptibly become living forces, productive of, indeed the constituents of, the concrete realities and simultaneities of which they were admittedly but the pale shadows and ever partial generalizations. Thus "the Ethical World, the World torn asunder into a Here and a Beyond, and the Moral conception of the World are the spirits whose 'outward' movement and 'inward' return develop into the simple life lived for Itself by the Spirit" (*Phaenomenologie*, ed. 1907, p. 287). And the "Logic" concludes with the transition from thought to Reality as follows: "The Absolute Idea," the highest category, "is still only logical. But inasmuch as

---

[1] A. Trendelenburg, *Logische Forschungen*, ed. 1870, vol. i. p. 38; A. Seth, *op. cit.* pp. 95–100.

the pure idea of knowledge is thus still shut up in." a kind of "subjectivity, it is so much *impulsion* to remove this limitation; and thus the pure truth becomes, in its last result, also the beginning of another sphere and science. The Idea, by taking itself as the absolute *unity* of the pure notion and its reality, hence by concentrating itself (*sich zusammennimmt*) immediately into *Being*, is, in the *Totality* of this form, *Nature*. This determination of itself is not, however, a process of *becoming* or a transition," such as the "Logic" has hitherto described. "Rather the Idea *freely lets* itself *go*, absolutely sure of itself, and at rest within itself." And "on account of this freedom, the form of its *determination* is likewise unconditionally free—namely, the *externality of space and time*, extant absolutely for itself without subjectivity." We have here "the *resolve* of the Pure Idea to determine itself as External Idea" (*Logik*, v. 352, 353; and Seth, *op. cit.* pp. 111–113).

We cannot, however, thus jump from Logic to Reality, and deduce Reality from Logic; and yet those critics and disciples of Hegel are, surely, right, who take such production of concrete existence by sheer thinking without a thinker, as an essential element of Hegel's (thus profoundly inconsistent) system. Face to face with such amazing mythology we can but exclaim, with the ex-Hegelian Professor Pringle Pattison: "No sophistry can permanently obscure our perception that the real must be *given*. Thought cannot make it; thought only describes what it finds" (*ibid.* pp. 125, 127).

(*b*) Hegel has, however, a still ampler identity —that of the human and of the Absolute Reason and Consciousness. Here again we can trace largely opposite intentions. Thus in the "Phenomenology" and in the "Logic" his fundamental object is to trace the concomitance of richness of content and of degree of "truth" (correspondence to reality) in the various categories successively described; but the descriptions of the elements, as though so many stages within these categories, are not originally intended for necessarily more than logically ordered analyses of the, presumably simultaneous, mental constituents of these mental conceptions. And we know how severe is Hegel's criticism of Fichte for not possessing somewhere an Absolute above all temporal flux and succession.

Yet, hand in hand with his hypostatizing of the categories, Hegel rapidly comes to treat the systematic analyses of these categories as so many historic accounts; and since Thinking now not only apprehends but produces Reality, and since the more general, shallower stages of thinking produce the higher and fuller, Thinking in general produces Absolute Thinking, and such Absolute Thinking produces the Absolute Reality. On looking back, this Absolute Reality is, in a sense, found to have been present from the first; yet Absolute Idea, Absolute Spirit, God, and human reason and spirit, and Reason and Spirit generally, are (at any of their corresponding stages) ever one and the same. And since Hegel's sense of the importance of History for man is admirably strong, he makes even premature and over-ambitious attempts to take the successive stages of human history as so many manifestations of those categories of the human mind, and thus as so many tests of their respective "truth." Indeed, the very range and slowness of such an immense, assumedly necessary, foretellable evolution further helps him to identify this continuous growth in richness of content with the self-explication, the attainment to full consciousness, of the Absolute Itself.

Thus Hegel can say: "The living Substance is truly real, only in so far as it is, not an original unity as such, but a division of the simple, and again the negation of this difference—a Becoming of Itself, a Circle which presupposes, and begins with, its end as its aim, and which is real only by the execution and its end" (*Phaenomenologie*, ed. cit. p. 13). We have here a kind of Neo-Platonist treble movement; and such a Self-Consciousness could, so far (if taken as unlimited in range and as complete and non-successive "from the first", *i.e.* as an Eternal Present), be well attributed to God, and to God alone. But the identification of the Absolute Reason and Consciousness with the admittedly historical, temporal doings, sufferings, and growth of mankind is here nearly complete. "The Life and Knowledge of God may doubtless be expressed as Love's playing with Itself; but this idea sinks to triviality, if the seriousness, the pain, the patience, the labour of the Negative are absent therefrom. *In Itself* that life may well be the untroubled equality and union with Itself, Which has no serious concern with being other and overcoming such otherness. But such *In Itself* is but the abstract generality, in which we have ignored that Life's nature—of being *For Itself*, and, therewith, the Self-Movement of the Form." All "existent Reality is movement and developed becoming; precisely this unrest constitutes the Self" (*Phaenomenologie*, ed. cit. pp. 14, 15).

Yet even Hegel does not venture entirely to carry our poor chequered human history into

God, nor to bring God directly into all this our human happening and doing. In the *Philosophy of Religion* he does, indeed, outline an identification of his Neo-Platonist treble movement of all reality with the three Persons of the Christian Trinity; yet he does not dare to take our actual and complete human history as the simple self-expression of the Son. In the *History of Philosophy* the Absolute Spirit is both *in* time and *out* of time, hence evolving *slowly* in time! "As to the slowness of this World-Spirit" in "achieving for itself a philosophy," let us remember that it has no need to hurry, "'a thousand years are before Thee as one day'; it has time enough, precisely because it is out of time, because eternal" (*Werke*, vol. xiii. p. 49). And, in the *Philosophy of Law*, the Preface (Berlin, 1820) even angrily insists upon the immediately divine character and work of and within the Prussian State as then and there extant. "Philosophy, as the penetration of the Rational, is, already therewith, a comprehension of the Present and Actual, and not the putting up of a Beyond supposed to be God alone knows where." "The Rational is the Real; and the Real is the Rational." Indeed, "those who live in the reality of the State, and find their knowledge and their will satisfied therein, are, at bottom, all men"; and "the Germanic monarchy" brings "the turning-point, the infinite positiveness of the Substantial," the Absolute, "Spirit" (*Werke*, vol. viii. ed. 1854, pp. 16, 17; 9; 428, 431). Yet Hegel thereupon promptly attempts to restrict philosophy to "the recognition, within the appearances of the temporal and transitory, of the Substance and the Eternal, there immanent and present." And as to the crucial point—how to discriminate between the two, this is haughtily waved aside: "The infinitely manifold circumstances, formed in this externality through the irradiation of the Substance,—this infinite material and its regulation,—are no subject-matter of Philosophy" (*ibid.* p. 17). Yet, surely, they *are* the subject-matter of an *Absolute* Philosophy.

The Hegelian system, indeed, in all its parts, presupposes, and culminates in, Absolute Knowledge, equivalent to Absolute Reality's Absolute Self-Consciousness. Religion is everywhere the penultimate, never the ultimate, end and standard of man. The end, as in Eckhart, is "the Spirit's Self-Knowledge in its pure, transparent Unity—not simply the contemplation of the Divine, but the Divine's own Self-Contemplation." "Truth," Reality, "is here not only completely coextensive with" the mind's "certainty, but truth exists here in the form of certainty peculiarly its own—it exists, for the knowing spirit, in the form of this spirit's own self-knowledge." "But this Spirit consists in its Becoming what it is from the first in Itself; and only this Becoming, in its reflection in Itself, is" (in full truth or reality) "Spirit." "Not then till the World-Spirit is complete in Itself can it attain completeness as Self-Conscious Spirit"; and "Comprehended History forms both the memorial and the calvary of the Absolute Spirit,—that without which It would be Lifeless Solitude" (*Phaenomenologie*, ed. cit. pp. 511, 514, 516, 521).

Here, as practically everywhere in Hegel, we have what, I take it, both life and thought persistently prove to be a dangerous identification of two very distinct and largely different things. There is a magnificent sense of the fundamental importance of History for man; of the mysterious presence and necessity of a negative, self-renouncing element and movement; of the Christian "dying to live," throughout such history; and of the presence, within this *durational* history, of a Concrete Reality, giving to this history its full worth and an abiding, indeed Eternal, meaning. And there is everywhere more or less an assumption, and sometimes a formal affirmation, that this history, this "dying to live," and this presence so profoundly necessary for us men, are as truly, directly, simply, indeed in the same sense necessary elements in the life (considered here as a development) of the Absolute, of God, as they are in man.

And thus here, at the end, we also find quite an accumulation of incompatibilities. Especially this: that a Completed Self-Consciousness was to be the centre, the measure, and the moving and directing force of the entire process; but now this Completed Self-Consciousness, supposed to be the *prius* and cause, is seen really to be the *posterius* and effect, of all this history. And such contradictions cannot here be taken simply as indications that the Reality sought after is more than our thought can comprehend. For here we have an Absolute System; we *think* the Absolute, because we *are* the Absolute—we but analyse what we are. Yet Self-Consciousness is nothing without Personality; and what gave Berkeley, Kant, Fichte their passion and *momentum* was precisely the maintenance and development of Personality, as against its dissolution by Materialism and Scepticism. But Hegel begins with the production, by mere categories of thinking, of Self-Consciousness and Personality; and he ends with an extension of the Self-Consciousness, thus strangely conjured out of an abstraction, into the widest and most ambitious, but again the thinnest and most unworkable, of categories. From abstraction, through the richest and most costly of Concretions, on to, indeed back into, abstraction—is such a Wheel of Generation reasonable and worth its terrible expense? Does such a scheme correspond to the deepest of Hegel's own convictions, to what is really impelling him, and us, to our divine unrest? We take it, decidedly *not*.[1]

(3) Probably the most impressive re-interpretation presented, in a predominantly positive direction and in entire lives and characters, since Hegel's death, of Hegel's doctrine, has been

---

[1] The excellent analyses and criticisms in Andrew Seth's *Hegelianism and Personality*, ed. 1893, pp. 188–193, 199–203, have, after careful study of Hegel's texts, been accepted above, except where Seth appears to the writer to fall into certain contrary extremes. Thus Seth declares: "In religion we are altogether on human ground" (p. 204). Yet religion's very errors postulate, we think, a dim but most real experience of that intensely actual and operative, prevenient Infinite Spirit to which those stammerings are the utterly inadequate response. And again Seth says: "The only sense which the term 'eternal' can bear to us," even with reference to the Divine Being, "is the abidance or persistence of the Ego through time" (p. 236, n.). Yet the Simultaneity of God, as against the Duration (the approximation to simultaneity) of Man, seems to the writer to be simply necessary in explanation and defence of the deepest experiences of the soul. But Professor A. S. Pringle Pattison himself appears fully to have outgrown both these positions in his admirable later writings—*Theism*, 1897, and "Martineau's Philosophy," in *The Philosophical Radicals*, 1907.

effected in England; especially by *Thomas Hill Green* (1836–1882) and *R. Lewis Nettleship* (1846–1892) at Oxford, and by the brothers *John Caird* (1820–1898) and *Edward Caird* (1835–1908) at Glasgow and Oxford. All who ever had the honour of learning much from, or of personal intercourse with, any of these rarely noble, spiritually sensitive, critically trained men, could not but feel how much Hegel was to them; yet also how much their specifically English and Scotch antecedents and characteristics had brought of sobriety, and of sense concerning life's difficulties and of man's limitations, to this their Hegelianism. The nobly moving Memoirs of Green, Nettleship, and John Caird, respectively by Nettleship, A. C. Bradley, and Edward Caird, exhibit, in their authors as well as in their heroes, Hegel's continuous search of the whole in every part of life and thought, and of parts in every whole; his profound respect for history, and continuous search for an orderly evolution of truth within and through it; and his deeply spiritual sense of man's continuous need of "dying to live"; and they do so with a massively impressive measure and reticence. And such work as Green's *Prolegomena to Ethics*, Nettleship's Letters, John Caird's *University Sermons*, and Edward Caird's book on Comte, much of his

*Evolution of Theology in the Greek Philosophers*, his paper, *Christianity and the Historic Christ* (1897), and several of his *Lay Sermons*, bring home to us still further the fine spiritual insight and wide outlook of these devoted men.

And yet the influence of Hegel, or indeed of Idealism generally, was, surely, not simply beneficent even here. For man's life is, after all, throughout its marvellous range (hence inclusively of the supply of materials for his thinking and of the very actuation of his consciousness and self-consciousness, and thus also of the awakening and persistence of his religious sense) profoundly dependent, not simply upon the activity and categories of his reason, but on the stimulation of his senses, on the action upon him, upon his body, of the material world. And the Infinite Mind and Spirit must be taken as somehow causing, and to be in some degree traceable by our minds within, what is lower than these our minds; indeed, we shall never vividly apprehend that Spirit as real, distinct from, and higher than, our own, unless we allow realities distinct from, and inferior to, these our own minds. Be superfine at this lower end, and you will, in the long-run, be sceptical or monistic at that upper end, of your mind's range and informations.

And, after all, religion, in its most articulate and

spontaneous utterances, is not directly a search for, or presentation of, the Whole; still less a finding of man's own mind, or of mind in general, within or as that Whole; nor a striving after self-realization; nor a sense that nothing really matters, except as merely out of place, or only for a time. But religion is, in such utterances, a sense, a love, an adoration, by spirits, conscious of their own distinctness and reality, of an Infinite Self-Conscious Spirit, a Reality distinct from and prior to themselves, though their original, infinitely penetrative, source; a seeking of conformity by these real minds and wills with that Real Spirit; and a consciousness of, a contrition for, Sin—a sense of the intrinsic difference between, and of the variously abiding results producible by, right and wrong volition and character-building. Especially is Green's elaborate hypostatizing of that abstraction, "consciousness in general," unsatisfactory; for thus neither God nor man is a complete whole—there is nowhere a full self-consciousness or personality.

And again, does their philosophy, as distinct from their lives, not merely allow, but insistently require, Institutional Religion as, after all, in *possession*, as the irreplaceable means of a special vigour and concreteness, and as furnishing that bond of socially spiritual intercommunion with our fellows, of higher and lower social and educational grades than our own, which is so profound a need for the fullest health of philosopher as of peasant? I think, it does not do so.

And finally, life, after all, at its deepest, is a stretching out of faith and love to God into the dark. Philosophy ends, surely, with certain *desiderata* and possibilities, which religion meets, exceeds, traverses, re-states; and religion is a circle of experience, possessed of its own character, contents, and conditions, which, as man's first and last and deepest experience, will indeed greatly exceed philosophy in richness but fall short of it in direct clearness and detailed articulation. Whereas these writers, *qua* Hegelians, give us, in and through philosophy, already the substance of what we get in religion; both these variants of the final light and word here are (seeing we are dealing with finite man's ultimate apprehensions of the Infinite) astonishingly clear and complete; and indeed, clearness and completeness being here the dominant, determining, character, philosophy cannot escape from being held the "truer," because the clearer and completer, form of outlook. And yet how can philosophy, or such a philosophy, be man's ultimate faith, an outlook that ignores or minimizes temptation, doubt, sin; that knows so little of the homeliness alone truly appropriate to man, the created and the weak; that is not centrally love seeking and finding Love in trial and in darkness? Gethsemane and Calvary, are they truly, fully here?[1]

(4) Dr. *J. E. M'Taggart's* positions as to Eternal Life have special interest in that they proceed from a mind which (in spite of its intense conviction of the unique importance and strict duty of Metaphysics and of consistency in general, and of the all-round truth of Hegel's main positions in particular) is still largely dominated by certain conceptions, and by the temper of mind, of the Enlightenment. Thus the category, not of Self-Consciousness but of Substance, is supreme at the critical points; all Theism is contemptuously dismissed, but a cheerful toleration is extended to a semi-modernized Deism; a family of interdependent (eternal but finite) spirits are finally taken as the true determinations and sole constituents of the Absolute, yet with an inevitable discontinuity in their self-consciousness; and finally, a very careful, largely original apprehension of the nature and inter-relations of Time and Eternity appears to fail, towards the end,

---

[1] For Green's "Consciousness in General," see Andrew Seth's *Hegelianism and Personality*, pp. 13-38.

simply through the Hegelian refusal to allow more than one (the simply human) centre and kind of consciousness.

(*a*) Dr. M'Taggart, then, impressively insists that "all other questions are abstract, as compared with metaphysical problems; and most, as compared with these, are unpractical. It will depend on our metaphysical beliefs whether we can regard the troubles of the present, and the uncertainties of the future, with the feelings of a mouse towards a cat, or of a child towards its father." "The world of our empirical knowledge is probably less capable of satisfying us than it used to be, for though it has doubtless improved, it has not kept pace with our increasing demands for improvement" (*Some Dogmas of Religion*, 1906, pp. 32, 33). And Religion is declared rightly to insist upon Metaphysics, and Dogma to be essentially distinct from morality, and to rest, as a minimum, on the conviction that "the universe is good on the whole" (pp. 1-32, 11).

And "the self is not a mere delusion, nor a mere collection of adjectives referring to no substance except the Absolute. It is substance existing in its own right. In the identity of the substance lies, it seems to me, the personal identity" (*Studies in Hegelian Cosmology*, 1901, pp. 36, 37). The conception of a non-omnipotent, non-creative God, "a person of appreciable importance as against the whole universe," is, in contrast with Theistic convictions, treated as worthy of serious consideration. "If we make God less than a creator, we make it possible that He should be a person and that He should be good. It is sufficiently certain that His wisdom and power would excel our own" (*S. D. of R.* p. 258). Yet there is no need even of such a God if (as indeed it does) "reality consists in a system of selves." "The perfect community is the true kingdom of the spirit. God, if represented adequately, is a community. A perfect community may be as complete a unity as any person. But a community cannot be a person; and the fact that it is a perfect community and a perfect unity does not make it at all more possible for it to be a person" (*S. D. of R.* p. 247; *H.C.* p. 210).

Immortality is considered to require coupling with Pre-Existence. "It is," indeed, "certain that in this life we remember no previous lives." Yet "exact similarity of attributes is always sufficient to prove personal identity." For "if the same self passes through" several "lives, any change happening to it any time must affect its state," directly or indirectly, "in all future time"; and this is enough "to make the identity between the different lives real,"—"in spite of the loss of memory, it is the same person who lives in the successive lives" (*S. D. of R.* pp. 130, 129, 128, 130).

And as to Time: "I cannot regard the question of unending existence with the contempt with which it is sometimes treated." Now, "in so far as substances and events are real at all, they exist." But, though "whatever is temporal exists" (Lotze indeed considers that "time is an essential characteristic of existence"), Dr. M'Taggart holds that also "timeless existence is possible"—"to exist and to be in time," he strikingly insists, "seem to me two characteristics, each quite distinct from the other" ("Relations of Time and Eternity," *University of California Chronicle*, 1908, pp. 4, 6, 7). And then the differences and relations between Time and Eternity are most carefully, in part very originally, developed, on the supposition of the reality of both. But Dr. M'Taggart's own final position is that; "in spite of the very great difficulties of the theory that all existence is really timeless, it must be accepted as true" (*ibid.* pp. 12, 11).

(*b*) Now in the above positions we can but admire the keen sense of man's need of Metaphysics, and of the Metaphysical element in religion; and of the necessity both for religion and

Metaphysics, indeed, for life in general, of existent, even of eternal, Reality. But it is strange, at first sight, to note how these our needs of Metaphysics and Reality, so characteristic of fully self-conscious spirit and, surely, only of such, are here made to seek and apparently to find, their satisfaction, not in Self-Consciousness, but in Substance.

Indeed, even here, we have all reality still largely conceived under the lurking image and connotations of an immense mirror, composed of an indefinite number of interfitting, interdependent, yet not only distinct but mutually impenetrable parts—a Monadism which somehow is, so far, less interior, less persistently self-conscious, than is Leibniz's own. The parts all really exist, they are all really immortal, indeed, at bottom, they are eternal; they are all really parts of one Whole, and however much their attributes may successively appear to vary under the varying conditions, their substances ever remain the same: what more can we possibly want? And we cannot, of course, have those parts, thus constitutive of the entire mirror, *and* another mirror, not made up of parts, and distinct from the first mirror and any of *its* parts. For in all these cases we have substances, and does not any one substance exclude another? True, these substances are all purely minds, spirits—matter does not exist anywhere; and (as against the *Esse* of supposed Matter, which is *percipi*) we have here the only true *Esse*, which is *percipere*, and indeed other activities held to be constitutive of *persons* such as are here alone considered to exist. Yet, all the same, these persons are primarily not centres of self-consciousness, but substances—spirits certainly of a strange kind. For these spirits have their self-identity, not in their self-consciousness and memory, their interpenetrativeness and spirituality; but in their substance, in the persistence of this substance, and in the outsideness of one to the other—their eternal quasi-materiality.

And thus the Realized Perfection, which Hegel required in the Universe, lies here, both as to reality and as to perfection (even if we admit the persistence and perfection of this society of spirits), not, at any one moment and continuously, in their self-consciousness, the highest of Hegel's categories, but in their substance, a lower amongst these same categories. The Absolute here exists, in its perfection, only intermittently. Indeed, without a Spirit of spirits other than, though penetrating and sustaining, these lesser spirits, such intermittence of self-consciousness is inevitable. And it is doubtless this grim alternative that has forced Dr. M'Taggart to find the persistence and identity of the Absolute in what, for Hegel and indeed for the deepest thought generally, is simply *not* the fullest and "truest" that we know.

Again, *what* a demand upon our belief, against all our evidences, all our instincts, is the absolute perfection of this poor little happy family of us poor little men! Nor let it be said that Christianity places man as high; for it does nothing of the sort. Whenever it places man high, it never places him thus alone, but only as, and in so far as, penetrated and sustained by another—*the* Other, *the* Reality, God; and only in so far as man's mind and will vividly apprehend, and fully endorse, this contrast, necessity, grace and Reality within and for man's entire existence.

And all through, Dr. M'Taggart takes God, not only as a person in the ordinary, human sense of the word, but indeed without any of that indefinitely penetrative and penetrable quality, that power of embracing and stimulating other minds and lives, which we know, from daily experience, constitutes the very character, actuation, and worth of these our spirits. The God here refused, and the God here considered possible, are not even men, they are but mannikins. At least the concept of God here nowhere gets beyond that of an orderer of matter from without, "a directing person" (*S. D. of R.* p. 245); hence here everywhere He is but one moving figure, one artificer, amongst so many other artificers or things, since He is nowhere conceived according to the deepest of what we really know and really want. The Roman Church has ever impressively taught what is here so strangely overlooked; for she who certainly never undervalued the power of Saints or of evil spirits, or the authority of ecclesiastical persons, has continuously insisted that One, and only One, possesses direct access to, and enlightening, moving power over, the depths of the human mind and will—the Spirit of spirits, God alone.

Thus this scheme leaves unutilized, indeed unexplained (except violently as a pure illusion), the sense of the Infinite, the Other, of Dissatisfaction in all and everything, however extended, however heightened, that is merely human—a sense that lies, undeniably, in the depths of the human soul. At this point no multiplication, no eternalizing, of human society, *minus* that sense and the Reality it indicates, is of any avail; the best and the most vital in man will ever overleap all such artificial limitations.

And precisely the admission of the operative presence within our spirits (as indeed everywhere) of such a Spirit of spirits can alone, we think, consistently explain the entirety of man's experiences and requirements with respect to Time. For thus, and thus only, do we find full recognition of our actual experience and necessity. This appears to be treble and as follows.

We recognize, then, *phenomenal* Time, the equable succession of mutually exclusive, ever equally long moments — *clock-time*, very clear but shallow, indeed largely artificial; *real* Time, a varyingly concentrated or extended succession of ever more or less interpenetrating, never equally long parts — *duration*, obscure or vivid and deep, but never very clear; and *Eternity*, this latter not owned, as such, by the human subject, yet indirectly, contrastingly experienced by him, since it is owned by the Divine Spirit which penetrates the human spirit, and since this human spirit lives in real Time (that is, in duration) and thus ever directly experiences some simultaneity, that quasi-eternity. In this way the vividness and dynamic force of man's ideal — Eternity, full Abidingness — is accounted for by man's real, however obscure, diffused, and predominantly indirect, experience of it. And all fanaticism is excluded by the two admissions, that this full Eternity is not, and never will be, man's own; and also that such experience as he has of it is never pure and separate, but ever of it only in, through, and over against, his various, ever more or less successive, directly human experiences. But no "orderer of matter," no "directing person," would here be of any avail; certainly the deeper religious consciousness does not itself, especially here, suggest to the religious mind such a curiously external and limited cause for such immense and profoundly interior effects.

We would only add, finally, that the Christian consciousness has notoriously, and ever more explicitly throughout the orthodox Churches, found a multiplicity of Persons to be constitutive of God's Unity; so that there is here a deep recognition of what Dr. M'Taggart so reasonably thirsts for, richness in Unity, indeed a Community as distinct from a single "person." But we see no gain in labouring this point, since God remains, in any case, for the deeper religious consciousness, neither "person" nor "persons" of the curious, non-penetrative and non-penetrable, intermittently self-remembering and self-conscious, kind so laboriously constructed by Dr. M'Taggart.[1]

[1] On Dr. M'Taggart's category of Substance, see Professor Pringle Pattison's *The Philosophical Radicals*, 1907, pp. 200-205. On his conception of Person, see Clement Webb's *Problems in the Relations between God and Man*, 1911, pp. 145-154. The above conception of real time was first clearly learnt from M. Bergson, *Essai sur les Données Immédiates de la Conscience*, ed. 1898, but also from Dr. James Ward—see now *The Realm of Ends*, 1911, pp. 306, 307. On the quasi-eternity of time, as really experienced by us, see also the fine passage in Dr. Bosanquet's *The Principle of Individuality and Value*, 1912, p. 339.

(5) The most impressive articulation and development ever given, by delicate psychology and ruthlessly *doctrinaire* reasoning (and at the terrible cost of a life's wreckage) to the destructive implications and elements of the Hegelian Absolutism and indeed of the preceding Idealisms, is doubtless furnished by *Ludwig Feuerbach* (1804–1872). Especially is the lesson cogent, if we consider and contrast, as two successive conclusions of the same mind from the same premises, Feuerbach's still ethically Christian, and psychologically often most penetrating and delicate, *Essence of Christianity*, 1841, 1843; and his completely naturalistic and cynical *Lectures on the Essence of Religion*, 1851. Our quotations shall be, all but exclusively, from the finer, earlier work in George Eliot's translation, 1854.

(a) "The inner life of man is the life which has relation to his general, as distinguished from his individual, nature. Man *thinks*, that is, he converses with himself." " The essential nature of man is not only the *ground*, it is also the *object* of religion. But religion is consciousness of the Infinite; thus it is, and can be, nothing else than the consciousness which man has of his own—not finite and limited, but infinite nature." "The consciousness of the Infinite is," then, "nothing else than the consciousness of the Infinity of the consciousness" (pp. 1, 2). Thus "The Absolute, the God of Man, is man's own nature"; "Consciousness of God is self-consciousness, knowledge of God is self-knowledge. . . . But ignorance of this identity is fundamental to the peculiar nature of religion." "Man first of all sees his nature as if *out of* himself, before he finds it in himself. Religion is the childlike condition of humanity; a man is then an object to himself, under the form of another man. Hence the historical progress of religion consists in this, that what, by an earlier religion, was regarded as objective, was worshipped as God, is now recognized as subjective, is perceived to be something *human*. The antithesis of divine and human is nothing but the antithesis between human nature in general and the human individual" (pp. 12, 13).

And again, "If the predicates of God are anthropomorphisms, if love, goodness, personality are human attributes, so also is the subject which you suppose here, the existence of God, the belief that there is a God, an anthropomorphism, a presupposition purely human." "Yet he alone is the true Atheist to whom the predicates of the Divine Being—*e.g.* love, wisdom, justice—are nothing, not he to whom merely the subject of these predicates is nothing. And in nowise is the negation of the subject necessarily also a negation of the predicates considered in themselves. These have an intrinsic, independent reality; they force their recognition upon man by their very nature. The idea of God is dependent on the idea of justice, of goodness, of wisdom . . . but the converse does not hold." "Religion," however, "knows nothing of anthropomorphisms; to it they are not anthropomorphisms. . . . They are pronounced to be images only by the understanding which reflects on religion" (pp. 17, 21, 24, 25).

(*b*) At this stage in Feuerbach's thought, we have still two ideal convictions—the higher human impulsions and ideals, with the bearer of them left uncertain within the human range; and the "divine" predicates, with any divine bearer of them denied. In both cases the Hegelian habits of intense abstraction are still at work,—*i.e.* the power and determination to give independent reality and prodigious operativeness to demonstrable abstractions, and to evade the question of who, or whether anything, is, after all, the bearer of such ideals and qualities. And here again man consists essentially of mind alone. And, here quite unambiguously, this human mind can penetrate and be penetrated by, it can really know, nothing whatsoever but itself; and it attains to this real self-knowledge never by means, or on occasion, of other realities than man himself—man, the human race, as distinct from the selfishly particularist in this particular individual.

Yet actual life teaches us, beyond reasonable doubt, that man is not merely mind, but also sense, imagination, feeling, will; that mind itself is not simply abstractive and discursive, but intuitive as well; that the human personality, when at all complete, holds and harmonizes all these forces in a generally difficult, ever rich interpenetration; that these various constituents of this one personality are developed, and slowly built up, by their possessor into his true manhood only by means, and on occasion, of his contact with other minds, other living beings, other things, and through the interaction between himself and them all; and that, however superior or inferior he may be to these other realities, and however different he may be from them, he ever achieves some real knowledge of them, whilst thus attaining some real knowledge of himself. The mind, a live force, finds itself in closest contact with the other energizings and impulsions within the human subject; this entire subject is ever, in the first instance, necessarily related, not to an idea or representation of itself or of anything else, but to some, to various, concrete realities distinct from, though not all unlike, itself. And it is the action of all that objective, variously interrelated world upon this human subject, itself a world within that world, and this human subject's response (from his senses up to his reason, feeling, will) to that world's action, which is primary; whereas the abstracting activity is secondary and instrumental, and necessarily never fully overtakes those primary informations. The more real the subject stimulated and reacting, and the more real the object stimulating and acting, the more "inside" does each possess, and the more rich, and the more difficult clearly to analyse, will be the result of such stimulus and response.

Hence, whether man's consciousness of the Infinite on occasion of the Finite is or is not, as a matter of fact, simply man's consciousness of his own truly infinite consciousness, we cannot, with Feuerbach, straightaway decide that "it cannot be anything else." For we certainly, concomitantly with our awakening to self-consciousness, acquire varyingly dim or vivid, but very real, experiences of the existence (indeed, to some degree, of the inner life) of other beings as well. And, as a matter of fact, the specifically religious consciousness cannot, even when thus challenged, discover in itself merely the prolongation (even if this be taken as simply potential) of the human individual's, or the human species', own achievements or efforts. But it finds, instead, an Infinite, *not the soul's own*, present and operative *here and now* in the world and in the soul; an Infinite different in kind from any mere prolongation, since the soul rests on It—on an actually present and operative Perfect Reality. "On ne s'appuie que sur ce qui résiste," said Napoleon; we cannot, and indeed we do not, lean upon a flux.

True, it appears certain that man has no religious consciousness, until his mind and senses are awake to their several objects and their activities. But this applies all round; I have to apprehend trees and stones or the like before, or simultaneously with, my awareness of, and my actual love of, my fellow-men. Every faculty I possess, and every object at all within my range, stimulates, feeds, checks everything else. And especially with regard to the Infinite Spirit, the ultimate ground and most intimate bond of all that is real at all, we cannot, from the nature of the case, expect to be able, apart from a review of the totality of our life's requirements and implications, to catch more than contrasting glimpses and impulsions, on occasion of the awakening and awakeness of all that life within and around us. But my consciousness of God is no more, because of this, simply my self-consciousness, than is my consciousness of a pebble, of a plant, of my friend.

Man's religious apprehensions and conceptions will ever necessarily be mixed up with considerable inadequacy, mostly even of the avoidable kind, and with much evil passion and positive error; hence at the later stages he considers the earlier stages as full of, sometimes as sheer, delusion. And these developments have, so far, moved, chiefly, away from external nature to the inner life of man. Yet also the much easier, because less deep, physical sciences have admittedly maintained, for millenniums, the most far-reaching, most fantastic errors, so that they readily appear, if we insist on this fact, as sheer, incorrigible illusions; nevertheless we rightly maintain them, as increasingly true and as possessed, from the first, of some real connection with Reality. And much points to man's again finding, in the future, and then with indefinite increase of precision, Spirit at work in the visible world. Unless the Irishman's argument was sound that, because a certain stove would save him half his fuel, two such stoves would save it all, there is no necessary consequence, from the admission of such an admixture of illusion with truth, to the negation of the operative presence of some reality within this long series of human apprehensions.

And the special conditions and effects of the religious attestation itself strongly point away from such a theory of all-illusion. For in this theory not any one particular impression, nor even some particular yet persistent concomitant of human experience in general, but an entire kind of life, one held by mankind at large to be the deepest, is declared to be a sheer projection, by the individual man, of his mind's contents,—of the general, but purely immanental, human requirements and ideals; and this whilst the projector is so entirely unaware of his own action as to consider himself (the projector) as the creation of this (his own) projection. And it is certain that man, when he comes to doubt or to reject this or that element, or apparently even the whole, of his present religion, does not necessarily and *pari passu* lose faith in trans-subjective, superhuman Reality as such. Also note how, in Feuerbach's scheme, it is *precisely* the illusion, the inversion, *it alone*, which gives religion its entire special power. Precisely the same content which, when in its "true" place and character, leaves man cold or but superficially moved, becomes, when seen in its "false" place and character, the greatest, often the most terrible, force known to history. And yet not all the childishness, abuses, trials, variously attributable to the different religions of the world, can permanently obscure the magnificent, indeed unique, services of religion. How can we retain Plato and Leibniz, Pheidias and Michael Angelo, Homer and Shakespere in highest honour, as revealers of various degrees and kinds of reality and truth, if Amos and Isaiah, Paul and Augustine, Francis of Assisi and Joan of Arc are to be treated as pure illusionists, in precisely that which constitutes their specific power and attestation?

It is, of course, most certain that our conceptions both of God's predicates, and of God their bearer, are anthropomorphic; as Aquinas (with Aristotle) ever insists: "Omne quod recipitur in aliquo, recipitur in eo per modum recipientis" —man cannot jump out of his skin. Yet this decides nothing as to how much the skin may hold or stretch, nor how much, and what, Reality really affects him, and can or must reasonably be admitted to be genuinely known by him. No one, certainly, has ever explained how, if man is completely shut up within a mode of apprehension bearing no real relation to reality, and hence without any ontological worth, he possesses a sense of the inadequacy of all merely human apprehension so fairly continuous, certainly so very spontaneous, often so acutely painful. Whence, *e.g.*, does Feuerbach get his contempt for even the generally human categories, as soon as they are made to claim trans-human truth? And this sense is so fundamentally human, and so much determines the admittedly noblest achievements, and the creaturely wistfulness, of Science, Philosophy, Art, Ethics, Life in general, that it is no less than gratuitously suicidal for man on principle to declare this sense mere illusion, or, equivalently, no more than the sheer projection of the simply human race-instinct.

We are thus face to face with the least tolerable and the most ruinous of all scepticisms. Well, against all subjectivist Idealism, we first simply admit the real existence and influence of countless realities, more or less different from, though lower than, or equal to, ourselves, and we contend that only by and in real contact with these realities do we ever awake to a consciousness and knowledge of ourselves. We require now to continue and to complete this apprehension and interpretation of life and existence. We admit, then, the real existence of a Perfect Reality which, prior to, the cause of, and present throughout, those other non-human realities and our real selves, is sufficiently like us for us to be (dimly and contrastingly yet most really) aware of this its presence and action. And this Reality is thus, though ever only in and through these lesser realities and through ourselves thus stimulated and expanded, the fundamental and persistent cause of this our noblest, most inalienable characteristic—our dissatisfaction with anything and with all things merely contingent and finite.

Religion thus, precisely as the sense of the Infinite, *does* know of anthropomorphisms; the consciousness of the depth and mysteriousness of life and reality is ever with it, *as* religion, from first to last. "How unsearchable are God's judgments, and His ways past finding out!" and "One of the greatest favours bestowed on the soul in this life" (thus like to the blessed in heaven) "is to enable it to see so distinctly, and to feel so profoundly, that it cannot comprehend God." These exclamations of the intensely onto-logical St. Paul and of the Spanish peasant St. John of the Cross, merely express, respectively, the very soul of religion and a delicate concomitant of all its deepest experiences.

(*c*) And finally, Feuerbach's own history is one more tragic proof that it *does* matter whether or no we deny a subject as bearer of the predicates "love, wisdom, goodness." For, in his latest stage, the two abstractions of the earlier time—man-in-general, and "divine" predicates considered as possessing a separate reality of their own—fall away; only empirical, individual men remain as real, and these appear to Feuerbach as far too weak, vain, false, lustful, cruel to bear and to exemplify (unless we add to all those vices a ghastly hypocrisy in this our estimate) such exalted virtues and ideals. These ideals must now be declared sheer illusions and impracticable ; such a declaration is the final truth attainable by man concerning man. " Man *is* what he *eats*."[1]

4. *Arthur Schopenhauer* (1788–1860), the deliberate antipode of Hegel, interests us here, in spite of his glaring inconsistencies and inadequacies, on account of certain of his convictions. Two of these, primarily epistemological, are concerned with the world as we find it, and with very un-Kantian developments of strictly Kantian positions; two others, primarily ethical and spiritual, with the darkness and sinfulness of the human self and the denial of this self, and with

---

[1] The above is mostly extracted from a paper by the writer, which appeared (in Italian) as "Religione ed Illusione," in the *Cœnobium*, Lugano, March–April 1911. The writer has learnt most from Professor Troeltsch's profound analysis of the true and the false in Feuerbach, in his " Die Selbständigkeit der Religion," *Zeitschrift f. Theologie u. Kirche*, 1895, pp. 392-427. *Das Wesen des Christenthums* has appeared excellently re-edited by Quenzel, in Reclam's Universal-bibliothek, 1904. Jodl's *Ludwig Feuerbach*, 1904, is a useful précis and description of the, still variously rich, psychology of Feuerbach's middle period; but is intemperately enthusiastic, and leaves practically unnoticed his last period, and its significant difference, yet development, from that middle period.

the possibility, indeed the shy conviction, of quite another life and reality, attained by man in and beyond *Nirvana*.

Already by temperament pessimistically, sceptically, dualistically inclined, with a nature as strongly sensual as aspiring, early left without a father and sent adrift by a clever, unprincipled mother, Schopenhauer, with ample means and leisure, turned to philosophy and art for at least occasional escape, from his clamorous lower self, into regions of abiding peace. *The World as Will and as Idea*, its first volume published in 1819, its second volume (as a commentary to the first) in 1844, is practically his sole work, since his other writings are simply preparations for, or elucidations of, this one book. And our present artistic and literary world is even now once more saturated with the feelings and ideas, with the atmosphere expressed and extolled, in consummate form, by this strange, strong, sincere, and stimulating, but quite incomplete and, systematically, impossible thinker.

(1) In his Epistemology Schopenhauer opens with Kant's Subjectivism and also with the same Kant's ready, though unconscious, transformation of this Subjectivism into a Metaphysical Dualism; but he promptly conceives this Dualism in a quite un-Kantian, Oriental, indeed Buddhist, fashion.

"Our consciousness alone is and remains the immediate; everything else is first mediated and conditioned by it, and hence dependent on it." "Everything, in being *in and for itself*, is necessarily *subjective*; this same thing, *in the perception of another*, is as necessarily *objective*; a difference which can never be completely resolved, for the thing has thus radically changed its entire nature, having entered into forms alien to its own essence, since these new forms belong to that alien subject, whose cognition of this thing becomes possible only through them." Hence "our cognition ever furnishes only appearances, never the nature of things-in-themselves" (*Sämmtliche Werke*, ed. Grisebach, Reclam; *Die Welt als Wille und Vorstellung*, vol. ii. pp. 12, 224, 225).

"The first among the many things," then, "which render the world so strange and alarming to man, is that, infinite and massive as may appear its existence, it hangs on a single fine thread—the particular consciousness in which, at the time, it stands. Thus the same cerebral function which, as though by magic, builds up, in our sleep, an entirely objective, tangible world, must have an equal share in the representation of the objective world of our waking life." "All that proceeds from" such purely subjective categories as "causes or motives is but the *Maja*, the" Buddhists' "veil of deception, which causes mortals to see a world of which one can neither say that it is nor that it is not." "The Vedas," as the Brahmanic and Buddhist literature generally, "breathe in Indian air and in a primitive world akin to nature. How the mind is here washed clean of all Jewish superstition," Libertarianism, Theism, Optimism, "and of all the philosophy that does it slave's service!" This literature "has been the consolation of my life, and will be that of my death" (*ibid.* vol. ii. 520; vol. i. 38, 39; "Zur Sanskrit-Litteratur," *ibid.* vol. v. 418).

We find here, as with Kant, the strangely instinctive, entirely unreasonable, assumption that nothing that is my perception can, in its content, resemble the reality; and even that, because, simply as *my perception*, it (of course) exists only in this my perception, the *content* of my perception cannot exist independently of this perception. A critical Realism alone appears to be here fully adequate to the facts. But then a turn—a quite un-Kantian, un-"practical," an æsthetic and Eastern, strangely floating and sentimental, turn —is given to this Metaphysical Dualism; reality, which Kant set out to find by Idealism, has here (as far as reality is to be apprehensible by the reason or to be reasonable in itself) been dissolved by Idealism into a dream.

Yet Schopenhauer's keen æsthetic instinct yields one admirable epistemological position,—the preference for intuition as against abstraction,—although coupled with an inadequate sense of the limited range within which intuition obtains. "General concepts are the material of philosophy, but only as marble is the material of the sculptor; it ought to work not *from* them, but *into* them." "In most books the author has *thought*, he has not *seen*" (*Werke*, ii. 87, 84). This continuous search for intuition and direct experience is one source of the perennial freshness of so much of Schopenhauer's work.[1]

(2) But then, with a strange inconsistency, which, however, has doubtless some of its roots in Kant, Schopenhauer finds the Thing-in-itself in the Will, a Will bereft of all reason and logic, and well known to us within our own selves. "The Will alone *is*, it, the Thing-in-itself, it, the source of all appearances. The Will's self-knowledge, and the Will's consequent self-affirmation or self-denial, is the sole event-in-itself." "Everywhere a reason can be given only for" different "appearances, for single things; never for the Will itself, nor for the Idea," the World at large, "in which this Will adequately objectifies

---

[1] See J. Volkelt's admirable *Arthur Schopenhauer*, 1900, pp. 64–127.

itself; an endless striving, eternal becoming, a boundless flux, are of its essence" (*Werke*, i. 250; 227, 229).

Schopenhauer sometimes admits that he has the "Ἐν καὶ Πᾶν in common with the Pantheists. Indeed, his predominant vehemence against the designation of "Pantheist" doubtless proceeds from his antipathy to Theism, and this again from his all-devouring subjectivism and pessimism. Since these latter excesses prevent his admission of Intelligence and Love, as present and operative, even though hiddenly and mysteriously, within this (at least superficially) often terrible world, he, with a striking consistency, still more emphatically refuses to believe that God could "transform himself into such a world as the one before us—countless millions of living beings which all subsist, for a while, only through the one devouring the other" (*Werke*, ii. 757, 758; "Ueber den Pantheismus," *ibid*. v. 112).

And if Hegel was determined to find fullest richness and life in supreme Reality, and knew not how otherwise to do so than by carrying Difference and Successiveness right into that Reality, Schopenhauer is athirst for absolute Identity and Rest—History is everywhere to be driven out. "All such historical philosophy takes Time as a determination of the Thing-in-itself";

whereas "the true philosophy asks not after the *Whence*, the *Whither*, the *Why*, but ever only after the *What*, the ever Self-Identical Essence of the world, which appears in all relations, but is not itself subject to them" (*Werke*, i. 358, 359).

We have here three fundamental self-contradictions. For man was to be utterly incapable of reaching the Thing-in-itself; but now he knows it thoroughly, in his Will, though not in his Reason. The Thing-in-itself was held to be quite cut off from all appearances; yet now the Thing-in-itself is recognized as a Will that unfolds and manifests itself in the visible world. And this Thing-in-itself, the Will, is held to be bereft of all Reason; yet now some of its appearances are found to be beautiful and reasonable. But indeed, as a question of fact, an absolutely irrational will is quite unknown to us men, since our various soul-forces never exist in this purely separate and entirely contradictory form. We have thus simply a projection of Schopenhauer's abnormally divided and unhappy interior life.

Yet two points are profoundly valuable here— the sense of the impossibility of an immediate, pure Optimism, since Pantheism turns out to be intolerable, precisely in the matters where already Theism finds its greatest difficulties; and, again, the sense that the Ultimate Reality must be conceived as Simultaneous, Eternal. The rejection of Theism, as the truth of the Ultimate Reality, and the denial of all reality to Time,—even concrete Time, that quasi-eternity,—prevent these two admirable points from here attaining to their full power.[1]

(3) "There is, in life, no final end of the striving, hence no limit to the suffering; all life is essentially suffering." "Thus each of these fleeting formations and shallow thoughts of the Infinite Spirit of Nature, that is, the individual, has to be paid for, by the persistent Will to live, with many deep sufferings and finally with a bitter death." "As little as any exterior power can alter or suppress this Will, so little can any exterior power free it from the tortures which proceed from the life which is the appearance of this same Will" (*Werke*, i. 402, 403; 416; 417; 421).

"This poor earthly happiness, howsoever fostered by men or favoured by fortune, is, at bottom, but a hollow, deceitful, sorry affair, which neither constitutions and legislation, nor steam-engines and telegraphs will ever make into something essentially better. Thus the glorifiers of history are foolish Realists, Optimists, and Eudæmonists, hence shallow fellows and incarnate

[1] See Volkelt, *op. cit.* pp. 159-176, 200-210.

Philistines. Indeed, at bottom, they are bad Christians; for the true spirit of Christianity, as of Brahmanism and Buddhism, is the knowledge of the nothingness of earthly joy, the complete turning away from it to an entirely different, indeed contradictory, existence; whence atheistic Buddhism is much more nearly related to Christianity than is optimistic Judaism and its variety, Islam."

And "Protestantism, by its elimination of asceticism and of its centre, the meritoriousness of celibacy, has, at bottom, abandoned the innermost kernel of Christianity. This has now become evident by its gradual transformation into a flat rationalism, modern Pelagianism." On the contrary, "all times, peoples, languages have ever sharply discriminated between a virtuous life and a reasonable one. Thus we would consider the designation of the sublime founder of Christianity as 'the most reasonable of men' to be a most unworthy, indeed blasphemous, expression, and similarly if men said that his maxims are the best instruction as to 'an entirely reasonable life'" (*Werke*, ii. 521, 736; i. 653).

Indeed "the myth of the Fall is the one thing in the Old Testament which reconciles me to it; for our existence resembles nothing so much as a consequence of a trespass and of a culpable desire.

The New Testament most wisely has promptly utilized that myth, without which it would have found nothing to which to cling in Judaism" (*Werke*, ii. 683).

Certainly nothing can be more true and necessary than a continuous keen sense of the suffering, misery, and guilt to be found in life; of the shoddy Philistinism of most journalistic, and of some philosophical, "progressiveness" and "enlightenment"; and of the splendidly irreplaceable fruitfulness of the ascetical, self-renunciatory movement, and of its essential place in primitive, indeed in all authentic, Christianity. The future is doubtless only with such convictions and practices of life as will find full room and work for these virile truths; and in this they will but continue the very spirit of Our Lord and of His closest followers. Yet all this will be on one condition, unfortunately almost entirely ruled out by Schopenhauer. This movement must stand within a larger whole, and be but one of two movements. For the other movement—that of seeking, of occupation with, of learning from and of teaching, of being stimulated by and of leavening and transforming, in a word, of loving, the actual world of time and space around us and within us, is also essential to Christianity, to all spirituality, to all deeper and the deepest human life.

And the outgoing movement is thus necessary, not only because we have duties to others and to things in time, which are co-ordinate to our duties to ourselves and to God, to things eternal; but also, and more fundamentally, because only through such occupation with the temporal, spatial, finite can we thoroughly wake up our sense and need of the Eternal and Infinite; just as, contrariwise, all this outward-going and time-and-space occupation inevitably disperses and empties the soul, unless the soul returns also to recollection, detachment, abandonment to God. For the fact is that somewhat as, in all our genuine knowledge, we have a given world of relations between realities—the real knower and the real known; and we have our concrete apprehension and abstractive reason and deductive reasoning rendered possible, and supplied with materials, by those previous realities, and made fully effective by our acceptance of, and belief in, their operations and intimations: so here, in all the deeper life in general, we have indeed an important, even an irreplaceable, negative, self-renunciatory movement, but this within a given system of movements—movements at work between previously extant, variously deep realities—spatial temporal things, finite durational spirits, and the Eternal Spirit, God.

Thus also, and especially, as to Marriage, Schopenhauer's asceticism is, at bottom, not Christian but Gnostic; it aims not at the spiritualization of the senses, and at the full articulation of the human spirit by means of the right use, as well as by the heroic continence, of the body, but at the entire suppression of the use, and at the extinction of, the body. Even the bodily functions essential to the race are here intrinsically impure and utterly incapable of being spiritualized. We thus leave behind all sane Monasticism, indeed the fundamental principle of every incarnational doctrine; only dervishes and fakirs would keep Schopenhauer company.

And this same excess renders him unjust to Judaism and Islam which, if insufficiently alive to the negative movement of religion, strongly realize the positive movement, and thus escape such dangerous parodies of Asceticism. The fact is that the full greatness, sanity, and fruitfulness of Christianity consists in the largest presence, and the deepest interaction, of *both* these movements; and indeed only thus will there be, in any and every life, a sufficient other-worldliness without fanaticism, and a sufficient this-worldliness without philistinism. And this again involves, at bottom, a difficult, heroic, an *ultimate*, yet thus all the more real, an inexpugnable, Optimism.

Theism thus remains in spite of, and is indeed actually strengthened by, all these obscurities, trials, renunciations; a Theism which—on this point in full accord with Schopenhauer — deliberately refuses to find man's full satisfaction in his life before the grave.[1]

(4) And this brings us to Schopenhauer's last word and dearest aspiration—the *Nirvana*, as something unspeakable, yet as hiding something positive after all. "No absolute Nothing is even thinkable; every nothing is such only with reference to something, and thus presupposes this other." Doubtless "with the free abandonment of the Will, also all the appearances of the Will are abolished—even the general forms of Time and Space, indeed Subject and Object; no Will, no Idea, no World. But that we so loathe the Nothing," *this* Nothing, "only means that we so intensely will life, and know nothing but just this will. Yet if we turn our gaze away to those who have overcome the world, who have freely denied themselves, and who then only wait to see the last trace of the will-to-live disappear with the body in which this last trace lingers, we find, in place of all that restless pushing, that never-satisfied yet ceaseless expectation, which composes the life-dream of man, a

---

[1] See Volkelt, *op. cit.* pp. 211-258.

peace which is higher than all reason, an Ocean-calm of the soul, whose bare reflection upon the countenance is already a full and sure Evangel; Knowledge alone has remained, the Will has vanished." "For this contrast" with our present world "we are without image, concept, or word; since all those we have are derived from the objectivation of the will, and hence they can in nowise express its absolute contrary, which latter thus remains standing as a simple negative." We can but use such terms as "Ecstasy, Illumination, Union with God." "Precisely at this point it is where the Mystic, in contrast with the Philosopher, proceeds positively; and indeed from hence onwards there remains to us nothing but Mysticism" (*Werke*, i. 526, ii. 717; i. 525, ii. 720).

Here, at last, we see clearly how intense a yearning after, indeed how real a faith in, an unutterable Perfect Life and Abiding Reality persists and works in this soul, which on the surface is so bitter, sceptical, and pessimist. For his conviction that there *is* such a Life and Reality appears here, although shy and indirect, to be almost as strong as that, if it is at all, it utterly differs from all and everything we are able to think or to imagine. And here we can grasp more plainly in what, as concerns religion, such dim and despairing outlooks, when compared with the clear and confident (such as that of Hegel), are weak, and in what they are strong.

Such an outlook as Schopenhauer's is weak. For it is certainly unnecessary, and, in the long-run, impossible, to seek and to find the religious realities thus entirely outside of all this visible world and of all our reason and its categories. Unless all the different departments of life and all the different levels of our own activity and experience, variously, in some degree and way, prepare, imply, contain, or show spiritual realities and spiritual necessities as somehow the deepest facts and final crown and justification of life's entire movement and travail, Religion in general is untrue. And especially is Christianity then untrue, with its incarnational conviction, its profound reverence for the individual soul, the historic fact, the social hierarchy, for spirit in matter, for God in the soul. So far, then, a reason-loving, immanental, clear, "civilized" outlook and philosophy is favourable to religion, provided there is here no doubt or denial of spirit as distinct from, and higher than, matter; and of the Spirit, God, as distinct from, and higher than, the world and man.

Yet, on the other hand, unless even all that those different departments and experiences can, of themselves, find in themselves, and all that philosophy can establish, still leaves something further, distinct, real, and vital, for specific, historical religion to develop, to infuse, and to produce, religion will remain bereft of its full power and persuasiveness. Something prophetic, pictorial, deeply personal; a great yearning and trust; a disquieting excess beyond our demonstrative p ocesses and immediate demands will rightly, necessarily characterize such revelations to man, and such attempts of man to articulate his deepest experiences and certainties. And, so far, an outlook and a philosophy of a "wild," dim, transcendental trend will be favourable to religion, provided it is not genuinely sceptical, and does not seriously weaken the necessary crispness of, and the friction between, the concrete facts and necessities of life.

And this double need of religion with respect to philosophy is to the advantage of philosophy also. For thus philosophy need not be asked to do more than lay certain foundations—than discover certain necessities for, and the *place* of, religion, and analyse, synthesize, and so far utilize, as carefully and loyally as possible, the materials offered by the religious experience and history.[1]

[1] See Volkelt, *op. cit.* pp. 128–138, 311–328, 344–358.

*Richard Wagner's* enthusiasm for Schopenhauer is well known. And *Leo Tolstoi's* affinity with Schopenhauer is probably as great as is this massive (but wayward and self-conscious) Russian's dependence upon Rousseau. Yet doubtless the Dane *Sören Kierkegaard* (1813-55) and *Friedrich Nietzsche* (active as a philosophical writer 1871-88) are, respectively, the religiously deepest, and the most widely (if probably not lastingly) influential, among the present-day apostles of an outlook akin to, or directly derived from, Schopenhauer.

(5) *Kierkegaard*, the deep, melancholy, strenuous, utterly uncompromising Danish religionist, is a spiritual brother of the great Frenchman, Blaise Pascal, and of the striking English Tractarian, Hurrell Froude, who died young and still full of crudity, yet left an abiding mark upon all who knew him well. Kierkegaard is specially interesting in that he, otherwise a modern of the moderns, is as massively *ontological* in his religion as any ancient; and that the tension of his spiritual life arises, not from any doubt as to *whether* or *what* God is, but from the keenest certainty both that God is the very source and home of man's spirit, and, yet, is utterly unlike this human spirit.

"What the conception of God, or of man's eternal beatitude, is to effect in man is that he shall remodel his entire existence according to it; but by this remodelling man dies to his entire immediacy. As the fish lies out of its element when left upon the sand, so is the religious man caught in his absolute conception of God; for such absoluteness is not directly the element of a finite being. No wonder, then, if, for the Jew, to see God meant death; and if, for the Heathen, to stand in relation to God portended madness. For if the conception of God is our one absolute help, it is also the sole conception capable of absolutely showing to man his utter helplessness" ("Final Unscientific Postscript to the 'Philosophical Crumbs,'" chap. iv. "How can an Eternal Beatitude be based upon an Historical Knowledge?" German translation of the *Gesammelte Werke*, Jena, 1910, vol. vii. pp. 170, 171). And this vivid sense of both the Reality and the Difference of God is (most consistently) combined with the strongest (indeed an excessive because exclusive) realization of the eschatological, the other-worldly, movement in Our Lord's teaching, a realization which, indeed, leads Kierkegaard finally to break with every and all ecclesiastical organization, as essentially a compromise and hypocrisy.

In Kierkegaard's ever occasional yet intense, diffuse yet over-concentrated, one-sided yet magnificently spiritual writings, especially in his profound *Postscript*, 1846; and in the short account and criticism of this difficult thinker and heroic life given us by his friend, the clear and elegant, over-immanental, yet here sympathetic and mostly very just, Professor Harald Höffding, *Sören Kierkegaard* (German translation, Stuttgart, 1896), we are given admirably fresh experiences and warnings concerning "Eternal Life." For here once more we see, most impressively, the all-importance for religion of Ontology and Difference, yet also of Likeness. Thus it is Kierkegaard's profound apprehension of the Ontology and the Difference which renders him religiously deep and powerful, beyond all the Subjectivists and Identity-thinkers put together; and it is his lack of insight as to the Likeness which leaves his life strained to the verge of insanity.

Ibsen's *Brand*, well translated into English by Dr. Herford, 1894, 1903, was admittedly suggested by the great Dane, and gives a vivid picture of his intense other-worldliness, and heroic straining and one-sidedness. Christ's self-renunciation is here, but not His expansive tenderness.

(6) *Nietzsche*, on the contrary, doubtless owes his recently immense, and now still great, vogue primarily, not to anything philosophical, still less to anything religious, but (probably even more than his original idol Schopenhauer) to his form—his brilliant and biting, witty, aphoristic, French *esprit* and style; to the ceaseless intensity, paradox, and transformations of his thought; and, not a little, to his piquant combination of an aristocratic aloofness from the herd of men with an (at least apparent) invitation to "heroic" selfishness and "superior" immorality. And, indeed, this clean liver and devoted brother is, as a writer, destined to endure, not by his last works, *The Twilight of the Idols*, and *The Antichrist*, 1888, with their wild and vulgarly violent attacks upon Christianity; but by many an exquisite saying or half-page in his booklets on Strauss, on the Use and Drawback of History, and on Schopenhauer; in his *Human, all-too-Human*; and on to his *Zarathustra*. Even in these writings we everywhere come upon excesses, yet excesses which, if often (in form) vehemently anti-religious, or even anti-moral, spring doubtless largely from a thirst and search for what religion alone can give. Especially is this the case with Nietzsche's favourite idea of the "Super-man,"—that pathetically hopeless mis-

application of our instinctive need of adoration, —in which Professor Aloys Riehl, himself for so long an aggressively negative philosopher, finds one of the many significant and powerful (because utterly sincere, indeed as yet unconscious) reawakenings of the religious passion and conviction in these our times.[1]

## CHAPTER X

### BIOLOGY AND EPIGENESIS

Introductory—Darwin's declarations concerning religion—Discussion of these declarations—Three religious gains from Evolution, conceived as a means and method—Bergson.

THE immense, seemingly all-pervading influence of such ideas as Descent, Selection, Struggle for Existence, indeed of Biology generally, as articulated by *Darwin*, is admitted by all men, and yet is probably even greater, for good or for evil, than any of us can estimate. And again, the

---

[1] The most instructive and just of the countless studies of Nietzsche is probably A. Riehl's *Friedrich Nietzsche*, Stuttgart, 2nd ed. 1898. William Wallace's two essays on Nietzsche, in his *Lectures and Essays on Natural Theology and Ethics*, ed. by Edward Caird, 1898, pp. 511–541, are, I think, wanting in sufficient sympathy for the good and true richly present in that wayward, chaotic man of letters.

touching greatness of Charles Darwin's character, the range and depth of his achievement in detailed observation and experiment, and the immense stimulation given by his theories to such research, wheresoever we deal with organisms and bodily and instinctive life at all, are equally patent. Here, however, we have but to consider the orientation of mind of Darwin, and of intellects specially influenced by his ideas and work, with respect to the facts, experiences, and necessities which we have found to constitute, or to be essentially connected with, Eternal Life. Direct quotations from Darwin himself shall give us our first material, and then developments and criticisms of our own and of others shall bring out the special truths, mistakes, helps, and hindrances here apparently involved.

1. *Charles Darwin*, surgeon, traveller, geologist, botanist, zoologist (1809-1882), in his winningly homely autobiography and letters, as carefully published by his son, Mr. Francis Darwin, writes of his own capabilities, in regard to our subject-matter, in 1876: "I do not think that the religious sentiment was ever strongly developed in me"; yet "formerly" he had "the firm conviction of the existence of God and of the immortality of the soul." And in 1881 he notes:

"Up to the age of thirty, or beyond it, poetry of many kinds gave me great pleasure; and even as a schoolboy I took intense delight in Shakespeare. Formerly pictures gave me considerable, and music very great delight. But for many years I cannot endure to read a line of poetry: I have tried lately to read Shakespeare . . . it nauseated me. I have also almost lost my taste for music and pictures. The loss of these tastes may possibly be injurious to the intellect, and more probably to the moral character, by enfeebling the emotional part of our nature." He also declares, in 1861: "I am not at all accustomed to metaphysical trains of thought"; and in 1879. "What my own views may be," on the subject of religion, "is a question of no consequence to anyone but myself" (*Charles Darwin*, by Francis Darwin, 1902, pp. 55; 60; 62; 50; 51; 62; 55).

As regards Theism, he writes (in 1876) of "the extreme difficulty, or rather impossibility, of conceiving this immense and wonderful universe, including man with his capacity for looking far backwards and far into futurity, as the result of blind chance or necessity. When thus reflecting, I feel compelled to look to a First Cause, having an intelligent mind in some degree analogous to that of man; and I deserve to be called a Theist. But then arises the doubt

—Can the mind of man, developed, I fully believe, from a mind as low as that possessed by the lowest animals, be trusted when it draws such grand conclusions?" And at other times: "There seems to be no more design in the action of natural selection than in the course which the wind blows." Again, "I am aware that if we admit a First Cause, the mind still craves to know whence it came and how it arose. Nor can I overlook the difficulty from the immense amount of suffering throughout the world"; and "the number of men in the world is as nothing compared with that of all other sentient beings, which often suffer greatly without any moral improvement" such as men may derive from their sufferings. Yet, in spite of his own sufferings ("I *never* pass twenty-four hours without many hours of discomfort when I can do nothing whatsoever"), he declares: "According to my judgment, happiness decidedly prevails" in the world. "In my extreme fluctuations I have never been an Atheist, in the sense of denying the existence of God. I think that generally (and increasingly as I grow older), but not always, that an Agnostic would be the more correct description of my state of mind." His son emphatically endorses this diagnosis (*ibid.* pp. 61, 64, 59; 57, 60, 56, 59; 55, 65 n.).

With respect to Immortality and "the view now held by most physicists that the sun with all the planets will in time grow too cold for life," he exclaims: "Believing as I do that man, in the distant future, will be a far more perfect creature than he now is, it is an intolerable thought, that he and all other sentient beings are doomed to complete annihilation after such long-continued slow progress. To those who fully admit the immortality of the human soul, the destruction of our world will not appear so dreadful" (*ibid.* p. 61).

And finally, as to Conscience, Duty, Sin, he writes in 1873: "Man can do his duty"; and in 1879: "As for myself, I believe that I have acted rightly in devoting my life to Science. I feel no remorse for having committed any great sin, but have often and often regretted that I have not done more direct good to my fellow-creatures" (*ibid.* pp. 57, 328).[1]

2. The following points appear to be specially important here:—

(1) Nothing can well be more different than Evolution as understood, of simple Organisms or Monads, by Leibniz, and in part already by

---

[1] See the delightfully sympathetic reminiscences of Darwin, in J. W. Judd's "Darwin and Geology," in *Darwin and Modern Science*, 1909, pp. 337-384; and in his booklet, *The Coming of Evolution*, 1911.

Cardinal Nicolas of Coes (d. 1464), or of the Logical Idea and of the entire Universe, by Hegel, on the one hand, and the Darwinian "Evolution" on the other. The former is simply an unfolding, an unpacking, of a content completely present in miniature from the first, or a differentiation of a unity; the latter is an integration of a plurality,—the parts here are not present, in the organism or its embryo, from the first, but are gradually superadded and organized, one after the other. With the great anatomist William Harvey (d. 1658), who prophetically anticipated the conception and coined the term, and with Professor James Ward, thus carefully discriminative, we shall call this latter process, not Evolution but Epigenesis (J. Ward, *The Realm of Ends*, 1911, pp. 97–99).

Now Darwin, in his misgivings as to the range of man's mind, confounds, and uses with strange inconsistencies and cross-purposes, these two very different senses of "Evolution." "Man is developed from the lower animals" seems here to imply for him, "man's mind is *still* somehow limited by that starting-point." Yet Darwin's own "Evolution," Epigenesis, postulates the integration of new organs and powers; and Leibnizian-Hegelian Evolution (rightly according to the logic of *that* view) looks to the end, and not to the beginning, of the unfolding for the true revelation of each organism's content. Thus Darwin here follows, not his own Epigenesis (for man in Epigenesis is indeed descended from the monkey, yet is not now a monkey, but a creature which, in the course of ages, has integrated much that is new into what has descended to it through the monkey), but the Leibnizian Evolution (where man is now what he was from the first). And yet Darwin here adopts the Leibnizian Evolution only directly to contradict the logic of *this* Evolution, which requires, should it come to hold man to be developed from a creature which in the past seemed to be no more than a monkey, that the apparent monkey was really a man, and not that the latter fully explicitated being is no more than a monkey.

But indeed, even if the logic of Darwin's argument be self-consistent, it is impossible to see what the kind or degree of intelligence possessed by man's earliest ancestors has to do with the nature and range of man's present intelligence, any more than Newton's capacity for apprehending the law of gravitation is called in doubt by our remembering his animal-like early infancy. I take this difficulty, which evidently was *the* obstacle to Darwin's full and continuous adhesion to Theism, to have attained to its great power over his mind, through his immense absorption in, and intense picturing of, the supposed earlier stages of living organisms. This absorption would, when he turned to those great, largely metaphysical questions, make him involuntarily conceive human beings as still facing these problems with powers not differing in kind, and hardly in degree, from those of the animals from which they sprang.

(2) If the evidence of Botany, Zoology, Anthropology, amply endorsed and extended within each of these sciences by Palæontology, have more and more recommended some degree and doctrine of Descent, the immense and varied observations and thought devoted to these questions since *The Origin of Species* (1859) have, ever more conclusively, shown how complex, and still predominantly obscure for us, has been the precise character and mechanism of this Descent. Certainly "Natural Selection" and the "Struggle for Existence" are now mostly admitted not to suffice as explanations. And Professor Weissmann has conclusively proved that "the kernel of the riddle, in selection," even if we adopt it, "*lies in the varying*," in the fact that "the necessary beginnings of a useful variation are always present" (*Darwin and Modern Science*, 1909, p. 27).

We are thus thrown back, here also, upon some Power—Theists will still conceive It as God—Which ever provides these variations in the right time and place, even if It does not directly determine their selection. Indeed, in whatever form we adopt Descent, we are ultimately confronted with similar conditions, and are driven to choose between this or that form of Descent, as simply the mechanism and means provided and used by Creative Intelligence and Power; or the direct attribution to Matter of Consciousness and Mind; or, at least, of the Spontaneous Generation of these. And by such attributions we are landed in pure Mythology.

(3) We all know of the beautifully generous friendship that existed between *A. R. Wallace* and Darwin, and how the former, admittedly a simultaneous and independent elaborator of "Darwinism," has, ever increasingly, combined with this his "Darwinism" a full and deliberate Theism. And probably the most valuable contribution of this most patiently probing and sincere biologist to the religious philosophy of the question is his elucidation of how man possesses certain faculties, the Mathematical, Musical, Artistic, special to himself; how these faculties cannot have been developed under the law of Natural Selection; and how no breach

of continuity, no sudden or abrupt change, is involved by the introduction, in the case of man, of new causes into the continuity of living beings. Indeed, as to this last objection, "there are at least three stages in the development of the organic world when some new cause or power must necessarily have come into action": the stage from inorganic to organic —from a mere complexity, however great, of chemical compounds, to *living* protoplasm, the first plant-cell, a new thing in the world, with its marvellous powers of growth, assimilation, reproduction, variation, vitality; the stage of sensation or *consciousness*, a thing, the animal, that feels its own existence; and the stage of *full self-consciousness*, reason, and volition, man. These stages "point clearly to a world of spirit, to which the world of matter is altogether subordinate." And the changes thus introduced "may be none the less real because absolutely imperceptible at their points of origin, as is the change that takes place in the curve in which a body is moving when the application of some new force causes the curve to be slightly altered" (*Darwinism*, reprint 1905, pp. 469–476).

We would only add to man's special characteristics the sense of the Infinite, the non-contingent, full Reality, the Perfect; and we would so frame our description of this Reality as to guard against any possibility of taking the Ultimate as perhaps, after all, some super-conscious, non-"personal" Spirituality, since what we here require is not even "Spirit," but *the* Spirit, or a family of Spirits.

In any case, Dr. Wallace's example is an impressive direct demonstration of how little even a lifelong devotion to, and pioneer work in, Biology and Epigenesis necessarily involve Atheism or even Agnosticism; indeed how much some such workers find their researches point to, and to require as their fully satisfactory *nidus* and explanation, Spiritualism and Theism.

(4) Many of us personally still remember Professor *Huxley's* Romanes Lecture, *Evolution and Ethics*, in 1893, the original main position of which (though practically retracted by the author in one of his notes added to the published text, and plentifully "answered" by various Naturalistic Evolutionists) has nowhere been refuted. Is, or is there not, "a sanction for morality in the ways of the cosmos"? he asks; any justification there for the artificial world built up by man within that cosmos, and which is in perpetual conflict with that spatially wider world? "Cosmic evolution may teach us how the good and the evil tendencies of man may have come

about; but in itself it is incompetent to furnish any better reason why what we call good is preferable to what we call evil, than we had before." "Cosmic nature is no school of virtue, but the headquarters of the enemy of ethical nature"; and hence "the ethical progress of society depends, not on imitating the cosmic process, still less in running away from it, but in combating it" (pp. 31; 27; 34).

The rough heroism of the address formed a striking contrast, and yet a frame and bulwark, to the deep and delicate ethical sense of Darwin himself. It was, however, nothing short of a direct challenge to the inevitable consequence, indeed concomitant, of every doctrine of Descent and Evolution which would insist upon itself as exhaustive and self-explanatory, and upon earlier and shallower stages of life as the true and complete explanation of the later and richer ones.

Professor *Andrew Seth* (*Pringle Pattison*) has admirably illustrated, completed, and guarded Professor Huxley's appeal. Especially does he finely discriminate between the two meanings of the word "nature" and their continual confusion and identification in all naturalistic thinking and feeling—the lower or narrower sense of "all that happens in the known world *except* the responsible activities of human beings," and the higher and wider sense of "the entire nature of things." And he insists that, "since the true nature of the cause only becomes apparent in the effect," we must, when we pass from one order of facts to another, ever be careful not to press the account of the preceding set of facts, out of which a fact of another set seems to arise, as this latter fact's true and full explanation. For "by so doing we identify the fact with its antecedents, whereas these antecedents, as understood by the naturalistic theories, are not the causes of the consequents, since here the antecedents are taken *in abstraction from their consequents*,—as we might suppose them to be if no such consequents had ever issued from them. Hence the futility of all attempts to explain human life in terms of the merely animal, to explain life in terms of the inorganic, and ultimately to find a sufficient formula for the cosmic process in terms of the redistribution of matter and motion." And yet we have no means for a satisfactory conviction both of the world's unity and of an intrinsically worthy end explanatory of existence, except the conclusion that the end which we recognize as alone worthy of attainment is also the end of existence as such (A. Seth's *Man's Place in the Cosmos*, 1897, pp. 14, 15, 32).

Here we would only ever keep it abundantly plain that we thus in no wise exclude the possibility, which is, surely, a great probability, that, in other planets and stars, quite other, higher beings than man may, simultaneously or subsequently, exist, who know and practise indefinitely more of Reality and of Love than man does or ever will do.

The Huxley-Seth positions here given, certainly alone, in spite of the admitted difficulties of their systematization and practice, find a sufficiently spacious and strong home and justification for Darwin's own touching sense of duty, of obligation, even of sin as possible, and above all, perhaps, of the sacredness of careful veracity in little things. Naturalism has really no logical room for these difficult and magnificent things, however sincerely individual "Naturalists" may practise them and may think themselves consistent in doing so.

(5) Anthropology and the Comparative History of Religions is, most understandably, still largely, though perhaps no longer increasingly, influenced by the "Naturalism" just considered, even when their votaries show a fine sense of the inadequacy of mechanical categories to all living, hence to all human, things, and when they discriminate, theoretically, between descriptive accounts and ultimate explanations. And indeed the earlier, ruder manifestations of man's social, ethical, and religious instincts and requirements

have been so much neglected and are so interesting, and man's mental and spiritual nature is so continuously and so closely awakened, nourished, limited, deflected by his physical antecedents, constituents, environment, and by the family, state, race, into which he is born, that the attaching even a proportionally excessive importance to such things is, in these still early days of those sciences, practically inevitable.

Such a pregnant little book as Mr. *R. R. Marett's Anthropology*, 1912, seems to us an instructive combination of all the insights and advantages, and of some of the imperfections, just indicated. "We anthropologists," he tells us, "are out to secure this: that there shall be but the same kind of history, with the same evolutionary principle running right through it, for all men, civilized and savage, present and past." "Anthropology is likely to bring us nearest to the true meaning of life, because the life of human beings must always be nearer to human students of life than, say, the life of plants." And again: "Let us look upon ourselves as if we were so many bees and ants, not forgetting, of course, to make use of the inside information that, in the case of the insects, we so conspicuously lack" (pp. 11, 12; 13, 18). These passages seem not free from the mistakes signalized above. But the following is refreshingly helpful: "Biology finds that it cannot conveniently abstract away the reference to time," nor "treat living things as machines"; "Anthropology is a history of vital tendencies which are not natural in the sense of merely physical"; and "the more you take in, the better your chance of really understanding" (pp. 14, 16, 17).

I will but briefly add how persistent is the writer's impression of the greater penetration and sympathetic evocation of present or past, civilized or barbarous, humanity offered by such work as that of Rohde, compared with that of the later Nietzsche; or, again, of Paul Wendland or Willamowitz Möllendorff, contrasted with that of more "biological" workers; and of the delicate justice of such criticisms as Professor Loisy bestows upon thought as brilliant as that of M. Salomon Reinach, and upon certain theses so learnedly maintained by Professor J. G. Frazer. In all these and similar cases the superiority, such as it is, appears to proceed from a more wakeful sense of man's specific differences from animals, plants, and inorganic things.[1]

---

[1] For Rohde-Nietzsche, see specially O. Crusius, *Erwin Rohde*, 1902, pp. 113, 158, 159. For P. Wendland, his *Die Hellenistisch-Römische Kultur*, 1907. For Willamowitz-Möllendorff, the beautiful preface to his *Griechisches Lesebuch*, i. 1, ed. 1907, p. viii. For Loisy, *A Propos d'Histoire des Religions*, 1911, pp. 1-99; 166-217.

3. Yet the increase of light furnished by the movement so predominatingly initiated by Darwin, concerning the closeness of the relations between man's spirit and man's body, between man and other living beings, and between the whole living world and its inorganic environment, has also brought, as all sincere research cannot fail to bring, much helpful criticism, confirmation, and growth to our apprehension, analysis, and formulation of the facts and requirements constitutive of our religious and moral experience. We take this to obtain in three ways.

(1) The movement, at its best, has brought the scientific attention back from physical, mechanical, chemical facts and laws, from *things*, to organisms, to *living beings*. And in such living beings we have inevitably a wondrous increase of significance and reality. Thus the young traveller Darwin is already especially absorbed in "the singular relations of the animals and plants in the several Galapagos Islands, and of all of these to the inhabitants of South America"; he ever loves "to exalt plants in the scale of organized beings"; and, as to Buckle's materialist and monistic *History of Civilization*, he "doubts whether his generalizations are worth anything" (*Charles Darwin*, pp. 29, 49, 35). The close interconnection, the upward trend and varying worth,

and the deep difference between living organisms and all mere matter and its mechanical laws, are thus vividly apprehended here.

Now all wholesome and fruitful Ethics, Religion, Life in general, and all balanced and circumspect Epistemology, combine in insisting upon precisely these mysterious differences, superiorities, and connections. And especially Religion, above all Christianity, awakens and develops its strength in contact with the visible, especially the organic · and, in such contact and awakening, discovers life, instinct, rudimentary or developed reason, increasingly like unto man's own, and all these as dim analogies of, and in real relation to, the Divine Spirit and Life. Here Darwin's rapt interest in the interrelated lives of plants and insects, in a bird's colouring and a worm's instincts, are, in their grandly self-oblivious outgoing to the humble and the little, most genuine flowerings of the delicate Christian spirit in this fierce, rough world of ours. Without such real love, bridging over such real differences between realities possessed of varyingly deep inner lives, such studies instantly become impossible, or dry and merely ingenious, or weakly sentimental.

And this deep, graduated glow of love for the graduated realities of our real world will succeed in withstanding the fierce flare of the ruinous passion for abstraction and for the logical pyramid as now again manifested in Professor *Haeckel's* vehement monistic propaganda. Here "the great abstract law of mechanical causality rules the entire universe, as it does the mind of man." Here, with the beginning of all things, we have "the homogeneous primitive matter, prothyl, at an enormous temperature"; then, with the cooling of the heavenly bodies, "protoplasm, that wonderful substance which alone, as far as we know, is the possessor of organic life," is evolved; the simplest organic beings, *e.g.* bacteria, arise, "by spontaneous generation from the nitro-carbonates" of those stars; "the radiation of heat into space gradually lowers the temperature until all water is turned into ice,—*that* is the end of all organic life." "At length the moons fall upon the planets, and the planets upon the sun. The collision again produces an intense heat . . . and the eternal drama of sun-birth begins again." This, the Professor insists, is "a sublime picture"; Darwin, we saw, found even the much milder monism of Buckle to be of doubtful worth, and this picture "intolerable."

"Over all this 'perpetual motion,'" continues the unconquerably cheerful Professor, "rules the law of substance." We do not know what 'substance' *is*; but "from the obscure problem of substance we have evolved the clear law of substance"; and "the monism of the cosmos which we establish thereon proclaims the absolute dominion of 'the great eternal iron laws' throughout the universe," and "shatters the three central dogmas of the dualistic philosophy—the personality of God, the immortality of the soul, and the freedom of the Will" (*The Riddle of the Universe*, 8th impression, 1911, pp. 129–132, 134, 135).

Thus, the more abstract and unreal the notions, the more they here oust and destroy the concrete, the experienced, the real; and man is invited to admire this his own self-strangulation by means of the thinnest cobwebs spun by his own brain! Such perversely clever feats are still very popular. Yet they thrive, not on any intrinsic adequacy or fruitfulness, but on the faults and excesses committed by the representatives of the richer and truer outlooks; upon the admittedly great triumphs, at shallower levels, of mechanical science; and especially upon the plausibility of "clear" thoughts.[1]

(2) The interesting attempt of the Rev. *F. R. Tennant*, in his *Origin and Propagation of Sin*,

---

[1] See the wise and firm discussion of Evolution in Professor Eucken's *Geistige Strömungen der Gegenwart*, 3rd ed. 1904, pp. 185–225.

1902, to elucidate the moral and religious experiences of Temptation and Guilt, and the theological definitions of these experiences, by means of the Descent Theory, shows at least how this Theory not only raises or intensifies difficulties, but can also resolve some of the obscurities attaching to these profoundly important matters.

"The further back we trace man, the less," says Mr. Tennant, "do we find him the person or even the individual"; "the 'tribal self' preceded the 'personal self'"; "the idea of moral personality, in terms of which theology has been wont exclusively to formulate its doctrine of the origin of sin, emerged extremely late in human thought." "The origin of sin, like other so-called origins, thus appears as a gradual process, rather than an abrupt, inexplicable plunge; and the first sin, instead of being the most heinous and the most momentous in the race's history, would rather be the least significant of all." And "if man's physical nature is necessarily endowed with instincts, appetites, impulsions, it contains abundance of raw material for the production of sin, as soon as these native propensities are brought into relation with any restraining or condemning influence." The universality of sin, in at least many of its most general forms, becomes thus attributed to "the self-assertion of powerful tendencies, with all their priority in time and fixity in instinct and habit, after the acquisition and superposition of a 'higher nature' which demands their subordination to less immediate and tangible ends." Hence "the human infant is simply a non-moral animal"; and "our lowest appetites are means of self-realization in the highest sense," whilst they are also "the fateful rocks on which so many human lives make shipwreck." "Indeed, it is because the mastery of appetite and emotion by the moralized man has always proved so difficult that human thought has generally considered the animal side of our nature to be positively evil." Or, as Archdeacon Wilson tersely puts it, "to the" evolutionist "believer sin is not an innovation, but the survival or misuse of habits and tendencies that were incidental to an earlier stage of development, and whose sinfulness lies in their anachronism"; and "this conflict of freedom and conscience is" precisely "what is related as 'The Fall,' *sub specie historiæ*" (*op. cit.* pp. 89–93; 95, 98, 100).

The deepest root of sin, and the deeper and deepest kinds of sin (such as self-centredness, pride of intellect, self-adoration) are surely apprehended or explained here only very inadequately. Yet it is certain that, of all the Christian Symbols concerning Original Sin, the definition of the

Council of Trent (1546) is the least in conflict with such a conception. And, in any case, it is clear that there is nothing here to weaken our sense of the profound duty and rightness of virtue, our conviction concerning the grim reality and wrongfulness of sin, or our longing for grace and help against sinfulness and self.

(3) And finally, as regards Epigenesis and Creation, a wider, and indeed deeper and richer, conception of Creation, especially a concentration upon, and vivid apprehension of, the continuity and immediacy of the Divine Action involved in any adequate doctrine of Creation, appears to leave sufficient room within Creation for all probable forms of Epigenesis, provided always that such Epigenesis or Evolution is content to be, not the all-sufficient reason and ultimate explanation, but simply a process and description.

Thus the Rev. *Philip Waggett* strikingly declares: " Science persistently presses on to find the universal machinery of adaptation in the planet "; and " in whatsoever Science may find this adaptation, it must always be opposed to the conception of a Divine Power here and there, but not everywhere, active. For Science the Divine must be constant, operative everywhere and in every quality and power, in environment and in organism, in stimulus and in reaction, in variation and in struggle, . . . in short, in the general wonder of life and the world. And this is exactly what the Divine Power must be for religious faith." And he points out that, "whereas 'God rested' has been long taken in the sense that God's activity, with respect to the formation of living creatures, ceased at some point in past time," "Creation, in the reformed language of religion, comes now specially to mean for us the mysterious and permanent relation between the Infinite and the finite, between the moving changes we know in part, and the Power, after the fashion of that observation, unknown, which is itself 'unmoved all motion's source'" (*Darwin and Modern Science*, 1909, pp. 491, 492; 489, 490).

I will but add that, in proportion as we move up in the scale of reality, the more we have to conceive the Divine Action as bafflingly rich and varied in the manner, the degree, and the restraint of its operation and aid; and that, in proportion as we insist upon God's Immanence within the sensible and the human world, in the same proportion does the problem of Evil increase in urgency and difficulty. Yet both these mysteries appear to be intrinsic to life, and religion, which has not caused or imagined them, can bear them; indeed only religion can, if not theoretically explain, at least practically utilize and surmount, the wondrous and dread capabilities and realities thus experienced by us in our lives and in the world.

4. Two philosophers, both largely followers of Darwin, but otherwise strikingly different in their entire orientation of mind and literary form, might be considered here—Herbert Spencer, with his *Unknowable*, and Henri Bergson, with his *Durée*. We will, however, restrict ourselves to M. Bergson, as by far the most penetrating, the most likely to live, and the most instructive in our particular subject-matter.

*Bergson's* form is so vibratingly alive and beautiful, his success against a merely mechanical or materialistic conception of life is so real, and his intentions in favour of Libertarianism and Spirituality are so evident and so worthy of respect, that it is difficult, for one who has long loved and learnt from him in all these ways, to take up an attitude towards him that is at all critical. And then, in spite of his admirable form, he is far from easy to analyse or to understand.

But first I would once more gratefully accept his cardinal distinction between Concrete Time (Duration) and Conceptional Time (Clock-Time), and the more restricted amongst his descriptions of both; and especially his insistence upon the essential, indeed immense, rôle played by Duration in the entire life of man. Other philosophers have indeed adumbrated these facts, but no one has so continuously and so profitably elucidated them. Let us here, then, only consider certain other, still more fundamental and original, applications or conceptions of Bergson, under the two rough headings of Time and Space, and of Finalism and the place and character of Transformism. Our texts shall come almost exclusively from his fundamental book, the *Essai sur les Données Immédiates de la Conscience*, 2nd ed. 1898, and from his most recent, largest, and most Darwinian work, *l'Évolution Créatrice*, 1907. My quotations are made directly from the originals.

(1) As concerns Bergson's fundamental antinomy of the Durational, Temporal, and Qualitative, and the Extensional, Spatial, and Quantitative, the *Essai*, in its first chapter, warns us that "we love simple things, and hence our language is but ill constructed for rendering the subtleties of psychological analysis"; and then attempts to show, in exquisitely developed examples, that our consciousness is ever qualitative, never quantitative, in kind. Thus "without the successive (muscular and other) reactions, the intensity of pain would be a" constantly varying

"quality, and not a quantity." But "in proportion as the sensation ceases to be affective and the reactions disappear, we come to perceive the external object, the sensation's cause. And this cause is extensive, *i.e.* measurable; hence we now associate the idea of a certain quantity in the cause with a certain quality in the effect; and we finally put that quantity into this quality." Yet in reality "there exists no contact between the unextended, quality, and the extended, quantity," although "Physics, which calculates the exterior causes of our internal states, deliberately confounds the two, and thus even exaggerates the illusion of common-sense in this matter" (pp. 10; 28; 31, 32; 52).

And then the second chapter attempts to establish that the sole reality experienced by us is "Time Quality, with mutual penetration of its parts, as against Time Quantity, with multiplicity of juxtaposition"; that "every clear idea of number implies a vision in Space," whilst "a complex feeling contains indeed a considerable number of simpler elements, but, as soon as the consciousness distinctly perceives them, the psychic state, the result of their synthesis, will, for that very reason, be changed"; and even that "the actual, not only virtual, apperception of subdivisions in the individual is precisely what we call objectivity." Thus, then, "we know two realities of different orders,—the one" purely "heterogeneous, the reality of Sensible Qualities; the other" purely "homogeneous, which is Space. It is Space which, clearly conceived by the intelligence, enables us to make precise distinctions, to count, to abstract, perhaps also to speak." And hence "in Duration there is never anything homogeneous, except what does not endure, namely, Space, in which alone simultaneities appear drawn up in line"; and "in Movement there is nothing homogeneous, except the Space which has been traversed, that is, Immobility. Hence Science operates upon Time and Movement only after first eliminating from Time Duration, and from Movement Mobility." In a word, "our perceptions, sensations, emotions, ideas are either clear and precise, but then they are impersonal; or they are confused and infinitely mobile, but then they are inexpressible" (*ibid.* pp. 57, n. 1; 60; 63, 64; 70; 74; 78; 86, 87; 97).

Now here we are, first of all, struck by the strange difference of method pursued with regard to Time and with regard to Space. For Time here is most real when most concrete; Space most real when most abstract. Again, Time here is real only when full of its characteristics, successions; Space is real only when empty of its characteristics, simultaneities. And again, Time here is real only when it effects something real within real beings that endure; Space is real only as a passive medium against which we, concrete beings, can project the thin ghosts of our real experiences, and can thus discriminate into clear simultaneities the obscure successions of our actual lives. Nor is it that Time, as Duration, is here primary and alone real, and Space secondary and everywhere subjective; but both are to be real, and yet they are to answer to directly contradictory standards of reality.

And, again, we are baffled by the intense abstractness of both these two sole realities. For pure homogeneous Space and pure heterogeneous Becoming are entirely beyond all human experience, which only knows Spatial and Temporal Objects, in which the Space is never purely homogeneous and the Becoming never purely heterogeneous. Certainly such wholesale Spatialization of Science would be the ruin of Science; for Science would then hover completely outside of the concrete reality which it would still claim to interpret. And such a complete Fluidification of Human Life would be the destruction of this Life, since there would be here no rational, spiritual necessities, no ideal, organization, or end which could lift the toil and trouble, the joy and sadness, above sheer, blind happenings and soulless things.

But indeed Bergson himself gives us two indications that we cannot take Duration as the sheer Change and Becoming which he usually declares it to be. For Duration ever consists with him in the interpenetration of its *various parts*. Take away all these *parts* (however obscurely discriminated and intimately interpenetrative) and the Succession of Duration has become as homogeneous as the Simultaneity of Space—which is precisely what the entire system does *not* want. Yet parts are ever parts of a whole, and sheer Becoming has no room for wholes, and hence none for parts. And again, Bergson himself sometimes clearly realizes that Metaphysics cannot simply consist in innumerable, utterly independent and differing, intuitions of an utterly disjointed, chaotically creative reality. Thus, in the " Introduction à la Métaphysique," he says : " Metaphysics is never fully itself, unless it emancipates itself from stiff and ready-made concepts, and creates representations that are supple, mobile, almost fluid, and are ever ready to mould themselves on the elusive forms of intuition " (*Revue de Métaphysique et de Morale*, Janv. 1903, p. 9). Here again, then, we are after a will-o'-the-wisp, unless the reality which intuition grasps, and which is thus to be conceptualized, contains some permanence, some tendency, requirement, or end within itself.

The fact is, doubtless, that Bergson has broken up the opposites, which together constitute our consciousness and life, into two separate worlds; which worlds, then, are each unreal and excessive, and refuse to come together again. For I, my Self, am not more a sheer Becoming or a sheer Creator than I am a mere Fixity or a mere Result; indeed my manhood consists precisely in the permanence, and in my consciousness of the permanence, of my one Self throughout its changes, and in the upbuilding of my abiding personality by means of these vicissitudes. Doubtless without such changes there would be for me, and for human beings in general (as these are known to us in this earthly life), no permanence, no upbuilding of the spiritual Self. Yet this Self is not simply those changes, nor simply their result, nor merely their contemplator; but it is I, myself, who, in and through those changes, maintain and build up this my personality.

(2) In the *Évolution Créatrice*, the utter heterogeneity, unaccountableness, unpurposive character of all Duration and Life, in precise proportion to its depth, is perhaps even more vehemently emphasized; *e.g.* " whether as Matter or as Spirit, Reality is a continual Becoming, it

makes or unmakes itself, but it is never something made" (p. 295). But in this work Bergson attempts to enforce this his central conviction by means of various, often exquisite, studies in biological adaptation and animal instinct, all tending to show that Evolution, Transformism, has ever followed, and still follows, that course of utter heterogeneity. He is attracted to Transformism, both because he thinks it adds greatly to the conclusiveness of the considerations to be derived from Duration against all mere Mechanism; and because he finds it to show that "life does not proceed by association and addition of elements, but by dissociation and distinction" (pp. 40, 97). Indeed, his entire second chapter here is devoted to "The Divergent Directions of the Evolution of Life."

And yet we read here that "this entire study tends to establish that the Vital is in the direction of the Voluntary"; and that "the Absolute endures like to ourselves, but, on certain sides, with infinitely greater concentration and recollection within itself." And as to our human faculties, Kant indeed considers all our intuitions to be only sensible, *i.e.* infra-intellectual. But Bergson proposes to find " Science increasingly symbolical, in proportion as it proceeds from the physical to the psychical through the vital"; so that, "since we must, in some manner, perceive a thing if we are to be able to symbolize it, there would exist an Intuition of the psychical, and more generally of the vital, which the Intelligence would indeed transpose and translate, but which, nevertheless, would exceed the Intelligence"—we would thus possess "a supra-intellectual Intuition" (pp. 244, 323, 388, 389).

Thus here again the same Flux and Becoming, which is generally presented as absolutely without purpose or aim, appears at times as moving in a particular direction, as infinitely differing in worth, and as most precious where most concentrated and most nearly a simultaneity, an Eternity. Yet here again, and on a larger scale than in the *Essai*, we usually find that the immense stress and struggle of life, and its various, simultaneous forms or successive stages (inert, instinctive, rational), are all only changes and growths in *the means to exist*, and in the degree and kind of liberty and capacity possessed by the various beings towards their self-concentration and self-creation *for such existence*. There is absolutely no change or advance in *the end* striven for; and no wonder, for, from first to last, no *end* is striven for at all, except existence, ever increasingly free indeed from all compulsion, yet bereft throughout of all rational, ethical, spiritual motive, aim, or ideal, however obscure and inchoate. Thus in Bergson's predominant view we struggle, suffer, live, and die, in order to exist, and only to exist; if we seek anything in and through our existence besides an ever more concentrated, an ever more existing, existence, we are supposed to court a Finalism less directly determinist than is Mechanism, but which, in the long-run, is as ruinous to liberty, and hence to life, as is Mechanism itself.

(3) To sum up. We are deeply grateful to M. Bergson for his great central discrimination between Conceptual and Real Time, and for his fine penetration into the irreplaceable function performed by Real Time in all specifically human activity and consciousness. But we must demand a similar discrimination between Conceptual and Real Space, and especially the admission of the strictly artificial character of M. Bergson's "Real" (*i.e.* Pure, Homogeneous) Space. These changes will necessarily modify Bergson's usual definitions, though not his occasional admissions, concerning Real Time (Duration). For Real Time will then be no more sheer Heterogeneity and Creation, than Real Space will be sheer Homogeneity and Emptiness. And thus we can ever discover, in our consciousness and activity, real Simultaneity as well as real Succession; and the first will not be pure fixity, nor the second pure

fluidity. But our life will have a range around in the present, as well as back into the past and on into the future; and it will have a variety in which the new will ever revivify the old, and the old will ever steady and extend the new. And this position alone will be fully justifiable by philosophy, since only thus do we systematically trust and follow the highest, richest, best-known, of our categories, Self-Consciousness and Personality—a category which essentially consists in precisely this mysterious union of opposites.

But even further. However real, however simply ultimate (for man) may be Duration (and this book strongly holds that Duration is indeed thus real and ultimate), Duration is, surely, at its highest, not in its element of Change, but in its element of Permanence. Bergson almost exclusively insists upon the Change, because only boundless, ceaseless Change can, to his mind, secure for Duration its free operativeness and truly Creative power. And he is doubtless right in his opposition to such a system as that of Leibniz, where our seemingly free acts are but the inevitable carrying out of a programme fixed in every detail. Yet a full and unforced analysis of the facts of our consciousness, and a careful consideration of Bergson's own position, show plainly, I think, that here again, in his idea of

Liberty, we are given a "pure," *i.e.* an artificial, a one-sidedly abstract, conception.

For, as to the facts of consciousness—all its tension, friction, movement, Bergson indeed admirably describes and defends them *qua* realities operative for their own perpetuation, but he fails fully to penetrate and to explain them, and hence even adequately to describe them in their deepest strivings. We have here nothing of Professor G. F. Stout's persistent conviction that "any specific activity must be thought of in relation to some result which it either maintains in existence or tends to bring into existence—an *end* to which it is directed" (*Analytic Psychology*, 1909, vol. i. p. 126); and nothing of his fine preoccupation with the relations between Interest and Attention (*ibid.* pp. 224–240). Indeed, the entire conception of the primary importance of Conation, and of the essentially teleological character of all Conation, is wholly absent from the mind of Bergson. And this absence is truly strange in a mind so delicately alert to all the lesser characteristics of life, and so keenly anxious to elucidate life's libertarian, spiritual character.

And as to the final result of Bergson's own general position, it is doubtless his too simple (because, in great part, only negative and naturalistic) conception of Liberty, and his consequent aversion to all genuine Finalism, which prevent his admirable beginnings and motives from attaining their own requirements. How impressive, for instance (as far as it goes), is, in the *Essai* (pp. 175, 176), the account of the Free Act, as an unusually extensive and close interpenetration of the successive parts of Duration—as a momentary, almost complete, Concentration and Simultaneity of the Agent's entire Succession. Yet the same writer will find the essence of this same Duration in an utterly heterogeneous flux, bereft of all parts or any wholeness; will oppose all Simultaneity, as so much Spatialization and hence as the destruction, of the living soul; and, above all, will (even in such otherwise exquisite descriptions) ignore the most fundamental of all the characteristics of full human self-consciousness, according to which the self-concentration of the soul is never sought as admirable or precious apart from the realization thereby of some end or ideal other than such self-concentration. If, in this free act, there is a self moved by necessities and ideals, ultimately by realities, of a rational, ethical, spiritual kind and worth; if it can, in endless degrees, affirm, seek, and actuate within its own life, or deny, evade, and almost forget, these indestructible necessities and realities; and if such a spontaneous affirmation effects this human self's full depth and happiness: then, indeed, can such a self-concentration be a fully moving spectacle for the human mind; then, but only then.

Bergson has thus, we feel, stopped half-way; he has removed the mechanical obstacles to Liberty, but he has not discovered the spiritual conditions and requisites for the same Liberty. Indeed, by his strenuous exclusion of all permanence, and of every aim and ideal, as of so many abstractions essentially hostile to Freedom, he has, most unintentionally, brought us back, in this anti-Finalism, to that Naturalism which he had so successfully resisted when it masqueraded as a sheer Mechanism. And thus the present writer can never get away for a little from the fascination of this exquisite and most brilliant mind, without feeling this distressing antagonism in his thought—a nobly sensitive awareness as to the active nature, the rich variety, the range, and the successiveness, essential to all life; and yet a strange insensibility to its purposive character, its profound unity, organization, and simultaneity. We thus get a spiritualistic beginning crowned by a naturalistic conclusion, a certain warmth with coldness, and depth with shallowness.

And especially as regards Eternal Life, the finest words yet spoken concerning Bergson's central conception are probably those of Professor Bosanquet: "Succession and Continuity are," indeed, "the two inseparable factors of a reality which is fundamentally temporal"; but once the dual nature of time is thoroughly admitted, "*Durée* is" seen to be "one with the relative timelessness of a finite self." "The finite *qua* finite has an aspect of succession"; yet "the distinctive being of the self is inversely as its dependence on successiveness" (*The Principle of Individuality and Value*, 1912, pp. 338-340).

Let us only here insist, once more, upon the right, privilege, and duty of Religion to experience and conceive full Eternity and Simultaneity, not simply as an ideal limit to which our quasi-eternity can ever increasingly approach, but as already fully extant—as the characteristic of the Spirit of spirits, God, Who acts within these our quasi-eternal spirits, and Who thus both awakens and slakes within us our noblest desire, a keen sense of Eternal Life.[1]

---

[1] On most of the points considered above, see J. M'Kellar Stewart's excellent *Critical Exposition of Bergson's Philosophy*, 1911, pp. 205-254, 300, 301; and Mr. Boyce's Gibson's wise and probing study, "The Intuitionism of Henri Bergson," *The Quest*, Jan. 1911.

## CHAPTER XI

SOCIALISM AND PRESENT SOCIAL PROBLEMS

Introductory—Marx's fundamental conceptions—Causes of the prevalence of secularism in contemporary social movements—Conditions and symptoms traceable here favourable to religion.

WE are, next, face to face with quite a different world, different difficulties, and yet also different helps, as regards Eternal Life, from those directly presented or supplied by the philosophers, singly or collectively. This world, and these difficulties and helps, are, in their special intensity, range, and complication, a genuinely new experience in the history of mankind. It is the world of the West-European and North-American workmen, with their special requirements, passions, and mentality, as these have been developed within the last sixty years. The advent of machinery, especially of steam and electricity; the huge increase of population and its concentration in great cities; the amazing swiftness and continuousness of international communication; the immense increase in the pace and range of men's living, thinking, desiring; the gigantic organizations of capital and of labour; the influence, both stimulative and repellent, of the great French Revolution, in the attempt of the *bourgeois* to remodel society and the State in accordance with the ideas of the sceptical Encyclopædists; and, still more, the propagandist force of the Marxist, utterly immanentist or directly irreligious, Socialism: all this, and the like, has unitedly produced conditions and problems of an acuteness and difficulty without a match in the human past.

Here, we are concerned with this huge complex of troubles and aspirations, now seething all around us, only in so far as it affects Eternal Life. Let us, then, first consider briefly the attitude of Marx to our group of experiences and convictions; let us next elucidate how and why not only Socialism, but our present social condition generally, is unfavourable, or directly hostile, to that deepest religious life; and, finally, what are the elements in this situation generally, and what are the symptoms observable amongst Socialists in particular, which are already satisfactory or hopeful for the future.

1. *Karl Marx* (born in Treves in 1818; died in London in 1883), as his collaborator Friedrich Engels tells us, made "the two great discoveries

of the Materialistic Conception of History, and of the Secret of Capitalist Production; and through these discoveries Socialism became a Science." That conception of History is simply the affirmation of the continuous process of Development of all things spiritual and material, a process in which nothing is permanent except this eternal Becoming and Dissolution, as Marx and Engels tell us they found it in Hegel. But they hailed with joy Feuerbach's elimination of the dualism (still retained by Hegel) between Spirit and Matter, and the same Feuerbach's latest, frank proclamation of the entire spiritual life of man as the product of mere matter. For Marx, as for Feuerbach, there thus exists no God; man is not essentially distinct from the brute; thinking is only a chemical process; death is the end of all.

Yet Marx and Engels consider that they have apprehended the evolutionary process more deeply, again, than Feuerbach, through their discovery that "production, and, next to production, the exchange of the products, is the basis of all social order"; that "in every society which arises in history the distribution of the products, and therewith the social articulation into classes or ranks, depends upon what, and how, men produce in such a society, and upon how these products are exchanged therein. Thus the final causes of all social and political changes are to be sought, not in Philosophy, but in Economics." And this fundamental law and vital movement, of itself and quietly, eliminates all religion. For with mankind's recognition of the fundamentally economic character of its entire life, a new social order arises, with a new law and a new morality; whilst religion disappears when man, thus fully awake, enters upon the Socialist period of human history.

We can here pass over the capitalistic question; but must, for a moment, remind ourselves how this system, in its original, Marxist form, wages a relentless war against all the natural organizations which are not the one (here sole and omnipotent) organization of the State. For the State here does not simply represent, co-ordinate, regulate, and supplement the narrower, yet deeper and more primitive, organizations of the family, the clan, the class, the nation, society; but obviously supplants them all, since it possesses, distributes, regulates, commands simply everything. And this action of the State operates according to rigidly equalitarian, strictly secularist standards: marriage becomes a shifting, temporary union; the family, a co-ordination of so-many citizens of the all-providing State; and education, a training in economics by the State, for the State.[1]

2. Now if we look around amongst the classes, the necessities, and the movements in view, we find, I think, that three causes are, varyingly, yet ever more or less, operative in the direction of Secularism—of the insistently, even angrily, *this*-world attitude here still so predominant.

(1) Man's capacity of attention and of persistent operative interest is essentially limited; and only great, unbroken traditions of spiritual experience and of mental training are, in ordinary circumstances, able somewhat to extend these limits. But those great traditions are, for the most part, practically unknown in the world we are now considering. Hence men will, here, whatever may be their deepest requirements, be absorbed in other, more shallow yet more immediate-seeming, needs.

These, the needs of physical existence, are, nowadays and especially in these classes, dependent, and are vividly seen to be dependent, upon national and international, financial and social con-

[1] The quotations are from F. Engels' *Die Entwicklung des Socialismus von der Utopie zur Wissenschaft*, 4th ed. 1891, pp. 26, 23; and from his *Dühring's Unwälzung*, p. 253. I take these quotations, and most of my description, from the very careful discussion, "Der Socialismus," in Victor Cathrein's *Moralphilosophie*, 2nd ed. 1893, vol. ii. pp. 117-219; pp. 124, 125.

ditions of the most various and varying, complex, and hardly calculable character. And again, all this is on a gigantic scale. Two years ago, the railway workers of France almost succeeded in suspending the entire traffic of the country, and were stopped only by the Army ordered on to the railway lines by an ex-Socialist Premier even more resolute than the Syndicalist leaders of that revolution. This year in Germany the Socialists have returned over one hundred representatives to the Reichstag; and, if Germany possessed proportional representation, they would avowedly occupy double that number of seats. And at the present moment England is in the throes of a coal strike with over one million miners idle, with all the mines at a standstill for a fortnight, and with already nearly a million of other workmen deprived of employment. And the problem of the chronically unemployed in all the great cities is more anxious still, and indeed appears to be practically insoluble.

What wonder, then, that those who find themselves the very subjects of such crushing necessities and of such immense excitements—necessities and excitements all well within the range of the senses and of the least-developed mentality—show little or no ethical or spiritual experience and requirement? We should be face to face with a great moral miracle, did the case stand otherwise.

(2) And to this absorption in the clear surface and away from the dimmer depths of life, is added a revulsion against the great Churches, and largely even against the Chapels and Sects, on grounds of political and social grievances, real or imaginary. The *bourgeois's* old hatred of the noble has, here, been in part continued, in part replaced, by the worker's hostility to the capitalist; and both these incensed classes still largely see in the Church the ally of the Castle, and in the Clergy the paid apologists of the exploiters and oppressors of labour. And such an alienation from organized religious worship and instruction, even where it is almost entirely political or social in its origin, cannot fail gravely to weaken the religious inclinations of those concerned. The comparative ease and peace which characterized the disestablishment of the Church in France speaks volumes upon this point.

(3) Nevertheless, neither the absorption nor the revulsion suffices fully to explain the phenomenon; we only get to its bottom if we add a widespread ignorance, often a grave misunderstanding, of the nature and history of religion and of mankind, and of the perennial character and necessities of the human soul. All that excited absorption in

the physical requirements, and in the social-economical basis, of our earthly existence naturally disposes men to materialistic, mechanical views, and to ignore, misunderstand, or silence the deepest demands of the soul. True, these demands have, in the past, time after time, victoriously surmounted, or swept away, all lesser necessities, howsoever tangible and urgent they may have seemed; and these same demands still appear in man's universal restlessness until he reaches those unfailing fountains of Eternal Life. Yet meanwhile, and on the surface, the majority of the men in question are still satisfied by such clever and clear superficialities as are offered by writers like Buckle, Haeckel, Clodd.

Indeed, the men of this mentality must also inevitably fail to understand the true nature of human society and the power of social arrangements, although these are the very things in which they are so absorbed. Thus they offer us, in *doctrinaire* Socialism, a distinct, indeed a highly militant and dogmatic, Creed, of an apocalyptic, millennial character. A time of universal peace and plenty, of absolute equality and entire contentment, is here quite certainly to come, and quite certainly by means of the Social Revolution alone; and all this is to be here below, entirely within, entirely through, our simply human powers and earthly lives. It is a sort of Kingdom of God, but without a King and without a God—an awakening of man to all his wants; a finding that these wants are all sublunar; and a satisfying of all these sublunar wants by purely sublunar means.

And all this is to be achieved with a completeness demanding a faith more difficult than any of the great religious faiths. For here we are not simply to achieve an amelioration of man's earthly lot, an insight into the spiritual utility of suffering and of trial, and a conviction that our final perfection and peace can only find their preparation here, and their full achievement only hereafter; but this our earthly life alone, and its non-religious elements alone, are to satisfy man, by the sheer perfection of their development and harmonization. John Stuart Mill could ask himself, when a richly cultivated young man of twenty: "Suppose that all your objects in life were realized; that all the changes in institutions and opinions which you are looking forward to, could be completely effected at this very instant; would this be a great joy and happiness to you?" And "an irresistible self-consciousness distinctly answered 'No'!" (*Autobiography*, ed. 1875, pp. 133, 134). But here we have souls, of much less development and self-knowledge, which proclaim an unhesitating "yes."

And finally, since happiness is here to arise entirely from the perfection of exclusively earthly conditions achieved by exclusively earthly means, it is plain that all other-worldly, invisible, eternal inclinations and seekings, even if any logical basis remained for them here, have to be rigorously suppressed. For that earthly perfection, and the consequent happiness, are indeed completely achievable, but they are very difficult to achieve. Hence no distractions, no waste of energy, are permissible here. Man, even in his holiday dreamings, is no more to be an amphibious creature, longing somehow for the boundless ocean; he is no more to be a denizen of two worlds and a link between them; but he is ever to be simply, exclusively, a land-animal, a creature of earth alone. We thus get an immense further enforcement of the secularism already furnished by the absorption and revulsion considered farther back.

3. Yet we can also trace three sets of conditions and symptoms, in this great social movement, which are full of promise for religion.

(1) First, there are certain general effects which in various degrees and ways, reach all men throughout the countries concerned. We all of us are here put face to face with great masses of men who, if without the strength, are yet also

without the maladies, of full education ; who are, thus, without the dainty, dreamy scepticism so largely prevalent amongst the leisured classes ; and who frequently manifest a crude and violent, yet sincere and simple, even self-sacrificing faith, however materialistic and anti-religious most of its form, and much of its substance, may still, unfortunately, be. Certainly, the perfection of the Socialist organization would be impossible without the presence of much personal unselfishness.

And again, all this Socialistic militancy certainly does some real good outside of the Socialist ranks, since it awakens and keeps awake the middle and upper classes in various much-needed ways, so that the complete disappearance of some such incitement would probably be almost as noxious as would be its triumph. Our social problem indeed is, in its substance, utterly real, natural, inevitable ; and the Socialists have no more caused this its substance than they could cure it. The Socialists, however, can and do call the forcible attention of the classes, and of the bureaucrats, ever so averse to facing reality, to the grave troubles and requirements of the masses.

(2) And this double gain, in reality of mind and in public-spiritedness, brought by the Social Problem to the general public, is, or can be, a

special advantage for religious souls and for the Churches, especially as regards the experience and conviction of Eternal Life. The advantage here is in two directions.

For one thing, this gigantic Social Problem brings home, even to the sleepy traditionalist or recalcitrant official, with demonstrative clearness and clamorous intensity, how large is the dependence of the growth and power of the religious experiences and requirements, amongst average human beings, upon a certain security and stability in the means and circumstances of physical existence, and especially upon some family life and leisure. The cases of the Galilean "poor," *i.e.* small fishermen and husbandmen, whom Our Lord declared to be blessèd, or, again, the Umbrian peasantry and workmen addressed by the *Poverello* of Assisi in his homely open-air discourses, are here nowise in point. The problem is not simply intensified for us, it is radically changed; and this change has made us realize, more clearly than ever before, the great dependence of the chances and articulation of religion upon the various social conditions of the average human beings addressed by it. This we now see to apply even to the Primitive Christian and Mediæval world and religion, and it is doubly applicable to our present conditions.

This indeed is the element of profound truth parodied, because taken as complete, by the Socialists, and almost as keenly, but more wisely, apprehended by the various Christian Social workers. For the latter, with whatever excesses or even errors, all strongly realize the necessity, for average man, of some social and sanitary roominess and decency, some home life, some assurance concerning the morrow, and some little leisure, as preliminaries for the growth within him of the religious instincts and of an echo to religious appeals. Cardinal Manning in England, Bishop Ketteler in Germany, and the distinguished M. le Play in France, all vividly apprehended this truth, as indeed did Pope Leo the Thirteenth himself. And the late Bishop Westcott and the present Bishop Gore, amongst Anglicans, have strenuously worked in the same direction.

And then, secondly, a large and close occupation with these masses of our fellows, and with these social problems, brings, in the long run and in the most unexpected, overwhelming ways, an admirable further revelation and example, to believers and unbelievers alike, of the costly twofold source of Christianity's perennial youth and renovative power. For Christianity is thus obliged to be, more than ever, busy with the

Temporal and Spatial, the Physical and Psychical, since now it has to be all this according to sciences, and in the midst of circumstances, and on a scale, unknown even a century ago; so that, more than ever, any exclusive Other-Worldliness, all quietistic suffering and listless waiting, would be treason against both man and God. Thus less than ever is the Immanentism and the Incarnational Doctrine of Christianity an empty theory; indeed, its insistence that spirit shall penetrate and transform matter, and shall thus awaken and develop its own self, has never in the history of the world had so gigantic a field, and such immense difficulties, in which to show and to develop its power, as it possesses now. In reality only a vivid faith in the utterly real and perfect God, only the experience and love of Eternal Life, are able, in the long run, to supply a sufficiently deep, steady, and tender love and service of our fellow-creatures, precisely where, in their actual condition, they most require, because they least deserve, such selfless devotion. No wise regulations, no scientific insight are here, by themselves, any substitutes for this most difficult and most essential, this alone creative, disposition.

This heroic love will thus be gained *for* men but not simply *from* men; it will be acquired in close union with God. And this union will demand, and will produce, a profound self-knowledge and self-hatred within the devoted lover of his fellows; a deep, genuine, daily turning away of the whole soul from the shallow, naturalistic self. Asceticism, in its noblest and widest sense and forms, will thus again operate as the great instrument of love; and will ever purify and replenish that expansive outgoing to creatures and intimacy with them. And the second, the Other-World movement, the sense of Eternal Life, will precisely correspond to, and continue, that Transcendence in Our Lord's life and teaching which the best historical criticism is again discovering as one (indeed as the chief) of the two driving forces operative there, and which ever anew reawakens the life of Christianity.

Yet it is only the two movements together, the Transcendence in the Immanence, and the Eternal in the Temporal—only this tension and duality in harmony and union, which constitute the Christian spirit's flower and strength. And surely never was there a finer field for the heroically joyous practice of these two movements together, for the fructification of each by the other, and for the full power of the Christian spirit which is their origin and their result, than lies before us now. Sir Charles Booth, in summing up his ten years' closest study of the conditions of the poorer and working classes of London, tells us, in spite of his very evident natural prepossessions against ecclesiasticism and celibacy: "The saintly life of a St. Martin, sharing his cloak with the beggar, is incompatible with family duties. But the saintly, self-sacrificing life is that which strikes the imagination of the poor as nothing else does. . . . To do effective work among the poor of London, a single life is essential." Hence, in discussing the causes of the alienation of the working classes from the Churches, Booth can declare: "The Secularist propaganda is not a very powerful influence; the last twenty years have witnessed a notable change in this respect. The successes at the polls (for the Board of Guardians, etc.) of men and women who, in the name of religion, are giving their lives to the service of the people, is one of the noteworthy facts of democratic rule." Indeed, "to live a life of voluntary poverty seems to be the only road to the confidence of the people in this matter" of religion (*Life and Labour of the People in London*, 3rd Series, "Religious Influences," vol. vii., Summary, 1902, pp. 24, 424, 428).

And let us note how this same religious conviction can alone save our enthusiasms, more necessary and more difficult than ever before, from Utopian fanaticism and from the inevitable reaction into indifference and cynicism. For only by such a faith do we obtain a motive for the most heroic action and devoted love, free from any denial or evasion of the dread facts of human life and human nature, and from any insincere idealization of the past, present, or future. Man here is to do his utmost to improve his fellow-man's earthly lot; but that lot, whilst greatly improvable with time and care, is deliberately held to find its completion in another life alone. And, in this faith, such completion can become real and abiding for each soul; whereas, in the Secularist systems, the perfection which they offer would (if attained) be, even as regards the entire race, only for that race's limited duration.[1]

(3) There are, indeed, symptoms amongst the Socialistic leaders and masses themselves, and especially in the working-class world generally, that certainly the angry secularism, perhaps also the quiet indifference to religion, still so preponderant, are in process of modification or disappearance.

Thus in Germany, Dr. Eduard Bernstein, the Revisionist Socialist leader, in his organ, the

[1] As to the importance of the social factor even for the religious life, and the irreplaceableness of Christianity, with its Transcendence and Immanence, precisely in our present Social troubles, see Professor E. Troeltsch's great book, *Die Soziallehren der Christlichen Kirchen*, 1912, pp. 975-977, 974, 978, 979. Sensible admissions and distinctions appear in V. Cathrein's article, "Sociale Frage," in the *Freiburg Kirchenlexikon*, 1899, vol. xi. coll. 431-436.

*Sozialistische Monatshefte*, now modifies Marxism in a more idealist and religious direction. Indeed, Professor Troeltsch, so circumspect and so profoundly experienced in the currents of German thought, can declare: " The element in Marx's doctrine which constituted a particular view of life, is now already in process of complete decomposition "; and " it is very probable that Social Democracy, the more its dreams of progress and its enthusiasm over development are damped by the facts of life and by disillusions, will hand over its believers to the Christian Sects— since the Socialists have presumably lost for ever all trust and all attraction towards the great Churches " (" Die Kirche im Leben der Gegenwart," in *Weltanschauung*, 1911, pp. 447, 436).

In Belgium, M. Van der Velde is certainly friendly to religion, although he still treats it as a simply individual concern.

In Italy, Giuseppe Rensi is the exponent of an ethico-religious Socialism; and Dr. Angelo Crespi, who lives as much in England as in Italy, has moved out of the Socialist system into an organic and spiritual conception of Society, and an explicit recognition of Institutional Christianity.

And in France, M. Georges Sorel, the Syndicalist leader, and a learned exponent of Marxism, presents us (in spite of considerable disjointedness of thought and not a few crudities and injustices as to past events and still living persons) with certain interesting aspirations, or even convictions, concerning Spirituality and Eternal Life. Thus in his article, *La Religion d'Aujourdhui*, 1909, and in his Preface to its Italian translation, 1911, he tells us: " The feeling of mystery is strictly allied to pessimism ; and pessimism is the unfailing source of ceaseless religious renovation "; indeed, "amongst ourselves to-day, the feeling of mystery continues highly adapted to excite the desire for the very highest activities, since a man's conviction is strong in proportion to the domination exercised within his soul by this feeling of mystery." And Sorel is alertly opposed to all Pantheism. Thus : " The religious man understands life only by referring it to a Power, superior to Nature, with Which he can enter into relation." " The problem of the relations between Religion and Science will, without doubt, ever more passionately interest our successors." " One of the grave consequences of the Pantheistic tendencies is a persistent elimination of the doctrine of Sin ; indeed, even Christianity, as we have it now, has singularly attenuated the old teachings as to Grace and Sin." " Modern piety would be quite content to find the essence of Religion, with Renan, in sentimental effusions." And he respects Institutional

Christianity: "Catholicism will, without doubt, live on in France, but it will undergo large restrictions; there will be only a limited number of believers, but these will be genuine Christians" (from the Italian translation, *La Religione d' Oggi*, 1911, pp. 8–10; 14, 15; 125).

In his *Les Illusions du Progrès*, second edition, 1911, we have a striking hatred of the *Encyclopédistes*, and a noble hunger for self-renunciation and spiritual greatness. Thus: "At the end of the Eighteenth Century the terror of Sin, the respect for Chastity, and Pessimism, disappeared more or less simultaneously; hence Christianity disappeared also." "All our efforts must tend to prevent the *bourgeois* ideas from poisoning the class which is now rising; we can never do too much to break every link between the people and the literature of the Eighteenth Century." Again: "Catholicism can regain its youth only if a crisis occurs within it, under the action of men formed to the spiritual life in the monastic institutions. History proves that such crises can provoke prodigious effects of" spiritual "greatness." "The present hour," indeed, "is not favourable to the idea of greatness; but other times will come, since history tells us that greatness cannot indefinitely be lacking to that portion of humanity which possesses the incomparable treasures of classical culture and of the Christian tradition" (pp. 32, 286, 329, 335). And in the *Réflections sur la Violence*, 1909, he admits that no historical movement is truly efficacious unless its end is accepted as an absolute finality.

Altogether, we are here not far from the experience and conception of Eternal Life, its bracing costliness and its irreplaceable greatness, as operative within the creaturely soul, the servant of the Perfect Reality, God.[1]

## CHAPTER XII

### INSTITUTIONAL RELIGION

Introductory—Strict necessity, yet apparently fatal decline, of Institutional Religion—Causes of this decline—Institutional Religion and Eternal Life.

WE have reserved, for this last chapter of our survey, the consideration of the Institutional Religions, in so far as these are the homes and training-grounds of the experiences and convictions concerning Eternal Life, and in so far as they bring helps, or occasion obstacles, to

---

[1] This last division owes much to the competence and kind aid of Dr. Angelo Crespi.

these convictions, or, contrariwise, are themselves checked and purified by these convictions.

Let us, then, first show clearly that religious Institutions are indeed the normal requirements, expressions, and instruments of the religious sense; that Religion and its Institutions cannot, if they would be strong in themselves and influential outside of their own special territory, stand aloof from the other ranges and levels of human life, with their corresponding organizations; and that, nevertheless, there are numerous, broad symptoms all around us of a deep-seated, widespread, and still spreading, alienation from all Institutional Religion.

Let us, next, explain the particular insights and aids, and the corresponding special insensibilities and deadlocks, traceable, as actually operative at present, within such Institutionalism. Here we shall take, as representative of the religious Institutions, the Roman Catholic Church, as by far the oldest, most widespread, and most consistent of all such bodies; and as alone, so it happens, known and well known from within to the present writer.

And let us finally show how and why the experiences and convictions concerning Eternal Life surround, penetrate, supplement, purify, and check the Durational, Institutional necessities, habits, and aids; and let us illustrate such an unconquerably deep and all-fructifying sense of the Eternal, Perfect God, as developed within and through such Institutions, by the life and utterances of a few recent spiritual seers and heroes at work under these conditions.

1. It is now ever increasingly clear, to all deep, impartial students, that Religion has ever primarily expressed and formed itself in *Cultus*, in social organization, social worship, intercourse between soul and soul and between soul and God; and in Symbols and Sacraments, in contacts between spirit and matter. Where we cannot trace this Institutional Element in a soul's life, we always find either that this soul's religion has constantly been weak; or that the soul is suffering under a reaction from some religious excess, and is losing its religion; or that it is in process of gaining some institutionalism; or, finally, that its religion, though non-institutional, is indeed delicate and deep, but that this religion was first awakened in this soul by some fervent institutional religionist. We certainly find the Institutional at work, both as cause and as effect (often all the more powerfully because everywhere assumed rather than anywhere formally expressed), in the great Israelitish and Jewish

Prophets; in our Lord and the Apostles, especially St. Paul; in Origen, Augustine, Aquinas; but also in Luther and Calvin; especially again in St. Teresa, in Pascal, Bossuet, Fénelon; and in Laud, Lancelot Andrewes, and William Law. And again in such modern philosophers as Nicolas of Coes, Leibniz, and Berkeley; and, in our own times, in Rosmini, Trendelenburg, Fechner, the Cairds. The same element of Institutionalism is, of course, observable in post-Christian Judaism, in Mohammedanism, in Brahmanism, in Buddhism. And this social-institutional need of Religion turns out to be threefold.

(1) There is the need of Common Worship. Professor Troeltsch has admirably shown that this necessity is rooted in the very nature of man and of man's religion, and hence is logically prior to, and more general than, any and every positive incorporation by the founders of the great historical religions. "It is a law of social psychology that nowhere can men exist alongside of each other, with merely parallel feelings and thoughts, but that thousandfold relations subsist between individual men; and that, out of these relations, there everywhere arise social circles, which contain superordinations and subordinations of their members, and

which all require a concrete centre. And this general law applies also to the religious life." Indeed, " one of the clearest results of all religious history and religious psychology is that the essence of all Religion is, not the Dogma and Idea, but the Cultus and Communion, the living intercourse with the Deity—an intercourse of the entire community having its vital roots in Religion and deriving its ultimate power of thus conjoining individuals from its faith in God." And hence " whatever the future may bring us, we cannot expect a certainty and force of the knowledge of God and of His redemptive power to subsist without Communion and Cultus. And so long as a Christianity of any kind shall exist at all, it will be conjoined with a Cultus, and with Christ holding a central position in this Cultus." Indeed, " the absence of Communion and of Cultus is the specific malady of modern Christianity and of modern Religion generally " (*Die Bedeutung der Geschichtlichkeit Jesu für den Glauben*, 1911, pp. 27, 25, 29, 25).

We know that Our Lord instituted a Preaching Band of Apostles, and that St. Paul (carrying out Our Lord's spirit and the necessities of His work) organized the Church with all the main outlines of the Institution as we have them still. But, in any case, the Church would have been, and is, a necessary consequence and necessary instrument of Christianity; the two, in the long run, ever rise and sink, stand and fall, together.

(2) But religious psychology and religious history testify, surely, in a similar manner, to another, closely connected point, which Professor Troeltsch will not allow. Like Harnack, Eucken, and modern German Liberal Protestants generally, Troeltsch is unfortunately very ready to see Magic, and exclusively Heathen Rites and Mysteries, in the attribution of any productive efficacy (as distinct from a representation of effects produced solely by the Spirit in spirits) to any Symbol or Sacrament whatsoever. And yet our study of the Idealist philosophers has probably already convinced us of the artificiality of every Theory of Knowledge which ignores or minimizes the essential, persistent contribution furnished by sense-stimulations and non-mental causes and objects to our entire knowledge and our most elementary self-consciousness. It would no doubt be Materialism were we to attribute a direct, exclusive efficacy, in the attainment of our knowledge and self-consciousness, to sense-stimulation and to material things; and were we to ignore our spirit, responsive and active here throughout. And similarly, it is Superstition if we attribute to sensible contacts and to material

things any direct and exclusive efficacy; and if we ignore the action and intention of the individual soul, or of the community of souls, which experience or apply such contacts. But, in either case, to ignore the body is, surely, as little in accordance with psychology and history, as it is to ignore the community.

The anti-sacramental passion, indeed, as it shows itself, *e.g.* in Wycliffe, seems to have been in its origin, and to have had as its very understandable causes, a revolt against, and terror of, interference and domination by a priestly caste, especially in matters social and political; and a conviction that the priestly power stands and falls with the sacramental claims. Yet, here as everywhere, to cut the knot is not to resolve the difficulty; and in fact the elimination of sensible impressions and of sensible things, as joint-awakeners and joint-vehicles of spiritual life, has against it all the analogies of the various departments of human existence. In any case, the appeal to psychology and history, as decisive in favour of Cultus, carries logically with it the admission of *some* Sensible Signs as contributing, when used by souls in and with this Cultus, to the spiritual awakening and sanctification of such souls.

Here again we have indications of the use and of the recommendation of such efficacious sensible signs in Our Lord's life; and we find them most explicit and prominent in St. Paul's life and writings, and everywhere implied or taught in the Fourth Gospel. Yet, in any case, such Signs belong to the necessities and fruitful functioning of general human psychology; and hence, in special forms and degrees, they belong to Religion also.

(3) And there is the third generally human, and specifically religious, necessity, which Professor Troeltsch again sees with admirable vividness—the need for Religion as a whole (although itself a distinct, and in its way complete, experience, life, and organization) ever to keep aware of, to accept or to combat, to assimilate or to reject, the various chief forms and conclusions presented by the other complexes and organizations of human life. Religion, indeed, is not directly either Ethics or Philosophy, Economics or Art; yet, at the peril of emptiness and sterility, it has to move out into, to learn from, to criticize, and to teach, all these other apprehensions and activities.

Here it is that Ritschlianism, still so vigorously represented by Wilhelm Hermann, is essentially artificial and inadequate. Thus Professor Hermann rejects all Mysticism, as a mere subjectivism which is ever incomparably beneath the great objects of Religion. Yet a particular capacity and disposition of the soul is simply necessary for the soul's apprehension of God; and the acknowledgment of this mediation need no more render me self-engrossed or conceited than I am thus influenced by my awareness that a particular sense of vision, in my diminutive eyes, is essential to my perception of that immense orb, the sun. Indeed, in both cases, these necessities and their supplies come from God, and I can love Him in these His ordinations and gifts.

And then Hermann insists upon Religion being complete in two experiences and acceptances alone —those of the Categorical Imperative of the Moral Conscience; and those of the Historical Jesus, as the uniquely perfect realization of this Imperative, and hence as the unique revelation of the depths of Reality, and the unique means towards the human soul's execution of that Imperative. Yet Religion, though closely related to Ethics, is not identical with them; nor are the Ethics to which it is thus related, the legalistic formalism of Kant. And there is an insufferable defiance to History, and to the affinities and genius of Christianity itself, in the restriction (so emphatic in Hermann's scheme) of every degree of genuine religion, of all true prayer, to those who explicitly know and formally acknowledge the historic Jesus's earthly life. Here even the Spanish Inquisitors were larger and more truly Christian.

The fact is that the Christian, indeed the man of any religion, who wishes to make and to keep his religion strong, will doubtless have to live it with all he is and has; but that Christians, and indeed religionists of any kind, cannot (all of them and in the long run) ignore the other activities of man's manifold life, nor simply sacrifice either their religion to these activities or these activities to their religion. Christianity in particular will be unable to do so, because Gnosticism is not true to life. God is the God of the body as He is of the soul; of Science as He is of Faith; of Criticism and Theory as of Fact and Reality. And thus, in the long run and upon the whole, man will, even *qua* spirit, have to grow and to be through conflict and temptation, through darkness and humiliation, and through a triumph hardly won.

Assuredly countless souls, who never heard of these questions and conflicts, have nevertheless become great friends of God: the *Poverello* of Assisi and Joan of Arc, what *did* these glorious spirits know of such trials? But the conditions of Western Europe have radically changed since those ages, and proofs are accumulating, with saddening rapidity, to show that religion cannot remain a joyous possession and a strong influence in these countries and in these times, without, on the part of its educated representatives and followers, any cognizance, acceptance, criticism, or rejection of current philosophical, scientific, economic and other influences and positions. True, the predominant, and apparently most characteristic, trend of the Saints has been towards an exclusive absorption in the direct relations between the soul and God and the soul and other souls. Yet we have already seen how large has been the occupation, of precisely some of the greatest of the Saints, with Philosophy, with the larger Politics, and with Economic questions. And the official Church especially has, from very early times, persistently conceived and practised life, not pietistically, but in a Catholic, *i.e.* an all-inclusive manner.[1]

(4) And yet, have not the institutional Religions, inclusive of those that have developed specially strong religious Organizations and Sacraments, and that have largely adopted or combated Philosophy and Science, lost ground now for many a day, and are they not now losing it very rapidly?

Thus there are now South German Catholic

[1] Concerning Professor Hermann's positions, see my *Mystical Element of Religion*, 1908, vol. ii. pp. 263-275, and the references there given. Dr. Hermann's book, specially considered in this work and in the present book, has now been translated into English as *The Communion of the Christian with God*, London, 1910.

towns, where at most 30 per cent., and North German Protestant towns, where only 3 per cent. of the population, go to Church; and probably not more than a third of the entire German population clings by conviction to Church and Clergy. In Westphalia and the Rhineland, in the Bavarian Highlands and the Austrian Tyrol, strongholds of immemorial, patriarchal faith, Socialism or other Secularisms are admittedly gaining ground.

In France, of the forty million Catholics only about eleven millions appear to attach any value to this profession; the State is, in the widest sense of the term, without religion, and the schools stand outside of all Churches and all Creeds. The number of students for the Priesthood has, up to quite recently, greatly diminished; and the number of Catholic clerics who leave the Church, mostly for some Deism or Scepticism, is considerable.

And especially in Portugal, but also in Spain, and to a considerable extent in Italy, the anti-clerical current is largely anti-Christian or even radically anti-spiritual, and remains powerful, intransigent, alert.

In the United States of America only some two-thirds of their hundred and one millions appear to belong to any of the numerous denominations there; and at least five millions confess themselves to be without religion.

And as to England, there is a marked decline in the social origin and the scholarship of the average Anglican cleric; the Nonconformist ministers appear, in considerable part, carried away, with their flocks, from all deeper and more delicate spirituality, into party politics and "Pleasant Sunday Afternoons"; and the conversions to Rome, so numerous and remarkable between 1845–70, have notably diminished, in both respects, especially during the last decade.[1]

Now the symptoms just described cannot one and all be simply ascribed to the perversity and wickedness of human nature. For it is obvious that human nature remains essentially what it was in the ages when the most institutional of the Churches now still extant was the most popular and the most generally influential of all the organizations within the very lands and races which now show the alienation just indicated. And least of all can a Roman Catholic attempt such an explanation, since his Church has never accepted, indeed has solemnly condemned, the doctrine of a total corruption and blindness of human nature.

But if Institutions, Sacraments, and relations,

[1] The figures for the continental countries given here are taken from the very careful article, "Die Zukunftsaufgaben der Religion," by the late Professor H. J. Holtzmann, in *Die Christliche Religion*, vol. ii. 2nd ed. 1908, forming part of *Die Kultur der Gegenwart*.

both friendly and hostile, towards the various manifestations within the other complexes of life, are right and necessary for Religion; if Religion is the deepest truth and the ultimate joy of life; and if men still everywhere possess some glimpses of truth and experiences of grace and of goodness, and some aspirations after more of such preveniences of God—where lies the mischief?

2. Now the present writer has long and profoundly benefited by Institutional Religion, and he watches wistfully its present-day operation and men's alienation from it; he does so from within the most ancient, the most powerful, and the richest of such Institutions, the Roman Catholic Church; and he is fully certain that what he may accurately diagnose here applies, *mutatis mutandis*, to all Institutional Religions throughout the world. He finds, then, that the essential strength and attraction, and the actual weakness and repulsiveness, of such Institutional Religion are closely intertwined; and that they can be presented in five pairs of nearly related power and defect. The first two pairs are primarily concerned with intellectual matters; the last three pairs, with moral affairs. I take them here approximately in the order of their increasing influence with the majority of men.

(1) The Roman Catholic Church continues the immemorially ancient tradition of a large and continuous utilization, discussion, acceptance or rejection of Philosophical Systems and Scientific Hypotheses on the part of Religion. What was right for the author of the Book of Wisdom, for St. Paul, and for the author of the Fourth Gospel, for Augustine, the Pseudo-Dionysius, and Aquinas, is right and good for this Church. It is the unity of this Church's Christian-Scholastic thought which doubtless largely accounts for the relative success of Roman Catholicism in Germany, against the Socialists, with *their* unified, materialistic outlook. And the future will (with a provisional and relative pacification of our modern, storm-tossed world) bring also, we may be sure, a great increase of this desire for some such coherency of thought. And, again, the maintenance of this Scholastic tradition has rendered more easily possible that sympathetic penetration and presentation of mediæval thought, which are so necessary for the clear understanding of our modern ideals and impulsions; and it has also helped men to unveil the very real insufficiencies of the Idealist Epistemology and other kindred weaknesses of modern philosophy. Bäumker and Denifle in Germany, Cardinal Mercier in Belgium, Toniolo in Italy, and Maher,

Walker, and Joseph Rickaby in England, are names genuinely respected by all competent workers.

And yet two great weaknesses and dangers are here intertwined with these considerable advantages. For the absolute need (on the part of Religion) of Philosophy in general, and the practical need (on the part of the Church, at any one period of its existence) of some particular system of Philosophy, have here nearly coalesced with the still deeper, far more delicate, and ever different, necessities and authority of the religious Experience and Tradition, and of the Church, their chief witness and interpreter. Philosophy, in itself, is essentially free; *i.e.* Philosophy may and does simply follow its own specific requirements and self-criticisms, or it is nothing.

This liberty of Philosophy leaves to the Church Authority the fullest right and duty to discountenance or condemn this or that philosophical doctrine, or even system, as incompatible with the Christian Faith. And it leaves this same Authority entirely untrammelled in the maintenance of some particular system of Philosophy, as the general intellectual starting-point of its clerical students. Philosophers constantly criticize each other, on the ground that this or that particular conception or system does not adequately recognize some general and persistent experience of mankind. Should not then the chief home and guardian of the religious and Christian life possess the right and duty of a far more authoritative criticism and condemnation? And as to the particular system adopted, he would, indeed, be a bold man who would insist, without hesitation, upon the systems of Kant or Hegel, or of Descartes or Leibniz, as, upon the whole, more adequate to the abiding necessities of the human mind and of the religious and Christian experience, and as more appropriately penetrative of the Christian theology throughout the centuries, than is an intelligent Neo-Scholasticism.

But the liberty of Philosophy is indeed incompatible with the acceptance, as obligatory, of a philosophical proposition or system as true, simply and directly because of its imposition by Church Authority. And yet it is plain that the apparent eternity and sanctity of Scholasticism is produced by such a conjunction and coalescence of ecclesiastical authority and philosophical appeal; and that the bitter, and often excessive reactions, which so readily turn against all Ontology in Philosophy and all Institutionalism in Religion, are, in considerable part, determined by this *bloc* system, this theological pressure in philosophical questions.

And then, Aristotelianism (even when enriched with certain Neo-Platonist doctrines and when modified by Scholasticism) is profoundly unhistorical, in its entire temper and outlook. It would certainly be possible to remedy this defect, now so dangerous, by the study of the most living parts of Plato, Aristotle, and Plotinus, and of the Ethics and spirituality of Aquinas, in a sympathetically historical and critical manner. Such a method would teach the student how to trace the growth of philosophical thought and the development of the Christian consciousness, and how to criticize and value the stages and formulations in each according to the central principles and substance of each. And these principles and this substance would be laid bare by a study of their entire historical growth and development, and would be known and relished in the daily practice and testing applied to them by a devotedly earnest and Christian life.

As regards discoveries and hypotheses in Physical and Natural Science, it is highly instructive to note how entirely silent concerning them the recent most strenuous papal campaign against all and every " Modernism " has remained throughout. Thus neither the Inquisition's Decree *Lamentabili*, condemning sixty-five propositions, nor the Papal Encyclical *Pascendi*, probably the longest Encyclical ever issued, says one word about them. Yet *there* lay, for centuries, the most dangerous " Modernism." Thus Galileo's proposition, " the sun is the centre of the world, and therefore immovable," was in 1616 unanimously condemned by the Inquisition, as " foolish and absurd in philosophy and formally heretical"; and in 1633 Galileo was obliged solemnly to abjure that doctrine before the same tribunal. And not till 1820 was permission given to teach that proposition as simply true; and only in 1835 did the Congregation of the Index withdraw Heliocentric books from its list. Mental Pathology and Biological Evolution have, indeed, also had their troubles since then; but, upon the whole, scientific workers have, since (and outside of) the Heliocentric controversy, suffered comparatively little. We can then reasonably assume that a tolerable latitude is assured to Physico-Mathematical, perhaps also to Biological, research and science, in the Roman Catholic Church, now and hereafter.[1]

---

[1] For Philosophy within the Roman Catholic Church, see Léon Ollé-Laprune, *La Philosophie et le Temps Present*, 2nd ed. 1894, especially pp. 333-360; and Professor Maurice Blondel, *Lettre sur les Exigeances de la pensée contemporaine en matière d'apologétique et sur la méthode de la philosophie dans l'étude du problème religieux*, 1896. And for Science and Church Authority, see Dr. F. X. Funk's very careful "Zur Galilei-Frage," in his *Kirchengeschichtliche Abhandlungen und Untersuchungen*, 1899, vol. ii. pp. 444-476:

(2) The next pair concerns History. This is doubtless, with the pair immediately to follow, *the* crux of every Institutional Religion, and especially of one so deeply Historical as is the Roman Catholic Church. Yet here again, indeed here particularly, there can be no doubt that the Religions, and Rome especially, are right in their general principles; since only in and through History, only by means of concrete happenings in time and space, does man awaken to, does he apprehend, Eternal Life and God, and do they penetrate and win him. Nor will any systematic or radical distinction between Historical Happenings and Dogmatic "Facts" or Doctrines really suffice here. For not only Rome, but all genuine Religion absolutely requires, at every stage, *Ontology*, a really extant God, and really *happened* Historical Facts and Persons. Indeed, Christianity's greatness resides especially in its all-pervasive and persistent Incarnational trend; since God, the Eternal Spirit, here reveals Himself to us, and touches us, in Duration and through Matter. Indeed, it has been under the influence of this same Christianity that man's

and, generally, Andrew White's copious *History of the Warfare of Science with Theology in Christendom*, 1903, 2 vols., especially vol. ii. pp. 97-167. Important reflexions suggested by the latter book are contained in George Tyrrell's "The Rights and Limits of Theology," in his *Through Scylla and Charybdis*, 1906.

apprehension has, slowly but surely, been deepened and refined concerning the difference between Historical Facts and purely Ideal Symbols; and that man, nevertheless, feels, in his Religion, the need, as imperiously as ever, of *some* assured instances of such Facts. And thus Rome, the chief representative of Christianity, which is itself so nobly Ontological and Factual, cannot but be and remain profoundly wedded to Reality and Facts.

But the difficulties here appear to be as follows. The Religions, as we are now getting more and more to know them in their historical growth, always indeed proceed from some actual Happenings; and the faith of the votaries of the Religions always necessarily includes a continuous conviction as to the historical character of these Happenings. But these same Religions also live, and live still more, by their penetration of the Spiritual Substance and Meaning of these Happenings, by their sense of the Eternal's Self-manifestation in these temporal events; and—here the difficulty comes in—they symbolize this their interpretation of the Factual Happenings by means of fact-like historical pictures which (once a keen discrimination between factual and non-factual becomes irresistible) cannot be taken as directly, simply factual in the manner and degree in which those Happenings can be taken. The later documents of the Hexateuch, and certain scenes in the Fourth Gospel, are probably the best illustrations of this process.

Now Rome's difficulties here are specially great, yet they are so, in large part, because Rome sees so firmly and so very far. Thus Rome is splendidly aware of Religion's absolute need of a Real God, manifesting Himself in Real Happenings and Effects. And Rome is finely free from all *Fideism* or Pietism; it appeals to historical documents—taken as common sense and good faith know and allow them—as historically cogent proofs of the historical Happenings whose historical character is fundamentally important for this religion. Thus Rome can neither let go the Happenings, *qua* Happenings; nor can it, without a deeply uncatholic pietism, withdraw these Happenings, *qua* Happenings, from the cognizance and criticism of historians. Yet, on the other hand, Rome cannot make the historical evidence other than what it is; nor appeal to it, and yet insist upon keeping it above all discussion; nor change the simple, broad facts that men in the past were but little alive to the difference between Factual Event and Symbolical Narrative, and that men in the present are keenly sensitive to this difference. And yet even to insist upon the strict Factualness of all the factual-seeming narratives, but to abandon the insistence upon the demonstrative force of the documents concerned, would already, no doubt, be a serious modification of the very ancient, predominant attitude of traditional theologians.

Again, there is no Church, with any large following in our Western lands, which has tolerated, or even encouraged, so many local legends, so much floating, uncertain, or even spurious history. And the still large, and relatively ever more influential, peasant element in the Church is very sensitively favourable to such secondary beliefs. And besides, considerable vested interests have grown around such, now mostly severely fixed, traditions. We need only refer to the supposed Apostolic Origin of the Episcopal Sees of France, and to the legend of the Transference of the Holy House from Nazareth to Loretto, beliefs which are late and without serious historical root, yet the challenging of which has required great courage, on the part of such thorough scholars as Monseigneur Duchesne and Canon Ulysse Chevalier; even though the question as to the Origin of the French Sees was already conclusively settled, in the critical sense, by the great Maurist Benedictines two centuries ago.

In such secondary questions the Church Authorities, when conclusive proofs have been furnished, can discover no grave intrinsic difficulties against the return to the earliest constituents or forms of such beliefs, forms which are generally sober and serious (as, *e.g.*, here, the sub-Apostolic origin of the Churches of Lyon and of Vienne, and a very ancient picture of the Madonna venerated at Loretto), and the encouragement of those constituents alone. But as to the far more difficult and important matters connected with Biblical, and especially with New Testament and Primitive Christian documents and evidences, the Authorities will doubtless ever insist upon the need for the reasonable and reasoned certainty as to the factual character of a nucleus in the Christian complex of doctrines, and upon the inclusion, within our faith in God and in His Church, of a full conviction that He will never deprive us of such certainty concerning that nucleus; upon all the great Christian doctrines as finally true, as interconnected, and as all either directly descriptive of actual spiritual Realities and Persons and factual Events, or as closely interpretative and protective of those Realities, Persons, or Events; and, finally, upon the possession by the Church, and by the Church alone, of the grace and the right fully to penetrate, and finally to decide, the spiritual truth and ultimate meaning of Scripture. Yet Theologians, both as Catholics and as reasonable men, will have not to insist upon historians finding more, or different, historical Happenings in documents put forward as historical proofs, than these documents will yield to careful and candid critical analysis. And though this may appear to us now to be far more difficult than were the discriminations so painfully and so slowly effected with respect to "heretical" Astronomy, it may well be that our difficulties do not really appear more difficult to us now, than *their* difficulties appeared to the astronomers and theologians of 1616 and 1633, and that some of these historical troubles of ours may last less long than the two centuries required for the full tolerance of Heliocentrism.[1]

(3) The third conjunction of power and of weakness doubtless affects many who know nothing of Philosophy or of Historical Criticism.

[1] On the general question of the Catholic position as to Holy Scripture (*qua* historical document) and Biblical Criticism, see Mgr. Mignot, Archbishop of Albi, *Lettres sur les Études Ecclésiastiques*, 1908, especially pp. 291–324. Also the friendly controversy between Maurice Blondel, "Histoire et Dogme," and F. von Hügel, "Le Christ Eternel et les Christologies Successives," both in *La Quinzaine* of Paris, 1904. On the legendary element in Church History, see the excellent monograph of Père Hippolyte Delehaye, the Bollandist, *Les Legendes Hagiographiques*, 1905 (English translation, 1910); Mgr. Louis Duchesne's *Fastes Episcopaux de l'Ancienne Gaule*, 3 vols., 1894-99; and Chanoine Ulysse Chevalier, *Nôtre-Dame de Lorette*, 1906.

The Roman Church here insists, with an, alas! increasingly rare, yet immensely true and precious, emphasis, upon the supreme importance of Religious Truth and Religious Unity, and upon the profound loss and wrong of religious error. Certainly the careless accommodation, the easy tolerance and indifference, the horror of all persecution on the ground that it deals with "merely" religious opinions, which is all around us now, cannot be the final word or true ideal for man. For man, at his deepest, longs for Eternal Life, for Abiding Reality and Ultimate Truth; and, if he is seriously religious at all, cannot but regard every further ray of religious light as precious beyond all other gifts. And indifference about religion ever tends either to render such a soul shallow and hard in its other interests and insights; or else to make it feverish and fanatical in sublunar matters, since it will expect from these more than they can possibly yield.

And yet here especially the corresponding trouble is very terrible. For has not this fervour found expression, throughout the centuries and throughout entire countries, in awful cruelties? There is Charlemagne's wholesale enforcement of Baptism upon the heathen Saxons; the extermination of the Waldensians and Albigensians; the Spanish Inquisition, with its thousands of executions; the

Dragonnades of the Huguenots. And we know how already St. Augustine (who died in A.D. 430) vehemently insisted upon the Church's right and duty to use physical force in matters of religious conviction; how Pope Gregory IX., the friend of St. Francis of Assisi, organized, in 1230, the General Inquisition; how numerous Popes, amongst them the grandly incorruptible St. Pius V., helped to render the Spanish Inquisition possible and actual, as a specifically, jealously *ecclesiastical* tribunal; and how the Roman Church, as such, has never renounced this attitude, and indeed actively applies it, in so far as the modern State permits such application. Can we wonder, then, if men shrink from forwarding such an authority?

Here, however, we can readily trace also another current in the Church's history, which admirably combines the deepest zeal and fervour with a sensitive shrinking from the application of physical force in spiritual things. Thus the Church before Constantine (A.D. 307–37) held, quite generally, that to force consciences to the truth is immoral and unchristian; and the Church Father Lactantius, well on in that reign, still insists: "Let the Heathen imitate us Christians; no one is retained amongst us against his will"; "religion is to be defended, not by killing, but by dying"; and "if you try to defend religion by blood, you violate it; for nothing is so much a matter of free willing as is religion" (*Div. Instit.*, bk. v. 19 (12, 22, 23)).

The first execution for heresy occurs in A.D. 385; but St. Martin of Tours and St. Ambrose of Milan protest against it. And St. Gregory the Great (d. 604), perhaps the greatest of all the Popes, peremptorily forbids certain Neapolitan zealots to interfere with the Jews' celebrations of their feasts, and sternly reproves various Bishops of Southern Gaul for compelling Jews to submit to Baptism (Epist. xiii. 12, viii. 27, ix. 6). And again Pope Alexander II., in 1068, and Pope Clement VI. (1342–52), with numerous other Popes, similarly protect the Jews. Indeed, up to 1284, and even still in 1322, the several millions of Castilian Jews were allowed, by Church and State, a separate organization under their own Rabbis, and the fullest observance of all their civil and religious laws.

And then as to modern high theological pronouncements, Cardinal de Lugo, the great Jesuit theologian (he died in 1660), insists that the members of the various Christian sects, of the Jewish and Mohammedan communions, and of the heathen philosophical schools, who achieve their salvation, do so, ordinarily, simply through the aid afforded by God's grace to their good faith in its instinctive concentration upon, and in its practice of, those elements in their respective community's cultus and teaching which are true and good and originally revealed by God (*De Fide*, Disp. xix. Nos. 7, 10; xx. Nos. 107, 194). And Pope Pius IX., the least "liberal" of Doctors, assures his Cardinals: "It is known to us and to you that those who labour under an invincible ignorance concerning our most holy religion, and who zealously observe the Natural Law written by God in the hearts of all men, can, with the aid of the divine light and grace, attain to Eternal Life"; and "Who will dare to draw the limits of such ignorance, in view of the existing immense variety of peoples, minds, and so many other circumstances?" (*Recueil des Allocutions de Pie IX.*, Paris, 1865, pp. 480, 340).

Indeed, the Church's grandly bold inclusion of the entire Old Testament in the Christian Canon, against the powerful and protracted hostility of the Gnostics, involves the admission that polygamy and the *Lex talionis* can be practised and proclaimed, at rudimentary stages of Revelation, by God's own Saints and Revealers; and hence that the various degrees of God's truth and light, and the difference of value between them, are nearly as unspeakable as is that truth itself.

Again, the Church's excommunications are admittedly fallible; hence exclusions and consequent schisms are not, of necessity, simply the fault of those thus excluded. And certainly, even where such fault seems clear, we very soon find unmistakable evidences of various degrees of truth and of grace in the souls that grow up in these separate organizations. Cardinal Manning, as is well known, strongly emphasized this fact, in his last years, with regard to Anglicans.

And finally, the very great variety amongst the types of spirituality represented, well within the Roman Church, by different periods, different religious orders, and different theological schools, also aids towards this, very important, indeed essential, breadth and many-sidedness.

It appears only necessary that all this larger, gentler, and deeply Christian current shall become universal and instinctive, for Roman Catholicism (thus most fervent without fanaticism and universally just and encouraging without indifference) once again, and more than ever, to become fully lovable and entirely trusted. In any case, not even bigotry and persecution must drive us into indifference or scepticism; since these latter diseases of the soul, amidst other great evils, furnish ready excuses, or provocatives for those contrary extremes, or, at the least, allow them a quite unchecked career. A deep vigilant love of

## The Roman Church and Canon Law 353

God in man and of man in God, a continuous sense of Eternal Life will, here also, alone be really adequate and constructive.[1]

(4) The next pair is, in parts, hardly distinguishable from the preceding one, and has, indeed, largely produced the peculiarities just considered. This pair concerns the Canon Law.

The Roman Church most rightly conceives Religion as also concerned with Law, and as having the need and right to some legal organization, amidst the civil laws and legislations of the world. Certainly the idea that everything legal is essentially evil is but a sorry Gnosticism, or a pathetic excess understandable as occasioned by the contrary excesses. For the spirituality and liberty of the Gospel have ever to develop, and to show, their full force in contact with, and through the transformation of, matter and law. And indeed there are entirely conclusive proofs in the very Acts of the Apostles that, *e.g.*, the community of goods amongst the first Christians was never universal, and that it never suspended the sense of the rightfulness, and

[1] For the action of Popes and of Councils, in respect to Conscience and Persecution, before, and in connection with, the Spanish Inquisition, see H. C. Lea's *History of the Spanish Inquisition*, 4 vols., 1906, 1907, especially vol. i. pp. 71–211; vol. ii. pp. 470, 471, 548–550; vol. iii. pp. 183–190; and vol. iv. pp. 516–534. A good short account is to be found in the Abbé Vacandard's *L'Inquisition*, 1906.

the free retention and use, of private property amongst those Christians. Not, then, the exclusion of the very idea of law, or even only of its actual application, but simply the spirit, character, position, and effects of such law, can reasonably be called in question. And indeed, the earlier parts of the Canon Law are often of a kind still strongly to appeal to every Christian conscience.

It is plain, however, that now, for many a day, the persuasiveness of the Church is in inverse ratio to her coercive character and action. Thus it is most instructive to follow the admissions and varying emotions of such a strongly anti-sacerdotal, but deeply religious and highly competent, jurist as is the Lutheran Professor *Rudolf Sohm*. He insists that "the essence of Catholicism consists in its not discriminating between the Church in the religious sense (the Church of Christ), and the Church in the legal sense"; and he opposes Rome precisely on this ground. Yet he has to admit that St. Augustine, and indeed numerous other Catholic authorities up to Luther, fully possessed the idea of the Invisible Church, and of its non-identity with the Visible Church; that a legal organization is already strongly at work in the First Epistle of St. Clement (between 93 and 97 A.D.), and is fully asserted by Pope Callixtus' Edict concerning marriage (in about

220 A.D.); and that the "Roman Catholic Church, alone amongst extant bodies, possesses the exterior connection with the legal organization which arose out of Primitive Christianity."

Above all, Sohm shows, with a fine insistence, how Christianity, from the first, owned "the conception of a Christendom—a community which, conjoined by love, forms a unity, a *body*, the body of Christ." Thus Primitive Christians knew "only the *one* Church of Christ, which energizes and appears (to the faithful) in countless 'Churches,' assemblies of Christendom, manifestations of the life of Christ." This Church is the Catholic Church, and not a separate community; "wherever Christ's spirit is, there is Christendom, the Ecclesia, always the *same* Christendom, the *same* Ecclesia." And precisely this fact, according to Sohm, is the reason why scholars have been unable to show how and when the primitive communities (supposed by them to have alone existed at first and to have at that time existed independently of each other) came to coalesce, or to be absorbed by one of them, and thus suddenly to appear in history as the full-blown, uniform Catholic Church. According to Sohm there existed, from the first, the Catholic Church, and it alone; and the only change that occurred was an all-pervading interior revolution, one of principle and disposition,—the transformation of this (ever single and Universal) Church, from an entirely free, purely charismatic body, into a predominantly coercive, legalist organization (*Wesen und Ursprung des Katholizismus*, Leipzig, 1909, pp. 13, 12, 14, 15, 24 n., 35; 14, 26, 27; 42).

Here the apprehension of the central quality of Christianity and of the Church, and of the excesses in its juridical development, is doubtless very true and deep. But it is certainly inexact to conceive even present-day Roman Catholicism as teaching (either officially or in the higher or even average belief of its adherents) the simple identity of the Invisible with the Visible Church. Sohm admits that the Primitive Christians saw the Invisible Church in the Visible, and that they did not distinguish between the two (pp. 23, 24). Well, the later Catholic Christians saw and see the Invisible Church in the Visible Church and connected with it, but certainly not as simply identical or co-extensive with it. "There are many souls within the Visible Church that do not belong to the Invisible Church; and there are many souls not within the Visible Church that belong to the Invisible Church" is still a thoroughly orthodox and common saying. Indeed, Luther's and Sohm's positions, where they become fully polemical, are as distinctly non-primitive, in their exclusion of all connection between the Visible and Invisible Churches, as is the extremer and more exclusive Legalism of such Roman Catholic theologians as, say, Cardinal Torquemada and some of the (now dominant) Italian and German Jesuit Canonists. The rich vitality of that primitive Christian conviction doubtless depended as truly upon those Christians *not* making the absolute distinction, insisted upon by Luther, as upon their *not* making the simple identification, almost fully reached by these Canonist theologians.

Here once more, then, we have to beware of all superfine Idealism — of "pure" spirituality, and again of "pure," "simple," "easy" counter-theories. For everywhere, and hence particularly here, we have to watch and to maintain the friction, the pain, and the cost of the Spiritual in and around the Material, and of the Eternal in the Temporal and Spatial, within man's quasi-eternal, durational life.

We must, however, admit that a considerable amount of the Canon Law bears the impress of the strongly theocratic later Middle Ages, from, say, A.D. 1230 to about 1480. Much even amongst these laws can be shown to have been appropriate and useful to those times; and besides, in those ages, Emperors, Cities, Bishops, Universities were strong and vigorous within the

Church; and, by their very excesses in a centrifugal direction, they justified or excused, and, in either case, they mostly checked or balanced, any centralizing excesses in this Canon Law. And the presuppositions of this Law were then all in the air, and deeply ingrained in the mental habits of the populations, trained in such ideas by the Roman Empire and by its Byzantine and early Mediæval copies, during a millennium and more.

But since the Protestant Reformation, and much more since the great French Revolution, those powerful checks, and those habits and instincts, have ever increasingly disappeared. And yet it is the strange but undeniable fact that not since the later Middle Ages has the Papacy, or rather the Curia, aimed so persistently, and never with so little interior check or hindrance, at the full development, codification, and detailed enforcement of this Canon Law. Such an address as that of the learned jurist, Dr. Fleiner, "On the Development of the Catholic Church Law in the Nineteenth Century" (an address welcomed by German Catholic Canonists as very accurate and penetrating), brings vividly home to us the unhasting and unresting absorption or elimination of all non-Papal, non-Curialist powers and activities by Rome throughout this time, until the Vatican Council, in 1870, placed all the Church's doctrinal and disciplinary powers in the hands of the Monarch Pope. Since the accession of Pius x. in 1903 the energetic execution of this policy appears, with startling plainness, in such acts as the abolition of the irremovableness of Parish Priests, and in the *Motu Proprio* pronouncements concerning Mixed Marriages and the Immunity of the Clergy from the civil tribunals. Indeed, Rome's action in the matter of the Separation of Church and State in France, and in the numberless condemnations of books, doctrines, and men during these eight years, also illustrates this pure autocracy.

Here we can find comfort in but three reflexions.

It was zealous believers, mostly laymen and non-Italians, such as de Maistre and Chateaubriand, Stolberg and Görres, Veuillot and W. G. Ward, who (keenly suffering under the dreary emptiness and ignorant contempt of Deism and Secularism, or under the insufficiencies of Protestantism) pressed this policy upon Rome. And zealous believers, perhaps again mostly laymen and non-Italians, may arise who will successfully aid the return to a wider and richer, a truly Catholic, action. After all, Rome depends upon its subjects as truly as its subjects depend upon Rome; and Rome will live, and deserve to live, only as the expression of the fullest religious life.

And again, the Curialist presentation of the situation, as a simple alternative between anarchy or autocracy, revolt or self-stultification, will not for ever terrify into nonentity or goad into scepticism the freely docile children of Jesus Christ and of His Vicar, the Servant of the servants of God. They will, on the contrary, come to feel with Rosmini the holy, and with Newman the far-sighted, and with many a great Saint down to our own acutely saddening times, that revolution and despotism are ever the fruitful parents of each other, and that no fellow-mortal, even if he truly represents, to the fullest degree possible amongst frail men, the authority and power of God, can ever come to be beyond learning and receiving from men and through men—those very men to whom he has so much to teach, and so much to give.

And finally, if we choose to look we shall find, still and already, amidst deplorable revolts and infidelities, corresponding to distressing autocratic acts and claims, much sincere and dignified Catholic loyalty and submission, and genuine, because humble and creaturely, freedom, operative amongst numberless souls, cleric and lay, persistently devoted lovers of the great Roman Church.[1]

---

[1] Professor Fritz Fleiner's address: *Ueber die Entwicklung des Katholischen Kirchenrechts im 19. Jahrhundert*, 1902. For

(5) There remains a last pair of complications. The Roman Church, probably more keenly than any other large Christian body, maintains that Religion cannot remain utterly unconcerned with Politics; but that Religion can and ought also to permeate and to sanctify political life. And certainly here again, taken in this generality, our complex life proves that Rome is right. For everything in man hangs together; and Politics, which, adequately conceived, are so profoundly and widely important, cannot stand utterly outside Religion. Edmund Burke, de Tocqueville, Ranke, did not think that they do. Economics certainly do not; and can we draw any sharp line between Religion and Ethics, Ethics and Economics, Economics and Politics? Did Lorenzo de' Medici's intrigues against the Florentine Republic, or Marie Antoinette's successful determination to secure the dismissal of the Ministers Turgot and Malesherbes, really have "nothing to do with religion"? I do not think we can maintain this.

Yet none of the attempted theocracies, in

---

Rosmini and Newman, see the Rev. William Lockhart's *Life of Antonio Rosmini*, 2 vols., 1890; and *The Life of Cardinal Newman*, by Wilfred Ward, 2 vols., 1912. And as to the relations between obedience to God and obedience to His representatives, see the Rev. George Tyrrell's " From God or from Men ?" in his *Through Scylla and Charybdis*, 1907.

modern times and in the West, have been long successful; and the evils they have provoked have probably outweighed the good which they have produced. And then, any persistent and direct mixing up of politics and religion becomes intolerable in proportion to the limited number, to the unchecked power, and to the secrecy of procedure, of the religious officials thus operating. It is precisely the most earnest and promising of the religious minds of our day that are the most sensitive concerning the very suspicion of the operation of strong sublunar motives in claims of a transcendental kind.

And yet all the world knows how apparently incapable of dying is the Roman Curia's thirst for the old Temporal Power over the Roman States, and its hunger for external, political recognition and influence amongst the governments of the world. Thus many Italians, in the middle of last century, knew (like Dante) how to combine a devoted Catholicism with an heroic patriotism—witness Rosmini and Manzoni, Pellico and d' Azeglio; yet their successors still have to live, at best intermittently and but half-acknowledged, and, in the long run, disavowed and condemned, by the Roman Curia in these their lives and convictions. Nevertheless, any serious attempt to restore to the Church any direct temporal and political power would destroy, perhaps for ever, such popularity as the Papacy still enjoys in Italy. And similarly, the political system of Papal Nuncios, and even, recently, of semi-secret political agents of small capacity and denunciatory procedure, has more and more crippled the authority of the Bishops in times and countries most in need of such an undisputed, public, essentially spiritual, authority representative of these Churches' special needs and wishes.

Here we can only do our best, and trust God and the interconnection (ever so real even when most obscure) of all men and classes and forces in this our wondrous existence. Providence may allow that the ruinousness of such a combination for these later ages of the world shall be demonstrated even more fully and at greater cost than heretofore, in one more bitter experience of mankind. Or it may utilize this very power, which now appears as though finally omnipotent, to give all the larger scope to some *Papa Angelico* who will know how to conjoin with the simple, traditional piety and goodness, still genuinely amongst us, a sensitive sympathy, as yet lacking or angrily suspected, with all that is true and generous in the very troubles and dim aspirations of our greatly altered world. Such a figure would in some way severely check, and perhaps for ever repress all directly political ambitions, through a great increase, in the Servant-Mistress of all the Churches, of the sense and practice of Eternal Life.[1]

3. Let us now conclude our survey with two difficult endeavours. Let us attempt to show how the experiences, conceptions, and habits concerning Eternal Life, which the Saints in especial teach us, can alone forcibly aid us to avoid, bear, mitigate, abolish, or utilize the evils we have found to be closely intertwined with the benefits of Institutionalism. And let us try to illustrate, by some recent examples, the supreme delicacy, vividness, and operative force of those experiences and convictions, where they have been awakened, deepened, and guarded, in heroic souls, by Institutional Religion.

But I would premise that we are dealing here with the Eternal-Life complex, only as this is an antidote to the evils incidental to Institutionalism. Again, the account thus attempted deals, not with the vague and intermittent aspira-

[1] On the above matters, see the delicately balanced, highly competent *La Politique de Pie X., 1906-1910*, by Maurice Pernet, 1910; the rougher, yet still honest and well-informed *La Separation des Églises et de l'État*, by M. de Narfon, 1911; and the deeply religious study, so frankly adverse to all easy solutions, *Die Trennung von Staat und Kirche*, by Professor Troeltsch, 1907.

tions which are (more or less) common to all men, but with the hunger and thirst of the human spirit after the Eternal Spirit where this thirst is keenly awakened and clearly articulated by Historical, Institutional Religion. And, finally, nothing simply hypothetic, or really new, is advanced here. But we shall only strive to put together, and clearly to show, the experiences and convictions in question, as these have been and are operating (to the writer's very certain knowledge or direct observation) in fully awake and deeply spiritual souls within the greatest of the Christian Institutions.

(1) The complex, then, of vivid, operative convictions connected with Eternal Life, as we have gradually come to understand it in this book, is fundamentally fivefold. And each of these convictions awakens and feeds special habits and capacities, which are so many true and potent antidotes to the evils considered above.

There is, first, a keen yet double sense of *Abidingness* — an absolute Abidingness, pure Simultaneity, Eternity, in God; and a relative abidingness, a quasi-eternity, Duration, in man (*qua* personality). And the Eternity is always experienced by man only within, together with, and in contrast to, the Duration. And both Eternity and Duration stand out, in man's deepest consciousness, with even painful contrast, against all mere Succession, all sheer flux and change.

Here the special value lies in the double sense that we are indeed actually touched, penetrated, and supported by the purely Eternal; and yet that we ourselves shall never, either here or hereafter, be more than quasi-eternal, durational. For only this double sense will save us from the perilous alternatives of an uncreaturely sheer fixity and an animal mere flux and change. We thus gain a perennial source of continuity and calm.

There is, next, the keen sense of *Otherness in Likeness*. We are genuinely like, and we are genuinely unlike, God, the Realized Perfection. Hence there is ever a certain tension, a feeling of limitation or of emptiness, a looking for a centre outside of, or other than, our own selves.

Here again this double sense will be profoundly helpful in our troubles. For thus we are never free to lose reverence for the deepest of what we are, since it is like God, and actually harbours God. And yet we may never lose humility and a thirst for purification, since even the deepest and best of ourselves never is, never will be, God; and since all that we actually are is full of weakness and of manifold sins and faulty habits.

And so we find a continual reason for self-respect, humility, contrition, each aiding and penetrating the other; and for a faith and certainty, which will never be arrogant, and for a diffidence, which will never be sceptical.

There is, thirdly, the keen sense of *Other-Worldliness in contrast with This-Worldliness.* There is here a lively conviction that our spiritual personality, and its full beatitude, can never be attained in this life, but only in the other life, after death; and yet that the other life can be begun in this life, indeed that we are, all of us, more or less solicited, here and now, by that other life, and that we cannot consummate it *there*, unless we begin it *here*. And, in this case, as everywhere, the greater and ultimate has to awake and to grow within us, in and through, and in contrast with, the lesser and (eventually) secondary.

This double sense is, again, a deep help in all our trials. For thus we are pricked on to labour energetically at the improvement of man's earthly lot, in all its stages and directions; but we do so without philistinism, impatience, or fanaticism, since we are fully convinced (even before beginning) that these attempts, could they all succeed, would not, could not, ever satisfy man, when once he is fully awake. And this applies, in its degree, even to our spirituality, even to the Church.

Even these are, in considerable part, preparatory, educative, during this our short schooltime, our years of training, upon earth—a necessary and noble function, and one that is fundamentally rooted in Him Who Abides and in the quasi-eternal within ourselves; yet one which (taken as it stands here on earth) is not throughout an end, *the* end, but is a mean, or, at best, *the* means. We thus find perpetual escape from all pedantry or feverishness, and this through the gain of an unconquerable, because sober, optimism.

There is, fourthly, the keenest sense of *Reality*. Our analyses, theories, hypotheses, our very denials and scepticisms, all presuppose realities which environ and influence us, real beings; realities which, together with us real men, constitute one real world. And throughout, and within, and over against, all these realities is *the* Reality of realities, the Eternal Spirit, God. Indeed, this Source and Sustenance of the other realities is apprehended by us ever with, and in, and through, and over against, those other, various realities that impinge upon our many-levelled lives. And thus our highest certainties awaken with, and require, our lower and lowest ones.

This double sense again will greatly aid us. For it will make us profoundly concrete, historical, incarnational, ontological, real; yet all this without a touch of inflation. And it will fill us with dauntless faith, courage, and joy, yet ever also with the creaturely temper—with respect for the body, for things, for matter; and will keep us ever averse to all abstract and subjectivist schemes.

And finally, there is the keen sense of *Unity in Multiplicity and of Multiplicity in Unity*—of the Organism. Everywhere we find in the real world only such organisms—systems, families, complexes; nowhere sheer, mere unity or units. God Himself (in the deep rich Christian orthodoxy) is a Trinity of Persons; Christ is a Duality of Natures; the Humanity of Christ and of all men is a Trinity of Powers. Our bodies are wondrous organisms, our minds are still more wonderfully organic; and the two together form an organization of an even more marvellous unity in multiplicity. And yet it is not even such a single man who is the true, fundamental social unit, but the family, in which the father, mother, and child are each *sui generis* and essential, as non-interchangeable parts of this rich organism. Thus from a lichen or seaweed up to God Himself—the unspeakable Richness (because the incomprehensibly manifold Unity and complete Organization)—we find ever increasingly rich, organized unities. And the great social complexes of Society and the State, of Economics, Science, Art, are all similarly possessed of specific laws of organization. They are strong and beneficent only as special wholes possessed of special parts, which wholes again have to grow and fructify in contact, contrast, and conflict with other such complexes without, and the ever more or less disorderly elements within, themselves.

Here, again, we find an immense help. For thus we are all taught Reverence for each other's spiritual individuality, and for the characteristics of all the great organisms; since each is necessary for all the others. And we gain in Public Spirit; since we feel keenly that no individual or organization, however essential and sacred, can live fully and fruitfully except by living also with and for other individuals and organizations. And, perhaps above all, the religious passion can thus, at last, more and more require and seek the scientific, and the other noble, passions of mankind. For here man has to grow with and through other men and other things, never simply within and through himself. And thus his very religion here drives him to find checks and obstacles even to his standards and ideals—sure, as he is, that he requires purification even in the best of what he is and has, and that God, Who has ordered all things to co-operate towards the good of those who seek and love Him, will ever help his soul to find His Peace and Eternity in even the severest storms and wreckage of its earthly times.

(2) With regard to specially precious manifestations of the experience and conviction of Eternal Life, of God with man, within the authoritative Institutions, in these our times, we can again point to the impartial testimony of Sir Charles Booth. In general, "the clergy and ministers" amongst the London poor, he tells us, "have no authority that is recognized, but their professional character remains . . . and their manner is somewhat resented. In the case of the Roman Catholic priesthood alone do we find the desired combination of professionalism and authority, resting not on the individual but on the Church he serves; and where most nearly approached, it is by the lives of some of the High Church clergy" (*op. cit.* p. 428). And in English literature generally we find poignant expressions of this Other-Worldliness fostered (in various yet everywhere real ways) by Religious Traditions and Institutions. Thus we get Claude Montefiore's moving pages upon Prayer, in his *Liberal Judaism*, 1907; Frederick Robertson's great sermon on "The Loneliness of Christ"; Dean Church's study of the sense of God in the Psalms, as contrasted

with the Vedas; and many an address in J. H. Newman's *Parochial and Plain Sermons* and *Sermons to Mixed Congregations*. Then for the Russian Church, we have the striking extracts from the Diary of Father John (Sergieff) of Cronstadt, published in English as *My Life in Christ*, in 1897.

And for deep spirituality and heroism in the Roman Catholic Church, the present writer's mind dwells ever specially upon four examples.

There is the rough uncultured Belgian, Father Damien, deliberately contracting and dying the loathsome, slow death of a leper, from love of God in men utterly without claims of any other kind upon him, away in an island lost in the ocean at the Antipodes, as Robert Louis Stevenson has unforgettably described the simple, splendid life.

And there is, again, Jean Baptiste Vianney, the now beatified simple peasant Curé of Ars. How impressive are the accounts by the Abbé Monnin, an eye-witness of the Curé's utter absorption in God and in souls, each ever inciting the other, and the joyous expansion of his entire nature through this keen sense and love! (*Le Curé d'Ars*, 12th ed., 2 vols., 1874, is before me). And in the "Spirit of the Curé d'Ars," chronicled by the same, we find numberless deeply spontaneous sayings, such as the following: " Time never seems long in prayer. I know not whether we can even wish for heaven!" Yet "the fish swimming in a little rivulet is well off, because it is in its element; but it is still better in the sea." "When we pray, we should open our heart to God, like a fish when it sees the wave coming." "Do you see, my children, except God, nothing is solid—nothing, nothing! If it is life, it passes away; if it is fortune, it crumbles away; if it is health, it is destroyed; if it is reputation, it is attacked. We are scattered like the wind." "You say it is hard to suffer? No, it is easy; it is happiness. Only we must love while we suffer, and suffer whilst we love. On the way of the cross, you see, my children, only the first step is painful. Our greatest cross is the fear of crosses" (English translation, pp. 28, 40, 114).

And then there is Eugénie Smet, the daughter of a burgher of Lille (1825-1871), who, as Mère Marie de la Providence, founded an Order of devoted women, at work, even before her death, as far as India and China; who insisted upon remaining in Paris throughout the siege and the Commune, 1870–71; and who slowly died there, in agonies of cancer, utterly absorbed with joy in God, the Eternal and utterly Real, and with tender and unceasing activity towards His poor and sick around her. In the midst of these immense trials she was wont to say: "Let us feel that Eternity is begun; whatever pain we are going through, let us make joy out of that thought." And: "In all things I can only see God alone; and, after all, that is the only way to be happy. If once we begin to look at secondary causes, there is an end of peace" (Lady Georgiana Fullerton, *Life of Mère Marie de la Providence*, 4th ed., 1904, pp. 241, 237).

And finally, there is before my mind, with all the vividness resulting from direct personal intercourse and deep spiritual obligations, the figure of the Abbé Huvelin, who died only in 1910. A gentleman by birth and breeding, a distinguished Hellenist, a man of exquisitely piercing, humorous mind, he could readily have become a great editor or interpreter of Greek philosophical or patristic texts, or a remarkable Church historian. But this deep and heroic personality deliberately preferred "to write in souls," whilst occupying, during thirty-five years, a supernumerary, unpaid post in a large Parisian parish. There, suffering from gout in the eyes and brain, and usually lying prone in a darkened room, he served souls with the supreme authority of self-oblivious love, and brought light and purity and peace to countless troubled, sorrowing, or sinful souls. His Curé, of St. Augustin, has spoken well of this great figure; Adeline, Duchess of Bedford, a devoted Anglican, has published a vivid, and almost entirely accurate, sketch of him; and now three volumes have been issued containing the careful reports, taken down by certain of his hearers, of familiar addresses which are full (at least for those who knew and loved the saintly speaker) of sudden gleams of the deepest spiritual insight and love.

Thus, in the "Conferences on some of the Spiritual Guides of the Seventeenth Century," he says, in connection with Saint François de Sales: "When once we desire a thing to be true, we are very near to finding it true"; and "a spirituality of the little-by-little is not an enfeebled spirituality." And, in criticism of Jansenism: "There exist families of souls which are determined to find the principle of tranquillity within their own selves; they want to cast anchor within their own depths. But we have to cast anchor, not below, but above; it is in God, in His goodness, that we have to found our hope." And finally: "God, who might have created us directly, employs, for this work, our parents, to whom He joins us by the tenderest ties. He could also save us directly, but He saves us, in fact, by means of certain souls, which have received the spiritual life before ourselves, and which communicate it to us, because they love us."

Of Père de Condren, Abbé Huvelin says: "He has hardly written any books; he wrote in souls"; "he experienced great interior derelictions and strange obscurities—a man is not called to form other souls without having to suffer much"; and "his call was not to live for himself, but to live utterly for Him who gave him all things."

In speaking of M. Olier, M. Huvelin exclaims: "Strip yourself of self, love God, love men; what are all these other things that seem of such importance to you?" And he declares: "The world sees, in this or that soul, the passions, the bitter waters which fill it; but we priests, we seek, beneath these bitter waters, the little spring of sweet waters, Arethusa, that little thread of grace, which, though deeper down and more hidden, is nevertheless most truly there." And again: "The true means to attract a soul, is not to attenuate Christian doctrine, but to present it in its full force, because then we present it in its beauty. For beauty is one of the proofs of truth."

As to Saint Vincent de Paul, he tells us: "See the reason why, in this life so devoted to his fellow-creatures, you will find something austere, and shut up in God: it is that the Saint feels the necessity, for himself and for others, thus to re-immerse, to temper anew his soul in the source of all love."

And lastly, with respect to the great Trappist Abbé de Rancé, he observes: "When something very high and inaccessible is put before human nature it feels itself impelled to attain to that height, by something mysterious and divine which God infuses into the soul." And: "There is ever something mysterious in every conversion; we never succeed in fully understanding even our own"; nevertheless, "the voice of God does not speak in moments of exaltation. Such converted souls would say: 'It was in the hour when I was most mistress of myself, most recollected, least agitated, that I heard the voice of God.'"[1]

Thus souls, who live an heroic spiritual life within great religious traditions and institutions, attain to a rare volume and vividness of religious insight, conviction, and reality. They can, at their best, train other souls, who are not all unworthy of such training, to a depth and tenderness of full and joyous union with God, the Eternal, which utterly surpasses, not only in quantity but in quality, what

[1] "The Abbé Huvelin," by Adeline, Duchess of Bedford, in *The English Church Review*, London, Jan. 1911; *Quelques Directeurs d'Ames au XVII. Siècle* (Paris, Gabalda, 1911), pp. 6, 12, 37, 38, 50, 64, 76, 101, 102, 113, 121, 201, 230, 234.

we can and do find amongst souls outside all such Institutions, or not directly taught by souls trained within such traditions. And thus we find here, more clearly than in any philosopher as such, that Eternal Life consists in the most real of relations between the most living of realities—the human spirit and the Eternal Spirit, God; and in the keen sense of His Perfection, Simultaneity and Prevenience, as against our imperfection, successiveness and dependence. And we find that this sense is awakened in, and with, the various levels of our nature; in society as well as in solitude; by things as well as by persons. In such souls, then, we catch the clearest glimpses of what, for man even here below, can be and is Eternal Life.

# PART III

PROSPECTS AND CONCLUSIONS

# PART III

## PROSPECTS AND CONCLUSIONS

## CHAPTER XIII

### FINAL DISCRIMINATIONS

Eternal Life, a religious experience and conception—Not a cause, but an effect: a relation between realities—The three things involved by Eternal Life; in their fulness they exist only in God, the Eternal—Eternal Life in man, only quasi-eternal, Durational—Man's highest ideals and deepest unrest caused by this his likeness in unlikeness to God—The sense of the Eternal is developed in the Durational—In the Spatial—In the Material—Eternal Life and Eternal Death of the human soul—Eternal Life, in man, requires sense of both weakness and of sin, in our Lord's way of conceiving both—Eternal Life requires a Cultus, and various outgoings into other departments—Three characteristics of deepest Religion at work to prevent its becoming oppressive—Three causes of simplification ever at work in practice of Eternal Life.

As regards the development of the consciousness of Eternal Life, and a fully fruitful conviction concerning it, we find that the history of Religion, and the deepest experiences and revelations vouchsafed to us, indicate the true lines to be as follows. (We here adopt, not the historical or psychical, but the logical order.)

1. Eternal Life, in its pregnant, concrete, ontological sense,—the operative conviction of its reality,— is not, primarily, a matter of Speculation and Philosophy, but reveals itself clearly only in the course of ages, and even then only to riper, deeper souls, as having been all along (in some manner and degree) experienced and postulated in all that men feel, will, do, and are of a characteristically human kind. It is only Religion that, in this matter, has furnished man with a vivid and concrete experience and conviction of permanent ethical and spiritual value. Philosophy, as such, has not been able to do more than analyse and clarify this religious conviction, and find, within its own domain and level, certain intimations and requirements converging towards such a conviction. It has not itself been able vividly to experience, or unshakably to affirm, a corresponding Reality as actually present and ever operative in the production of these very intimations and requirements.

2. Eternal Life, as thus operative in man's life and discovered for us there by Religion, is not an ultimate cause, a self-subsisting entity, which (accidentally or necessarily) evolves a living subject or subjects; but it is simply the effect, the action, of a living Reality, or the effect, the interaction,

of several such realities. Hence Eternal Life is no substitute for either God or man; but it is the activity, the effect, of God, or of man, or of both.

3. Eternal Life, in the fullest thinkable sense, involves three things—the plenitude of all goods and of all energizings that abide; the entire self-consciousness of the Being Which constitutes, and Which is expressed by, all these goods and energizings; and the pure activity, the non-successiveness, the simultaneity, of this Being in all It has, all It is. Eternal Life, in this sense, precludes not only space, not only clock-time—that artificial chain of mutually exclusive, ever equal moments, but even *duration*, time as actually experienced by man, with its overlapping, interpenetrating successive stages. But Eternal Life precludes space and clock-time because of the very intensity of its life. The Simultaneity is here the fullest expression of the Supreme Richness, the unspeakable Concreteness, the overwhelming Aliveness of God; and is at the opposite pole from all empty unity, all mere being—any or all abstractions whatsoever.

4. Eternal Life, in a real, though not in the fullest sense, is attributable to man. This lesser eternal life appears to have its range between the pure Simultaneity of God, and mere Clock-Time,

and to have its true form in *Duration*—an ever more or less overlapping succession, capable of being concentrated into quasi-simultaneities. And this lesser eternal life, although unending, is never boundless; nor does it (here below at least) ever become entirely actual.

5. Now, owing to this our likeness in unlikeness to It, the Eternal Living Spirit (though necessarily incomprehensible by our own) can be, and is, continuously apprehended by us—since that Spirit really penetrates us and all Its creatures. And this our apprehension occurs, not separately, abstractively, clearly, statically; but ever more or less in, or contrasting with, finite, contingent, changing things; and it does so obscurely, yet with an immensely far-reaching dynamic operativeness. From hence alone can spring our unquenchable thirst after the Eternal and Abiding, the Objective, the Final; and our intolerable pain at the very idea of being entirely confined to the merely fleeting, subjective, momentary—a pain which persists even if we extend the validity and permanence of our life's experience to all humanity, taken simply as such. For this thirst and pain could not be so ineradicable and so profoundly operative, and could not constitute so decidedly the very flower and test of

our fullest manhood, did it not proceed from a Reality or Realities deeper than any exclusively human projection or analysis whatsoever.

Nor will it suffice to refer this experience to the operation, within us, of Spirit in the making—to the gradual and painful coming to self-consciousness of the one concrete Universe (of which we form an integral part) precisely through our spirits and their growth. For we have no other instance of an unrealized perfection producing such pain and joy, such volitions, such endlessly varied and real results; and all by means of just this vivid and persistent impression that this Becoming is an already realized Perfection. Religion would thus deceive us precisely in the conviction and act which are central in all its higher forms and stages—Adoration. And the noblest root and flower of the Jewish-Christian religion and of European civilization,—the sense of *Givenness*, of grace, of dependence upon a Reality other and higher than ourselves, singly or collectively—would also have to go. For such a habit of mind requires (logically, and in the long run also practically) my belief in a Reality not less but more self-conscious than myself—a Living One Who lives first and lives perfectly, and Who, touching me, the inferior, derivative life, can cause me to live by His aid and for His sake.

6. Thus such a sense of the Divine Eternity or Simultaneity will be developed by man within, and in contrast to, *duration*. And it will be strengthened in proportion as man effects, in others and in himself, results spiritually real within this (for him) real duration ; and as he collects his spirit (in alternation to such action) away from all particular strivings, and concentrates it, more exclusively, upon the Divine Living One—the ever-present Background and Support of his little life. *Time* then, in the sense of *duration* (with the spiritual intercourse and the growth in spiritual character which we develop and consolidate in such time), is, for us men, not a barrier against Eternal Life, but the very stuff and means in and by which we vitally experience and apprehend that Life. Man's temporal life is thus neither a theory nor even a vision ; nor something that automatically unrolls itself. Nor, on the other hand, is it, even at its deepest, itself the Ultimate experienced by man. But man's life is one long, variously deep and wide, rich and close, tissue of (ever more or less volitional) acts and habits—instinctive, rational, emotive ; of strivings, shrinkings, friction, conflict, suffering, harmony, and joy ; and of variously corresponding permanent effectuations in and by the spirit thus active. And hence man's life is full of cost, tension, and drama. Yet

such an individual life never experiences, indeed never is constituted by, itself alone; but it is ever endlessly affected by the environment and stimulation of other realities, organisms, spirits; and it ever itself correspondingly affects such other realities. And the whole of this inter-connected realm of spirits is upheld, penetrated, stimulated, and articulated by the one Infinite Spirit, God. Thus a real succession, real efforts, and the continuous sense of limitation and inadequacy are the very means in and through which man apprehends increasingly (if only he thus loves and wills) the contrasting yet sustaining Simultaneity, Spontaneity, Infinity, and pure Action of the Eternal Life of God.

7. But also *spatial* concepts and imagery play two important rôles in the full and normal consciousness of Eternal Life. For whether or no the spatial category abides with man in the Beyond, in this earthly life at least he cannot persistently and vividly apprehend even the most spiritual realities, as distinct and different from each other, except by picturing them as disparate in space. Now a vivid consciousness of the deep distinction and difference (within all their real affinity and closeness of intercourse) between God and man, and the continuous, keen sense that all man has, does, and is of good is ever, in

its very possibility, a free gift of God, constitutes the very core of religion. Hence the spatial imagery, which, by picturing God as *outside* the soul and Heaven as *above* the earth, helps to enforce this fundamental truth, is highly valuable —as valuable, indeed, as the imagery (spatial still) which helps to enforce the complementary truth of God's likeness to the soul and His penetration of it, by picturing God as *within* the soul and Heaven as *in* this room.

And again, the principles, ideals, and picturings of Mathematics and Physics (with their insistence upon ruthless law, utter interchangeableness of all individual instances, and flawless determinism) have a very certain place and function in the full spiritual life of the soul. For they provide that *preliminary* Pantheism, that transition through fate and utter dehumanization, which will allow the soul to affirm, ultimately and as ultimate, a Libertarianism and Personalism free from all sentimentality or slovenliness, and immune against the attacks of *ultimate* Pantheism, which can *now* be vanquished as only the caricature of the poorer half of a far richer whole. Yet for the sufficient operativeness of that Mathematico-physical world and outlook, vivid pictures of space and of quasi-space—clock-time—are absolutely necessary.

8. Finally, *material* things (however dead or seemingly dead) and abstract propositions (however empty if taken alone) can, and do, continually thwart or stimulate human spirits—within this life at least. Because God is Spirit, and because man is spirit and is more and more to constitute himself a personality, it does not follow that man is to effect this solely by means of spirits and personalities, divine and human. Nor does man require material things only for the expression and communication of a personality already developed independently of such material things. But, as in all mental apprehension and conviction there is always, somewhere, the element of the stimulation of the senses, so also does the spirit awaken to its own life and powers, on occasion of contact and conflict with material things. Hence Eternal Life will (here below at least) not mean for man aloofness from matter and the bodily senses, nor even a restriction of their use to means of spiritual self-expression; but it will include also a rich and wise contact with, and an awakening by means of, matter and *things*.

9. All this costly acceptance and affirmation of Eternal Life will be found to form the sole self-consistent alternative to a (more or less obscure, but none the less real and immensely operative)

refusal of man's true call, and the election of the (always easier) course of evading the soul's deepest longings and requirements. This evasion will strengthen the animal instincts and chaotic impulsions of the man's complex being; and will weaken those higher claims of human reason and of spiritual organization and transfigurement. And the soul may at last arrive at an abiding disintegration and self-contradiction, and be alive only in a superficial, distracted degree and way. And this shrinkage and pain of self-contradiction and self-stultification, which the soul itself has (at least indirectly) willed, would be the soul's death.

In any case, it seems clear that, with regard to a self-stultifying soul, neither Total Annihilation nor a consciousness equal, though contrary, to that of the soul which practises and experiences Eternal Life, meets the various facts as well as does the doctrine that the effects of such full self-determinations indeed abide both for good and for evil, but that they differ not only in quality, but also in intensity. Thus, though no soul would ever cease completely, and none of its fullest spiritual and moral self-determinations would ever, in their effects upon such a soul itself, be as though they had not been, the contrast between the saved and the lost soul would be between two different quantities, as well as qualities, of life.

And whereas the sense of Time, in the most fully *eternalized* of human spirits, would be so *Durational* as almost to lapse into Simultaneity, the sense of Time with *phenomenalized* human souls would lose almost all Duration and be quite close to Clock-Time—to the mechanical movement of soulless matter. This is certainly the case in this life; here we are merely assuming that what already *is*, as the deepest of our experiences, will continue to obtain as long as we last at all.

10. Eternal Life, conceived as above, will be found to include and to require a deep sense of human Weakness and of man's constant need of the Divine Prevenience, and again of the reality of Sin and of our various inclinations to it; but also to exclude all conceptions of the total corruption of human nature, of the essential impurity of the human body, or of the utter debilitation of the will. The Pauline, Augustinian, Lutheran, Calvinist, Jansenist trend, impressive though it is, will have to be explained, in part, as a good and necessary (or at least as an excusable, temporary) corrective of some contrary excess; and, for the rest, it will have to suffer incorporation within a larger whole, which, in appearance more commonplace, is yet in reality indefinitely richer—the doctrine and practice of Jesus Christ Himself.

"In my flesh abideth no good thing," will have somehow to be integrated within "the spirit indeed is willing, but the flesh is weak."

11. And lastly, Eternal Life will not be simply a Moralism, with just the addition of a theoretical or practical reference to God, as the sanction and source of morality. Such a Religion has, fortunately, never existed except in the heads of some Philosophers. In its central consciousness and action, this Life will be indeed religious, hence Adoration, a Cultus—a deep, rich, spiritual Cultus, but a Cultus still. This for the ingoing, recollective movement. And the outgoing movement will not only discover God as hidden in the deepest ideals, necessities, and impulsions of Ethics, but also in the fullest strivings of Art and in the widest and most delicate attempts of the speculative and analytical reason. God is no less truly the ultimate Source, Sustainer, and End of perfect Beauty and of utter Truth than of complete Goodness and of the purest Self-Donation.

12. The sense, then, of Eternal Life requires, for its normal, general, and deepest development, *Duration*, history; Space, institutions; Material Stimulations, and symbols, something

sacramental; and Transcendence, a movement away from all and every culture and civilization, to the Cross, to asceticism, to interior nakedness and the Beyond. Thus our very sense of, and search for, Eternal Life will, apparently, re-enforce or re-instate all the exclusive ecclesiastical claims, the dread oppressions and persecutions of the past. The bitterest of all earthly hatreds would thus seem to be an essential condition of heavenly love. Yet Religion, taken as here supposed, would, in three ways, powerfully counteract these very certain and most grave dangers.

Religion is here assumed, on the evidence of undeniable history, to exist and to function in various stages and degrees of depth, purity, and articulation, and with variously intense and true revelations from God through prophets inspired by Himself. And men who are in the fuller, truer, purer stages and degrees may increasingly learn to recognize, in the positive and fruitful constituents and effects of other religions, something good and from God—fragments and preparations for such fuller truth as they themselves possess.

Again Religion, even in its totality, is here supposed to be indeed the deepest, yet not the only activity of man's spirit; and each of these several activities is taken to possess its own immanental laws, duties, and rights. And Religion has the difficult, yet quite feasible and supremely fruitful, task of ever respecting, whilst ever more and more harmonizing, purifying, and utilizing, each and all of these various realms, under penalty of finding, otherwise, that itself is more and more bereft of necessary material and stimulation, and that all the other activities of man's many-levelled nature escape more and more into a wilderness of rank secularism.

And finally, in this scheme of life the first cause, and the ultimate unity, of all things is found in God, as the supremely rich, self-revealing, self-giving Eternal Life. This ultimate Living Unity is trusted, and, in the long run, is mysteriously found, to permeate all, and to bring fruitfulness to any one good activity, from the other levels and kinds of goodness, even though apparently most distant or most contrary. And it is just because of this fundamental, ineradicable interconnection, and of the soul's conviction of it, that man's spirit can drive home this or that research or interest, and can remain sure of contributing (in proportion to his selfless attention to the immanent necessities and prophetic hints of its subject-matter) something of abiding value to the other departments and levels of man's energizings, and, ultimately, to his further seeking and finding of Eternal Life.

13. The many requirements thus articulated cannot fail to appear intolerably complex both to those who attempt to stand aloof from all Religion, and to those who, with little or no analysis or theory, are directly absorbed in its practice. Like all living realities, living Religion possesses a sovereign spontaneity and rich simplicity which seem to render all attempts at analysis an insult. Indeed, Religion in particular possesses three essentials, which continually bring expansion and simplicity to its tension and complexity.

Religion is essentially Social *horizontally*; in the sense that each several soul is *therefore* unique because intended to realize just *this* post, function, joy, effect within the total organism of all souls. Hence no soul is expected to be a "jack-of-all-trades," but only to develop fully its own special gifts and *attraits*, within and through, and for, that larger organism of the human family, in which other souls are as fully to develop their own differing gifts and *attraits*, as so many supplements and compensations to the others. The striving of any one soul can thus be peaceful, since limited in its range to what this particular soul, at its best, most really wants and loves.

And Religion is essentially Social *vertically*— indeed here is its deepest root. It is unchangeably a faith in God, a love of God, an intercourse with God; and though the soul cannot abidingly abstract itself from its fellows, it can and ought frequently to recollect itself in a simple sense of God's presence. Such moments of direct preoccupation with God alone bring a deep refreshment and simplification to the soul.

And Religion, in its fullest development, essentially requires, not only this our little span of earthly years, but a life beyond. Neither an Eternal Life that is already fully achieved here below, nor an Eternal Life to be begun and known solely in the beyond, satisfies these requirements. But only an Eternal Life already begun and truly known in part here, though fully to be achieved and completely to be understood hereafter, corresponds to the deepest longings of man's spirit as touched by the prevenient Spirit, God. And hence, again, a peace and simplification. For that doubly Social life I try to lead here (though most real, and though itself already its own exceeding great reward) constitutes, after all, but the preliminary practice, the getting ready, for ampler, more expansive, more utterly blissful energizings in and for man, the essentially durational, quasi-eternal, and God, the utterly Abiding, the pure Eternal Life.

# INDEX

[Subject-matters and Authors discussed in the text at some length are printed in *Italics*; ordinary type indicates such Subjects and Authors as appear only in shorter references or remarks—mostly in the notes alone.]

## I

## SUBJECT-MATTERS

|  | PAGES |
|---|---|
| *Abidingness*, sense of, a twofold degree of | 365, 366 |
| *Above*, all true existence is, in Johannine writings | 74 |
| *Absolute*, the, God as, sporadically affirmed by Fichte | 176 |
|    *Knowledge* in Eckhart | 112, 113; 117, 118 |
|       in Hegel | 203; 211-213 |
|    *Philosophy*, the, in Hegel | 215 |
|    *Spirit*, in Hegel | 202, 203 |
| *Abstract character* of Parmenides' philosophy | 31, 32; 34 |
|       of middle period of Plato | 36, 37 |
|       of God in Aristotle | 41 |
|       of one current in Philo | 53 |
|       of Greek philosophy from Plato onwards | 85 |
|       of much in Plotinus | 85 |
|       of parts of the Fourth Gospel | 79, 80 |
|       of form of St. Augustine's great experiences | 89, 90 |
|       predominant in Proclus | 96 |
|       and in Pseudo-Dionysius | 97 |
|       of one current in St. Thomas | 107, 108 |
|       predominant in Eckhart | 112; 118, 119 |
|       in Spinoza | 134 |
|       of Kant's fundamental epistemological question | 139, 140; 153 |
|       of his Ethics | 146, 147 |
|       of Schleiermacher's pure Intuition-Feeling | 189-195 |
|       of Hegel's identification of Thinking with Reality | 207-211 |
|       and of human with the Absolute Reason | 211-216 |

|  | PAGES |
|---|---|
| *Abstract character* of T. H. Green's "consciousness in general" | 215 |
| of much in Feuerbach | 223 |
| Schopenhauer's fight against | 248 |
| intensely, of Haeckel's propaganda | 281–283 |
| largely, of Bergson's conception of Duration and of Space | 291, 292 |
| of Life | 299 |
| of Liberty | 301 |
| *Activity*, the pure, (Action) of God in Aristotle | 38–40 |
| in Philo | 51 |
| in Fourth Gospel | 73 |
| external, and religion, according to Schleiermacher | 189; 190; 192 |
| *Adoration*, as centre of religion in Isaiah | 17, 18 |
| in the Psalms | 48 |
| in Our Lord's utterances | 63, 64 |
| in Fourth Gospel | 73 |
| in St. Augustine | 89, 90 |
| in Pseudo-Dionysius | 98, 99 |
| ignored in the *critical* Kant | 158–160 |
| final affirmation, by author, of | 392 |
| *Aevum* in St. Thomas | 105, 106 |
| *Anthropology* amongst worshippers of Dionysus | 26 |
| of Orphics | 28 |
| Plato | 38 |
| Aristotle | 40, 41 |
| Stoics | 45, 46 |
| Philo | 52, 54 |
| in Our Lord's teaching | 65, 66 |
| of St. Paul | 68 |
| Fourth Gospel | 75; 79, 80 |
| in Spinoza | 132, 133 |
| the English Hegelians | 220 |
| Feuerbach | 233–236; 243, 244 |
| Darwin | 266, 267; 270 |
| *Anthropomorphism*, excessive reaction against, in Fichte | 174, 178 |
| a critical, urged against Hegel | 204–206 |
| found everywhere by Feuerbach | 234, 235 |
| *Apathy*, the Stoic | 45, 46 |
| in Philo | 54 |
| Aristotelianism, its unhistorical temper | 340 |
| *Asceticism* in Our Lord's utterances and life | 65 |
| in Schopenhauer | 252, 253 |
| favoured by Sorel | 321, 322 |
| its abiding importance | 253 |
| its true place and measure | 253–255 |

# Index

*Atheism*, Fichte accused of . . . . 177, 178
   of Feuerbach, profoundly important  234, 235; 243, 244
   of Haeckel . . . . . 281–283
*Attention*, man's limited capacity of, seen in Secularist
   Socialism . . . . . . . 307

*Becoming*, everything sheer, not Being, in Primitive Buddhism  8–10
      all Reality without any, in Parmenides . . 31, 32
      a pure, in Bergson . 289–291; 293, 294
*Biology and Epigenesis*, Darwin's confessions regarding, in
        relation to religion . 265–268
        consideration and criticism of 268–279
        three religious gains from recent 280–288
        Bergson's utilization of, its strength
          and weakness . . 288–302
        freedom of research in, within
          Roman Catholic Church . 341
*Body, the human*, perfection sought outside, in Dionysiac Cult  26
        in Orphism . 29
   image of human society found in, by Stoics 47, 48
   and of Church, by St. Paul . . 71, 72
   distinguished from the Flesh by St. Paul  68
   its high importance in Spinoza . 132, 133
*Brahma*, his nature and relations to world and single souls,
   in Ramanuja . . . . . . 10–12
*Buddhism*: sheer Becoming and *Nirvana* strictly inter-
     related . . . . . 8–10
   Orphic constituents akin to . . . 28, 29
   Eckhart's affinity to . . . 113, 114
   primitive, a spiritually attuned moralism, not
     yet a religion . . . . 165 *n.*
   in Schopenhauer . . . 246, 247; 256

*Category, the dominant*, in Buddhism: Becoming . . 9
      in Zarathustrism: two Coequal Posi-
        tive Forces of Good and of Evil 12, 13
      in Israelitish religion: the Spiritual-
        Ethical "This-life" Experiences 21, 22
      in Aristotle: *Energeia* . 38–41
      with Our Lord: the Kingdom of God 56
      in St. Paul: *Pneuma*, the Spirit . 67
      in Fourth Gospel: Eternal Life 75; 77, 78
      in Spinoza: Substance . . 125
      in Schleiermacher's *Reden*: Intui-
        tion-Feeling for Infinite 183, 184
      in his *Glaubenslehre*: Feeling of
        Unconditional Dependence 195, 196
      in M'Taggart: Substance . 224; 227
      in Bergson: Duration . 288–294

|  | PAGES |
|---|---|
| Categories, Hegel's ordering and estimating of the | 203 |

Change, see *Becoming*.
Christocentrism in Schleiermacher . . . 197, 198
    in Wilhelm Hermann . . 331, 332
*Church, the Christian*, its preformation in Jesus's personal
                utterances . 62, 63 ; 326, 327
        its conception in St. Paul 70–72 ; 326, 327
                St. Augustine . 93, 94
                Pseudo-Dionysius 97
                St. Thomas 101, 102
            and Eckhart . . . 110, 119
            and Kierkegaard . . . 261
            and Socialism . . 309, 315, 320
            in Georges Sorel . . 321, 322
            Troeltsch . . . 326–328
            Sohm . . . 354–358
        is in part only preparatory, a
            means . . . 367, 368
*Circle*, the, through which the Many move from the One back
        to the One
        in Stoic teaching . . . . . 44
        in Proclus . . . . . . 95, 96
        in Pseudo-Dionysius . . . 98
        in Eckhart . . . . . 117, 118
        in Spinoza . . . . . . 131
        in Hegel . . . . . 212, 213
*Circle*, the, of Necessity, "the wheel of births"
        in Buddhism . . . . . 8–10
        Orphism . . . . . 28, 29
        Schopenhauer . . . 246, 247, 249
*Clearness*, passion for, as test and measure of truth,
        in Descartes . . . . . 125
        in Spinoza . . . . . 125
        in Eckhart . . . . 111–113
        its limited range apprehended by Leibniz and
            Kant . . . . . 142, 143
        ruinous thirst for, in Haeckel . . 281–283
        its fascination for the half-educated . . 310
        contrasted with Richness . . . 134
Conation, no sense of, in Bergson's philosophy . . 299
Consciousness, stage of, was introduced by creative act,
    according to A. R. Wallace . . . 273
"Consciousness in general," in T. H. Green . . . 221
*Contact* between soul and God, in Plotinus . . 83, 84
            St. Augustine . . 90
            Pseudo-Dionysius . 97, 98
            Schleiermacher . 184–188
    between soul and material things
        insisted on against Kant . . 163–185

*Index* 401

|  | PAGES |
|---|---|

*Contact* between soul and material things insisted on against
- Fichtean school . . 179, 180
- Feuerbach . . 236, 237
- apprehended even excessively by Naturalistic Anthropologists . . 277–279
- persistently demanded by Institutional Religions . . . . 328–330
- required by this book . . . 389

Council of Nicæa . . . . . . 166
- Chalcedon . . . . . . 166
- Trent . . . . . 285, 286
- Vatican . . . . . 358, 359

*Creation*, according to Eckhart . . 115; 117, 118
- its operation in Epigenesis,
  - according to A. R. Wallace . 272–274
  - Philip Waggett . 286, 278

*Creaturely spirit*, the, strong in St. Paul . . . 72
- weak in Hegelians . . 222, 223
- absent from M'Taggart . . 229
- expressed by Curé d'Ars . . 373
- present in experience of Eternal Life 368, 369
- final insistence upon . 385; 387; 391, 392

*Critical Philosophy*, the, as founded by Kant . . 137–144
- rendered more radical by Fichte 173, 174
- developed by Schopenhauer 245–248
- modified by Bergson . 295, 296
- criticism of, in Kant 139–144; 146–149; 153–155; 161–166
- Schleiermacher 186–188
- Feuerbach . 235–243

*Curialism*: its predominance in Roman Catholic Church 358, 359; 364 *n*.
- mediæval checks upon . . 357, 358
- present-day hopes for its limitation . 359, 360

*Decline, apparent present-day, of Institutional Religion*
- in Germany . . 333, 334
- France . . . 334
- Portugal, Spain, Italy . . 334
- United States . . . 334
- England . . . 335
- its causes: not sheer perversity of human nature . . . 335
- social-political . . 307–312
- ecclesiastical . . 337–364

*Deification* of human soul, affirmed by Plotinus . . 96
- denied by Proclus . . 96
- affirmed by Pseudo-Dionysius . 100

26

## Index

|  | PAGES |
|---|---|
| *Dependence, feeling of unconditional*, the soul of religion in Schleiermacher's *Glaubenslehre* | 195, 196 |
| *Determinism* in Stoicism | 44 |
| in Spinoza | 129 |
| need and place of, in spiritual life | 133–135, 388 |

*Dim and despairing, and clear and confident outlooks*, their
    weakness and strength as regards religion . 258, 259
*Dionysiac Cultus*, Rohde's account of . . . 23–26
         author's additional observations on . 27

*Dissatisfaction with all things finite*
    keen in Our Lord . . . . 58, 59
        St. Augustine . . . 91
    weaker in St. Thomas . . . 103
    insufficient in Schleiermacher . 188, 189
    strong in Troeltsch . . . . 200
    wanting in M'Taggart . . . 230
        Feuerbach . . 241–243
    its operation in Schopenhauer 256, 257
            Kierkegaard 260–262
            Nietzsche . 263, 264
    absent from Secularist Socialism . . 311
    acutely experienced by John S. Mill . . 311
    persistently felt by the Curé d'Ars . . 373

"*Dogmatic*" *subjectivism* in Kant . . . 140, 141
        Schopenhauer . . 245, 246

*Dualism*, intense ethical, of Zarathustrism . . 12, 13
    of body and soul, in Orphism . . . 29
    as to good and bad men in Stoicism . . 46
            Philo . . . 52
            St. Augustine . . 93, 94
    metaphysical, in Kant . . . 141
        Schopenhauer . . 245, 246

*Duration*, no sense of, in primitive Buddhism . . 10
    gropings after, in St. Thomas . . 105, 106
    not recognized by Spinoza . . . 127
            Kant . . . 143, 144
    specially discriminated and valued by Bergson . 106; 288–291
    criticism of his positions concerning 297, 298 ; 299–301 ; 301, 302
    distinguished from Time and from Eternity 231, 232
    final insistence upon 383, 384 ; 386, 387 ; 390, 391

*Ecstasy*, as sense of Non-Succession, Eternity, in Dionysiac
    experience . . . . . 24–27
    God's love for the creature an, in Johannine writings 73
    the creature's love for God an, in Pseudo-Dionysius 98
*Egyptian Religion*, the old, articulates little or nothing
    concerning Eternal Life . . . . 14

## Index

|  | PAGES |
|---|---|
| *Energeia, the Unmoving,* in Aristotle | 38–41 |
| Philo | 51 |
| *Epigenesis,* very different from Evolution proper | 268, 269 |
| confounded by Darwin with latter | 269, 270 |
| *Epistemology,* Kant's greatness in | 136 |
| motives in his | 137, 138 |
| positions in | 139–144; 150–153 |
| criticism of 139, 140; 141; 142; | 153–155 |
| Fichte's radically *critical* | 173, 174 |
| Schleiermacher's, its subjectivism | 186–188 |
| Feuerbach's radical subjectivist | 233, 234 |
| criticism of | 235–239 |
| Schopenhauer's, a metaphysical dualism | 245–247 |
| criticism of | 247 |
| Darwin's fluctuations in | 266, 267 |
| criticism of | 269–272 |
| Bergson's, tends to a supra-intellectual Intuition | 295, 296 |
| *Eternal Life,* a certain indirect sense of, in Buddhism | 10 |
| apprehension of, in Ramanuja's Brahmanism | 12 |
| traces of, in Zarathustrism | 13 |
| hardly articulated in ancient Egyptian religion | 14 |
| roots of sane apprehension of, in Israelitish religion | 22 |
| of God, and man's approach to it, in Aristotle | 39, 40 |
| no logical room for, in Stoicism | 43–45 |
| of God, in Philo | 51 |
| in Jesus's personal sayings | 57, 64, 65 |
| Fourth Gospel | 75–78 |
| St. Augustine | 89, 90 |
| love of, in Spinoza | 123, 124 |
| no room for, in Spinozism | 127 |
| in Eucken | 179, 180 and *n.* |
| Schleiermacher | 189 |
| Troeltsch | 199, 200 |
| M'Taggart | 226 |
| threefold | 231, 232 |
| constituents of the experience found to be five couples of intuitions and feelings | 364 |
| Abidingness, absolute and relative | 365, 366 |
| Otherness in Likeness | 366, 367 |
| Other-Worldliness contrasting with This-Worldliness | 367, 368 |
| Reality of two degrees | 368, 369 |
| Organization of all reality within infinitely rich Concretion of God | 369–371 |
| experienced most fully in Institutional Religion | 377, 378 |
| present-day examples of such experience | 371–378 |

|                                                      | PAGES      |
|------------------------------------------------------|------------|
| *Eternity* in Orphics                                | 25–27      |
| Parmenides                                           | 31, 32     |
| Plato                                                | 36, 37     |
| Philo                                                | 51         |
| St. Augustine                                        | 88, 89     |
| Boëthius                                             | 104, 105   |
| St. Thomas                                           | 105, 106   |
| *Evil*, positive in Zarathustrism                    | 12, 13     |
| in Israelitish religion                              | 18         |
| indications of a positive conception of, in Orphism  | 29         |
| in Plato                                             | 35         |
| positive in Jesus's preaching                        | 63         |
| in St. Paul                                          | 68, 70     |
| in one current of St. Augustine                      | 93, 94     |
| negative in Pseudo-Dionysius                         | 100        |
| mostly negative in St. Thomas                        | 109        |
| simply negative in Eckhart                           | 115        |
| Spinoza                                              | 129        |
| positive, even radical, in Kant                      | 144–146    |
| problem of, increases in difficulty with insistence upon God's immanence within sensible and human worlds | 287, 288 |
| *Evolution* in strict sense and *Epigenesis*, different | 268, 269 |
| yet confounded by Darwin                             | 269, 270   |
| and Theism (Weissmann)                               | 271, 272   |
| Creative acts (Wallace)                              | 272-274    |
| Ethics (Huxley–Seth)                                 | 274–277    |
| Anthropology (Marrett and others)                    | 277–279    |
| brings three aids to religion :                      | 280        |
| a graduated love of graduated reality                | 280, 281   |
| suggestions as to origin and nature of sex-sins      | 283–286    |
| a deepening of conception of creation                | 286–288    |
| Excommunications, ecclesiastical, admittedly fallible | 351, 352  |
| *Existence*, no fixed point for, in primitive Buddhism | 9, 10    |
| the Absolute of Ramanuja not mere                    | 11         |
| the Fourth Gospel emphasizes the, of God and of Christ | 80       |
| of the First keenly realized by Plotinus *qua* religious soul | 82–84 |
| of God, sense of, all-pervasive in St. Augustine     | 88–92      |
| Proclus declares the First to be above               | 96         |
| of God, St. Thomas on man's knowledge concerning     | 104        |
| of Substance, in Spinoza, different from existence of Modes | 126, 127 |
| Ontological argument for, of God, Kant's opposition to | 151, 152 |
| its treble abiding value                             | 153, 154   |

# Index

*Existence*, Ontological argument for, of God, its imperfections and limits . . 152, 153; 155, 156
of God as central certitude of religion, insisted upon in discussion of Kant . . 160, 161
irritation against very idea of, where proposed as not somehow the human mind itself or this mind's creation, strong in Fichte . . 173
    in Münsterberg . 174
    traceable in Eucken . 179, 180
sense for, in Schleiermacher . . 184–186
    religious imperfection of this sense 186–189
    his aloofness from affirmation of, of God in the *Reden* . . 192, 193
of God treated by Feuerbach as purely human presupposition and of no importance . 234, 235
Feuerbach's own history shows profound importance of the belief . . 243, 244
finally affirmed by Schopenhauer . 256, 257
intense realization of, of God, by Kierkegaard 260–262
Darwin's fluctuations as to, of God . 266, 267
keen sense for, within Roman Catholic Church 342, 345
strong instinct of, as part of experience of Eternal Life . . . . . 368
final affirmation of . . . 382–387; 394–396

*Factual Happenings* and *fact-like historical pictures*, necessity (yet difficulty) of admission of this distinction for Roman Catholic Church . . . 343–347
*Fall*, doctrine of the, reinterpreted by F. R. Tennant and J. M. Wilson . . 283–286
    enthusiastic adhesion to, by Schopenhauer . . . 252, 253
Feeling, religious, two contradictory estimates of, in Schleiermacher's *Reden* 183–185; 189, 190
    estimate of, in the *Glaubenslehre* 195, 196
    classical Christian estimate of . 191, 192
Fideism rejected by Roman Church (see Pietism) . . 344
Fierceness, religious (see also *Persecution*)
    in Johannine writings . . . 19
    in St. Augustine . . 93, 94; 192
    Schleiermacher's obtuseness concerning 189, 192
*Final Discriminations* of book:
    Eternal Life, an effect from interaction of Realities 382, 383
    three things involved in fullest, *i.e.* in God's 383
    still real, but no more full, in man . 383, 384
    effect from operation of full, within our slighter . . . . 384, 385
    Time, as Duration, no barrier, but necessary means to human sense of . 386, 387

PAGES

*Final Discriminations* of book—*continued*
   Eternal Life, Spatial concepts and imagery also required
              for full human consciousness of    387, 388
            Material things also necessary for develop-
              ment of this sense . . .   389
            achieved as alternative to Spiritual Death :
            probable characteristic of latter, as to
              Time (Duration) . . 389–391
            what experience of, requires with respect
              to consciousness of human weakness,
              need of God and sense of sin and
              with regard to conceptions of total
              corruption of human nature .   391, 392
*Finalism*, Bergson's aversion to all . . .   299–302
*Formalism* in Ethics, in Kant . . .   146, 147
*Freedom*, Bergson removes mechanical obstacles, but fails
   fully to apprehend spiritual requisites of . .   299–302

Gnosticism, apparent approximation yet vehement antagon-
            ism to, of Fourth Gospel . . . 74, 75
            in Schopenhauer as regards marriage . . 255
            is untrue to life . . . . . 332
            its rejection of O.T. condemned by Catholic
              Church . . . . . 351
            its condemnation of Law as essentially evil . 353
*God* in the Psalms . . . . . . 48
        Philo . . . . . . 51–54
        Jesus's personal utterances . . . 64, 65
        St. Paul . . . . . 68, 69
        Johannine writings . . . . 73, 74
        Plotinus . . . . . 83, 84
        Pseudo-Dionysius . . . . 97–99
        St. Thomas . . . . 107–109
        Eckhart . . . . . 113–115
        without reality in Spinoza's system . . 125–132
        precarious position of, in Kant's *critical* system   150–156 ;
                                        157, 158
        only sporadically admitted by Fichte . 174, 175, 176
        indifference to, in Schleiermacher's *Reden* . 192, 193
           conceived Spinozistically in his *Glaubenslehre*   197
        Hegel carries history into . . . 213–215
        M'Taggart and a non-omnipotent, non-creative   224, 225 ;
                                        229, 230
        Feuerbach finds, to be man's own nature . 233–235
        Schopenhauer even more opposed to, of Pantheism
           than to God of Theism . . . 249, 250
        Kierkegaard's profound sense of Reality and Differ-
           ence, but not of Likeness, of . . 260–262
        place of, in doctrine of Selection and Descent . . 272

|   |   |
|---|---|
| **God**, love of, sole sufficient motive for love of man where latter most required | 316, 317 |
| His absolute Abidingness | 365, 366 |
| His Likeness in Unlikeness to us | 366 |
| *the* Reality of realities | 368 |
| the unspeakable Richness of | 369 |
| the Curé d'Ars on | 373 |
| Abbé Huvelin on | 375–377 |
| cause, and sole full possessor, of Eternal Life | 382, 383 |
| adoration of, the centre of religion | 160, 161; 385, 395 |
| **Godhead** and God contrasted in Eckhart | 113–115 |
| **Grace**, sense of, absent from Gautama's teaching | 12, 29 |
| present in Ramanuja | 11, 12 |
| in Isaiah | 18 |
| Ezekiel | 20 |
| Orphism | 28, 29 |
| its presence doubtful in Plato | 34, 36 |
| absent from Stoicism | 46 |
| in the Psalms | 48 |
| Philo | 53, 54 |
| Jesus's teaching | 57, 59, 64 |
| St. Paul | 68–70, 72 |
| Fourth Gospel | 76–79 |
| Plotinus | 84 |
| St. Augustine | 90–92 |
| St. Thomas | 108, 109 |
| Kant's suspicious attitude towards | 156, 157 |
| criticism of | 160–162, 167 *n*. |
| obscure in, or absent from, Schleiermacher | 196, 197 |
| approximation to, in Schopenhauer | 256, 257 |
| in Kierkegaard | 261, 262 |
| Sorel's keen | 321 |
| noblest root and flower of religion | 385 |
| *Hellenic Experiences*, the, their five stages | 23–42 |
| *Hellenistic, Jewish-, Times,* | 42–54 |
| *Christian-, Times.* | 81–100 |
| Hexateuch, later documents of the | 344; see also 16, 19, 20 |
| *Hindooism*, as represented by Ramanuja | 10–12 |
| *Historical element of religion:* | |
| St. Augustine's sense of | 92, 93 |
| insensibility of Kant to | 158, 159; 164–168 |
| slightness of sense for, in Fichte | 177 |
| strength of sense for, in Eucken | 179, 180 *n*. |
| Schleiermacher | 192 |
| keen instinct of Roman Catholic Church for | 342, 343, 344 |
| difficulties in | 343–345 |
| possible solutions of | 346, 347 |
| fundamental necessity of | 342 |

|  | PAGES |
|---|---|
| *History* found by Hegel in God Himself | 211–216 |
|     criticism of this | 216, 217 |
|     driven out everywhere by Schopenhauer | 249–251 |
|     conceived materialistically by Marx | 304–307 |
|       the element of truth present here | 314, 315 |
|     Scholasticism without sense of | 340 |
|     achieved by Durational man with aid of Eternal God | 386, 387 |
| *Identity* of thought and being, in Eckhart | 312 |
|     in Hegel | 201, 207–211 |
|     of human and Absolute Reason in Hegel | 211–216 |
| *Illusion*, religion taken by Feuerbach as all | 233–235 |
|     criticism of this | 235–243 |
| *Immortality of the soul*, its late apprehension amongst the Jews | 21, 22 |
|     its first apprehension as Eternity in Greece | 23–26 |
|     conceived as accompanied by memory, in Orphic Tablets | 29–31 |
|     in Fichte | 176 |
|     in Schleiermacher's *Reden* | 193, 194 |
|     conceived by M'Taggart as coupled with Pre-existence and possessed of only intermittent memory | 225, 226 |
|     Schopenhauer's aspirations and shy convictions concerning | 256, 257 |
|     conviction of, wholesome where based upon faith in God | 21, 22 |
| *Individualism*, excessive, in Kant's Ethics | 147–149 |
| *Individuality*, dignity of right, in St. Thomas | 109 |
|     finally affirmed | 395 |
| *Infinite, the*, in Schleiermacher, rather the Spatial Infinite | 188 |
|     in Feuerbach, man's own nature | 233, 234 |
| Inquisition, the General | 349 |
|     the Spanish | 348, 349 |
| *Institutional Religion*, how far here considered | 323–325 |
|     threefold necessity of | 325–333 |
|     present-day movement away from | 333–335 |
|     five pairs of aids and difficulties brought by: | |
|       as to Philosophy | 337–344 |
|       History | 342–347 |
|       Authority and Freedom | 347–353 |
|       Law and Initiative | 353–360 |
|       Politics | 361–364 |
|     awakens, and yet is checked and supplemented by, Eternal Life, in five ways | 364–371 |

## Index

|  | PAGES |
|---|---|
| *Institutional Religion*, contemporary examples of before-mentioned operation within Roman Catholic Church | 371–378 |
| *Intellectualism*, in Aristotle | 40, 41 |
| in Eckhart | 112, 113 |
| in Hegel | 215 |
| a certain, in English Hegelians | 222 |
| how far helpful to religion | 258 |
| *Intuition*, a sudden, comes to purified soul, in Plato | 36 |
| in St. Augustine | 90 |
| of Universe, as essence of religion, in Schleiermacher | 183–186 |
| preferred to abstraction by Schopenhauer | 248 |
| a supra-intellectual, sought by Bergson | 295, 296 |
| *Israelitish Religion*, its range | 15, 16 |
| three stages | 16–20 |
| concentration upon God as experienced in this life | 21, 22 |

| *Jewish-Hellenistic experiences and conceptions* | |
|---|---|
| in the Psalms | 48 |
| Book of Daniel | 49 |
| Ecclesiasticus, Second Book of Maccabees, Apocalypse of Baruch, and Psalms of Solomon | 49, 50 |
| Wisdom of Solomon | 50 |
| in Philo of Alexandria | 50–54 |
| Judaism attacked by Schopenhauer because of its optimism | 252, 253 |
| its merits here | 255 |

| *Kingdom of God*, the, in Jesus's personal utterances | 56–63 |
|---|---|
| its four characteristics in its apocalyptic, transcendent presentment | 56–59 |
| its characteristics in its prophetic, immanental presentment | 59–63 |
| Troeltsch on this double presentation | 199, 200 |
| how both these two presentations or movements are necessary still | 315–317 |
| *Knowledge*, the Pneuma of God alone has, of the things of God, in St. Paul | 68 |
| taken as intuitive and akin to physical sight in Fourth Gospel | 75 |
| is apprehension of like by like in Sextus Empiricus | 75 |
| the One is apprehended through a Presence above, in Plotinus | 83 |
| God known to soul because He Himself is present within it, in St. Augustine | 91, 92 |
| we know clearly *that* God exists, we know confusedly *what* He is, in St. Thomas | 104 |

PAGES

*Knowledge*, man blessed because he *knows* how near God is to him, in Eckhart . . . . . 112
    can be conceived as independent of an object, according to Kant . . . 129, 140
    of *Noumena* impossible, yet we know they are utterly heterogeneous to our conceptions of them, according to Kant . . 140, 144
    is mind's recognition within object of what itself has placed there, according to Kant 141, 142
    man's, ever only of himself, according to Feuerbach . . . . 233, 234
      criticism of this . . . . 235–238
    of its own continuous anthropomorphisms denied to religion by Feuerbach . 234, 235
      criticism . . . . . 242, 243
    Darwin's misgivings as to range of man's powers of . . . . 266, 267
      criticism . . . . . 268–271
    our, not attained without stimulation of the senses . . . . . 328, 329
    of Eternal Life, final determinations concerning our . . . . . 382–394

*Law*, the Mosaic, its growth . . . . 16, 19, 20, 50
    the Canon, and the Church . . . 353–360
      very ancient and wise acceptance of Law in general by Church . . 353, 354
      rights and excesses of later developments of Canon Law studied in connection with Sohm's contentions . 354–357
      in Middle Ages . . . 357, 358
      as leading to utter centralisation and curialism . . . 358, 359
      three reflections upon this . . 359, 360
Legalism, largely present in *Priestly Code* . . . 20
Logic, position of, in Stoic system . . . . 43
    Hegel's jump from, to Reality, described and criticised . . . . . 207–211
*Logical pyramid*, the, taken as representing actual condition of Reality in Proclus . . . . . 96
    Eckhart . . . . . 118
    Haeckel . . . . . 282
    not always so taken by Pseudo-Dionysius . . 99
    rejected in his personal work by Darwin . 280, 281
*Logos*, the Stoic . . . . . . 45
    the, in Philo . . . . . . 52
    in Fourth Gospel . . . . 73, 74; 76
*Longing after God*, as present in man, affirmed by Plotinus . . . . . . 84

|   |   |
|---|---|
| | PAGES |
| *Longing after God*, affirmed by St. Augustine | 91 |
| less vividly apprehended by St. Thomas | 103 |
| Loretto, legend as to transference of Holy House of | 345, 346 |
| Magic and Sacraments, weakness of Liberal Protestantism concerning | 328, 329 |
| Man, object as well as ground of religion, in Feuerbach | 233, 234 |
| criticism of this position | 235–243 |
| Materialism of Stoics | 43–45 |
| Hume | 138 |
| last stage of Feuerbach | 243, 244 |
| Marx and Engels | 304, 305 |
| Haeckel | 282 |
| *Material things*, position of Locke concerning reality of | 138 |
| of Berkeley | 137, 138 |
| an effectuating function denied to them in moral and religious life by Kant | 158 |
| Troeltsch | 328 |
| affirmed by Primitive Christianity | 329, 330 |
| Roman Catholic Church | 328–330 |
| final determinations of book concerning | 389 |
| *Mathematical Physics* are found a place and function within Spiritual Life, by Spinoza | 124, 125 |
| estimate of this scheme | 133–135 |
| *Metaphysics* in Philo | 51, 53 |
| St. Paul | 71, 72 ; 191 |
| Fourth Gospel | 73–75 ; 191 |
| St. Augustine | 87 ; 93 |
| Pseudo-Dionysius | 97, 99 |
| St. Thomas | 101, 103, 107 |
| position of Kant towards | 137, 138 |
| of Schleiermacher | 184–191 |
| M'Taggart | 223, 224 |
| Darwin unaccustomed to | 266 |
| and Religion interrelated in Roman Catholic Church | 337, 338 |
| according to final discriminations of this book | 392 |
| "Modernism," Heliocentrism formerly a | 340, 341 |
| Modes, the, in Spinoza | 126, 127 |
| *Monism*, a modified, in Ramanuja | 11, 12 |
| a pure, in Parmenides | 31, 32 |
| in one current of Eckhart | 111–120 |
| a pure materialist, in Haeckel | 281–283 |
| Moravian Brethren, the | 180, 181 |
| *Movements, the two*, in Religion in Our Lord's life and teaching | 64–66 |
| insisted upon by Troeltsch | 199, 200 |
| only one of, in Schopenhauer | 253–256 |

|                                                                           | PAGES |
|---|---|
| *Movements, the two*, alone a match for present-day social problem | 315–319 |
|     insisted upon as part of experience of Eternal Life | 367 |
| *Multiplicity in Unity and Unity in Multiplicity*, sense of, in experience of Eternal Life | 369–371 |
| Mysticism of Fourth Gospel | 73 |
|     in Plotinus | 83 |
|     Schopenhauer | 257 |
|     rejected by Wilhelm Hermann | 330, 331 |
| Mythology, where we sink back into, according to Schleiermacher | 185 |
|     the sole alternative to a Critical Anthropomorphism, as seen in constructions of Hegelians of the Left | 205 |
|     of Materialism | 272 |
|     in Haeckel | 282, 283 |
| Natural and Revealed Religion first systematically distinguished in Christian theology by St. Thomas | 102, 103 |
| *Naturalism in Anthropology* | 277–279 |
| *Negative Movement*, the, in Plato | 33, 34; 37, 38 |
|     absent from Aristotle | 38 |
|     in Our Lord's teaching | 58, 59; 65, 66 |
|     St. Paul | 70 |
|     Plotinus | 82, 86 |
|     Pseudo-Dionysius | 100 |
|     Eckhart | 115, 117 |
|     Spinoza | 123, 133 |
|     Hegel | 213, 216 |
|     Schopenhauer | 251–253; 256, 257 |
|     criticism of | 253–256; 257–259 |
|     absent from secularist Socialism | 311 |
|     necessary in struggle with present-day social problem | 316, 317 |
|     part of experience of Eternal Life | 367 |
|     present in writings of Institutional Religionists | 371, 372 |
|     in the Curé d'Ars | 373 |
|     Abbé Huvelin | 376, 377 |
| *Neo-Platonism*, anticipations of, in Philo | 53 |
|     its richest exponent, Plotinus | 81, 82; 85 |
|     its systematizer, Proclus | 95, 96 |
|     in Pseudo-Dionysius | 97, 98 |
|     St. Augustine | 87, 88 |
|     Eckhart | 115 |
|     Spinoza | 122, 131 |
|     Hegel | 212, 213 |
|     Schopenhauer | 257 |

## Index 413

| | PAGES |
|---|---|
| *Neo-Scholasticism*, its strength and its weakness | 337–340 |
| *Nirvana*, the, of Gautama | 9, 10 |
|     Schopenhauer | 256, 257 |
| *Nothing, the, Nothingness*, in Eckhart | 114 |
|     absolute, denied by Schopenhauer | 256 |
| Nunzios, Papal, the system of | 363 |

*Obscure Apprehension* or Obscure Knowledge
    of the blessed life, in St. Augustine . . 91
    God, in St. Thomas . . . . 104
    generally, in Leibniz . . 142, 143, 143 *n*.
    in Kant . . . 142
    its weakness and its strength as regards religion . . . . 258, 259
Old Testament, the Church's inclusion of, in Christian Canon, lesson of . . . . . 351
*Ontological Argument*, the, for God's existence, Kant's rejection of . . 150–152; 155, 156
    its significance and value . . 152–154
*Ontological Sense*, the religious,
    strong in Plotinus . . . . . 83
    St. Augustine . . . 88, 91
    halting and weak in Kant . . 154, 155, 160, 161
    restricted in scope in Fichte . . . 173–175
    Eucken . . 179, 180
    its vivid, yet limited and inconsistent, operation in Schleiermacher's *Reden* . . . 184–189
    treated as illusion by Feuerbach . 233–238; 241–243
    supremely strong in Kierkegaard . . 260–262
    strong in Roman Catholic Church . . 342, 343
    final insistence upon fundamental importance of . . . . . 385; 395, 396
*Optimism*, Spinoza possesses too much immediate . 133
    Kant opposed to immediate . . 144–146
    Eucken's opposition to . . . 179
    Schleiermacher's, largely immediate . . 197
    Troeltsch discovers, to be final, not preliminary, in Christianity . . . . 199, 200
    found to be too predominant even in the religious English Hegelians . . . 222, 223
    Schopenhauer's rejection of . . 247, 251, 252
    crude, of secularist Socialism . . 311, 320
Orderer, a non-omnipotent, held to be a reasonable belief by M'Taggart . . . . . 224, 225
Ordering, a cosmic active, but not an Orderer, accepted by Fichte . . . . . 174, 175
Organic, apprehension of reality as, in proportion to depth of the reality, in experience of Eternal Life . 369–371
*Organic conception* of human society by Stoics . . 47, 48

|   |   |
|---|---|
| | PAGES |
| *Organic conception* of Kingdom of God, in Jesus's teaching | 62, 63 |
| future life, in same | 63, 64 |
| Church in St. Paul | 70–72 |
| world of Spirits in Johannine writings | 78, 79 |
| human society and Church in St. Augustine | 93, 94 |
| Pseudo-Dionysius | 98, 99 |
| St. Thomas | 109 |
| human society in Spinoza | 132, 133 |
| M'Taggart | 225, 232 |
| *Organic life*, everything in intention of religion to be, according to Schleiermacher | 192 |
| *Organic, love of the*, strong in Darwin | 280, 281 |
| eliminated by Haeckel | 281–283 |
| *Origin* of Episcopal sees in ancient Gaul, question of | 345 |
| Sin, according to Tennant and Wilson | 283–285 |
| reflexions on theory | 285, 286 |
| *Orphics, the,* their first appearance | 27, 28 |
| doctrine | 28, 29 |
| like and unlike Buddhism | 29 |
| the tablets of | 29, 30 |
| various constituents and probable experimental origin of doctrine of | 30, 31 |
| *Otherness*, sense of, of God, strong in Israelitish religion | 21, 22 |
| wanting in M'Taggart | 230 |
| unchecked in Kierkegaard | 260–262 |
| a constituent of experience of Eternal Life | 366, 367 |
| *Other-Worldliness and This-Worldliness,* double sense of, in Troeltsch | 199, 200 |
| part of experience of Eternal Life | 367, 368 |
| finally insisted on in this book | 396 |
| *Overflow, the, of the One* in Plotinus | 84 |
| Proclus | 98 |
| modified in direction of Self-Revelation by Pseudo-Dionysius | 98, 99 |
| | |
| *Pantheism* of Stoics | 43–45 |
| Spinoza | 125–129 |
| Schleiermacher in his life | 181, 182 |
| *Reden* | 188; 190–193 |
| *Glaubenslehre* | 197 |
| Schopenhauer's affinity with, yet objection to | 249–251 |
| Sorel's opposition to | 321, 322 |
| preliminary, a, advocated | 134, 135; 388, 389 |
| *Papa Angelico*, possibility and power of a | 363, 364 |

## Index 415

*Parables of Our Lord*, the, two kinds:
    parables of immediate expectancy . 57
    of slow growth . . 60, 61
*Penetration*, power of, possessed by spirits, supremely by God,
    taught by St. Paul . . . . 69
    emphasized by Fourth Gospel . . . 78
    insisted upon by Roman Catholic Church . 229
    ignored by M'Taggart . . . 227, 229
    final affirmation concerning, in this book 386, 387
*Permanence*, as highest element of Personal Life, insisted
    upon by Aristotle . . . . 38-41
    indicated by Our Lord . . . . 64
    proclaimed by Fourth Gospel . . . 77, 78
    St. Augustine . . . 88-91
    taught by St. Thomas . . . 105, 106
    Eckhart . . . 114, 115
    insufficiently apprehended by Bergson 298, 301
*Permanence*, fully understood by Bosanquet . . 301, 302
    final insistence upon, in this book . 383, 384
*Persecution and Patient Zeal*, two currents in Roman
    Catholic Church . . . . 348, 349; 349-353
*Personality*, its dignity insisted upon, as diversity of natures,
    by St. Thomas . . . . 109
    insufficiently guarded by Hegel . . 217, 218
    is without memory of its own past in
    M'Taggart . . 224, 225; 227; 230; 232
    inadequately apprehended by Bergson . 294-298
*Pessimism* in Gautama's teaching . . 8-10; 165 *n.*, 392
    Our Lord's life and preaching . . 59, 60; 391
    St. Paul . . . . 391, 392
    St. Augustine . . . 93, 94; 391
    absence of a sufficient, in Spinoza . 133-135
    as to man's ethical dispositions and doings, in
    Kant . . . . 144-146
    insufficient, in Schleiermacher . . . 197
    strongly operative in Troeltsch . . 199, 200
    slight, in M'Taggart . . . . 229
    excessive, of Schopenhauer 249; 251, 252
    entirely absent in Haeckel . 281-283
    insufficient, in secularist Socialism . 309-311
    a preliminary, insisted upon by author 249; 253-255; 315-319
*Philosophy*, its relation to Religion
    in Philo . . . . 50, 51
    Fourth Gospel . . . 73, 74
    St. Augustine . . . 87, 88
    Pseudo-Dionysius . . . 95
    St. Thomas . . . 101-103, 107
    takes first place in Eckhart . 112, 113, 119

416    *Index*

|  | PAGES |
|---|---|
| *Philosophy*, takes first place in Hegel | 215 |
| Hegelians | 222, 223 |
| its vicissitudes within Roman Catholic Church | 337–341, 341 *n.* |
| Pietism, its influence upon Schleiermacher | 181, 182 |
| not Catholic | 333, 344 |
| *Prayer*, vocal, rejected by Kant | 157, 158 |
| held to affect only man, by Schleiermacher | 197 |
| Claude Montefiore on | 371 |
| the Curé d'Ars upon | 373 |
| final insistence upon, as essential to Religion | 395, 396 |
| *Presence of God within human soul in this life* | |
| concentration of Israelitish religion upon | 21, 22 |
| insisted upon by St. Paul | 68 |
| Fourth Gospel | 78 |
| vividly apprehended by Plotinus, in spite of his philosophy | 83, 84 |
| proclaimed by St. Augustine | 90, 91 |
| sense of, weakened by doctrine of Deification of human soul in Dionysius | 100 |
| eliminated by Monism, in Eckhart | 115 |
| affirmed as against Kant | 153, 154 |
| M'Taggart | 229–232 |
| Feuerbach | 242, 243 |
| secularist Socialism | 311 |
| sense of, a constituent of experience of Eternal Life | 366, 367 |
| final insistence upon | 384, 385 |
| *Prevenience of God* | |
| absent from Plato | 36 |
| operative in Philo | 53, 54 |
| insisted upon by Our Lord | 57, 64 |
| proclaimed in Johannine writings | 78, 79 |
| absent from Plotinus *qua* philosopher | 84, 85 |
| continuously operative in St. Augustine | 91, 92 |
| sense of, weak in Kant | 160 |
| its rudiments strong in Schleiermacher | 184–186 |
| vividly realized by Roman Catholic Church | 342–344 |
| by Abbé Huvelin | 375, 376 |
| insisted upon by author | 368 ; 382, 383 ; 385 ; 387, 388 ; 391 ; 396 |
| Protestantism, Schopenhauer on, in so far as anti-ascetical | 252 |
| *Purification of the Soul* | |
| in Orphism | 29, 30 |
| Plato | 35, 38 |
| Our Lord's teaching | 65, 66 |
| Pseudo-Dionysius | 100 |
| Spinoza | 122, 123 ; 134, 135 |
| sense of its need, a constituent of experience of Eternal Life | 366, 367 |

# Index

**Realized Perfection**
    centre of Our Lord's experience and teaching . 64–66
    insistence upon, by Fourth Gospel . . 80
    sense of, slight in Kant . . 157, 158; 160
    admitted in one passage by Fichte . . 176
    demanded by Hegel . . . . 211
    not furnished by M'Taggart . . 228, 229
    eliminated by Feuerbach . . 233, 234
        criticism of this elimination . . 235–243; 244
        final insistence upon, as fundamental in religion 385

**Reality**, man's knowledge is knowledge of, as against
    Kant    139, 140; 141, 142; 149; 150, 151; 153–156
    keen sense of, in Schleiermacher . . 184–186
    but not followed up by him . . 186–189
    degrees of, apprehended by man, as against
        Feuerbach . . . 242, 243
    graduated love for graduated, characteristic of
        Darwin . . . . . 281, 282
    sense of two depths of, involved in experience of
        Eternal Life . . . . 368, 369

**Religion**, the place of
    in Eckhart penultimate . . . 112, 113
    in Kant . . . . . 150–167
    in Schleiermacher's *Reden* . . 183–190
                  *Glaubenslehre* . 195, 196
    in Hegel penultimate . . . . 215
    in English Hegelians . . . 222, 223
    partial dependence of, upon Social Conditions . 314
    requires intercourse with other complexes of life, as
        against Hermann . . . 330–333
            with Philosophy . . . 337, 338
                History . . . 342–347
                Law . . . . 353–360
                Politics . . . 361–364
    its two movements according to Our Lord 58, 59; 65, 66
            insisted upon by Troeltsch 199, 200
            as against Schopenhauer . 253
            required in struggle with the
                present-day social problem 315–318
    its three characteristics which operate against
        fanaticism . . . 392–394
    the two constant causes of simplification at work
        within . . . . . 394–396

**Richness in Attributes** as co-related to degree of elevation in
    scale of Reality
    exceptionally affirmed, generally denied, by Plato . 34–36
    denied, as regards God, by Aristotle . . 39, 40
    admitted also as to God in lesser part of Pseudo-
        Dionysius . . . . . 99

|                                       | PAGES |
|---|---|
| *Richness in Attributes* as co-related to degree of elevation in scale of Reality | |
|   St. Thomas sometimes ignores | 107, 108 |
|     sometimes proclaims | 108, 109 |
|   Spinoza generally denies | 126, 129 |
|     yet occasionally affirms | 130 |
|   Hegel proclaims principle of | 202, 203 ; 211 |
|     but then denies this principle in his positions | 207, 208 ; 217, 218 |
|   affirmed against Feuerbach | 236, 237 |
|   insisted upon by Wallace | 272, 273 |
|   instinctively assumed and applied by Darwin | 280, 281 |
|   ruthlessly denied by Haeckel | 281–283 |
|   intermittent affirmation of, by Bergson | 295, 296 |
|   sense of, is part of experience of Eternal Life | 369, 370 |
|   final affirmation of | 383 ; 386, 387 ; 395 |
| *Rigorism, Ethical,* in Stoicism | 45, 46 |
|   Kant | 146, 147 |
|   overcome by Fichte | 176, 177 |
| *Roman Catholic Church*, the, adopts St. Thomas as its dominant exponent | 101, 102 |
|   condemns Eckhart | 119 |
|   its future according to Georges Sorel | 321–323 |
|   its present-day position | 334, 335 |
|   and Original Sin | 285, 286 ; 335 |
|   its attitude towards Philosophy | 337–340 |
|   Natural Science | 340, 341 |
|   History | 342–347 |
|   Persecution and Tolerance | 347–353 |
|   Law | 353–360 |
|   Sohm on antiquity of | 354, 355 |
|   its attitude towards Politics | 361–364 |
|   witnesses to Eternal Life within, in recent times | 372–377 |
| *Sacraments* as productively operative | |
|   no place for, in Kant's Critical Philosophy | 162–164 |
|   opposed by Liberal Protestantism | 328, 329 |
|   cause of Wycliffe's passion against | 329 |
|   their place and necessity | 328, 329 |
|   Our Lord and | 329, 330 |
|   St. Paul and | 330 |
|   Fourth Gospel and | 330 |
| *Scepticism,* Kant's general intentions are against | 137, 138 ; 159, 160 ; 167 |
|   operation of, in Kant's Epistemology | 140, 141 |
|   Ethics | 147 |
|   Religion | 150, 151 ; 154, 155, 156–159 |

## Index

|  | PAGES |
|---|---|
| *Scepticism*, operation of, in Kant's, Religion, criticism | 159–167 |
|     in Fichte | 177, 178 |
|     Schleiermacher | 185 ; 192–194 |
|     criticism | 186–188 ; 194, 195 |
|   intense, of Feuerbach's latest stage | 243, 244 |
|   Schopenhauer's | 245–248 |
|   Sorel's hatred of | 321, 322 |
|   pure, impossible | 154, 155 |
|   religious, the most ruinous of all | 236–243 |
| Scholastic Philosophy in the Roman Catholic Church, its strength and its weakness | 338–340 |
| Science, Mathematico-Physical, its place in the spiritual life | 123 ; 133–135 |
|   considered in connection with Spinoza | 122 |
|   finally affirmed | 388 |
| *Secularism*, three causes of | 307–312 |
|   movement away from | 319–323 |
| Selection, Natural, and Struggle for Existence, insufficient as explanations of Origin of Species | 271 |
| *Self-consciousness*, loss of, in the *Nirvana* of Gautama | 9, 10 |
|   regaining of, in the Beyond, according to Orphic tablets | 29, 31 |
|   denied and attributed to the First by Plotinus | 82, 84 |
|   denied and yet implied as highest category by Spinoza | 127, 128 ; 131 |
|   treated lightly and yet strictly required by Schleiermacher's *Reden* | 192–195 |
|   implications of human, according to his *Glaubenslehre* | 195, 198 |
|   of God, Hegel's fundamental principle | 202–204 |
|   insistence upon fruitfulness of this principle | 204–206 |
|   Hegel's identification of human and Divine, ruins his principle | 215–218 |
|   man's awaking to, described as against Feuerbach | 236–239 |
|   Schopenhauer's unhappy, affects his philosophy | 244, 245 ; 247–256 ; 256, 257 |
|   Darwin's high esteem of | 268, 280 |
|   stage of, due to a Divine, creative act, according to Wallace | 272, 273 |
|   Haeckel's contempt for | 281–283 |
|   final affirmation of high worth of | 383, 384 |
| Self-seeking, in Spinoza | 133 |
| *Simultaneity*, no sense of, in Primitive Buddhism | 10 |
|   sense of, as central in Dionysiac experience | 27 |
|   central in Aristotle's Pure Energeia | 38–40, 41 |
|   of God, in Our Lord's teaching | 64 |

## Index

|  | PAGES |
|---|---|
| *Simultaneity*, of God, in Fourth Gospel | 77, 78 |

of God, and possibly at last of human soul's
    knowledge, in St. Augustine . . 90
        St. Thomas . 105, 106
      denied by Hegel . . . 215–217
      affirmed of all real existence by M'Taggart . 226
            by Schopenhauer 249, 250
      insisted upon by Bosanquet against Bergson 301, 302
      final propositions concerning . . 382–385, 396
*Sin*, doctrine and practice of Our Lord as to . . 65, 391, 392
            St. Paul . . 391, 392
            St. Augustine . . 94; 391
    imperfect sense of, in Eckhart . . . . 115
            Schleiermacher . . . 197
    profound sense of man's impurity in Schopenhauer 252, 253
    conception of, still retained by Darwin . . 268, 277
    origin of, according to Tennant . . . 283, 284
    reality of, affirmed by Sorel . . . 321, 322
    sense of, affirmed as part of experience of Eternal Life 366, 367
    final insistence upon reality of . . . 391, 392
Social Conditions, their influence upon chances of religion
    with average men . . . . . 314
*Social Element* in Plato . . . . . 37, 38
        Stoic teaching . . . . 47, 48
        Our Lord's preaching . . . 63, 66
        St. Paul . . . . 70–72
        Fourth Gospel . . . 78, 79
        St. Augustine . . . 93, 94
        Pseudo-Dionysius . . . . 98, 99
        St. Thomas denies . . . 107, 108
            affirms . . . 108, 109
        in Spinoza . . . . 132, 133
        insufficiently apprehended by Kant . 147–149
        fully realized by Schleiermacher in his
            *Glaubenslehre* . . . . 198
        recognized by M'Taggart . . 225
        exaggerated and travestied by Marx 304, 306
        as practised by Institutional Religion 326, 327
        in Religion, double . . . 294–396
*Socialism*, doctrinaire and secularist, formulated by Marx
        and Engels . . . . 304–307
        its three causes . . . . 306–312
        double general gain to be derived from militant 312, 313
        element of profound truth parodied by . 314, 315
        religion, in its two movements, alone sufficient to
            cure . . . . . 315–319
        indications of the abatement of . . 319–323
*Social Problem, the Present-day*, in its relation to sense of
            Eternal Life . . . 303–323

|  | PAGES |
|---|---|
| *Social Problem*, its novelty | 303, 304 |
| general beneficial effects | 312–315 |
| beneficial effects upon religion | 315–319 |
| Social workers, Christian | 315 |

*Soul*, the sensual, distinguished by St. Paul from the Mind,
       and still more from the Spirit . . . 66
   *the human*, separated, in Plotinus, from other souls, not
         by Space but by Difference . . 83, 84
       and longs after God by necessity of
         its nature . . . 84
       non-spatial in St. Augustine . . 87, 88
       can grasp even here for a little the ever
         abiding Eternity . . 89, 90
       possesses the blessed life and God in a
         real, though obscure manner . 91, 92
       and necessarily longs after God . . 91
       higher and lower powers of, respectively
         touch Eternity and Time, in Eckhart 111, 112
       the little spark, the increate light of 112, 114
       is all things . . 115
       God generates His Son in . . 117

*Space*, the soul and God without, in Plotinus . . 83, 84
                St. Augustine . . 87, 88
                Eckhart . . . 115
   sense of, allotted no function in spiritual life by Kant 143, 144
   sense of, keen in Schleiermacher . . 188
   treatment of, by Bergson . . 291–294; 297, 298
   insistence upon need of distinguishing between Con-
      ceptual and Real . . . 297, 298
   final affirmation of important rôle played by concepts
      and imagery of, in consciousness of Eternal Life 387, 388

*Spirit*, the, in St. Paul. . . . . . 67–72
   Absolute, in Hegel . . . 202, 203, 209
         and human spirit . . 212
         and History . . 212–216
         criticism . . 217, 218

Stages of Revelation, an essential doctrine of Catholic
   Church . . . . . . . 351

State, the World-, of the Stoics . . . 47, 48
   in St. Augustine . . . . 93
   Hegel . . . . 214, 215
   Marx . . . . . 306, 307

*Stoicism*, Oriental origin of earlier chiefs of . . 43
   materialistic Pantheism of . . . 43–45
   ethical Rigorism of . . . . 45, 46
   organic conception of human society entertained
      by . . . . . 47, 48
   its renunciation utterly surpassed in delicacy and
      range by Our Lord . . . 65, 66

## Index

|  | PAGES |
|---|---|
| *Stoicism*, traces of influence of, in Philo | 52, 54 |
| St. Paul | 72 |
| Fourth Gospel | 73–75 |
| Spinoza | 122, 132, 135 |
| Kant | 161 |
| its self-sufficingness rejected | 161; 385 |

Subject, a self-subsisting, absent from primitive Buddhism . 9, 10
   no transition possible between, and object in
      Schopenhauer . . . . . 246
   the general form of, and object abolished with re-
      nunciation of Will, according to Schopen-
      hauer . . . . . 256, 257

*Subjectivism* of Kant . . 139–144; 150, 151; 157, 158
      criticism 139, 140; 141; 142; 153–156; 160, 161
      of Fichte . . . . 173, 174; 177, 178
      Eucken's stand against . . . 179, 180
      of Schleiermacher . . . 186–188
      Feuerbach . . . . 233–235
      criticism . . . . 235–243
      Schopenhauer . . . 245–248

Temporal Power, the Roman Catholic Church's claim to, over
   Roman States . . . . . 362, 363

*Theism*, primitive Buddhism without, because not yet a
   religion . . . . 8–10; 165 *n*.
   Ramanuja approaches . . . 10–12
   Israelitish . . . . . 16–20
   excludes speculations as to Beyond . 21–23
   intermittent, imperfect glimpses of, in Plato 33, 34; 35–37
   Aristotle distant from, in all but the conception of
      Pure *Energeia* . . . . . 38–42
   Jewish pre-Christian, in Psalms, Daniel, Ecclesi-
      asticus, Wisdom of Solomon . . . 48–50
      in Philo . . . 51; 53, 54
   of Our Lord's teaching . . . 64
   St. Paul . . . . . 68, 72
   Fourth Gospel . . . . 73, 80
   approach to, of Plotinus . . . 82–84
   of St. Augustine . . . . 87–92
   Pseudo-Dionysius . . . . 97–99
   St. Thomas . . . . 103–109
   largely supplanted by Monism in Eckhart . 111–115
   Spinoza the philosopher eliminates . . 124–129
      the great soul implies . . 130–132
   of Kant, its philosophically hypothetic character 150–159
      criticism . . . . 159–166
   Fichte generally falls short of . 174–176; 177, 178
   Schleiermacher indifferent to, in the *Reden* . 192, 193
      criticism . . . . 194, 195

|                                             | PAGES |
|---|---|
| *Theism*, Schleiermacher still predominantly Pantheistic in the *Glaubenslehre* | 197 |
|     of Troeltsch | 199 |
|     Hegel is full of, in his fundamental principle | 202–206 |
|         contradicts, in his two identifications | 206–211 |
|     of deceased English Hegelians | 220, 221 |
|     opposition of M'Taggart to | 224, 225 |
|         criticism | 227–230 |
|     Feuerbach's radical denial of | 233–235 |
|         criticism | 235–244 |
|     Schopenhauer's antipathy to | 249 |
|         criticism | 253, 254 |
|         his shy implication of | 256, 257 |
|     Nietzsche's groping after | 263, 264 |
|     Darwin's fluctuations as to | 266, 267 |
|         criticism | 268–271 |
|     Doctrine of Descent and | 271, 272 |
|     of Wallace | 272–274 |
|     Haeckel's cheery "refutation" of | 281–283 |
|     Marx's elimination of all | 304–306 |
|         criticism | 307–312 |
|     Sorel's trend towards | 320–323 |
|     implied in full experience of Eternal Life | 368–369 |
|     final affirmation of | 382–387; 395, 396 |
| Theocracies, Modern and Western, never long successful | 361, 362 |
| *Things, material*, necessity of mind's contact with, imperfectly apprehended by Kant | 163, 164 |
|         Eucken | 179 |
|     its precise place missed in Schleiermacher's *Reden* | 194, 195 |
|     ignored by Feuerbach | 235–239 |
|     affirmed for Religion as against Liberal Protestants | 328–330 |
|     final insistence upon | 389 |
| *Thing-in-itself*, the, in Kant, unknown to us yet somehow known to be utterly unlike what it appears to us | 140, 141 |
|     criticism | 141; 153–155 |
|     This principle applied by Kant to Religion— Grace, Worship, History | 156–159 |
|         criticism | 159–166 |
|     in Fichte | 173, 174 |
|         applied to Religion | 177, 178 |
|     in Schleiermacher | 184, 185 |
|         criticism | 186–188 |
|     in Schopenhauer unknown, yet known as the Will | 245–247, 248–249 |
| *This-Life, This-World* religious experiences Israelitish concentration upon | 21, 22 |

424 *Index*

*This-Life, This-World* religious experiences

|  | PAGES |
|---|---|
| the Psalms upon | 48 |
| Philo | 53, 54 |
| insisted upon in one of Our Lord's two outlooks | 59–62 ; 64, 65 |
| in St. Paul | 68, 70 |
| Fourth Gospel | 77, 78 |
| Plotinus | 84 |
| St. Augustine | 89, 92 |
| Pseudo-Dionysius | 97–99 |
| St. Thomas | 104 |
| Eckhart | 112, 113 ; 115 |
| Spinoza | 115 |
| haltingly affirmed by Kant | 156–159 |
| criticism | 159–167 |
| in Fichte | 174–177 |
| Schleiermacher | 183–186 |
| Troeltsch | 199, 200 |
| Feuerbach, illusions in so far as they claim to intimate transubjective realities | 233–235 |
| in criticism | 235–244 |
| a touch of, in Schopenhauer's *Nirvana*-aspiration | 256, 257 |
| massive in Kierkegaard | 261, 262 |
| Nietzsche and | 263, 264 |
| apparently never strong in Darwin | 265 |
| deeply respected by Sorel | 320–323 |
| required by Roman Catholic Church | 342, 343 |
| vigorously flourish within | 372–377 |
| a keen sense of, enters into complex of Eternal Life | 367, 368 |
| final affirmation as to need of | 396 |

*Thumos*, the, in Plato . . . . . 37, 38
    present in Our Lord's life and teaching . 65, 66
        in St. Paul . . . . 72
    largely absent from Fourth Gospel . 79, 80
    present in Plotinus, the living soul, absent from his system . . . . 82–84
    abundant in St. Augustine . . . 88–92
    active in temper of Pseudo-Dionysius, excluded by his predominant theory . 97, 99
    absent from one current of St. Thomas 107, 108
    present in other current . . 108, 109
    Eckhart in his Monistic mood limits, to intellectual thirst after utter unity and clearness . . . . 110–114
    Spinoza introduces, in contradiction to his system, at culmination of his course 130–132

# Index

|  | PAGES |
|---|---|
| *Thumos*, the, Kant eliminates, from Ethics | 146, 147 |
| and largely from Religion | 159–161 |
| reintroduced by Fichte | 175, 176 |
| by Schleiermacher, as specially pertaining to Religion | 190 |
| insufficiency of, in deceased English Hegelians | 222, 223 |
| in M'Taggart | 229 |
| Tennant recognizes and requires | 284, 285 |
| *Time*, meaning of its exclusion, in Dionysiac ecstasy | 27 |
| completely excluded by Eternity, according to Parmenides | 31, 32 |
| Plato | 36, 37 |
| Philo | 51 |
| St. Augustine | 88, 89 |
| Boëthius | 104 |
| St. Thomas | 105, 106 |
| and Space, concrete and abstract, in Kant | 143, 144 |
| all existence really outside of, according to M'Taggart | 226 |
| utterly unreal, according to Schopenhauer | 249–251 |
| discriminations as to, in Bergson | 288–291 |
| criticism of | 291–294; 297–299; 301, 302 |
| human experience of, threefold | 231, 232 |
| sense of concrete, Duration, part of experience of Eternal Life | 365, 366 |
| final discriminations concerning Abstract Time, Concrete Time (Duration), and Eternity | 382–384; 386, 387; 390, 391 |
| *Totum Simul*, the, of Eternity in Parmenides | 31, 32 |
| Plato | 37 |
| Aristotle | 39, 40 |
| Philo | 51 |
| St. Augustine | 89–91 |
| Boëthius | 105 |
| St. Thomas | 105 |
| sense of, enters into experience of Eternal Life | 365, 366 |
| final insistence upon, as directly characterizing God's life alone | 383 |
| *Transcendence* of God, the, theoretically utter in Plato | 34, 36 |
| Philo | 53 |
| Plotinus | 82–84 |
| Proclus | 95, 96 |
| Pseudo-Dionysius | 97, 98 |
| Kierkegaard | 261, 262 |
| of Kingdom of God, as one of two movements in Our Lord's life and teaching | 56–59 |

# 426　　　　　*Index*

|  | PAGES |
|---|---|
| *Transcendence* of Kingdom of God, insisted upon by Troeltsch | 199, 200 |
| maintained here thus against Schopenhauer | 253–256 |
| secularist Socialism | 315–319 |
| Transformism in Bergson | 295 |
| *Triadic movement* of the Many in Proclus | 96 |
| Pseudo-Dionysius | 98 |
| Hegel | 212, 213 |
| *Truth*, in the Johannine writings | 74, 75 |
| tests of, not clearness but richness and fruitfulness | 125, 134 |
| religious, its supreme importance realized by Roman Catholic Church | 348 |
| *Uniqueness* as attaching to all History and Personality admitted by St. Thomas in one current of his teaching | 109 |
| denied and admitted by Spinoza | 129, 130 |
| mostly combated by Kant | 165, 166 |
| imperfectly recognized by Fichte | 177 |
| even excessively apprehended by Schleiermacher in his *Reden* | 189, 192 |
| Variations, useful, constant presence of, kernel of riddle in Selection | 172 |
| Variety of spiritual types within Roman Catholic Church | 352 |
| Washing of the feet, the, in Fourth Gospel | 80 |
| *Wheel of Generation*, the, in Buddhism | 8–10; 165 *n.* |
| Orphism | 28, 29 |
| Schopenhauer | 251 |
| *Worship*, Religious, not understood by Kant | 157, 158; 162–164 |
| men and religions replete with | 325, 326 |
| law of human soul which necessitates | 326, 327 |
| historical foundation and abiding need of | 327, 328 |
| final insistence upon | 392 |
| *Yasht Hymns*, the | 13 |
| *Zarathustrism*, its chief documents | 12 |
| doctrines | 13 |
| its merits and its indication of Eternal Life | 13 |

## II

### PERSONS AND AUTHORS

|  | PAGES |
|---|---|
| Adam, James, on Stoics at their religious best (the Hymn of Cleanthes) . . . . . . . . | 48 *n*. |
| Alexander II., Pope, protects the Jews . . . | 350 |
| Ambrose, St., of Milan, protests against first execution for heresy . . . . . . . . . | 350 |
| *Amos, the prophet*, his deeply ethical Theism . . | 17 |
| Andrews, Lancelot, Anglican Bishop, as religious Institutionalist . . . . . . . . | 326 |
| Archer Hind, R. D., on Plato's *Timæus* . . | 37 *n*. |
| *Aristotle* on the Unmoving *Energeia* . . . | 38–41 |
|     his insight and limitations . . . | 41, 42 |
|     on man's inevitable anthropomorphisms . | 241 |
|     elements derived from, in Pseudo-Dionysius | 99 |
|                         St. Thomas . | 103, 107 |
|     and the Roman Catholic Church . . | 337–340 |
|     unhistorical temper of mind of . . | 340 |
| Arnim, Johannes von, his edition of *Fragments of Stoics* | 48 *n*. |
| *Augustine, St., of Hippo* . . . . . | 87–94 |
|     conditions of his life and times . . | 87 |
|     his great indebtedness to Plotinus . | 87, 88 |
|     on God, the soul, and their inter-relations as non-spatial . . . . . . | 87, 88 |
|         Eternity of God as excluding Time . | 88, 89 |
|             yet as vividly apprehensible by man in Time . | 89, 90 |
|         God's immediate presence in men's souls | 90–92 |
|     his sense of Historical Element of Religion | 92, 93 ; 326 |
|         of Organic Character of Society and Church . . . . . | 93, 94 |
|         of Sin . . . . . . | 93, 94 |
|     distinguishes between Visible and Invisible Church . . . . . . | 354 |
|         yet at times insists upon a practical identity between the two . . . | 93, 94 |
|     his attitude towards human nature demands mitigation and completion by Our Lord's fully balanced, richer outlook . | 391, 392 |
| Azeglio, Massimo d', as a zealous Catholic and Italian patriot . . . . . . . | 362 |
| Bäumker, Clemens, his valuable studies in Mediæval Philosophy . . . . . . . | 337, 338 |
| Bedford, Adeline Duchess of, on the Abbé Huvelin . | 375, 377 *n*. |

|   | PAGES |
|---|---|
| Benedictine edition of St. Augustine, its Index | 94 *n.* |

Benedictines, the Maurist, on Origin of French Episcopal Sees . . . . . . . . 345
Bergson, *Henri,* on *Dureé* and on Liberty . . 288–302
    distinguishes between Duration and Clock-Time . . . . 106, 232 *n.*
    finds Duration alone real . . 288, 289
    excesses and defects in presentation of this great doctrine in the *Essai* 289–294
    in the *Évolution Créatrice* . 294–297
    at his best demands by implication three modifications of his ordinary contentions :
    Space to be discriminated into Real and Conceptual, in same manner as Time is already discriminated . . . 297, 298
    highest element in Duration to be ever found in Permanence or Quasi-Permanence, not in Change . . 298, 299
    a wide, elastic Finalism to be accepted, as alone giving Content, Aim, and Steadiness to Libertarianism . . 299–302

Berkeley, George, Anglican Bishop
    central motive of his philosophy . 137, 138
    as a religious Institutionalist . . . 326

Bernstein, Eduard, his modified, more idealist Socialism 319, 320

Blondel, Maurice, upon Philosophy within Roman Catholic Church . . . . . 341 *n.*
    relations between History and Dogma . . . . 347 *n.*

*Boëthius* on Eternity as Complete Simultaneity . 104, 105
    in St. Thomas . . . . 104, 105

Booth, *Sir Charles,* on Christian self-sacrifice as sole cure for popular Secularism . . 317, 318
    unique value, in face of acute social trouble, of strongly Institutional Religion . . . 371, 372

Bossuet, Bishop J. B., as a religious Institutionalist . . 326
Bradley, A. C., his Memoir of R. L. Nettleship . . 219
Buckle, H. T., Charles Darwin's opinion concerning views of 280
    his popularity amongst secularist Socialists . 310
Burke, Edmund, ever conscious of connection between higher Politics and Religion . . . . 361

Caird, *Edward,* on Plotinus . . . . . 87 *n.*
    Spinoza . . . . 135 *n.*
    as an English Hegelian . 218–223
    a religious Institutionalist . 221, 222 ; 326
Caird, John,   as an English Hegelian . 218–223
    a religious Institutionalist . 221, 222 ; 326

## Index

|   | PAGES |
|---|---|
| Callixtus, Pope, his Edict concerning Marriage | 354, 355 |
| Calmes, Père Th., on doctrine of Fourth Gospel | 81 *n.* |
| Calvin, John, as a religious Institutionalist | 326 |
|     his attitude towards human nature found excessive | 391, 392 |
| Cathrein, Victor, S.J., on secularist Socialism | 307 *n.* |
|     profound reality and vast range of Social Problem | 319 *n* |
| Charles, Prof. R. H., on Israelitish attitude towards experience of God and belief in a Future Life | 21, 22, 22 *n.* |
| Chateaubriand, F. A. de, as one of the lay influences towards the recent reinforcement of Curialism | 359 |
| Chevalier, Canon Ulysse, on translation of Holy House of Loretto | 345, 347 *n.* |
| Chrysippus, the Stoic | 43 |
| Church, Dean R. C., as example of deepening of religious life through Institutionalism | 371, 372 |
| Cicero, M. Tullius, on the Stoic doctrines | 43–47 |
| Cleanthes, the Stoic | 43 |
| Clement, St., of Rome, First Epistle of, already shows legal organization strongly at work | 354 |
| Clement VI., Pope, protects the Jews | 350 |
| Clement of Alexandria on Dionysiac worship | 26 |
| Condren, Charles de, Père, Abbé Huvelin upon | 376 |
| Crespi, Dr. Angelo, moves away from secularist Socialism | 320, 323 *n.* |
| | |
| *Damien, Father J.,* the Missionary to the lepers | 372 |
| *Daniel, the Book of,* on Everlasting Life | 49 |
| Dante combines Catholicism and patriotism | 362 |
| *Darwin, Charles,* on Theism, Immortality, Conscience | 265–268 |
|     criticism of these utterances | 268–271 |
|     his graduated love of graduated reality contrasted with Haeckel's monistic passion for reduction of all things to emptiest abstraction | 280–283 |
| Delbos, Prof. Victor, on the surreptitious self-contradiction of Spinoza's Ethics | 135 *n.* |
| Delehaye, Hippolyte, Bollandist, upon the legends of the Saints | 347 *n.* |
| Denifle, Father H. S., upon Eckhart | 111 *n.*, 120 *n.* |
|     his studies in mediæval thought in general | 337, 338 |
| *Deuteronomy,* author of *Book of,* insists upon man's entirety as called to love of God | 19 |
| Dilthey, Wilhelm, on Stoic constituents of Spinoza's philosophy | 135 *n.* |
|     Schleiermacher | 198 *n.* |
| Diogenes Laertius, on the Stoics | 43, 44 |

|                                                                                      | PAGES       |
|--------------------------------------------------------------------------------------|-------------|
| *Dionysius, Pseudo-*                                                                 | 94–100      |
| his times and probable circumstances                                                 | 94, 95      |
| dependence upon Proclus                                                              | 95, 96      |
| transcendental outlook                                                               | 97, 98      |
| Christian and Aristotelian, as against Neo-Platonist, constituents of                | 98, 99      |
| Deification of human soul in                                                         | 100         |
| absence of historic sense and attribution of purely negative character to Evil as defects of | 100 |
| insistence upon need of purification by soul that would experience and obtain Eternal Life nobly distinguishes | 100 |
| *Drummond, Dr. James*, upon Philo the Jew                                            | 54 *n.*     |
| *Duchesne, Mgr. Louis*, on Origin of Episcopal Sees in France                        | 345, 346    |
| *Ecclesiasticus, Book of*, upon God and Life                                         | 49          |
| *Eckhart, Joannes*                                                                   | 110–120     |
| his circumstances and tendency                                                       | 110, 111    |
| Psychology, the little spark of reason                                               | 111–113     |
| sharply contrasts "God" and "Godhead"                                                | 113, 114    |
| his monistic drift                                                                   | 114, 115    |
| two currents in his Ethics                                                           | 116, 117    |
| the circle and its triadic development                                               | 117, 118    |
| the three thirsts in Eckhart; causes of his turning away from all history and concreteness | 118, 119 |
| his condemnation by Rome objectively deserved; experience since his time has still further rendered his abstractiveness unworkable | 119, 120 |
| especially as concerns Eternal Life                                                  | 120         |
| *Elijah, the prophet*, witnesses to One Holy Power                                   | 16, 17      |
| *Engels, Friedrich*, Marx's collaborator in secularist Socialism                     | 304–307, 307 *n.* |
| *Eucken, Prof. Rudolf*, on Spinoza                                                   | 135 *n.*    |
| in his own rich doctrine, and the Fichtean influences which somewhat limit it       | 179, 180; 180 *n.* |
| on Evolution                                                                         | 283 *n.*    |
| *Ezekiel, the prophet*, on the Living God                                            | 16          |
| God the Good Shepherd                                                                | 20          |
| God as the Healing Waters                                                            | 20          |
| the "Priestly Code," its kinship with                                                | 20          |
| *Fechner, G. T.*, the philosopher, as religious Institutionalist                     | 326         |
| *Fénelon, Archbishop F. de Salignac Lamotte*, as religious Institutionalist          | 326         |
| *Feuerbach, Ludwig*                                                                  | 233–244     |
| two stages of his scepticism                                                         | 233         |

## Index 431

PAGES

*Feuerbach, Ludwig*, two stages of his scepticism—
    first stage . . . . 233–235
    criticism of . . . . 235–243
    last stage, its significance . . 243, 244
    his influence upon Marx and Engels . . 305
Fleiner, Prof. Fritz, on steady development of Canon Law and centralization within Roman Catholic Church in nineteenth century . . . 358, 359 ; 360 *n*.
François de Sales, St., Abbé Huvelin upon . . 375, 376
Frazer, Prof. J. G., naturalistic attitude towards man in anthropological works of . . . . 279
Froude, Richard Hurrell, the Tractarian, his affinity to Kierkegaard . . . . . . . 260
Funk, F. X., Dr., on the Galileo case . . . 341 *n*.

Galilei, Galileo, his condemnation . . . 341, 341 *n*.
*Gatha Hymns*, the, teaching of, concerning the two Spirits and their creations . . . . . 12, 13
*Gautama, the Buddha*, teaches the *Nirvana* . . 8–10
    the concomitant of this doctrine ; significance of the complex—a spiritually attuned moralism, not yet directly a religion . 10 ; 165 *n*.
Gibson, Prof. W. R. Boyce, upon Bergson's Intuitionism . 302 *n*.
Goerres, Joseph von, as one of the lay influences towards intense centralization of Church . . . . 359
Goethe, Wolfgang von, his change from Institutional Christianity to Spinozist habits . . . . 181, 182
Gore, Charles, Anglican Bishop, as Christian social worker . 315
*Green, Thomas Hill*, as an English Hegelian . 218–223
    his "consciousness in general" . 221
Gregory I., the Great, Pope St., condemns interference with the Jews' practice of their religion, and forbids compulsory baptism of Jews . . . . . 350
Gregory IX., Pope, founds the General Inquisition . . 349
Grill, Prof. J., on " Life " in Philo . . . . 54 *n*.

*Haeckel, Prof. Ernst*, vehement Monism of . . 281–283
    criticism of . . . . 283
    his popularity with secularist Socialists 310
Harrison, Jane, upon Orphism . 23 ; 29, 29 *n*. ; 30, 30 *n*.
Harvey, William, the Anatomist, the first clearly to conceive and name *Epigenesis* . . . . . 269
*Hegel, G. W. F.* . . . . . 201–218
    profound early influence of Schelling's Philosophy of Identity upon . . 201, 202
    this Philosophy deliberately contradicted by fundamental principle of . . 202–206
    but admitted in two positions of 207–211 ; 211–218

| | PAGES |
|---|---|
| *Hegel, G. W. F.*, like Eckhart puts Religion in penultimate place | 215, 216 |
| his influence in the deceased English Hegelians | 218–223 |
| M'Taggart | 223, 224 ; 228 |
| Feuerbach | 233, 235 |
| opposed by Schopenhauer | 249, 250 ; 251, 252 |
| and Evolution and Epigenesis | 268, 269 |
| his influence in Marx and Engels | 305 |
| Herford, C. H., his translation of Ibsen's *Brand* | 262 |
| *Hermann, Prof. Wilhelm*, restricts Religion to recognition of Categorical Imperative and of the Historical Jesus | 330–332 |
| artificiality of this restriction | 331–333 |
| Herodotus on the Dionysiac worship | 26 |
| Hesiod upon *Lethe* as evil | 30 |
| Hoeffding, Prof. Harald, upon Kierkegaard | 262 |
| Holtzmann, H. J., on the Kingdom of God in Our Lord's teaching | 62 *n.* |
| social character of this kingdom | 62, 63 |
| St. Paul's teachings as to the Spirit-Christ | 72 *n.* |
| doctrine of Fourth Gospel | 80 *n.* |
| decline of Institutional Religion | 335 *n.* |
| Huegel, F. von, in works other than the present, on Plato's Purgatorical teaching | 35 *n.* |
| Ontological Argument | 156 *n.* |
| Religion and Illusion | 244 *n.* |
| Wilhelm Hermann's theology | 333 *n.* |
| Factual and Symbolical constituents of Scripture | 347 *n.* |
| *Huvelin*, the *Abbé* | 374–377 |
| his character and influence | 374, 375 |
| sayings concerning Eternal Life | 375–377, 377 *n.* |
| Ibsen, Hendrik, his *Brand* suggested by figure of Kierkegaard | 262 |
| *Isaiah of Jerusalem, the prophet*, the vision at vocation of, | 17, 18 |
| his simile of God and His vineyard | 18 |
| Jackson, Prof. Henry, upon sequence of Plato's *Dialogues* | 35 *n.* |
| Jacobi, Friedrich W., writes against Spinoza | 182 |
| *Jahvist*, the, writes full of sense of God's living presence | 16 |
| *Jeremiah, the prophet*, upon God as fountain of living waters | 19 |
| the Lord, the Living God | 19 |
| *Jesus Christ*, actual earthly life and utterances of | 55–66 |
| their general occasion and character | 55, 56 |
| the Kingdom of God— its four characteristics in the transcendental movement | 56–59 |

*Jesus Christ*, actual earthly life and utterances of—*continued*
    the Kingdom—
        its characteristics in the immanental movement . . . . 59–62
        in both movements the Kingdom a social organism in this life . . . 62, 63
            and in the next life . . 63, 64
    God everywhere here awakens and purifies feeling, motive, action, in widest range . 64, 65
    interaction of the two movements within . 65, 66
    institutes a Preaching Band . . 327, 328
    uses and commends efficacious sensible signs 329, 330
    His attitude towards human nature contrasted with that of St. Paul . . . 391, 392
    in St. Paul . . . 67; 69; 70–72
        Fourth Gospel . . 73, 74; 79, 80
        St. Augustine . . . . 92, 93
        Eckhart . . . . . 113
        Spinoza . . . . . 130
        Kant . . . . . 165, 166
        Fichte . . . . . 177
        Schleiermacher . . . . 182
        Hegel . . . . . 214
        Schopenhauer . . . 252
        Kierkegaard . . . . 261, 262
        Hermann . . . . 331, 332
Jodl, Prof. F., upon Feuerbach . . . 244 *n.*
*Johannine Writings*, the . . . . 73–80
    their general antecedents and character 73, 74
    "Truth" and "Knowing" in . . 74, 75
    their culminating category and conviction: Eternal Life . . 75–78
    their insistence upon interpenetration between God, Christ, the souls of the faithful, and upon God's prevenience 78, 79
    their limitation of range yet profound sense of the two great concrete Realities, the living God and the historic Jesus . . . 79, 80
    great symbolic pictures in . . 344
John of the Cross, St., on incomprehensibility of God . 243
John, Father, Sergieff of Cronstadt, as example of deepening of religious life by Institutionalism . . . 372
Judd, Dr. J. W., on Charles Darwin's character . . 268 *n.*
Juvenal, his Stoic teaching . . . . 46

*Kant, Immanuel* . . . . . 135–168
    specific greatness, origin, three periods, and dominating motive of . . 135–138

                                                              PAGES
Kant, Immanuel, his Epistemology: five positions dis-
               cussed    .    .    .       139–144
               Ethics: their noble sense of moral
                 guilt; their formalism; their ex-
                 cessive individualism   .    144–149
               Religious Philosophy as regards
                 Ontological Argument    .    150–156
                 Grace, Worship, History .    156–167
               his Critical Philosophy rendered more uni-
                 formly radical and subjective by
                 Fichte   .    .   .   173, 174; 176, 177
    as operative in Schleiermacher    .    . 182, 184, 192
                 Hegel    .    .   .    .       217
                 Schopenhauer .    .    .     245–248
                 Bergson  .    .    295, 296; 297, 298
                 Wilhelm Hermann     .    .    331, 332
               final positions against the *Critical*     387, 388;
                                      389; 391, 392; 395, 396
Kautzsch, Prof. E., on Apocrypha and Pseudo-epigraphic
     Writings of Old Testament    .    .    .    50 *n*.
Ketteler, W. E. von, Bishop, as Christian social worker    . 315
*Kierkegaard, Soeren* .    .    .    .    .    260–262
               his affinities and special complex of insights .  260
               keen sense of Reality and of Difference of
                 God      .    .    .    .    .    261
               insufficient sense of the Likeness    .    .  262
               the original of Ibsen's *Brand*    .    .    262
Koch, Dr. Hugo, on Pseudo-Dionysius and his dependence
     upon Proclus    .    .    .    .    .    120 *n*.

*Lactantius*, the African Father of the Church, forbids applica-
     tion of force in religion    .    .    .    349, 350
Lange, Prof. H. O., upon Ancient Egyptian religion    .    14
Lask, Dr. E., on Fichte's attitude towards History    .   180 *n*.
Lasson, Prof. A., on Eckhart    .    .    .    .    120 *n*.
Lasson, Dr. G., on Hegel's early life .    .    .    202 *n*.
Laud, William, the Anglican Archbishop, as a religious
     Institutionalist    .    .    .    .    .    326
Law, William, the Non-Juring Divine, as a religious
     Institutionalist    .    .    .    .    .    326
Lea, H. C., upon Spanish Inquisition    .    .    . 353 *n*.
Lehmann, Prof. Edv., upon Buddhist *Nirvana*    .    . 8–10
                              Ramanuja    .    .    11, 12
                              Zarathustrism    .    . 12, 13
Leibniz, G. W., on obscure apprehensions    .    142, 143; 143 *n*.
               his Monadism compared with that of
                 M'Taggart    .    .    .    .    .    227
               his Evolution no Epigenesis    .    .    268–270
               as a religious Institutionalist .    .    .    326

|                                                                              | PAGES |
|---|---|
| Leo XIII., Pope, his social teaching | 315 |
| Le Play, Frédéric, as sociological thinker | 315 |

Lessing, G. E., the contradiction in main theme of his
    *Nathan* . . . . . . 166, 167
Locke, John, his denial of secondary qualities of Matter as
    half-way house to Berkeley's Idealism . . . 138
Lockhart, Rev. W., on Antonio Rosmini . . . 361 *n.*
Loisy, Prof. Alfred, on Kingdom of God in Our Lord's
                    teaching . . . . 62 *n.*
                    doctrine of Fourth Gospel . 81
                    his penetrating anthropological
                      method . . . 279, 279 *n.*
Lugo, John de, Cardinal, S.J., on ordinary process by which
    souls in good faith are saved outside of visible Catholic
    Church . . . . . . 350, 351
Luther, Martin, as a religious Institutionalist . . 326
            his attitude towards human nature requires
            correction and completion by Our Lord's
            own teaching . . . 391, 392
            deliberate differentiation from . . 335

*Maccabees, Second Book of*, on God as the Lord of Life . 49
M'Taggart, Dr. J. E.. . . . . . 223-232
          instructiveness of his combination of
          doctrines . . . . 223, 224
          on Metaphysics, Theism, Immortality and
          Pre-existence, and Time . 224-226
          criticism of . . . 226-232
Maher, Rev. Michael, S.J., as an impressive worker of the
    Neo-Scholastic School . . . . 337, 338
Maistre, Count Joseph de, as one of the lay founders of
    recent Curialism . . . . . . 359
Manning, H. E., Cardinal, as a Christian social worker . 315
            upon supernatural life amongst
            Anglicans . . . 352
Manzoni, Alessandro, as fervent Catholic and ardent Italian
    patriot . . . . . . . 362
Marie Antoinette, Queen, of France, and the inter-related-
    ness of politics and religion . . . 361
Marie de la Providence, Mère (Eugénie Smet), her dis-
    positions and sayings concerning Eternal Life . 373, 374
*Marrett*, Dr. R. R., strength and weakness of his anthropo-
    logical method . . . . . 278, 279
Martin, St., of Tours, protests against first execution for heresy 350
*Marx, Karl* . . . . . . 304-307
          derivation of his philosophy . . 304, 305
          his formulation of secularist Socialism . 304-307
Medici, Lorenzo de', and the inter-relatedness of politics and
    religion . . . . . . . 361

|                                                                    | PAGES      |
|--------------------------------------------------------------------|------------|
| Medicus, Dr. Fritz, upon J. G. Fichte.                             | 180 *n*.   |
| Mercier, Désiré, Cardinal, his important labours in philosophy     | 337, 338   |
| *Micah, the prophet*, upon the ethical character of God            | 18         |
| Mignot, E. J., Archbishop, upon the Church and Biblical Criticism  | 347 *n*.   |
| *Mill, John Stuart*, his vivid experience of Eternal Life          | 311        |
| Moellendorff, Prof. Ulrich von Willamowitz, his anthropological method | 279, 279 *n*. |
| Montefiore, Claude G., as example of religious life strengthened by Institutionalism | 371 |
| *Muensterberg, Prof. Hugo*, his Neo-Fichteanism                    | 178, 179, 180 *n*. |
| Murray, Prof. Gilbert, on Orphic Tablets                           | 23, 30 *n*. |

Narfon, E. de, on policy of Pope Pius X. . . . 364 *n*.
*Nettleship, R. Louis*, as an English Hegelian . 218–223
Newman, J. H., Cardinal, as combining self-respect
          with loyalty to Church
          authority . . . 326
      example of deepening of religious life by Institutionalism
                                      360, 361 *n*.
Nicolas (Kryffs), Cardinal, of Coes, and Evolution . 268, 269
              as a religious Institutionalist . . 326
*Nietzsche, Friedrich* . . . . . 263, 264
        causes of his great vogue . . . 263
        his exquisite sayings and vulgar attacks 263, 264 ; 279

Oldenberg, Prof. H., upon the Buddhist Nirvana . 9, 10 *n*.
Olier, M. Jean Jacques, Abbé Huvelin upon . . 376
Ollé-Laprune, Léon, upon Philosophy within Roman Catholic Church . . . . . 341 *n*.
Origen, as a religious Institutionalist . . . 326

*Parmenides*, the first clear formulator of the *Totum Simul* of Eternity . . . . . 31, 32
        spatial, abstract, monistic character of his outlook . . . . . 32
Pascal, Blaise, as spiritually related to Kierkegaard . . 262
        a religious Institutionalist . . . 326
*Paul, St.* . . . . . . . 66–72
        training and exceptional Christian experience of . 66, 67
        his dominant category, Spirit . . . 67
        Pneumatic anthropology of . . . 67–69
        interaction between experiences and conceptions of the Christ and of the Spirit in . . 69
        the Kingdom of God partly present, partly future in . . . . . . 70

## Index

*Paul, St.*, the Christ-Spirit in, is medium of universal brotherhood of mankind; profoundly organic character of this brotherhood . . . 70–72
    amazing range of volitional and emotional life in . 72
    his attitude towards human nature requires incorporation within, and mitigation by, larger and richer teaching of Our Lord . 391, 392
Pellico, Silvio, as fervent Catholic and ardent Italian patriot 362
Pernet, Maurice, on policy of Pope Pius X. . . . 364 *n.*
Pfleiderer, Dr. E., on sequence and three periods of Plato's *Dialogues* . . . . . . . . . 35 *n.*
Pfleiderer, Otto, upon the Pantheistic trend of Schleiermacher . . . . . . . . 198 *n.*
*Philo, the Jew* . . . . . . . . 50–54
    constituents of his philosophy; deeply religious, theistic motive of his entire teaching . . . . 50, 51
    God conceived by, in accordance with Aristotle, as Pure *Energeia* . . . . . . 51
    His Eternity conceived by, in accordance with Plato, as exclusive of Time . . . . . 51
    God as above Life, and God as Life . . . 51–53
    in his abstractive current largely anticipates Plotinus, perhaps even Proclus . . . . . 53
    God's prevenient operation in man's soul affirmed by . . . . . . . . 53, 54
    spontaneity and richness of Jewish religion mostly predominate in, over Stoic apathy and general Hellenistic abstractiveness . . . . 54
    ingredients like the teachings of, in St. Paul . 66, 67
        Fourth Gospel . 73
Pius V., St., Pope, aids consolidation of Spanish Inquisition 349
*Pius IX., Pope*, on reality and wide range of good faith, grace and salvation outside Visible Church . . . 351
Pius X., Pope, his *Motu Proprio* pronouncements . 359, 364 *n.*
*Plato*, his description of the Dionysiac ecstasy . . 25, 26
    the Orphics . . . 29, 30
    his own conceptions concerning Eternal Life . 32–38
    three stages of his mental growth and three corresponding groups of his writings . 32, 33; 35 *n.*
    Eternal Life in his second stage . . . 33–35
        in his third stage . . . . 35–37
    his doctrine of the soul's purgation . . . 35
    four abidingly great convictions—unique thus within one soul throughout pre-Christian antiquity . . . . . . . 37, 38
    influence of, upon writer of Fourth Gospel . . 74
        St. Augustine . . 89, 90, 93
        Pseudo-Dionysius . . . 97
*Plotinus* . . . . . . . . 81–87

|  | PAGES |
|---|---|

*Plotinus*, his strength as a religious soul, his weakness as an over-abstractive philosopher . . 81, 82
    God here utterly transcendent yet experienced by human soul in an immediate contact . 82–84
    non-spatiality, interpenetration of souls . 83, 84
    the soul longs for God, God longs not for the soul . . . . . . 85
    what to retain in . . . . . 86
    what to abandon in . . . . . 85–87
    in St. Augustine . . . . . 87, 88
    Pseudo-Dionysius . . . . 97
Prichard, H. A., on Kant's theory of knowledge . 142 *n*.
*Priestly Code*, the, its kinship with Ezekiel . . 20 (344)
*Pringle Pattison, Andrew Seth*, on Fichte . . . 180 *n*.
    Hegel . 206 *n*., 209 *n*., 218 *n*.
    M'Taggart . 232 *n*.
    Naturalism—two senses of the term "Nature" 275–277
*Proclus*, the Neo-Platonist . . . . . 95, 96
    his times and mental character . . . 95
    rigorously carries out circular process of all things, as conceived by Plotinus, in its triadic development . . . . . . 95, 96
    places First even above being . . . 96
    but increases number of realities intermediate between man and the One, and number of man's own constituents . . . . . 96
    denies that the soul can ever become the very One 96
    in Pseudo-Dionysius . . . 94, 95 ; 97, 98
*Psalms*, the, upon (spiritual) Life . . . . 48
*Psalms of Solomon*, the, upon Life . . . . 49, 50
Pünjer, Dr. G. Ch. B., his critical edition of Schleiermacher's *Reden* in their successive texts . . . . 183 *n*.

*Râ*, the Egyptian Sun-God, apparently conceived as purely successive . . . . . . . 14
*Ramanuja* . . . . . . . 10–12
    his significant modification of Vedantic Monism 10, 11
    as to Brahma, the World, the Soul . . 11, 12
    how far Eternal Life is to be found in . . 12
Rancé, A. le B. de, the Trappist Abbot, Abbé Huvelin upon . . . . . . . 377
Ranke, Leopold von, and inter-relation between Politics and Religion . . . . . . 361
Reinach, Solomon, his attitude in anthropology . . 279
Rensi, G., his religiously tempered Socialism . . 320
Rickaby, Rev. Joseph, S.J., as a helpful expositor of St. Thomas . . . . . . 337, 338
Rickert, Prof. Heinrich, upon Fichte as accused of Atheism 180 *n*.

## Index

PAGES

Riehl, Prof. Aloys, upon Nietzsche as indication of reawaking of religious passion . . . . 264, 264 *n*.
Robertson, Frederick W., as example of strengthening of religious life by Institutionalism . . . . 371
*Rohde, Erwin*, his *Psyche* upon Dionysiac Cult . 23–26, 26 *n*.
          composition of Plato's *Republic* . . . 35 *n*.
          his attitude in anthropology . . 279, 279 *n*.
Rosmini, Antonio, as a religious Institutionalist . . 326
          combining self-respect and loyalty towards Church authority 360, 361 *n*.
          a saintly Catholic and ardent Italian patriot . . . . 362

Schelling, F. W. J., his influence upon Hegel . 201–20
Schiller, Dr. F. C., upon Aristotle's Unmoving *Energeia* 38–40, 40 *n*.
Schleiermacher, *Friedrich* . . . . 180–198
    his character, education, two periods: of the *Reden* and of the *Glaubenslehre* . 180–183
    in his *Reden* . . . . . 183–195
        Religion is Intuition-Feeling of Infinite 183–186
        criticism . . . 186–189
        Religion is utterly distinct from all Philosophy and Ethics . . 189, 190
        criticism . . . 190–192
        History is emphasised; belief in God and Immortality is treated with indifference . . . 192–194
        criticism . . . 194, 195
    in his *Glaubenslehre* . . . 195–198
        Religion now Sense of Unconditional Dependence . . . 195, 196
        God now everywhere accepted but Spinozistically conceived . . 197
        Religion now intensely Christo-centric . 198
        and religious experience now sought in and through Community . . 198
    Professor Troeltsch's very limited succession to, and great superiority over . 199
Schopenhauer, *Arthur* . . . . . 244–259
    four sets of his convictions to be considered 244, 245
    nature, circumstances, practically single work of 245
    turns Kant's Epistemology into an Eastern Metaphysic . . . . 245–248
    finds the Thing-in-itself in a Will bereft of al reason and logic, yet vehemently protests against being designated a Pantheist, and yet again is athirst for Absolute Identity and Rest . . . . 248–251

# 440    Index

|   | PAGES |
|---|---|
| *Schopenhauer* insists upon intense Pessimism and quite Gnostic Asceticism . . . | 251–256 |
| and culminates, in his *Nirvana*, in a shy yet deep conviction of an utterly other, ultimate, timeless, mystical Life and Union . | 256, 257 |
| shows weakness and strength for religion of dim, despairing outlooks . . | 257–259 |
| his influence upon Richard Wagner and Leo Tolstoi . . . . . | 260 |
| affinity with, of Sören Kierkegaard . . | 260 |
| and of Friedrich Nietzsche | 260, 263 |
| Schütz, Dr. Ludwig, on terminology of St. Thomas . | 110 *n.* |
| Schweitzer, Dr. Albert, on Kingdom of God in personal teaching of Our Lord . | 62 *n.* |
| on origin and character of St. Paul's conceptions . | 72 *n.* |
| Scott, Prof. E. F., on teaching of Fourth Gospel . | 81 *n.* |
| Seneca, Lucius Annæus, expresses Stoic belief in interdependence and organic structure of human society . | 47 |
| *Seth, Prof. Andrew,* see *Pringle Pattison.* | |
| Seth, Prof. James, upon Kant's Ethics . . | 149, 150 *n.* |
| Sextus Empiricus, his doctrine that like is only apprehended by like . . . . . . . | 75 |
| Simmel, Dr. George, upon evasion by Kant, *qua Critical Philosopher*, of Religion as known to us in real life . | 167 *n.* |
| *Sohm, Prof. Rudolf* . . . . . | 354–358 |
| his positions concerning relations between Visible and Invisible Church, the Catholic Church and the local Churches . . . · . | 354–356 |
| criticism . . . . . | 356–358 |
| *Sorel, Georges,* the Syndicalist, his sympathy with Mystery, Theism, Christianity, Asceticism . . | 320–323 |
| Spencer, Herbert, as a follower of Darwin . . . | 288 |
| *Spinoza, Baruch* . . . . . | 121–135 |
| circumstances of his life and four main constituents of his thought . . . | 121–123 |
| end, method, fundamental category of his philosophy . . . . . | 123–127 |
| utter Determinism of his system . . | 128, 129 |
| broken through by author's ethical greatness | 130–132 |
| lessons taught by . . . . | 132–135 |
| influence of, over Goethe . . . | 181, 182 |
| Lessing . . . | 181, 182 |
| Schleiermacher 181, 182 ; 190, 191 ; 197 | |
| Stevenson, R. L., on Fr. Damien . . . . | 372 |
| Stewart, Dr. J. M'Kellar, on Bergson's Philosophy . | 144 *n.*, 302 *n.* |
| Stobæus, Joannes, fragment preserved by, concerning the Perfect Sage, according to the Stoic . . . | 46 |

# Index

| | PAGES |
|---|---|
| Stolberg, Friedrich Leopold, Count, as layman who helped on intense centralization of Roman Catholic Church | 359 |
| Stout, *Prof. G. F.*, upon all specific activity as always directed to an end | 299 |
|     upon relation between Interest and Attention | 299 |
| | |
| *Tennant, Rev. F. R.*, on Evolution and Sin | 283–285 |
|     criticism | 286, 287 |
| Teresa, St., as expressing classical Christian attitude towards religious feelings and decisive motives of action | 191 |
|     a religious Institutionalist | 326 |
| Thibaut, G., his translation of Ramanuja's commentary on the *Vedanta-Sutras* | 12 *n.* |
| *Thomas, St., Aquinas* | 101–110 |
|     circumstances and character of | 101, 102 |
|     contrasted with St. Augustine | 102, 103 |
|     admits possession by soul of confused knowledge of *what* God is | 103, 104 |
|     on Eternity, *Aevum*, Time | 104–106 |
|     current of a solitary and current of a social character in teaching of | 106–109 |
|     right and dignity of true individuality according to social current of | 109 |
|     Evil predominantly treated as negative by | 109 |
|     his estimate of human nature | 109, 110 |
|     on anthropomorphism | 241 |
|     as a religious Institutionalist | 326 |
|     as a Saint who utilized in largest measure philosophy in service of religion | 337 |
|     possibility and advantage of treating especially Ethics and Spirituality of, in sympathetically historical and critical manner | 340 |
| Tocqueville, Alexis de, on necessary interconnection between higher Politics and Religion | 361 |
| Tolstoi, Count Leo, his affinity with Schopenhauer | 260 |
| Toniolo, Professor, Dr., as helpful worker in ancient and mediæval philosophy | 337, 338 |
| Torquemada, John, Cardinal, his profoundly legalist conception of the Church | 357 |
| *Trendelenburg, Adolf*, on Hegel's surreptitious transition from Logic to Reality | 208, 209, 209 *n.* |
|     as a religious Institutionalist | 326 |
| *Troeltsch, Prof. Ernst*, upon the two interdependent and mutually compensatory movements of Christianity | 66 *n.* |
|     Ontological Argument for existence of God | 156 *n.* |

## Index

|  | PAGES |
|---|---|
| *Troeltsch, Prof. Ernst*, upon necessity of worship for religion | 167 *n*.; 326, 327 |
| need of History for religion | 167 *n*. |
| his doctrine of tension and polarity within all deeper religion | 199, 200 |
| fullest works of | 200 *n*. |
| upon Feuerbach | 244 *n*. |
| importance of social factor in religion | 317 *n*. |
| irreplaceableness of Christianity in our present social troubles | 319 *n*. |
| prospects of secularist Socialism | 320 |
| readily sees Magic in attribution of any productive efficacy to any sensible Sign or Sacrament | 199, 328 |
| criticism | 328, 329 |
| upon separation of Church and State in France | 364 *n*. |
| *Tyrrell, Rev. George*, on conflict between Science and Theology | 342 *n*. |
| obedience to God and obedience to His representatives | 361 *n*. |

| *Ueberweg, Friedrich*, as edited by Max Heinze on St. Thomas Aquinas | 110 *n*. |
|---|---|
| Kant's Ethics | 149 *n*. |
| J. G. Fichte | 180 *n*. |

| *Vacandard, the Abbé*, upon the Inquisition | 353 *n*. |
|---|---|
| *Van der Velde, E.*, his Socialism is respectful to religion | 320 |
| *Vianney, J. B.*, the beatified Curé of Ars, his character and sayings | 372, 373 |
| *Vincent de Paul, St.*, Abbé Huvelin upon | 376, 377 |
| *Volkelt, Prof. Johannes*, upon Kant's Theory of Knowledge | 142 *n*. |
| Schopenhauer's Epistemology | 248 *n*.; 251 *n*. |
| Pessimism and Nirvana | 256 *n*.; 259 *n*. |
| Dim and clear outlooks in their use to religion | 259 *n*. |

| *Waggett, Rev. Philip*, on continuous Creation | 286, 287 |
|---|---|
| *Wagner, Richard*, the musical composer, as enthusiast for Schopenhauer | 260 |
| *Walker, Rev. Leslie J., S.J.*, his distinguished work in Epistemology | 337, 338 |

# Index

*Wallace, Dr. Alfred Russel*, on the three stages of life where Creative action has to be postulated . . . 272, 273
   proposed addition to, and further guarding of this description . . . 273, 274
   significance of combination in, of pioneer work in Biology and Epigenesis and fervent Theism . 274
Wallace, William, upon Nietzsche . . . . 264 *n.*
Ward, Prof. James, on Real Time . . . . 232 *n.*
   Epigenesis as contrasted with Evolution in strict sense . 269
Ward, Wilfrid, his *Life of Cardinal Newman* . . 361 *n.*
Ward, Dr. W. G., as lay worker for intense centralization of Roman Catholic Church . . . . . 359
Webb, Clement C. V., upon Ontological Argument for existence of God . . 156 *n.*
   Kant's attitude towards Grace . 167 *n*
   M'Taggart's conception of Person . . . 232 *n.*
*Weissmann, Prof. August*, upon the *crux* in the theory of selection . . . 271
   religious significance of this point 272
Wendland, Prof. Paul, penetrative character of his anthropological method . . . . . 279, 279 *n.*
Westcott, B. F., Anglican Bishop, on teaching of the Johannine writings . . . 81 *n.*
   as Christian social worker . . 315
*Wellhausen, Prof. Julius*, upon character of Elijah's teaching . . . . . . 16, 17 ; 17 *n.*
White, Dr. Andrew, on Conflict between Science and Theology . . . . . . . 342 *n.*
Wilson, J. M., Archdeacon, upon Sin as an anachronism . 285
*Wisdom of Solomon*, the *Book of*, upon incorruption and immortality . . . . . . . 50
Wycliffe, John, origin of anti-sacramental passion of . 329

*Zarathustra* . . . . . . . 12, 13
   his probable date ; parts of the *Avesta* which may reach back to him . . . 12
   main doctrines of these parts . . 12, 13
   traces of apprehension and conception of Eternal Life in . . . . 13
Zeller, Eduard, upon the Stoics . . . . 48 *n.*
   Proclus . . . . 96 *n.*
Zeno, the Stoic . . . . . . 43

www.ingramcontent.com/pod-product-compliance
Lightning Source LLC
Chambersburg PA
CBHW022055150426
43195CB00008B/145